Spring 76

PSYCHE & NATURE
Part 2 of 2

A Journal of
Archetype
and
Culture

Fall 2006

SPRING JOURNAL
New Orleans, Louisiana

CONTENTS
PART 2 OF 2

JUNGIANA

FILM REVIEWS

BOOK REVIEWS

SUDDENLY BLUE

A leaf wind asks for nothing,
with the whole of winter before it.
It brings its own gifts, as last night
I slept the sleep of wintering bears;
the sky suddenly blue with kingfishers,
their feathers flame-bright and true,
kindling the dark;
the firmament inside me,
turning inside out,
black into blue.

—Michael Whan

EXCERPTS FROM *C. G. JUNG AND THE SIOUX TRADITIONS: DREAMS, VISIONS, NATURE, AND THE PRIMITIVE*

VINE DELORIA, JR.

EDITED BY PHILIP J. DELORIA AND JEROME S. BERNSTEIN

Editor's Note:

In 2007, Spring Journal Books will publish *C. G. Jung and the Sioux Traditions: Dreams, Visions, Nature, and the Primitive* by Native American scholar, activist, and writer, Vine Deloria, Jr. (1933-2005). Below is (1.) an excerpt from the Introduction to *C. G. Jung and the Sioux Traditions* written by the author (2.) an editor's introduction, with biographical information about the author, written by Philip J. Deloria, Vine Deloria, Jr.'s son, who is a Professor of History and American Studies, the Director of the Program in American Culture at the University of Michigan, and the author of *Playing Indian* (Yale, 1998), *Indians in Unexpected Places* (Kansas, 2004), and co-editor of *The Blackwell Companion to American Indian History* (2001); and, (3.) a second excerpt from *C. G. Jung and the Sioux Traditions*: Chapter Two, "Meeting Grounds: Jung's Indian Experiences and Symbolic Interpretations." Chapter Two examines Jung's actual encounter with the Indian people of Taos Pueblo, his understanding of the symbolic importance of Indians in an American national psyche, and the ironies produced by the juxtapositions of such symbolism with the realities of Indian dispossession. Chapters three and four of the book address the equally important contextual issue of "the primitive" and its place in the thought of Jung and of other scholars.

FROM THE AUTHOR'S INTRODUCTION TO
C. G. Jung and the Sioux Traditions

Vine Deloria, Jr.

For several decades I have been struck by the interest shown by some Jungians in the traditions and practices of the Plains Indians.[1] I have often been approached by people who have immersed themselves in Jungian thought and come away from that experience wanting to know more about Plains Indian religion. Their interest indicates a good intuitive sense because at many levels there is indeed a connection. In some instances, however, they believe they can move directly from a Jungian background to an immediate understanding of the ceremonial life and religious beliefs of the Plains people without any effort to translate the ideas from one context to the other. Over two decades ago, I sought to locate where this interest might originate within the Jungian system. When I found several Jungian concepts used to describe psychological states that seemed similar, if not identical, to the Sioux Indian beliefs and experiences, it seemed to me that a book discussing the possible points of agreement between Jung and the Sioux might be useful and enlightening.

At least three major concerns emerged as I pondered the possibility of an extensive comparison of, and dialogue between, the two cosmologies and two bodies of thought. Jung has had his share of critics and detractors within his own culture. He has often been accused of sneaking metaphysics and superstition back into Western intellectual thought, as if that body of knowledge had absolute boundaries that could not be violated. While Jung has been thoroughly discussed by his Western peers, he has not, to my knowledge, been compared or critiqued by someone from an American Indian culture—someone Jung would have referred to as being "a primitive." That kind of analysis may help to illuminate parts of Jungian psychology that have not been well received in western intellectual circles. Indeed, such a critique could provide additional insights and data to some Jungian concepts that were more intuitive than empirical.

Secondly, Sioux culture and its beliefs and practices are complex and, despite long histories of assertions of Indian inferiority, they do in fact meet the most rigorous standards of intellectual discourse and understanding. Though different, they are equal to those of Western peoples. Demonstrating through the framework of Jungian psychology the nature of the great complexity of Sioux cosmology and culture might help people to learn about the Plains Indians and to understand this unique system of thought. It would, at the least, enable them to avoid errors in interpretation and help them see the kinds of discipline and relationships that constituted the old traditions and enabled the Sioux to handle certain kinds of psychological problems easily.

Finally, cross-cultural exchanges, particularly in the United States, are often no more than the appropriation of concepts and beliefs of the smaller culture by those people of the larger one interested in the subject. Rarely does an idea from the smaller culture have any effect or influence on the beliefs and practices of the larger culture. Today we have a great revival of traditions in many Indian tribes and this movement has attracted people from the dominant culture who seek to find something of value. Ideas, of course, cannot be confined to any one group of people. Cross-cultural work, if it is to prove useful, should also subject the ideas of the larger culture to critique by those of the smaller in such a manner as to help create a new intellectual framework that partially transcends and contributes to each culture.

In producing that thing we call western culture, humans have at the same time cut themselves off from understandings of nature as a source of spiritual and psychological life.[2] Sioux culture—and the cultures of other indigenous peoples—contain certain understandings that can help us rethink and redress this lack. The long history of appropriations from Indian people, however, requires us proceed with caution. My intent here is to establish a balanced dialogue between the two cosmologies and the spiritual and psychological dynamics that derived from them.

NOTES

1. Readers often raise the question of naming and proper word use in connection with American Indian people. There are a range of possibilities, each with its pitfalls and virtues: Native, Native American, American Indian, Indian, indigenous, aboriginal, First Nation, tribal, as well as specific names such as Sioux, Dakota, Navajo, etc. Vine Deloria's usage here was consistent with his other writings: "Indian" was his preferred marker of generic Indian identity.

2. Editor's note: For an exegesis of this thesis that western culture was born at the cost of a dissociation from nature, see *Living in the Borderland: The Evolution of Consciousness and the Challenge of Healing Trauma* by Jerome S. Bernstein (Routledge, 2005), Part I.

FROM THE EDITOR'S INTRODUCTION, WITH BIOGRAPHCIAL INFORMATION ABOUT VINE DELORIA, JR.

Philip J. Deloria

The preceeding pages were written to introduce the forthcoming book, *C. G. Jung and the Sioux Traditions*, which my father, Vine Deloria, Jr., had contemplated for over three decades. I well remember being a senior in high school, and having my father present me with a copy of Carl Jung's *Memories, Dreams, Reflections* and an admonition to read it. "This is loaded with interesting stuff," he said. "It is particularly useful in thinking about families, ours included. You'll see that, like our family, Jung had a set of clergymen in his past. Like us, he sometimes wondered if he were answering questions posed by his ancestors." Equally to the point, at least as far as my father was concerned, Carl Jung had been willing to open his mind to new ways of thinking about the world, about history, and about our human relation to it: "Be sure you meditate on that passage where he is making his way through a series of cellars deeper and deeper into the earth," he said, "and read the passage on his visit to Taos Pueblo too." My father thought that *Memories, Dreams, Reflections* was the perfect book for a young man on the edge of adulthood, and so I read it.

I see now that he recommended it to me because the book was tremendously important to him. I had not been thinking about whether our family was answering questions posed by our ancestors, but my father surely was contemplating exactly that possibility. His forthcoming book, *C. G. Jung and the Sioux Traditions,* from which these excerpts are taken, reveals the ways in which Jung's thinking profoundly influenced his own. Indeed, the task of this book, as he saw it, is to establish the grounds upon which mutual influences—between Sioux traditions, practices, and ways of thinking, and those emanating from Jung and those writing in the Jungian tradition—might be recognized and fostered.

Such a dialogue did not come easily to my father. He devoted years to a thorough reading of Jung's entire *Collected Works* (the full set still remains in his library in Colorado), and he reveled in the moments when Jung seemed to be speaking my father's conceptual language. At the same time, however, he was inevitably disturbed by the seeming omnipresence of the intellectual legacies of European colonialism, naturalized in many of Jung's utterances concerning "the primitive" and the place of "primitives" in contemporary society, and in Jung's developmentalist understanding of the transformations of society, culture, and the psyche. A staunch critic of both colonialism and evolution, my father had a difficult time squaring his appreciation for Jung's cosmology with Jung's culturally-inflected discourse. Some of that difficulty inevitably shows up in his writing.

My father believed deeply in the power of the spirit, and when he confronted setbacks in the writing of the Jung book, he took those troubles deeply to heart. On at least two occasions, he suffered from severe writer's block. My memory is that, in both instances, he reached the same page number, and found that he could go no further (the actual page is lost to my memory, but it was something over 200). He experienced a devastating office fire in the early 1990s, health issues later in that decade, and a repeated disinterest on the part of publishers for a book that was not only tightly specialized, but also a sometimes-confusing blend of critique and appreciation, and of psychology, philosophy, and ethnography. His excitement about this material was such that he did not always pause to translate from his "thinking language" to one more attuned to communication with a reading audience. Nancy Cater, Jerome Bernstein, and I have worked to move the work more precisely through that translation.

Vine Deloria Jr., (1933-2005) was born and raised in South Dakota, the son and grandson of Dakota Sioux Indian leaders in the Episcopalian missionary church. His aunt, Ella Deloria, had done ethnographic work under the auspices of Franz Boas and the first generation of female anthropologists, and his great-grandfather, Saswe, had been an important spiritual and political figure among the mid-nineteenth century Yankton people. Even as Vine Deloria acquired a solid "western" education at boarding schools, and later, Iowa State University and the Lutheran School of Theology, he grew up surrounded by the stories and cultural contexts of his Lakota and Dakota Sioux Indian people. In 1965, he began serving as the Executive Director of the National Congress of American Indians, and worked tirelessly to mobilize tribes and Indian people in general toward effective participation in the American political process. Drawing on these experiences, he wrote the 1969 bestseller *Custer Died for Your Sins: An Indian Manifesto*, which used wit, humor, and biting critique to awaken Americans of all stripes to the persistence of American Indian people. Though he is best known for the political, legal, and historical writings that followed *Custer*, Deloria never retreated from questions of metaphysics and spirituality, and his explorations took concrete shape in books such as *God is Red* (1973) and *The Metaphysics of Modern Existence* (1979). The present work ought properly be seen as a continuation of those explorations that brings together the many strands of his interests.

If the words that began this excerpt introduced my father's desire for comparison and dialogue between two intellectual traditions, those that follow represent some of the basic contextual groundwork necessary to begin that dialogue. In *C. G. Jung and the Sioux Traditions*, Vine Deloria Jr. considers the cosmologies of Carl Jung and Sioux people, as well as their respective views on animals, dreams, visions, and the family. In preparing for that exploration, however, he felt it important to outline certain histories: the actual contacts Carl Jung had with North American Indian people (the episode in Taos in particular), Jung's understanding of Indians as symbols, and the ironic linkages existing between such symbolic uses and the historical processes of dispossession. He discusses these issues in Chapter Two, "Meeting

Grounds: Jung's Indian Experiences and Symbolic Interpretations," excerpted below.

From Chapter Two, "Meeting Grounds: Jung's Indian Experiences and Symbolic Interpretations," of *C. G. Jung and the Sioux Traditions*

Vine Deloria, Jr.

In 1920 Jung visited Algeria and Tunisia. He sensed immediately that he was in a radically different social and physical environment, one that did not fit with his narrow European psychology. His perceptions broadened; he began to reflect on what other cultures might represent and teach him.

> When I contemplated for the first time the European spectacle from the Sahara, surrounded by a civilization which has more or less the same relationship to ours as Roman antiquity has to modern times, I became aware of how completely, even in America, I was still caught up and imprisoned in the cultural consciousness of the white man. The desire grew in me to carry the historical comparisons still farther by descending to a still lower cultural level.[1]

So in the winter of 1924-25 Jung came to America, and as part of his tour visited the Indians of Taos Pueblo in New Mexico.

At the time, Taos was the playground of the 1920s version of the Beatniks and New Agers. Mabel Dodge Luhan was the unofficial hostess of the town, sponsoring important visitors and trying to duplicate her earlier salon success in Greenwich Village. D. H. Lawrence was Taos' resident intellectual and mystic, the Taos school of painting was well under way, and the cultural avant garde of the time had to make an obligatory journey to northern New Mexico as part of their personal spiritual quests. Mabel Dodge Luhan seized the opportunity of Jung's trip to have the famous psychoanalyst visit her domain and so a hasty side trip to New Mexico from Chicago was arranged. During this trip, Jung was able to visit Taos Pueblo and hold long conversations with some of the Pueblo elders and representatives. In *Memories, Dreams, Reflections,* Jung included a few pages of an unfinished manuscript on the Pueblo Indians that reflected on his trip and experiences. Those pages reveal a man profoundly changed in his view of the history of Western culture. Jung seems to have seen for the first time the dark shadow of "progress" and "civilization."[2]

The landscape of Taos is itself magnificent, and gives visitors a more realistic perspective about themselves than they typically experience in everyday life: we are but dust compared to the mountain and rivers of that plateau. Jung, too, was similarly affected and he remembered both the mountains and the physical setting of the pueblo:

> Behind us a clear stream purled past the houses, and on its opposite bank stood a second pueblo of reddish adobe houses, built one atop the other toward the center of the settlement, thus strangely anticipating the perspective of an American metropolis with its skyscrapers in the center.[3]

He would later pose a rhetorical question in "The Complications of American Psychology:"

> Have you ever compared the skyline of New York or any great American city with that of a pueblo like Taos? And did you see how the houses pile up to towers towards the centre? Without conscious imitation the American unconsciously fills out the spectral outline of the Red Man's mind and temperament.[4]

Here was a psychic apprehension he had not anticipated, an experience that challenged his psychology in new ways.

Jung's American experiences made a deep impression and would always stay with him. These reflections suggest that the psychological impact of the Indian was emotionally significant and transcended his critical and scholarly analysis. At one level, Jung was impressed by how the American unconscious had been influenced by Indians and was projected onto its landscapes. Jung decided that the Indians with their multi-storied pueblos had anticipated the later creation of large cities with massive buildings, so that the whites were unconsciously fulfilling ideas first generated by the Indians. Undoubtedly he had seen adobe villages in Algeria and Tunisia that closely resembled the pueblos of New Mexico so the idea of piling rooms on top of each other was not novel. Yet because it was American Indians who had built this structure, it seemed to offer him a different opportunity to examine a particularly American unconscious, one that linked immigrant non-Indians with indigenous psyche and culture.

The stay in Taos, although brief, greatly affected the psychoanalyst, and he alluded to his experiences at Taos several times in his seminars, particularly when he wished to describe and illustrate psychological maturity and stability. Upon reflection he remembered,

> It was astonishing to me to see how the Indian's emotions change when he speaks of his religious ideas. In ordinary life he shows a degree of self-control and dignity that borders on fatalistic equanimity. But when he speaks of things that pertain to his mysteries, he is in the grip of a surprising emotion which he cannot conceal—a fact that greatly helped to satisfy my curiosity.[5]

The apprehension of a calm yet intense religious feeling made a deep impression on him and he sought to get the Indians to explain their deepest religious beliefs to him.

Jung's host for the occasion was Ochiway Biano (Mountain Lake), a man designated by the Pueblo elders to represent them before the famous psychoanalyst. As a typical non-Indian, Jung mistakenly believed Biano to be the head chief of the Pueblo and always thereafter referred to him as his friend the Chief. The two men played a cat and mouse game with each other. When Jung would comment on some phase of Pueblo life, he would watch Biano's face, seeking to interpret the Indian's reaction to his observations. If a hint of emotion showed, Jung believed that he had raised an important question and counted the topic as one to be pursued. But Biano was no amateur, being the person designated by the elders to deal with outsiders, and he rarely offered to explain his beliefs or responses. Instead he spoke to Jung primarily about the sun and how it was the father of us all. This belief explained why the men of Taos sat on the roofs of their homes at sunrise. Biano said they were giving their personal energy to the sun, helping it begin to move across the sky. The idea was preposterous to non-Indians learned in celestial mechanics, but Jung, approaching this devotional setting from a psychoanalytical perspective, quickly saw the connection.

Jung later recalled:

> Never before had I run into such an atmosphere of secrecy; the religions of civilized nations today are all accessible; their

> sacraments have long ago ceased to be mysteries. Here, however,
> the air was filled with a secret known to all the communicants,
> but to which whites could gain no access.[6]

He needn't have fretted about his exclusion; at Taos no outsider is allowed to know anything about the religious practices of the Pueblo. Exclusion, however, was a new experience for Jung and he continued to attempt to uncover the Pueblo's religious secrets. In a letter to Biano in October 1932, seven years after his visit, Jung was still trying to discern the inner core of Taos religious life:

> I wish you would write to me at once, what your religious customs
> are in order to secure a good harvest. Have you got corn-dances,
> or other ways by which you make the wheat and corn grow? Are
> your young men still worshipping the Father Sun? Are you also
> making occasionally sand-paintings like the Navajos? Any
> information you can give me about your religious life is always
> welcome to me. I shall keep all that information to myself, but it
> is most helpful to me, as I am busy exploring the truth in which
> Indians believe.[7]

Something happened while Jung was at Taos that might have helped him in his efforts to gain psychological knowledge of the Indians. Unfortunately, Jung missed the point and tended to pass the incident off as a joke. As a matter of courtesy he was allowed to climb on the roofs and watch the men greeting the rising sun. When he began to climb down, like the typical outsider, Jung turned around and climbed down facing the ladder. The Pueblos walk down the ladder as if it was a stairs. Jung's everyday European behavior presented a humorous spectacle to the people of Taos.

> The Pueblo Indians declared in a matter-of-fact way that I
> belonged to the Bear Totem—in other words, that I was a bear—
> because I did not come down a ladder standing up like a man,
> but bunched up on all fours like a bear. If anyone in Europe said
> I had a bearish nature this would amount to the same thing, but
> with a rather different shade of meaning.[8]

The characterization of individuals in relation to the traits of an animal served as an Indian way of classifying and understanding strangers. And in Jung's case it was accurate, not only in terms of his performance on the ladder but in terms of his physical body and his own character as a powerful healer. Jung missed the subtlety of the depth to which their perception of character had penetrated him. Had he recognized that, it might have brought the discourse to a new and psychologically deeper level.

There is inferential evidence that Jung left Taos believing that he had acquired knowledge of the essential elements of the American Indian psyche sufficient to use in the practice of comparative scholarship. Yet, many of his statements concerning Indians and "other primitives" carry a sweeping, all-knowing style and an authority he had not necessarily earned through close study over a long period of time. Still, the Taos experience clearly haunted Jung and remained with him all his life. Writing to Miguel Serrano in 1960 as a feeble old man, a year before his death, Jung wistfully reflected: "We are sorely in need of a Truth or a self-understanding similar to that of Ancient Egypt, which I have found still living with the Taos Pueblos."[9] Remembering how brief and accidental his visit to Taos was 35 years before, we can but marvel at the impact that American Indians made on him. His visits to Algeria, Kenya, and India, while providing him with insights into different cultures, did not seem to have the same impact as his brief time at Taos. Thus comparing the Jungian psychological system with American Indian traditions has a basis in Jung's own emotional experiences.

We can easily chart the Indian influence on Jung after his American visit. In a lecture in his seminar on Visions, held in the fall of 1930, Carl Jung said, "the realization of Indian values by an American is an asset, not a liability. The Red Indian has great qualities *despite the fact that he is a primitive.*"[10] (Emphasis added) Jung made many comments like this during the course of his life, which encapsulate the complications inherent in his relation to Indians. On the one hand, the Taos experience had been transformative, giving him a sense of the possibilities to be understood in terms of Indian people. On the other hand, Jung was part of the intellectual discourse of his moment, which emphasized a kind of social evolutionary framework, in which "primitive" had intellectual explanatory power. "Primitives"— such as Indian people—were the living examples of earlier stages in evolution. Jung's own sense of development over time was complex, but it is not surprising that he would adopt the word "primitive,"which carried a host of ambiguities and multiple meanings. These contradictory positions—encapsulated here in the space of a single sentence—form a consistent thread in Jung's thought, as they did in much intellectual discourse of the period. Here, Indian values are offered to Americans: emulate these people and you will develop great qualities. But always remember that the Red Indian is a primitive. This was a contradiction that haunted many people besides Carl Jung: How do you explain the presence of great qualities in a person that has not moved up the cultural evolutionary incline? Jung never answered this question, which had already played itself out over two centuries of American history.

In effect, Jung was giving gratuitous advice to an audience already obsessed with Indian myth. Americans had long since begun to devour Indians in a genocidal policy of land confiscation while simultaneously applauding their virtues. In 1833, American men founded the Improved Order of Red Men, a fraternal order that traced its lineage to "Indian" clubs dating from the American Revolution. This organization was devoted to American Indian values and beliefs, although no one with Indian blood was eligible for membership because it was, after all, an effort to improve what Indians themselves had accomplished. It must strike students of the unconscious as ironic that concurrent with the popularity of Indian virtues, Congress passed the Indian Removal Act in 1830, which forced the Indians of the eastern United States to sell their lands and move across the Mississippi into the Great Plains because they were savages and not fit for civilized living. This belief prevailed even though the Cherokees, for example, had already devised an alphabet and established a written constitution. Before most of the Indians could even begin their journey into exile, whites were already organizing a society to celebrate their virtues. Clearly, the psychological achievements of, and idealized projections onto, the Indian were far more appealing than real Indians in the flesh and inhabiting the neighborhood.[11]

In the late 1920s, almost coincident with Jung's Visions seminar, the Improved Order of Red Men organization reached its peak membership of 500,000. Members were adopting fake Indian names such as "Running Deer" and "Pale Moon," dressing in outlandish brown canvas costumes decorated as if they were buckskins, engaging in a host of made-up Indian "ceremonies." The organization went into decline during the 1920s and 1930s when fraternal orders of this type lost membership across the country. Or perhaps people had discovered that no matter how hard they tried, they really were not Indians—nor were they much of an improvement.

Another organization founded earlier, but espousing the same goals as the Red Men, had better results. On February 8th, 1910, the Boy Scouts, founded by William Boyce and Dan Beard, received a charter in the District of Columbia and parents were urged to enroll their sons so they could learn the manly virtues of the Indian. The organization expanded with the founding of the Girl Scouts in 1912. There has been steady growth in these groups ever since their founding, perhaps because Indian values are cherished for young people. Even in today's politically correct climate, and in spite of the conservative Boy Scout practices, membership runs into the millions. Other organizations such as the YMCA with its Indian Guides program and the Camp Fire Girls joined in the imitation movement and also began applauding the values and virtues of the Indian. Just how much money was squandered on these pale imitations while the real Indians were starving on reservations is unpleasant to contemplate. The fact that countless Americans grow up participating in these organizations reflects the continuing idealization of American Indians.

Carl Jung perhaps missed that he was joining the long parade of people who claimed to find enduring values by honoring and/or emulating the American Indian. He differed from many others who wrote about the American Indian in that Indians for him possessed an understanding of deep psychological truths that he could find nowhere else.[12] Scattered throughout his collected works, seminars, and lectures are any number of statements on Indians, some derogatory, some back-handed compliments, some clearly extolling their virtues, but always, it seemed, casual and spontaneous references as if the Indians had affected him at the deepest psychological level.

A recounting, as above, of Jung's actual encounters with Indian people is critical to our understanding of the possibilities of dialogue and comparison. So too is the representation of Indian people—both positive and negative—in Jung's own theoretical corpus. It is also the case, however, that we need to understand some of the ways Indian images made their way into both symbolic expressions and into the richer and more subtle depths of the collective unconscious. What are some of the ways that Jung saw Indians appearing in the utterances of his patients, and in American and European culture in general? Jung often remarked that he had become aware of American Indians in therapy in the dreams and fantasies of his American patients. "I have found in my American patients," he wrote,

> that their hero-figure possesses traits derived from the religion of the Indians. The most important figure in their religion is the shaman, the medicine man or conjurer of spirits. The first American discovery in this field—since taken up in Europe— was spiritualism, and the second was Christian Science and other forms of mental healing.[13]

Spiritualism and Christian Science were movements that emphasized self-reliance in healing, and that saw the individual as capable of drawing from hidden sources of energy and spirit within the universe without the intercession of others. Like the skyscrapers that evoked Pueblo architecture, Christian Science and spiritualism may have refigured Indian spiritual practices at a deep, unconscious level, reflecting Jung's developing ideas concerning the collective unconscious. He perceived that these traits of American Indian religions and practices were echoed in the newly founded American religions and in the revivals of established American churches.

Jung's perceptions did not coalesce just because Indians appeared in the dreams of a few American patients. He recognized a number of additional phenomena, pointing out, for example, that the American unconscious "chooses the Indian as its symbol, just as certain coins of the Union bear an Indian-head. This is a tribute to the once-hated Indian, but it also testifies to the fact that the American hero-motif chooses the Indian as the ideal figure."[14] Although startling, it does not take much reflection to appreciate the profound effect Indians had on white settlers. Indians had confronted the United States as a powerful indigenous presence since its founding and provided more than enough reason to be included in the American cultural pantheon. Indians are everywhere in American cultural expression, from the dome of the United States capitol to its money to its literary fiction.

It is worth noting that the Indian on the penny, modeled in an eastern Indian headdress. was later replaced by the Buffalo nickel which featured a western Indian profile with different feathers on one side of the coin and a buffalo on the other. Had Jung known something of the Sioux Indians he would have smiled. This coin curiously represents the Sioux Indians' belief that in a higher cosmic dimension they and the buffalo are one spirit, split into two separate entities upon taking physical form. The particular figuring of this coin might be seen to reflect Jung's ideas concerning the significant effects of Indians at a deep level of the collective American psyche, as well as the psyches of its citizens.

Jung made a wide range of comparisons between Indians and American whites. Thoroughly accustomed to the civilized manner in which Europeans engaged in sport, for example, (before the soccer riots of recent times), Jung recoiled at the way in which Americans ferociously pursued athletic excellence. "The American conception of sport goes far beyond the notion of the easy-going European," Jung observed, adding, "Only the Indian rites of initiation can compare with the ruthlessness and savagery of a rigorous American training." He also suggested that in the much praised American trait of the "can do" pioneer spirit and tenacity, we are really catching a glimpse of the Indian.

> His [the American's] extraordinary concentration on a particular goal, his tenacity of purpose, his unflinching endurance of the greatest hardships—in all this the *legendary virtues of the Indian find full expression*.[15] (emphasis added)

While many might credit the ever-present frontier as the primary source of American inspiration, Jung saw American virtue at its deepest level as an expression of rigorous discipline and a profound willpower that was best seen in American Indians.

He was also fascinated by the idea that particular areas of the earth seemed compatible with one people and not another.[16] He warned that invaders or intruders of any land would find themselves vulnerable to its power and that that power would change them to resemble its aboriginal peoples. "The mystery of the earth is no joke and no paradox," he warned. "One only needs to see how, in America, the skull and pelvis measurements of all the European races begin to indianize themselves in the second generation of immigrants. That is the mystery of the American earth."[17] Franz Boas, the noted American anthropologist, had done some studies of first and second-generation immigrants that suggested that these physical changes were actually occurring. Though now regarded as questionable, Jung seized on these

as evidence that Americans were undergoing a unique change—
although no one recognized what was happening to them.[18] Boas
himself was operating out of the framework of environmental
determinism, but it may be that Jung was also seeing such changes in
terms of the power of the earth, and the resonance that he had formed
with American Indian religions in the development of his own ideas.
As important as the prospect of physical bodily changes, the immigrant
psyche was changing as it gradually adopted the psychology of the
aboriginal peoples. Despite their best efforts, fragments of the American
Indian soul were now appearing in the dreams and fantasies of American
whites. "Thus the American presents a strange picture," Jung said, "a
European with Negro behavior and an Indian soul. He shares the fate
of all usurpers of foreign soil."[19]

Barbara Hannah recalled that Jung believed that the European
possessed a safe and predictable unconscious that he described by
analogy as the cellar in a comfortable old home that could be safely
explored. In psychoanalysis the therapist opened the cellar door and
helped the patient proceed systematically down the steps, sequentially
recounting the historical experiences of the Europeans. But it was not
so with the Americans. "'When the American opens a similar door in
his psychology,'" Jung used to say,

> there is a dangerous open gap, dropping hundreds of feet, and
> in those cases where he can negotiate the drop, he will then be
> faced with an Indian or Negro shadow, whereas the European
> finds a shadow of his own race.[20]

Jung accurately perceived significant and complex psychological
differences between the native and the transplanted white European.

Taking such instances as the ground for our own speculations, we
can in fact draw some valuable conclusions about Jung's relationship
to American Indians. After an initial cultural shock in Algeria and
Tunisia in which he was forced to recognize his narrow European
perspective, Jung determined to make the acquaintance of the so-called
primitive peoples. There was no question that he initially regarded
tribal/primitive peoples as culturally and psychologically inferior to
Europeans. When the opportunity suddenly presented itself in the
winter of 1924-25, he journeyed to Taos Pueblo. While there, he
experienced a different way of life with a highly developed sense of

religious commitment that transcended his European experiences. He remembered that difference the rest of his life. Thereafter on the occasions when he mentioned Taos, it was always with great admiration. When, in his lectures and seminars, he wanted to use a living example of a mature personality, Jung always cited Biano, the spokesman of the Pueblo whom he had mistaken for a chief.

Jung's spiritual quest to Indian country has been duplicated by succeeding generations of his followers. Some people familiar with Jungian writings look to Indian reservations in search of spiritual enlightenment since they are influenced by Jung's admiration for Indians and the intuitive insights that he thought could inform and enlighten psychology. A few casual remarks by Jung about Taos would not ordinarily trigger this kind of sustained desire to experience Indians as part of the missing element of Jungian psychology. There must be a great kinship between Jungian psychology and the American Indian traditions that has been emerging, will continue to develop, and is worth the time and energy of our investigation. A major component of that kinship is Jung's strong sense of a dissociation in western culture due to its separation from nature and the Indian psyche that has never experienced such a separation and for whom nature is a living experience and spiritual presence.

NOTES

1. C. G. Jung, *Memories, Dreams, Reflections* (New York: Pantheon, 1961), 247.

2. *Ibid.*, 247-249. It is worth noting that these pages are not Jung's only writings on Taos. We do not know what additional material may be in others of Jung's papers to which we do not have access at the present time.

3. *Ibid.*, 249.

4. C. G. Jung, *Collected Works of C. G. Jung* (Princeton: Princeton University Press, 1960), Vol. 10, para. 356 [the *Collected Works* are hereinafter referenced as "*CW,*" followed by the volume number and the paragraph number].

5. *Memories, Dreams, Reflections*, 250.

6. *Ibid.*, 249.

7. C. G. Jung, *Letters, Vol. 1, 1906-1950,* "To Antonio Mirabal ("Mountain Lake,") 21 October 1932, p. 101.

8. *CW* 10 § 132. Later Jung would discover that a bear had been a part of his family's crest of arms many centuries before, but he did not further reflect on this coincidence.

9. C. G. Jung, *Letters II,* "To Miguel Serrano," 14 September 1960, p. 596.

10. *The Visions Seminar, Book One, Part Seven,* 242.

11. For an extended treatment of this dynamic, see Philip J. Deloria, *Playing Indian* (New Haven: Yale University Press, 1998).

12. This is not to say that others did not adopt the same or similar positions. Indeed, future Commissioner of Indian Affairs John Collier was in Taos at roughly the same time and he too wrote of Indians possessing the deepest secrets of the human development of personality and community. Mabel Dodge herself probably belongs in this group, as does Mary Austin and others.

13. *CW* 10 §101.

14. *CW* 10 § 99.

15. *CW* 10 § 100.

16. See, for example, Vine Deloria, Jr., *God is Red: A Native View of Religion,* 2d. edition (Golden: Fulcrum Publishing, 1994).

17. *CW* 10 § 18. Strangely, Arnold Toynbee also noted that the invaders of a land had a difficult time adjusting to new lands. In *An Historian's Approach to Religion,* he makes the following statement: "The colonists planted by the Assryian Government on territory that had been cleared of its previous human occupants by the deportation of the Children of Israel soon found, to their cost, that Israel's undeported god Yahweh had lost one of his local potency; and they had no peace till they took to worshipping this very present local god instead of the gods that they had brought with them from their homelands." (see 2 Kings. xvii 24-41), 35.

18. Not surprisingly, Boas's studies have come into question. Jung remarked, however, when he arrived in America to receive an honorary degree from Clark University, that there must have been significant intermarriage with Indians to achieve facial and skeletal similarities to Indians.

19. *CW* 10 § 103.

20. Barbara Hannah, *Jung: His Life and Work* (New York: A Perigee Book, 1976), 163.

LAND MINDS:
IMAGES OF PSYCHE AND SHADOW
IN TWO AMERICAN INDIAN NOVELS

RINDA WEST

The ecological crisis we face today, from habitat loss to global warming, flows in part from our culture's strained relationship with what is "natural" in human beings. In many ways, western culture has cast what is animal about humans into shadow. Projecting this shadow onto the natural world and onto native people has rationalized their conquest. In this essay I will argue that fictions can expose what shadow obscures. Retrieving shadow projections can offer new energies and ways of knowing that can serve individuals and the planet.

In its desire to harness and subdue the power of the earth, western capitalism declared the Earth inanimate and disowned the affiliation, respect, and affection for nature that characterize cultures that avow a more reciprocal relationship with their habitat. As the west industrialized, the need for a disciplined work force combined with the protestant work ethic to declare the human body just another

Rinda West was a Professor of English at Oakton Community College before becoming a landscape designer. She has been involved with the C. G. Jung Institute and Center in Chicago for 20 years. Her book, *Out of the Shadow: Ecopsychology, Story, and Encounters with the Land,* will be published in the fall of 2007 by the University of Virginia Press.

"resource" to be controlled and exploited. To control human production, some mental processes came to be called inferior, such as imagination, daydreaming, and experiences of the numinous. Around this time, also, the colonial ambitions of Western Europe resulted in bloodthirsty practices of extraction and conquest in Africa and the Americas. European adventurers and colonizers absolved themselves of the brutality of their own behavior by calling the conquered people "primitive" and "savage." These shadow projections, rationalized by the notion of a civilizing mission, shielded Europeans from acknowledging the shame of their own conquests. But they also deprived the colonizers of energies in the unconscious that constitute our human "nature," estranging them from the rest of the natural world and alienating them from themselves. Theodore Roszak, who coined the term "ecopsychology," argues that "our sense of being split off from an "outer" world where we find no companionable response has everything to do with our obsessive need to conquer and subjugate."[1]

I believe that fictions can promote the healing of both nature and psyche by offering images of reconciliation between human beings and the rest of the natural world. Awareness of environmental degradation is an essential part of any movement for change, but it can become what Andrew Samuels calls the environmental movement's "unrelenting litany of humanity's destructiveness," which can lead to self-disgust and depression.[2] Instead, the environmental movement needs to proclaim the joy and the healing that can be found in intimacy with the natural world. James Hillman maintains that individuation, or soul-making,

> does not seek a way out of or beyond the world toward redemption or mystical transcendence....The curative or salvational vision of archetypal psychology focuses upon the soul in the world which is also the soul of the world.[3]

In equating the soul in the world with the soul of the world, Hillman locates unconscious human "nature" in the realm of extra-human nature.

The philosopher, Vine Deloria, Jr. of the Standing Rock Sioux, concurs. Deloria argues that

> The living universe requires mutual respect among its members. The willingness of entities to allow others to fulfill themselves,

> and the refusal of any entity to intrude thoughtlessly on another,
> must be the operative principle of this universe. Consequently,
> self-knowledge and self-discipline are high values of behavior.
> Only by allowing innovation by every entity can the universe
> move forward and create the future.[4]

For Deloria, too, the world and all its entities are alive, ensouled, and entitled. Respect, restraint, and love are the principles that guide the relationship between humans and nature, and extending rights to others is the prerequisite for health. Because the relationship between humans and the land is central in American Indian cultures, Indian novels offer a valuable lens through which a contemporary reader can explore other ways of knowing and of being part of the natural world.

Although few people today would call Indian people "primitive" or "savage," the historical treatment of Indians is part of the American cultural shadow. In its relentless colonizing thrust, the United States made war on Indian people, their land, and culture. Many millions of Indians died. American laws transformed Indian land into property, forced Indian people onto reservations, and took Indian children away from their families, depriving them of their language and religion. Yet American histories rarely confront this legacy of devastation. Dealing with this shadow has to be part of our willingness, as Deloria puts it, "to allow others to fulfill themselves." To read contemporary American Indian fiction is to see the world from the shadow.

Traditional cultures believe the universe is animate, they acknowledge their dependence on other creatures, and they practice habits of mind that keep them close to the land. They respect myth, practice ritual, and rely on dream as a source of knowledge. These ways of knowing, generally undeveloped today, also occupy the American cultural shadow, leaving an absence of the numinous that continues to estrange people from the rest of life. Thus while it may be a cliché to describe American Indian cultures as ecologically sensitive, people rarely examine the beliefs and practices of those cultures that linked them to the earth. By looking at shadow in several forms in two American Indian novels, I hope to explore what they can teach us about developing an ecological conscience.

I will begin with James Welch's novel *Fools Crow*, a coming-of-age story of the Pikuni tribe of Blackfeet in the years just following the Civil War. Welch's novel presents a picture of a culture before conquest, in which a reader can become immersed in traditional values, beliefs, and ways of knowing. It covers a large swath of Blackfeet land in what is now western Montana, and it demonstrates a way of living with the land that honored the nature of which humans are one part. I will turn, then, to Leslie Marmon Silko's *Ceremony*, whose shell-shocked hero, Tayo, has returned from World War II to a land suffering a terrible drought. This novel explores many levels of shadow, from the personal to the archetypal, in the process of recounting the ritual through which the hero reconciles psyche and the land. Finally, I will look at the ways both of these novels explore the value of ritual in acknowledging, absorbing, and containing shadow.

FOOLS CROW AND TRADITIONAL WAYS OF KNOWING

Published in 1986, *Fools Crow* tells the story of White Man's Dog, a young would-be hunter and warrior, who, after several raids, takes on the new name, Fools Crow. Welch translates Blackfeet names for animals literally, so buffalo are "blackhorns." Months are "the moon of the burnt grass," "first thunder moon." Places are "the Backbone of the World" or "Woman Don't Walk Butte," and the power of nature is embodied in such terms as "Cold Maker," a designation that suggests more than the bland English abstraction "winter." In this use of language, Welch constructs a reading experience in which the Blackfeet reader is centered in his culture and a white reader pushed to the margins. In this way he inverts the usual assumption in western culture that the western world view is the norm, and all other readers must accommodate themselves to its presumptions. The narrative immerses the reader in Blackfeet consciousness, exploring potentials of psyche that often occupy shadow today.

In the beginning, white people are little more than an occasional threat, but their intrusion into Blackfeet country becomes increasingly more present, more unavoidable, and more destructive. Dread colors the story but never quite overwhelms it. What keeps despair at bay is Welch's performance of the traditional culture, which is thereby preserved from extinction. Welch explores ways of knowing enacted in the novel through the power of dreams, myths, ceremonies, and animal helpers. In representing rituals associated with shadow, the novel underlines the values of respect, restraint, and compassion.

In *Fools Crow*, a dream is not simply a subjective experience. On a horse raid to a Crow camp early in the novel, the young Fools Crow, who at this point is still called White Man's Dog, has a powerful dream, which he keeps to himself. He dreams, several times, of a lodge in an enemy camp filled with naked white-faced girls, who carry an erotic charge. By keeping his dream private, White Man's Dog withholds vital information from the raiding party. This exposes its leader, Yellow Kidney, to danger. In the Crow encampment, Yellow Kidney initially escapes detection, when the watch is roused, by ducking into a lodge filled with young people with smallpox. In the dark, he cannot tell that they are diseased, however, and in the heat of the moment, he rapes one of the girls. As a result, he contracts smallpox. When the Crows capture him, they cut off his fingers and send him out in the snowy night to be a warning to the Blackfeet.

White Man's Dog's dream illustrates the social quality of dreams. Later in the story, White Man's Dog hears Yellow Kidney's account of his experience in the Crow raid, and he feels responsible for the older man's condition. He confides in his father his feelings of guilt, and his father responds,

> It is true that you should have told Yellow Kidney about your dream, and it might be true that he would have turned back. But I believe that it would have been too late. Already the world was out of balance. You were too close to the Crow camps to see reason and so you proceeded, knowing the risks. No, do not blame yourself. At most, you made an error in judgment.[5]

A dream is a public responsibility. White Man's Dog "should have" told his dream. But his proximity to danger, and the excited state of mind this prompted, blinded him. His altered subjective state changed his perceptions, but more, it changed everything. "Already the *world* was out of balance." His father suggests here the close relationship of inner and outer in Pikuni culture. The dream places the subjectivity of the dreamer on view and links it to the common imagination. It makes a person responsible not only for his actions, but also for what he channels from the unconscious. In this respect, the traditional culture could absorb into public life energies that are locked within the individual in much of contemporary life.

POWER ANIMALS

In addition to dreams, *Fools Crow* features power animals. The numinosity accorded such animals indicates the respect in which humans held other creatures in nature and their acknowledged dependence on them. White Man's Dog rescues a wolverine from a trap. In the narrative, this represents a development in his consciousness and his capacity. Subsequently, he has a dream in which again he frees Wolverine, who instructs him thus:

> When you kill the blackhorns, or any of the four-leggeds, you must leave a chunk of liver for Raven, for it was he who guided you to me. He watches out for all his brothers and that is why we leave part of our kills for him.[6]

This powerful dream asserts a deep kinship between the man and the animal: each hunts and each honors the hunted. To live, each must take life, so each honors both those powers that guide the hunt and those that give their lives for the survival of the hunter. In leaving some of the liver for Raven, White Man's Dog sacrifices some of his bounty to acknowledge his dependence and complicity. This represents an example of the principles of self-knowledge and self-discipline articulated by Vine Deloria, Jr. The hunting ritual ensures that the act of taking life will be mindful, so the violence of the hunt does not withdraw into shadow and the dependence of humans on animal sacrifice remains conscious.

Wolverine reciprocates White Man's Dog's kindness by conferring power on him, specifically the power of song. The power song is a very special kind of utterance, akin to prayer. In *American Indian Literatures,* A. LaVonne Brown Ruoff writes of the emphasis American Indian people placed on "living in harmony with the physical and spiritual universe, the power of thought and word to maintain this balance, a deep reverence for the land, and a strong sense of community."[7] In song people vocalize the thoughts that maintain the balance. Song invokes the presence of the spiritual in the physical; it speaks to the singer; it promises; it celebrates. David Abram, in *The Spell of the Sensuous*, argues that for traditional people, language is not exclusive to humans. Trees, animals, even rocks speak. Wind and rain speak, and human speech involves a dialogue with the other beings.

> To such people, that which we term 'language' remains as much
> a property of the animate landscape as of the humans who dwell
> and speak within that terrain.[8]

Songs use repetition, both within the song and in singing it over and over, that can alter states of mind. Like prayer, a song is not intended to communicate information; instead, it "establish[es] or consolidat[es] relationship through intensifying the 'presence' of one being to another."[9] Song also brings deep parts of the self into relationship with the living physical world.

Later in the narrative, after the raid which resulted in his new name, White Man's Dog, now Fools Crow, and Red Paint, his wife, visit the mountains. There Raven instructs him to kill a white man who has been slaughtering animals and leaving them. At first Fools Crow resists, because he knows that to kill a white man at that point is to expose his people to danger, but Raven persuades him that his allegiance to "his brothers, the four-leggeds and the flyers"[10] demands that he rid the mountain of this menace. We see how song works when Fools Crow is stalking the Napikwan (the term used consistently for white people) who leaves his kill. He

> breathed deeply and saw a red wall come up behind his eyes. He felt sick and weak. He closed his eyes and called out to Sun Chief, to Wolverine, his power, to give him strength, to let him die with honor. Slowly, almost silently, a sound entered his ears. As the sound increased in volume, the red wall behind his eyes receded. Now he saw the slope clearly, the red bushes, the slender yellow grasses—and his gun. The sound was in his head and in the small meadow surrounded by the great mountains of the Backbone. The sound flowed through his body and he felt the strength of its music in his limbs, in his hands, in his guts, in his chest. He sprang to a crouch, then made a dive for his weapon. A *boom!* kicked up a patch of duff inches from his head. But the music had reached his heart. The weapon was in his hands, against his cheek, and he watched the greased shooter leave his rifle and he watched it travel through the air, between the trees, and he saw it enter the Napikwan's forehead above the startled eyes, below the wolfskin headdress, and he squatted and watched the head jerk back, then the body, until it landed with a quivering shudder in the bear grass, the lupine, the windflowers. Then the sound was no more. Fools Crow's death song had ended.[11]

The song seems almost involuntary, an agency that enters his ears, clears his sight, inflames his courage, strengthens his body, and guides his hand. It comes when he is nearly hobbled by fear, and it gives him the power of Wolverine to keep him mindful of his responsibility to all the animals. The song is in his head, but it is also in the "the small meadow," in him, and in the world. His death song, the reminder of his mortality, inspires him with the courage to do what's right. At the same time the song enables him to take life, not rashly, but in accord with moral principles. It contains and channels energy from the shadow into an appropriate act.

RITUAL

Fools Crow gets his new name after counting coup on the Crow for their treatment of Yellow Kidney. But before that can happen, when he is still White Man's Dog, he dances the Sun Dance to thank the sun god for his success in the earlier horse raid. On that occasion, however, he also killed a Crow boy, and he feels a need to cleanse himself. The ordeal at the Medicine Pole serves as a ritual transition for him, giving both thanks and sacrifice and thereby moving him toward his role as a warrior and his new name.

Like hunters, warriors must know their kinship with those they kill. Both kill, and both risk death in the process. The Sun Dance ritual allows White Man's Dog symbolically to take some of the violence he has performed and embody it, to contain the tension between his love of life, with whatever shadow elements of cowardice that may imply, and his desire for glory, with whatever shadow elements of hubris that may imply. Because it is symbolic, the ritual allows him to accommodate extreme desires and hold them simultaneously in his body, increasing the likelihood that he will grow in consciousness as a consequence. It helps to transform White Man's Dog from a young horse raider into a warrior and a man.

PERSONAL AND CULTURAL SHADOW

The character Fools Crow embodies the values of his culture, as Louis Owens points out.[12] Because Welch uses him as an icon, Fools Crow does not have a fully drawn shadow, but Welch acknowledges the shadow of the culture in other characters, such as Fast Horse and Owl Child. These young outlaws are individualistic, boastful, and unrepentant. They want to resist and punish whites for encroaching on their territory, and they take risks that endanger their community in doing so. The community could use their energy, but it cannot tolerate their adventurism.

On the way to the Crow camp early in the novel, Fast Horse also has a powerful dream, in which Cold Maker comes to tell him that the raid will only be successful if they remove a rock that has fallen over a spring on Woman Don't Walk Butte. When Fast Horse tells his dream, he translates it from the private to the communal. It requires a response, and the horse raiders interrupt their journey to pursue it. Puffed up at his big dream, Fast Horse brags that Cold Maker has chosen him for this important message. But the raiders cannot locate the spring. Yellow Kidney prays for guidance and decides to continue the raid, but with extra caution. Later, when Yellow Kidney steals down to seize a prize horse from the Crows, Fast Horse rides into the camp shouting boasts, exposing Yellow Kidney to the Crows, with the disastrous results reported earlier.

Fast Horse represents a shadow figure for the exemplary Fools Crow, and also for the tribe. When Yellow Kidney finally returns to the Pikuni camps and tells his terrible story, the elders of the tribe decide to banish Fast Horse for his boasting. He joins Owl Child, who, with his band of marauders, takes revenge on individual whites for acts of aggression or simply for their occupation of the Blackfeet land.[13] Fast Horse and Owl Child advocate all-out war against the whites, but they also become more and more involved with frontier habits, drinking, whoring, and adventuring, which all carry shadow in Pikuni culture. Banished from the tribe, they scorn the cautious debates that characterize tribal responses to white encroachment. Their absence also prevents tribal councils from receiving the benefit of their energy and refusal to submit.

Part of the shadow quality embodied in Fast Horse is individualism. Fools Crow becomes conscious of its appeal when Fast Horse's father persuades him to search for his son:

> ...suddenly, unexpectedly, [Fools Crow] felt excited. He was enjoying himself. He had not been without another person for some time. He did not feel sad or lonely... instead, he felt the freedom of being alone, of relying only upon himself....The thought came into his mind without warning, the sudden

> understanding of what Fast Horse found so attractive in running with Owl Child. It was this freedom from responsibility, from accountability to the group, that was so alluring. As long as one thought of himself as part of the group, he would be responsible to and for that group. If one cut the ties, he had the freedom to roam, to think only of himself and not worry about the consequences of his actions. So it was for Owl Child and Fast Horse to roam. And so it was for the Pikunis to suffer.[14]

Welch makes the dominant value system the Other in his narrative, and if a reader sympathizes here with the individualist Fast Horse, the narrative shortly forces her to confront the consequences of her point of view. Fast Horse and Owl Child murder recklessly and they endanger their people. Throughout the narrative, Fast Horse refuses to acknowledge any responsibility for the Crows' mutilation of Yellow Kidney. Near the end of the novel, United States forces destroy the village of Heavy Runner, one of the most peaceable of the chiefs; in the narrative this appears to be a direct retaliation for the self-indulgent violence of Fast Horse and Owl Child. We come to see their individualism as a terrible hubris, not romantic and free but reckless and cold. Their refusal to accept responsibility for their murders confronts a white reader with the silence in American culture that surrounds the expropriations involved in achieving the nation's "Manifest Destiny." At the same time, Owl Child and his band scorn the Pikunis for their refusal to fight the invading white settlers. It's hard not to feel some sympathy with their desire to stave off the invaders, and this raises questions about the vulnerability of a culture that excluded the energy of these wild young men.

The treatment of women in the novel also exposes Pikuni cultural shadow. Yellow Kidney's rape of the sick girl in the Crow camp exposes him to smallpox, but it is Fast Horse's bragging that occupies the group's attention. The treatment of Kills-by-the-Lake, Fools Crow's father's youngest wife, also suggests the powerlessness and sadness of some of the women. In other female characters, however, such as Red Paint and Heavy Shield Woman, Welch shows the religious and personal power many women enjoyed. Thus, while gender issues are not his primary concern, he does not shrink from exposing ways the culture's shadow may have rendered it vulnerable in this area.

Cultural and Archetypal Shadow

Near the end of the novel, in the midst of a smallpox epidemic, Nitsokan, dream helper, instructs Fools Crow to make a journey. He does not know his destination, only that he must ride for three days and three nights without food. He rides through the country of his enemies into Feather Woman's land. Feather Woman is a figure from Pikuni myth, central to their cultural identity. In this section, Welch evokes shadow at the archetypal level. This compresses the pain of a century's experience of colonization into a few pages and thus forces the reader to confront history that has been stored in shadow.

Fools Crow's visit to Feather Woman is a kind of descent into dread and grief. While victims of colonial violence often blame and hate themselves and each other, the conquerors and their heirs have ignored or romanticized this past. Thus this episode gives each reader, Indian and Anglo, the opportunity to stare into shadow. Welch confronts the Indian reader with at least the possibility that some flaw in the culture, represented by Feather Woman's original sin, brought about its own ruin. This device allows a contemporary Indian reader to encounter shadow rather than self pity. Self pity cannot lead to change, but out of the painful, shameful experience of shadow can come renewed energy. He also confronts the Anglo reader with a powerfully condensed account of the damage done by whites to the Blackfeet, and its emotional cost.

Feather Woman recounts her story, which tells how an act of disobedience cast her out of her home in the sky. Like Eve, Feather Woman broke the one rule she was given, and her curiosity set her at odds with the divine powers. Her downfall, however, comes not from a desire to be godlike, but rather from her homesickness, and the Pikunis who follow her also feel that bond of community at the center of their experience. Once she has been banished to earth, she can no longer return to her husband, Morning Star. Her son, Poia, however, makes his way back to his father, and after earning the gratitude of Sun Chief, he brings the Sun Dance ceremony to his mother and her people. Still, Feather Woman feels responsible for the people's current misery.

Fools Crow's journey to Feather Woman's camp—a journey into myth—is presented without explanation. He rides for days without stopping or eating. He passes through country that is dreamlike, and he struggles with self-doubt. The narrative captures well here the feeling tone of the encounter with shadow: energy leaves, hope departs, and shame and hopelessness weigh one down.

Feather Woman brings Fools Crow out of himself by her proclamation of faith that one day she will return to her husband and son "and your people will suffer no more."[15] Fools Crow fills with compassion for her loneliness and shame. He embraces her shadow and this allows him to see the designs Feather Woman has been making on a yellow skin, four visions—of smallpox, massacre, the extinction of the blackhorns, and finally, of Pikuni children watching the happy white children playing in the white school yard:

> He had been brought here, to the strange woman's lodge in this strange world, to see the fate of his people. And he was powerless to change it, for he knew the yellow skin spoke a truth far greater than his meager powers, than the power of all his people.[16]

This vision endows Fools Crow with a consciousness hidden from his people, prophetic and tragic.

What saves the narrative from despair is myth itself. The tragic vision concludes with Feather Woman's reassurance to Fools Crow:

> Much will be lost to them....But they will know the way it was. The stories will be handed down, and they will see that their people were proud and lived in accordance with the Below Ones, the Underwater People—and the Above Ones.[17]

This foregrounding of the role of myth and stories as ways of maintaining balance in the world will reappear in *Ceremony*. The old stories, for an oral culture, knit time and space, ancestors and the living, humans and the more than human world. Story does not tell us how to think. It draws us in to a meaningful sequence that reframes experiences so that we come to a new perspective, placing individual experience in the context of a larger narrative. Myth ensures that culture will persist; myth, thus, is in shadow for the missionary-school consciousness, a trickster. Myth is power. It recalls experiences banished from history and consciousness and offers a vessel to hold the pain. Welch is able to end the novel on an optimistic note because the reanimation of the myths presages a renaissance of the Blackfeet culture, and the ways of knowing performed in the novel offer even his Anglo readers insights that may foster their own individuation.

CEREMONY AND THE POWER OF MYTH

Shadow in Leslie Marmon Silko's novel *Ceremony* takes the form of an archetypal evil that has estranged humans from the land and induced the kind of madness that led to the bombing of Hiroshima and Nagasaki. The novel explores shadow at the personal, cultural, and archetypal levels, and it uses culturally central myths and stories as a framework to explore the ritual reconciliation that will ultimately heal land, culture, and the individual.

STORY, MYTH, AND SHADOW

Tayo returns from World War II to a land choked by drought. He believes he has caused the drought by his urgent prayers for an end to rain on the Bataan Death March, a belief that grows from his understanding of the responsibilities of humans to the land. At the outset, Tayo's mind is a stewpot of voices, "Japanese voices…Laguna voices…fever voices…women's voices…a language he could not understand,"[18] and throughout the narrative a story of despair vies for his allegiance, displacing the cultural myths that center him in the land. Feather Woman's prophecy has come to pass. The story told by the white schools, the army recruiters, and the government has produced atomic blasts, a deracinated land, and an alienated mind. Like the land, Tayo needs a new story to heal him. Psyche and land, anima and *anima mundi*, are not separable in this novel. Recovery entails psychological, ecological, and cultural healing.

Destructive stories obscure connections and erode hope, producing a numb and isolated mind. Tayo and his veteran friends gather in bars where they "repeated the stories about good times in Oakland and San Diego; they repeated them like long medicine chants, the beer bottles pounding on the counter tops like drums."[19] These rituals suck Tayo into passivity, shame, and self-hatred. Tayo and his friends all suffer from the U. S. military's distortion of their traditional warrior role. According to Eduardo and Bonnie Duran, psychologists whose primary practice is with American Indians, the Indian male's loss of his role as warrior results in a shadow filled with feelings of loss and rage that get acted out in alcoholism, intratribal violence, and suicide.

These men absorb the shadow projected onto them and their land by the white culture.[20] They believe that their land is "dried-up" and worthless, and that they are themselves without hope. For most of the novel, they are Tayo's only peer group.

To return to health, Tayo has to encounter shadow at three levels: personal, cultural, and archetypal. His friends, Emo, Harley, and Leroy, all bear witness to the cultural shadow. They both envy and scorn white America. Emo also carries Tayo's personal shadow capacity for violence. He attracts Tayo's rage so much that at one point Tayo tries to kill him with a broken beer bottle. Emo is also linked with archetypal shadow. Silko amplifies this aspect of shadow by associating him with the mythical Ck'o'yo gambler who steals the rainclouds and fattens himself at the people's expense.

Archetypal evil gets expressed culturally in a word that translates into English as "witch" or "witchery." The Navajo healer, Betonie, accounts for the origin of the current crisis in his story of the "long time ago" conference of witches. Betonie explains that witchery works through its own stories, the worst of which is a story about the coming of white people who view the world as dead matter, without soul. "They fear the world./They destroy what they fear./They fear themselves."[21] In these three lines Betonie summarizes the western industrial relationship with nature. However, Silko assigns the embodiment of this attitude to Emo, who is a full-blooded Indian, not to a white character. In this way she refuses to depict Indians only as victims and acknowledges the archetypal power of the shadow. When Tayo confronts Emo at the end of the novel, then, he confronts personal, cultural, and archetypal shadow.

Shadow in the novel has many faces: alcohol, despair, and self-hatred, but also insensibility and envy. Witchery erodes hope, "so that the people would see only the losses."[22] Witchery divides the people, setting full-bloods like Emo against half-breeds like Tayo, compounding Tayo's misery with ostracism. But it also makes them blame whites for all evil, absolving themselves of responsibility. Silko makes clear that witchery is something that happens to you, but it is also something that exists in you and in the world. War is witchery, at least wars like the one Tayo just fought, where there was "killing across great distances without knowing who or how many had died."[23] If all of nature is ensouled, then even nature has its shadow side, represented in the yellow veins of uranium that are the witch's mirror image of the sacred pollen. Witchery acts upon the soul, to shape what people see and how they feel. The witch in the story does not grind his evil into powder or tie it in bundles. All he does is tell a story and, as he tells it, it begins to happen. Thus Silko emphasizes the power of myth and story to construct consciousness and bring the world into being.

Tayo suffers a lack of positive feminine energies in his soul, the personal version of the damaged mother earth. The war unbalanced his mind, but the damage had begun in his childhood when his auntie saw in him, her sister's half-breed child, the shame of the family. Like Corn Woman, Auntie is self-righteous, and her pride rests on the shame she projects onto Tayo.[24] Auntie is an image of what Marion Woodman calls

> the old petrifying mother…a great lizard lounging in the depths
> of the unconscious. She wants nothing to change. If the feisty
> ego attempts to accomplish anything, one flash of her tongue
> disposes of the childish rebel.[25]

Auntie's strategy of estrangement and the absence of Tayo's biological mother from the narrative mean that Tayo believes he belongs nowhere, a man out of place, in a land gone dry, among people who want to escape their condition. He believes himself responsible for his cousin Rocky's death, for his Uncle Josiah's death, for the drought. The shame that Auntie succeeds in inculcating in Tayo, his sense of personal failure, gets reinforced every time he sees Harley, Leroy, and Emo. Their repetition of the stories of the colonizer feeds his weakness and erodes the power of the stories of the land. So powerful is the American mantra of booze and babes and bitterness that even as he gains in grounded wholeness, Tayo backslides again and again into self-doubt, which is Joseph Henderson's word for the personal shadow.[26] Sucked into seeing himself from the point of view of the colonizing culture, he sees only failure, inadequacy, and impotence.

CEREMONY AND HEALING

If witchery acts through story, so does healing. Through ceremony, Tayo is able to contain the pain stored in shadow and thereby reclaim his lost warrior energy for use in service of life. The narrative shows Tayo going through a process that leads ultimately to his healing himself, the land, and the culture. At the same time, the novel, through its incorporation of traditional stories that parallel and amplify the main action, can lead a reader through a healing process as well. Silko's interwoven poems/stories/chants act as a form of prayer and song for the reader which, together with the central story, can realign vision.[27] Like *Fools Crow, Ceremony* leads a reader through alternate ways of knowing. If the reader allows the novel to work upon her, the novel itself is a kind of ceremony.

There are two major rituals in *Ceremony,* a tribal healing performed by the local shaman, and a longer, more complicated ceremony performed by the Navajo healer Betonie. But the novel is also filled with smaller ceremonies, both rituals of offering and respect and dark rites performed by shadow forces. As the barroom rituals deaden feeling, the healing ceremonies in the novel align recovery in Tayo's mind with healing in the land. They establish a culturally centered story that can compete with the tales of despair. While there is not time here to detail all these rituals, one example will illustrate the connection between psyche and land.

Early in the novel, Tayo gains strength as he recalls particular places that connect him both to his own past and to the powers of local spirit beings. He tells himself a story about an earlier dry spell when he went to a spring to construct a ritual for rain. Sitting very still, he watched as first a spider and then a frog emerged from their hiding places to drink from the pool, and he remembered the old stories, how "Spider Woman had told Sun Man how to win the storm clouds back from the Gambler so they would be free again to bring rain and snow to the people."[28] In the next thought, the battle for his mind recurs: "He knew what white people thought about the stories. In school the science teacher had explained what superstition was, and then held the science textbook up for the class to see the true source of explanations."[29] But the white people's theories pale when he remembers "the feeling he had in his chest" when his Grandma told him about the time immemorial. Linda Hogan remarks that in creation stories, "life was called into being through language, thought, dreaming, or singing, acts of interior consciousness."[30] In this passage Silko illustrates Tayo's attempts to call his own life into being and into harmony through just such an act of interior consciousness. Central to it is the regeneration of feeling.

At the spring, practicing ritual slowed Tayo down and let him enter a state of mind in which the stories and the land could work on him. As the spider, the frog, and finally the dragonfly came to the pool, Tayo reflected, "Everywhere he looked, he saw a world made of stories, the long ago, time immemorial stories, as old Grandma called them."[31] Silko links the "world made of stories" with the archetypal or mythic experiences of the people; realigning himself culturally helps Tayo resist the false stories told by the school. At the same time, the "world made of stories" *is* what we see with the naked eye. Throughout Silko's work, nature forms the bridge between the everyday and the mythic world that gives it meaning. In this, Tayo's homemade ritual echoes the workings of other ceremonies in the novel, which provide access to a non-rational kind of wisdom that asserts the kinship of people and the land. Telling himself the story of that ritual helps him gain energy.

CEREMONY, FEELING, AND SKILL

The primary ceremony that structures the novel is the one performed by the Navajo Betonie. It is a white corn sand painting, assisted by a young man who acts the bear while recounting the story of a retrieval of spirit. Silko describes the ceremony itself, but she is more interested in the action Tayo must perform afterwards to bring about the healing. Ceremony, in other words, creates the conditions for healing, but conscious human action, aided by many powers resident in the land, brings it about.

Betonie also retells the story of the origin of the ceremony and its continuation through generations, reassuring Tayo that he is not alone, and he does not act only for himself. This history surrounds Tayo with forebears and descendents for whom his actions will have consequences, and this increases his burden, but seeing himself as part of a larger pattern allows him to share that burden with others. The historical and mythical contexts relieve his isolation and provide a way for him to make meaning of his life.

The remainder of the novel traces Tayo's pursuit of his beloved Uncle Josiah's cattle, which had disappeared after Josiah died, while Tayo was in Bataan. In the process he encounters two supernatural beings who aid him, Ts'eh Montaño, a powerful anima figure, and her husband, the hunter, Mountain Lion. In Ts'eh, Tayo encounters what

Robert Nelson calls "a form of the spirit he seeks to reestablish within himself."[32] She is an earth-based anima, and when Tayo makes love with her, as many critics have pointed out, she seems to merge with the earth itself: "He eased himself deeper within her and felt the warmth close around him like river sand, softly giving way under foot, then closing firmly around the ankle in cloudy warm water."[33] In this narrative, the anima mediates not only the unconscious dimensions of Tayo's story but also the earthly, physical energies he needs to access in order both to succeed in his mission and, afterwards, to live in the land. Anima gives him access to feelings, which help to combat the anesthesia that characterizes the veterans. Here, and in his meetings with Ts'eh later, anima acts as guide and mediator for Tayo, strengthening him for his encounter with the final incarnation of Shadow in Emo's killing ritual.

He has been introduced to the feminine energy of connection, but Tayo also needs courage and stealth: he is, after all, "stealing" the speckled cattle in the eyes of the cowboy and the Texan who guard them. At his low point he encounters the mountain lion:

> Relentless motion was the lion's greatest beauty, moving like the mountain clouds with the wind, changing substance and color in rhythm with the contours of the mountain peaks: dark as lava rock, and suddenly as bright as a field of snow.[34]

Nelson argues that the mountain lion is a "shadow-self in this shadow-place, an animal 'helper' figure"[35] for Tayo, and Silko's language foregrounds the liminal qualities of the lion, its trickster capacity to blend with the land. The lion offers a kind of animus energy that had been lost in Tayo's shadow but is now available to save him from his captors, and he makes his escape by imitating a deer, lying in a shallow depression covered with leaves until he regains his strength.

As he trails the cattle southeastward down the mountain, Tayo encounters a hunter, the husband of Ts'eh, who is explicitly associated with the mountain lion. The natural-supernatural quality of these two characters suggests the way that ceremony works to infuse the ordinary with the numinous. Louis Owens, in *Other Destinies*, says that this portion of the novel echoes a story from Pueblo mythology in which Yellow Woman (Ts'eh), the wife of Winter (the hunter), meets Summer (Tayo), and invites him to sleep with her. In the conflict that ensues, an agreement emerges that Yellow Woman will spend part of the year with Winter and part with Summer.[36] Robert Nelson, by contrast, understands Ts'eh and the woman Tayo meets at the mountain cabin as two distinct avatars of the same "'spirit of place,' a more-than-human being who represents the land's own life, who knows How Things Work and who is willing to share this knowledge with the People."[37] Whether we see her as one person or two, as anima or as *anima mundi*, the text insists that we acknowledge her reality, her power, and her affection for Tayo. When Ts'eh appears to Tayo the following spring, first in his dreams and later at the ranch where the earth is greening, Tayo realizes he has lost nothing:

> The snow-covered mountain remained, without regard to titles of ownership or the white ranchers who thought they possessed it. They logged the trees, they killed the deer, bear, and mountain lions, they built their fences high; but the mountain was far greater than any or all of these things. The mountain outdistanced their destruction, just as love had outdistanced death.[38]

Faith counteracts the stories of destruction and envy that consume Leroy and Harley. Tayo's mind has returned to a right relation with the land.

In the final ritual of the novel, Tayo confronts Emo at the uranium mine, where personal, cultural, and archetypal shadow converge. The power he needs, finally, is the capacity of restraint. His refusal to kill Emo represents his rejection of both inflation and contamination. Silko closes the novel with Tayo's ceremony of initiation in the kiva and a final invocation of the spirits that complete the circle of a year.

Ritual and Shadow

In these two novels, power comes to people through their receptivity to their interior realities, which are linked with the land. I think it's fair to say that the capacity to access wisdom through non-rational means is undeveloped in Western culture. In part this is a function of early childhood messages that we need to pay attention and not daydream, and in part the contemporary divorce from psyche flows from our divorce from external nature. Where we have fairly rigid boundaries of self and not-self, consciousness and the unconscious, traditional American Indian cultures seem to have had more permeable boundaries.

In each of these novels, ritual contains the confrontation with shadow, making it bearable to the ego. Although rituals differ from tribe to tribe, American Indian cultures understood the power of ritual to mediate between humans and the rest of nature, between one human and another, and between ego and the unconscious. Rituals performed respect and bred compassion. In these and other ways, rituals connect people to place, to the other animals, to spirits, and to instinctual or unconscious energies. The energy that inspires a ritual comes from primal sources, and the repetition gives a container or a form for that energy.

Rituals practiced over time provide containers for shadow energies and ways of acknowledging human investment in the natural world. Perhaps the most basic ritual is that of the hunter, who honors the prey and expresses his gratitude and dependence. Even in an advanced industrial culture, we can make some rituals part of our daily lives to provide us with the forms of mindfulness. Acknowledging the lives around us, both human and more than human, we can embrace our interdependence and remember those with whom we share the planet. I have some hope that such a practice, along with social action and even fictions like these, can foster an ecological conscience. This argument resonates with the claims of E. O. Wilson in *Biophilia* that humans have a natural affinity for life. "We are human in good part," Wilson concludes,

> because of the particular way we affiliate with other organisms. They are the matrix in which the human mind originated and is permanently rooted, and they offer the challenge and freedom innately sought.[39]

So in honoring our kinship, rituals help to form a bridge that permits, contains, and renews that affiliation.

NOTES

1. Theodore Roszak, *The Voice of the Earth: An Exploration of Ecopsychology* (New York: Simon & Schuster, 1992), 42.

2. Andrew Samuels, *The Political Psyche* (London: Routledge, 1993), 103.

3. James Hillman, *Archetypal Psychology: A Brief Account* (Dallas: Spring Publications, 1983), 26.

4. Vine Deloria, Jr., *Spirit and Reason* (Golden, CO: Fulcrum Publishing, 1999), 50-51.

5. James Welch, *Fools Crow* (New York: Viking Penguin, 1986), 85.

6. Welch, *Fools Crow*, 118.

7. Lavonne Brown Ruoff, *American Indian Literatures* (New York: MLA, 1990), 2.

8. David Abram, *The Spell of the Sensuous: Perception and Language in a More-than-Human World* (New York: Pantheon, 1996), 139.

9. Tom F. Driver, *The Magic of Ritual* (New York: HarperSanFrancisco, 1991), 96.

10. Welch, *Fools Crow*, 165.

11. *Ibid.,* 171.

12. Louis Owens, *Other Destinies: Understanding the American Indian Novel* (Norman: Oklahoma UP, 1992), 165.

13. Welch draws on history to base several incidents in the novel on the 1869 murder of a settler named Malcolm Clark.

14. Welch, *Fools Crow,* 211.

15. *Ibid.*, 352.

16. *Ibid.*, 358.

17. *Ibid.*, 359-60.

18. Leslie Marmon Silko, *Ceremony* (New York: Viking Penguin, 1977), 6.

19. *Ibid.*, 43.

20. Eduardo Duran and Bonnie Duran, *Native American Postcolonial Psychology* (Albany: SUNY Press, 1995), 37.

21. Silko, *Ceremony*, 135.

22. *Ibid.*, 249.

23. *Ibid.*, 36.

24. As Stuart Cochran remarks, "As a mixed blood, Tayo has internalized the ridicule of the dominant white culture through the hostility of his aunt…and the assimiliationist aspirations of his favored cousin Rocky. He will eventually see his own malaise in communal terms as a function of colonialism and Christianity. Stuart Cochran, "Ethnic Implications of Stories, Spirits, and the Land in Native American Pueblo and Aztlan Writing," *MELUS*, Vol. 20, No. 2 (Summer, 1995): 76.

25. Marion Woodman, *The Ravaged Bridegroom: Masculinity in Women.* (Toronto: Inner City, 1990), 17-18.

26. Joseph L. Henderson, *Shadow and Self: Selected Papers in Analytical Psychology* (Wilmette, IL: Chiron, 1990), 70.

27. The Acoma poet and critic Simon Ortiz argues that prayer and song constitute "the only way in which event and experience,…can become significant and realized in the people's own terms." Simon J. Ortiz, "The Historical Matrix Towards a National Indian Literature: Cultural Authenticity in Nationalism," in Richard F. Fleck, *Critical Perspectives on Native American Fiction* (Pueblo, CO: Passeggiata Press, 1997), 65-66.

28. Silko, *Ceremony,* 94.

29. *Ibid.*, 94.

30. Linda Hogan, *Dwellings: A Spiritual History of the Living World* (New York: Simon & Schuster, 1995), 80-81.

31. Silko, *Ceremony,* 95.

32. Robert Nelson, "Place, Vision, and Identity in Native American Literatures," in Dane Morrison, ed., *American Indian Studies: An Interdisciplinary Approach to Contemporary Issues* (New York: Peter Lang, 1997), 7.

33. Silko, *Ceremony*, 180-181.

34. *Ibid.*, 195-196.

35. Nelson, "Place, Vision, and Identity," 9.

36. Owens, *Other Destinies*, 187.

37. Nelson, "Place, Vision, and Identity," 3.

38. Silko, *Ceremony,* 219.

39. E. O. Wilson, *Biophilia* (Cambridge: Harvard UP, 1984), 139.

RECONCILIATION & REGENERATION: BUILDING BRIDGES FOR WOUNDED CULTURES AND WOUNDED EARTH

PETER BISHOP

Any understanding of the relationship between psyche and nature must engage both with wounded cultures and with wounded nature. This applies across virtually all contemporary cultures, from western ones, who might not define themselves as being wounded, to those who try to maintain a traditional life and for whom the wounding is an integral, inescapable part of their daily struggle to survive. I specifically want to address western cultures and their relation to a wounded earth. In particular, I want to explore the imaginal demands placed upon western cultures when, in their search for a viable earth-ethic and practice, they turn to indigenous cultures for help. Such a move could equally come if we turn the question around. When western cultures turn to indigenous cultures in a spirit of reconciliation, then inevitably questions of land, of nature, of country are similarly inescapable.

Peter Bishop is Associate Professor in Communication & Cultural Studies at the University of South Australia. He has written extensively about archetypal pychology, and his book, *The Greening of Psychology: The Vegetable World in Myth, Dream and Healing*, was published by Spring Publications in 1991.

The Double Wound

That both the world of nature and western culture's relationship to it are deeply wounded has long preoccupied the hearts and minds of many. For some the wounding, both physical and imaginal, is almost irrevocable. So, Annie Dillard laments:

> It is difficult to undo our own damage, and to recall to our presence that which we have asked to leave. It is hard to desecrate a [sacred] grove and change your mind … We doused the burning bush and cannot rekindle it; we are lighting matches in vain under every green tree. Did the wind used to cry, and the hills shout forth praise? Now speech has perished from among the lifeless things of earth, and living things say very little to very few.[1]

Despite such pessimism, numerous people, including Dillard herself, have searched for ways in which to both rekindle an intensely intimate and numinous relationship to nature and to heal the wounds inflicted upon nature. In this quest, many in modern western cultures have turned to indigenous peoples of the planet looking for an ancient eco-wisdom and guidance apparently uncontaminated by the malaise of modernity. I would not be the first to suggest that this can be a deeply problematic turn.[2] However, I believe it is a necessary one, albeit not for purely environmental reasons.

This turning to indigenous culture and its numerous eco-wisdoms is not a simple balm, for it exposes a double wounding. Turning towards indigenous culture for guidance in trying to heal a wounded relationship with nature reveals yet another raw wound, an accusation of cultural oppression, even genocide, from the world's First Nations towards those who now look to them for help. It is impossible to begin a healing dialogue between indigenous and non-indigenous cultures that does not address the wound of oppression and dispossession.

There is no need to detail at any length the numerous attempts to "borrow" eco-notions from indigenous cultures. At times respectful, at times commercial, often desperate, I'm not simply criticizing or dismissing these attempts. They can and have been important not only in developing a viable earth-ethic, practice, and imagining, but in providing sparks for building hope. But most of the borrowings bypass or circumvent the wound, the responsibility, the guilt or shame, the suspicion that lies between the cultures.

My argument is therefore simple. There can be no healing engagement with nature by western cultures that does not simultaneously involve reconciliation with the world's indigenous peoples. This is not because indigenous people are "closer" to nature, or because they have superior eco-wisdom-knowledge or eco-practices. Each of these may or may not be true. Nor is such a double healing required because indigenous peoples are more a part of nature—a view propounded both from a racist identification of such traditional cultures with native fauna or from a faux-romantic notion of the noble savage. No, it is the simple fact that both the wounding of indigenous cultures and that of the western relationships with nature are inextricably related and intertwined. Any healing must be in the form of an eco-justice, and the imaginal plays a critical role in both re-imagining what has happened and in creating transformative visions of what is possible. Also, there are parallels between a colonizing of indigenous cultures and a colonizing of nature, indeed, in many cases, of the very ancestral land inhabited by indigenous peoples.

Difficult Crossings: Burt Creek & Hindmarsh Bridges

A short drive north of Alice Springs, the unofficial capital city of Australia's desert center, sits Burt Creek Bridge. It is a low, unremarkable reinforced concrete structure about 40 meters long that carries a newly completed railway. This 2720 kilometer, north-south transcontinental crossing joins the city of Adelaide with its Mediterranean climate of the southern coast, through the aridity of Central Australia's semi-deserts, to the tropical north and the city of Darwin.

Burt Creek is typical of the rivers of Central Australia. A broad sandy bed, lined by large river Red Gums, it rarely carries much water, but is periodically subject to flash floods. Few travellers on the recently constructed transcontinental express would even know they were crossing Burt Creek Bridge. A small concrete railway bridge may seem an unlikely starting point for an imaginal study about psyche and nature, but it gathers together many of the key themes I wish to address. As someone who not just loves but "needs" to be in contact with wilderness, or with quasi-wilderness, Central Australia holds a special place in my heart. So, my encounter with Burt Creek Bridge just over a year ago, while not unexpected given I was doing research on the cultural impact of the new railway line, nevertheless still engendered a sense of surprise. I experienced an almost surreal feeling of incongruity at the technological intrusion into a vast and fierce landscape in which humans are scarce, a site where there is a sharp encounter between western modernity, indigenous culture, and wild nature.

By choosing Burt Creek Bridge I have deliberately chosen a difficult focus, one that does not easily allow a direct meditation on nature or on indigenous culture. It forces a refractive approach, one that fragments and deflects any attempt at simple, direct answers. While Burt Creek Bridge poses many questions for a western eco-reflection, its presence is even more significant for the small group of indigenous peoples whose home has been the Burt Creek country for probably tens of thousands of years. At Burt Creek — a "well equipped outstation [of] … tin houses, and one substantial new wooden house … a solar generator, reliable water"[3]— concerns were expressed about noise and the effect of vibration from the railway on the water bore. The tin sheds have no sound insulation. Adequate passage across the tracks needed to be ensured for hunting and for visiting ceremonial sites. Not far away, at Harry Creek, another bridge site, there were similar concerns about noise, safety, and access, about wildlife management. It was acknowledged already to be a disrupted community in need of healing. More disruption was not welcome.[4] Burt Creek Bridge reminds us that questions about nature and psyche always occur in and around issues of culture, power, and technology.

The precise locating of the bridge site therefore had to take into account a whole array of other "crossings." These ranged from sacred dreaming tracks to those of everyday life in the local indigenous communities, plus the eco-pathways of various fauna and flora. As an impact report points out:

> The Burt Creek area not only hosts a well-established outstation, but also dangerous sites associated with mpwere (maggots) and amenge (blow fly) Dreamings. If the mulga trees, which are understood to be the amenge (blow flies), are disturbed, maggots will rise from the ground and infest the genitalia of train passengers and anyone else who ventured near the damaged trees. The concerns of the custodians of these sites have been consistent over a long period of consultation about the railway and work

> restrictions have been put in place as a condition of approval of
> construction in this area. The concerns that custodians have about
> protection of particular trees in this area require that these trees
> be identified and fully protected during construction.[5]

I would suggest that few in the west could easily integrate such a story
into any recognizable form of eco-imagining. The minimal best outcome
that could be achieved was a practical respect. The wishes of the local
traditional owners needed to be adhered to. The maximum best
outcome would have been, in response to the indigenous story, a
profound reflection on western knowledges and fantasies about nature
and its relationship with technologies, in this case the railway and its
bridge.

Certainly, in the contemporary climate of reconciliation and legal
empowerment, the minimum result was achieved. The rail, both
symbolically and practically, is a site of intense renegotiation of
Australian settlement. There were many field inspections and
consultations. "It is essential that work restrictions aimed at preserving
the integrity of these sites is adhered to during construction activities."[6]
Construction crews were accompanied by a team of appropriate
indigenous custodians. In many areas traditional owners insisted that
construction workers receive localized cross-cultural training.

The outcomes were far more contentious at another bridge site in
Australia, which dramatically brought together questions of nature,
imagination, power, and reconciliation. In the late 1980s and well into
the 1990s, a desperate struggle occurred around the Hindmarsh Island
Bridge in South Australia. Initially given the go-ahead as part of a real
estate and marina development on an underpopulated island near the
mouth of the Murray, Australia's longest river, the proposal was the
focus of bitter protests from indigenous women of the Ngarrindjeri
people. In conjunction with concerns about the bridge's impact on
the environment and about disturbing indigenous heritage sites in the
vicinity, the women insisted that the bridge would catastrophically
affect sacred women's rituals and imaginal geography. Controversially,
the precise knowledge of the ritual meanings was classified as secret
women's business, and the findings of the anthropologist appointed
to study the matter were placed in a sealed envelope, unavailable except
to initiated and appropriate women. Indirectly it was reported that
the secret business had something to do with fertility, that the shape

of the river channel between the island and the mainland resembled a uterus, and that the women, drawing on traditional spiritual beliefs and knowledge, feared that a bridge would block this passage. As a place where salt and fresh water meet, the bridge site was of special significance. The story became complicated with increasingly bitter struggles between the indigenous women and the developers, plus their respective supporters, through the media, court cases, and demonstrations. In the end the bridge was built, along with the housing and marina. The indigenous community was left, once again, to heal its wounds. A deep gulf was confirmed between two divergent ways of knowing and of imagining human participation in the natural world.[7]

RECONCILIATION AND IMAGINATION

I've been doing a lot of work around reconciliation over the past few years, particularly in the context of the healing process between indigenous and non-indigenous peoples within societies such as Australia, South Africa, and so on. I've been struck by the critical place that nature and psyche has in this process. Each culture brings very different ways of imagining their relationship to nature, and reconciliation between cultures also involves, in fact forces, a profound re-imagining, a reconciliation *with* nature. In nearly every case of reconciliation that I've come across, questions of the "land," of place, are inextricably part of it.

Broadly speaking, reconciliation involves memory-work and an acknowledgment of wrongs, often some kind of amnesty or forgiveness, plus a measure of reparation and restitution. It requires an imagination of healing, of moving on, of hope. By refusing either to adopt a cycle of revenge or a regime of denial or despair, reconciliation constitutes a very specific, perhaps archetypal, imaginal state. It aims to heal the effects of traumatic events that have produced guilt, anxiety, depression, resentment, and injustice. Involving a struggle towards dialogue, often in contexts of fear, anxiety, and even violence, it requires a re-imagining of reflexive spaces for listening to silenced, anxious, or angry voices. It confronts what is often unspeakable or irreparable and gives rise to complex difficulties around the narrating of pain and trauma. It can be a search for forgiveness without necessarily forgetting. Guilt, resentment, anxiety, and a sense of injustice often accompany or motivate a move to reconciliation. Formal reconciliation projects in numerous countries, such as South Africa, Australia, Canada, Rwanda, New Zealand, and Bosnia, are complemented by multifaceted grass-roots reconciliation activities and sensibilities.

Such an agenda places extreme demands upon the imagination. A reconciliation imagination concerns itself with issues such as: the difficult challenges faced in a double process of acknowledgment and forgiveness, of grief and trauma alongside hope and healing; the complexities of acknowledging different ways of knowing, valuing, and experiencing in an inter- or trans-cultural dialogue; the struggle to re-imagine responsibility, shame and grief, land and identity; how to heal the imagination in the face of tragedy; how to imagine hope and transformation; plus, how imagining itself functions in the struggles for such things. A utopian vision of a possible alternative, even if small and fragmented, even just as a glimpse, is a crucial healing fiction, a necessary soul-spark. However, a reconciliation imaginal needs to avoid short-circuiting the process of descent by a premature optimism and an avoidance of disturbing truths. Along with hope, a reconciliation imaginal must, by necessity, engage with disturbing emotions, memories, responsibilities, and a messy lack of closure.

RECONCILIATION WITH NATURE

I want to suggest that the notion of reconciliation can be applied to healing the relationship between western culture and nature. Certainly there are deep similarities in emotions and denial between western culture's relationship with indigenous cultures and with nature.

Shierry Nicholsen writes about a constant sense of loss experienced in the West's relationship with nature, of a wounded-ness that inevitably accompanies any eco-awareness. She points to a "terrible despair" and suggests that a "symptom of acute grief is guilt."[8] Elsewhere there is a deliberate refusal to acknowledge connectedness, plus a desire to "traumatize the natural world as we ourselves feel we have been traumatized."[9] Nicholsen writes of "trauma" and "apathy," of a refusal or inability to acknowledge the scale and intensity of the wounding, let alone an acceptance of responsibility.[10]

She draws on the Holocaust, on Hiroshima, and other large-scale social catastrophes, or just the threat embodied in these examples, in order to help imagination grasp the magnitude of the experience of environmental destruction. Yet few think of it in these terms. Here are direct parallels which confront any reconciliation between western and indigenous cultures, the ability to imagine and acknowledge, even to witness where possible, what actually happened and is happening — its scale and depth. There is an "intertwining of guilt and victimization," a "wish to shut off the emotional pain on the one hand and the urgency to reintegrate and make meaning on the other."[11]

Nicholson invokes an apocalyptic psyche, which, as many have insisted, is integral to the bedrock of contemporary western *ars memoria*.[12] We constantly live with the degradation both of the environment and of many indigenous or First Nation cultures. Nicholson is unrelenting, insisting that all people in the developed world are "in some degree both perpetrators and victims."[13] "Guilt is an experience of failed responsibility, and failure is inevitable in these situations."[14] Trauma, she writes, "obliterates hope and desire."[15] The sense of loss need not be confined to such vast imaginings but is also present in the daily, often small, everyday interactions with nature.

Certainly, many enjoy benefits of a system that causes massive damage—both in the past and ongoing. How do we live in an unjust and wounded world? How do we live with awful thoughts? Yet even Nicholson can find hope. She suggests that there is a need to mourn, to experience the pain of remembering. That despair plays a crucial role in transformation. Importantly, she points to a struggle to witness, insisting that nature is not just the subject of our gaze but looks back at us, teaching us.[16] This is crucial. Reconciliation demands that nature too plays an active part in the healing, that nature is imagined as an active partner in such a project, although the imagining may not be what we expect. So, a young man, engaged in alternative Eastern & eco-oriented spirituality, has a dream: *I am carrying water in the desert when I meet a monster ape. He pours out the water. Then he picks up a handful of black peat-bog and says: "This is from Mother Nature. Drink/ take this."* The monster ape as personal messenger from "Mother Nature," like the "black peat-bog," may not have been exactly how the young man imagined the reconciliation process to unfold.

THE NATURE OF TECHNOLOGY

As was suggested with Burt Creek Bridge, it would be misleading to reduce local indigenous concerns to the protection of their sacred sites and "songlines," to confine their eco-wisdom to a traditional knowledge about a relationship to a natural world unmediated by modern technology. At the same time it would simplistic to demonize modern technology and society, to dismiss western eco-relationships as being superficial at best and arrogantly indifferent to both nature and indigenous culture at worst. For example, in Bruce Chatwin's best-selling travel book *The Songlines*, Aboriginal dreaming trails are imagined to be the exemplar of sacred tracks.[17] The "songlines" connect ritual sites and are considered to be sacred places in their own right. However, another set of tracks in the book constantly runs as a shadow to the songlines. These tracks belong to the proposed Alice Springs-to-Darwin railway. As a product of a technological mass society, and in particular as a form of transportation that seems to work against walking and nomadism, the rail tracks are the very opposite of Chatwin's vision of a sacred harmony between body, land, and movement. No matter what the railway engineer does, or how careful and respectful he is, the railway stands condemned. An absolute gulf is posited between the two Australian communities, Aboriginal and white. The engineer's task is deemed to be futile, even if well meant. According to Chatwin, from an Aboriginal perspective the whole of Australia is a sacred site and the scarring caused by the construction of the rail corridor is considered tantamount to wounding the earth and hence yourself, "and if others wound the earth, they are wounding you. The land should be left untouched: as it was in the Dreamtime, when the Ancestors sang the world into existence."[18] Within such a fundamentalist and erroneous scenario, the railway is beyond hope of redemption. In *The Songlines,* bulldozers and other earth-moving equipment being used to survey and mark the proposed rail route cut and churn the land like demons.

    This absolute polarization between a sublime Aboriginal sacred connection to the land and a superficial, crass, non-indigenous relationship reveals a prevalent Rousseau-like fantasy in western society about both indigenous culture and nature. It simplifies and even effaces the multifarious and often creative contemporary engagement between a diversity of Aboriginal communities and the products of high-tech culture.

Keeping Connection

Attempts to draw inspiration and guidance directly from the heart of indigenous cultures' store of eco-wisdom can too often short-circuit psychological complexity and darker imaginal associations. Instead I suggest a focus on the creative struggles by indigenous peoples both to survive and to engage with modernity whilst keeping the connection to traditional imaginal eco-knowledges and practices intact.

I believe the West can learn from contemporary indigenous struggles to sustain connection and to reinhabit a wounded earth. Kathi Wilson & Evelyn Peters, for example, note that almost half of First Nation people in Canada live in urban areas.[19] They describe how the Anishinabek peoples stress a relationship to the land "for maintaining *mno bmaadis.*" This Ojibway phrase roughly translates "living the good life"—physical, emotional, mental, spiritual.[20] Urban Anishinabek people "create small-scale places of cultural safety in urban areas to express their physical and spiritual relationship to the land."[21] In addition, they struggle to keep a mobility that enables a connection to be maintained between their everyday urban habitations and the traditional lands outside the urban centers. Every opportunity is taken to participate in ceremonies that remember and honor the earth and land. In a practice of "smudging," tobacco, along with other sacred medicine and herbs, is placed at trees and bushes, in backyards, and parks. By such practices the links between the people and the land, even in a state of "exile," are constantly maintained and renegotiated. While the situation is vastly different in western cultures, the use of micro-sites for enacting imaginal rituals of eco-connection helps to sustain a link, however tenuous, between an alienating modern world for which a viable eco-ethic is still in the process of desperate invention and a hopeful reserve of scarcely remembered fragments of various eco-ethics that can seem to lack contemporary viability.

Over a thousand kilometers north of Burt Creek, deep in the tropics, the railway crosses an impressively large span over the broad Katherine River. This is Nitmiluk, the country of the Jawoyn people. Reconciliation is a critical part of their attempts to rebuild the Jawoyn Nation after a devastating period of colonization. Through music they sing of sharing their country, tell stories of survival and celebration. They have proposed a kind of multiple sovereignty,

Forgive the white man
They're our brothers and sisters
Let's join hands together
Share one earth together … .[22]

However, the naming of the country is particularly critical as
indigenous peoples seek to have their language, their poetics, reinscribed
on the landscape after a long history where it has been effaced. So, the
Jawoyn Association, in addition to insisting on the protection of
"culturally significant paperbark trees in the vicinity of the railway,"
also wanted traditional owners and native title holders to be
"acknowledged as having a right to name places along the entire rail
route."[23] The poetics of language and naming, as Heidegger has
reminded us, are intrinsic to dwelling, to what he calls "the gathering
of earth and sky, divinities and mortals."[24]

The way in which indigenous knowledge is encountered, let alone
used, needs careful re-imagining. Stephen Muecke, for example, has
stressed the importance of the way Aboriginal land/country is visited.
"Seeing oneself as a visitor on the lookout for stories," he suggests, is
significantly different to visiting in search of neat theories or solutions.[25]
In describing how the imagination needs to be trained "to go visiting,"
Muecke cites Hannah Arendt who suggested that training the
philosophical imagination is like thinking "without a banister."[26] The
plurality of selves and others, the fluidity of stories—their tellings and
translations—can only be embraced when guiding handrails are
abandoned.

A DOUBLE HEALING: SINGING THINGS

Nature, culture, and technology are defined in a mutual
relationship. As James Hillman pointed out many years ago, not only
are there multiple definitions of "nature," (over 60 at one count), but
nature has come to be contrasted with human-made, as if "nature is
objectively pure, without subjective artifice."[27] Nature is often
imagined as "God-given;" however, nature is always to some extent
human-made, "if not directly with our hands, certainly always with
our minds."[28] Human culture is natural. It is as much human nature
to construct as it is to imagine. I'm not saying that the bridge is part
of nature, but it is somehow involved in the relationship between

psyche and nature. The way we imagine the bridge—say, as a structure for the soul to find beauty—is profoundly implicated in the way we imagine Nature. The consequences of ignoring this relationship are often profound. Idealizing wilderness and literalizing it "cast a shadow on our daily world, trashing it yet further," warns Hillman.[29] In particular, the relationship between psyche and nature constantly interfaces, rubs up against, or is mediated through culture and technology. It is here that our imaginality is often so deficient, leading to strangely abstract and rarified ideals.

A double move is required to heal a double wound. How to re-inhabit wounded land and places, how to engage with modernity in a creative, imaginative way? Western reflexivity has to re-imagine the complex interweavings of technology/nature.

Gaston Bachelard has called for a "material imagination" and warns:

> Because we fail to de-objectify objects and deform forms—a process which allows us to see the matter beneath the object— the world is strewn with unrelated things, immobile and inert solids, objects foreign to our nature.[30]

Our task is to move soul back into the world of things and of nature. Every thing has innerness. And it is to things, common everyday things that surround and imaginally support us, whether "natural" or technological, that we should turn our care and responsibility.

Some years ago I was at a conference on Tibet. One participant gave a wonderful talk about her research and the traditional songs that Tibetans sang whilst working in the fields. Such songs, she said, were heard less since the introduction of tractors. What about songs for the tractor, I asked, whimsically remembering the excitement of my young children as they climbed over old tractors at a farm. I was told that there are no songs for the tractor. I don't believe this. We surely need such songs, such singing? Isn't this the lesson from Frankenstein? That to reject the things we have made and their stories is to create monsters? Among other things, I want to listen to the song of bridges and railways, in both Aboriginal and non-Aboriginal culture(s). If we can't sing the things we have made, how can we sing the things of nature?

The railway bridge at Burt Creek provides an apt focus for reflections on the interweavings of nature, culture, and technology, plus on the double wound. The modest dimensions, its lack of sublime or picturesque qualities, and its banal concrete form preclude any spiritual or aesthetic flights of fancy so often associated with other bridges. Such fantasies would allow a short circuiting of disturbing complexity. In particular, the bridge and the railway, as in other countries from the USA to Africa, are haunted by past indifference and oppression, by a relative failure of a development process driven by a techno-imagination that celebrated the conquest and subjugation both of nature and First Nations.

So how can white Australian culture sing the railway, particularly in conjunction with nature and indigenous culture? It is not easy. Some diesel engines of the railways have been decorated with dot paintings, apparently showing Aboriginal motifs. Promotional literature for the railway shows the colorful trains crossing vast expanses of desert, sometimes with a frilled-necked lizard or kangaroo in the immediate foreground. Are we being asked to imagine the train inserted into the Outback on a par with native fauna and Aboriginal culture? Is this simply a tourism ploy, or a superficial token that substitutes a feel-good factor for real social and imaginal change? Does it somehow, even remotely, address complex debates and uncertainties in contemporary Australian culture? I might be naïve, but I like to think that somewhere in all this superficiality something viable, no matter how tenuous, is beginning to happen.

John Olsen, one of Australia's most respected modern artists, perhaps provides another angle on singing the rail and its relationship to nature. In 1982 he visited the Outback regions of Western Australia. His painting, *Pilbara Train*, shows an aerial view of a freight train snaking its way across the desert.[31] There are no horizons to this flat perspective. As with an earlier, similar image, *Night Train and Owls* (1980), the train is just another, rather diminutive, pattern in the vastness, its sinuous shape wriggling across almost half the canvas, suggesting either a great serpent or a dried-up river bed. For Olsen, with his deep involvement in traditional Chinese philosophy and art, the purpose of such landscape painting was to express a complex interconnectedness—natural, cultural, philosophical, and aesthetic. Therefore, rather than simply reiterating the trope so common in Australian art and literature whereby modern technology is either mocked and rendered impotent by the immensity or cast as oppositional to the natural world, Olsen integrates the train into the patterns of landscape. In his painting, modern technology is not alien to the place. Like the human presence in Chinese landscapes, while dwarfed and hence relativized, the train belongs there.

RE-IMAGINING KNOWLEDGE

As the indigenous Northern Land Council emphasized, nearly all the 1414 kilometers of land being traversed by the new section of railway from Alice Springs to Darwin is Aboriginal. Questions and fantasies about land ownership in Australia are crucial for any equal dialogue. Helen Verran insists that questions about claims of "ownership" can only be resolved through a shared imaginary. In her discussion of the encounter between indigenous Australians and pastoralists over the meanings of land ownership, Verran argues that

> by restoring imaginaries to modern theories of knowledge, we rediscover the capacity to re-imagine ourselves and devise ways … [of working] with other communities—human and non-human.[32]

In other words not only must traditional paintings, dances, and stories be understood and respected as knowledge, it is the task of mythopoetics to re-mythologize western systems of knowledge.[33] Western legalities of land ownership are our (sacred) fictions, our myths. Land titles are working in a performative mode, as scripts, as imaginal texts.

REGENERATION

In a famous passage, Heidegger uses the example of a bridge to illustrate the gathering qualities of things.[34] In a similar way, Burt Creek Bridge has gathered western and indigenous cultures, technology and nature, imagination and power, psyche and spirituality. At the same time, the bridge has created new spaces, not just physical but imaginative ones that allow for reflection on the complex and contradictory encounters produced in such a gathering.[35]

In order to begin healing the double wound (with First Nation peoples and with nature), western cultures need to find ways to reconnect with their own eco-imaginal traditions, especially ones that are creatively engaging with the modern world, need to find ways of re-animating a wounded world of nature and of things. Ways must also be found of re-inhabiting such a world.[36] A young man dreams: *A "giant man" standing on the Earth catches meteors and hurls them onto the planet so as to rejuvenate the crops.* The giant acts as agent of both connection and transmission, of drawing primordial re-animation from imaginal cosmology, of connecting the Earth and the Heavens. Reconciliation without regeneration falls short of a sustainable healing. Reconciliation takes its place alongside other images of our relationship with nature, such as stewardship, kinship, custodianship. But reconciliation can only occur between active participants. Only when the world in all its varied complexity is experienced as ensouled can this happen.

NOTES

This paper is part of a research project on reconciliation funded by an ARC Discovery grant.

1. A. Dillard, *Teaching a Stone to Talk* (London: Picador, 1984), 70.

2. J. Jacobs, "Earth Honouring: Western Desires & Indigenous Knowledges," in R. Lewis & S. Mills (eds.), *Feminist Postcolonial Theory: A Reader* (Edinburgh: Edinburgh University Press, 2003), 667-691.

3. R. Howitt, S. Jackson, & I. Bryson, *A Railway Through Our Country* (Macquarie University, NSW: Macquarie Research Ltd, 1998), 102.

4. *Ibid.*, 99-100.

5. *Ibid.*, 101.

6. *Ibid.*, 101.

7. K. Gelder & J. Jacobs, "Promiscuous Sacred Sites," *Australian Humanities Review* (1997), http://www.lib.latrobe.edu.au/AHR/archive/Issue-June-1997/gelder.html

8. S. Nicholsen, *The Love of Nature and the End of the World* (Cambridge, MA: The MIT Press, 2002), 43.

9. *Ibid.*, 123.

10. *Ibid.*, 129.

11. *Ibid.*, 123-4.

12. E.g., see, V. Andrews, R. Bosnak, & K. Goodwin, *Facing Apocalypse* (Dallas: Spring Publications, 1987); and M. Tumarkin, *Traumascapes* (Melbourne: Melbourne University Press, 2005).

13. Nicholsen, 141.

14. *Ibid.*, 143.

15. *Ibid.*, 147.

16. *Ibid.*, 123.

17. B. Chatwin, *The Songlines* (London: Picador, 1988).

18. *Ibid.*, 13.

19. K. Wilson & E. Peters, "'You can make a place for it:' remapping urban First Nations spaces of identity," *Environment & Planning D: Society & Space*, (2005), 395-413.

20. *Ibid.*, 403.

21. *Ibid.*, 403.

22. C. Gibson & P. Dunbar-Hall, "Nitmiluk: Place and Empowerment in Australian Aboriginal Popular Music," *Ethnomusicology* (vol. 44, no. 1, 2000), 53.

23. *Ibid.*, 145.

24. M. Heidegger, *Poetry, Language, Thought* (New York: Harper Colophon, 1975), 153, 215.

25. S. Muecke, "Visiting Aboriginal Australia," *Postcolonial Studies* (vol. 2, no. 1, 1999), 53.

26. *Ibid.*, 52.

27. J. Hillman, "Natural Beauty Without Nature," *Spring 1985* (Dallas: 1985), 51.

28. *Ibid.*, 52.

29. *Ibid.*, 54.

30. G. Bachelard, *Water and Dreams* (Dallas: The Pegasus Foundation, 1983), 12.

31. D. Hart, *John Olsen* (Sydney: Craftsman House, 1991).

32. H. Verran, "Re-imagining land ownership in Australia," *Postcolonial Studies* (vol. 1, no. 2, 1998), 249.

33. E.g., see D. Rose, "An Indigenous Philosophical Ecology: Situating the Human," *The Australian Journal of Anthropology*, (vol. 16, no. 3, 2005).

34. Heidegger, 152-4.

35. P. Bishop, "The Soul of the Bridge," *Sphinx 1: A Journal for*

Archetypal Psychology and the Arts (London, 1988).

36. L. Yoneyama, "Taming the Memoryscape: Hiroshima's Urban Renewal," in J. Boyarin (ed.), *Remapping Memory* (Minneapolis: University of Minnesota Press, 1994).

MASKS

Filling my dreams,
the memory of forests,
where I once took other shapes,
of subtle deer, badger, bird,
the red spectacle of fox,
vanished with quick stealth.
I'm alone in this quiet skin,
dancing the ghost-dance
of long-dead wolves,
my paws feeling the cold
of frost on the winter earth;
a formless self out of some hidden future,
flowing in the dark heat
of animal blood;
and, undone, I conceal myself
in creaturely hides
of feather and fur;
at home
in the elemental poem
of forgotten places.

—*Michael Whan*

Tending the Dream is Tending the World

STEPHEN AIZENSTAT

We stand at a critical moment in Earth's history, a time when humanity must choose its future. As the world becomes increasingly interdependent and fragile, the future at once holds great peril and great promise . . . It is imperative that we the peoples of Earth, declare our responsibility to one another, to the greater community of life, and to future generations.

These are the opening lines of the preamble to the Earth Charter, an international initiative endorsed by the United Nations, and to which I dedicate this essay.

INTRODUCTION

We all know the consequences. The dominant patterns of production and consumption, rooted in the psychological predisposition of humans, are causing environmental

Stephen Aizenstat, Ph.D., is the founding president of Pacifica Graduate Institute, a private graduate school offering M.A. and Ph.D. programs in depth psychology, mythological studies, and the humanities. A clinical psychologist whose research centers on a psychodynamic process of "tending the living image," particularly in the context of dreamwork, he has conducted dreamwork seminars for over 25 years in the United States, Canada, Europe, and Asia. Believing that tending the dream is tending the world, Dr. Aizenstat brought the insights of depth psychology and dreamwork to the Earth Charter International Workshop in 1995, and he participated in the "Earth Charter +5" international convocation at Amsterdam in 2005. He is involved with local environmental projects, such as Santa Barbara's annual Earth Day, the Heal the Ocean campaign, and Sustainable Santa Barbara.

devastation, the depletion of resources, and a mass extinction of species. How many times do we need to say this, to hear these words? Again and again, until the controlling images of greed and domination, with their tenacious stranglehold on our consciousness, give way to a new awakening.

In our desire to survive into the future we are in search of new, more generative images. These innate ways of knowing are imbedded in the fertile ground of the deep psyche. Each night when our eyes close and the rational mind goes to sleep, dreams come. Sourced in a deeper intelligence, the dreaming psyche offers us the seed images of a new vision.

To harvest these images is our task of tasks. To do so, we must return to a more "indigenous" sensibility, one that is informed by the psyche of nature—an awareness that our own essential psychological spontaneities are rooted most deeply in the psyche of the natural world. We are born out of the rhythms of nature, and to ignore these rhythms is, ultimately, to deny our psychic inheritance and our ethical obligation to a sustainable world.

In this essay I describe how "DreamTending," as an ecological approach to dreams, is a method which awakens a long forgotten way of knowing, a way of listening that remembers the world, too, is alive and always dreaming. DreamTending is offered as a praxis that opens the heart and mind to the deeper stirrings of Nature's dream. It is more than a traditional person-centered approach of dream interpretation. When tending to a dream, we consider a broader, more inclusive realm of imagination, a ground of Being from which all life evolves. The forces of nature that make existence a demanding and uncertain adventure also provide the conditions essential to life's evolution.

DreamTending is a way of tilling the deeper dimensions of indigenous knowledge located in the "natural mind" of all the world's phenomena. To tend a dream is to hear what the world is asking of us. Earth, our home, through the dreams of its unique community of life, is making its voice known. Listening to dreams of the others is a way of attending to their call.

Below, I present five eco-psychological principles central to the craft of DreamTending. I assert their relevance in building a just and sustainable global society. I discuss how, from an eco-psychological perspective, dreams include the knowledge of the other creatures and things with whom we share the planet.

But, first a story: In 1987 the United Nations World Commission on Environment and Development issued a call for the creation of a new charter that would set forth fundamental principles for sustainable development. The drafting of an Earth Charter was part of the unfinished business of the 1992 Rio Earth Summit. In 1994 Maurice Strong, the secretary general of the Earth Summit and chairman of the Earth Council, and Mikhail Gorbachev, president of Green Cross International, launched a new Earth Charter initiative with support from the Dutch government. I was invited to the Peace Palace in The Hague to begin the dialog. One of just three representatives from the United States, I was given the unique role of bringing the depth psychological perspective into the proceedings. For a little over a week, we worked all hours to craft the framework of what would ultimately become, after more than a decade-long, worldwide, cross-cultural conversation, a peoples' treaty that sets forth an expression of the hopes and aspirations of the emerging global civil society.

Again and again, my challenge was to understand clearly and communicate simply insights that depth psychology could contribute to this noble undertaking. It is not surprising that I offered the value of listening to the deep psyche, and more specifically, the language of dream. I introduced a new, yet quite old, concept of dream work. I presented an approach to dreams, DreamTending, that reaches beyond the person-centered, well-reasoned ways of the Western model to a more holistic vision shared almost universally by indigenous peoples. To my surprise, articulating the germ ideas of DreamTending to a group of environmentally-oriented world leaders was easier than communicating these notions to graduate psychology students in the United States. In the academy, for the most part, psychology students are schooled in theories of human development and methods of measuring the ups and downs of human behavior. These person-centered systems of understanding have merit, no doubt. Their appeal is also good for radio and television talk shows. But, they are bad for the environment! There is no regard given to the creatures and landscapes of the world. So, there I stood, leaning into the foundation of a more inclusive depth psychology that takes into account the psyche of the natural world.

With conviction, I asserted a number of ideas central to the practice of DreamTending:

DreamTending is initiated by one species, human beings, in recognition of and response to the call of the world's other inhabitants, animate and inanimate, who have need of us—as we do of them. In a world alive with the psychic presence of all beings, we humans are viewed as one species of dreamers among the many, particular members of an indivisible, interdependent psychic ecosystem—merely one of the constituents of a world alive with psychic vibrancy. As the question of how to listen to the world's other voices reverberates in the psyche, we discover that a more inclusive orientation to dreamwork is needed— an approach that is open to hearing the dreams of the non-human inhabitants as well as the dreams of persons.

The problem of talking in such psychological language was obvious. There were folks in the room from over 30 countries, and translations being delivered in 14 languages. So, as I was soon to discover, simple is better. Returning to the "child's mind," which is always a challenge, particularly when on an international stage, I addressed the gathering by "talking story." I told of when I was a child of twelve growing up on the West Coast of Southern California. I mused about walking on the beach one afternoon, leaving my family, and making my way to the other side of the point, away from the crowds, parking lots, and concession stands. There, around the bend, in the quiet of a more natural beach, I sat down on a large rock in a tide pool. After a while, a rather tall, strong-bodied, high-school-aged surfer walked right by me. Given that I was still one year from adolescence, he was like a god. As he passed, he said words that have echoed through my soul ever since. In a nonchalant way, in a hushed tone, he whispered in passing, "did you know that rocks can talk?" At that moment, my world was shaken. I already knew of this "secret," but growing up in the modern world, devoid of ritual and story, I did not know that anybody else could hear those kinds of voices.

Two hours later, as the tide came in, I made my way back to the other side of the point, changed forever. The ocean sparkled with new color, people seemed more alive, even the cars took on new wonder. Through the messenger of the "gods" and the "elder" of the wilderness places, I was initiated into one of the oldest mysteries known to native peoples: the things of the world are alive, each containing a life spark, an essential inner nature, and the capacity, therefore, to dream. In fourteen languages this story was transmitted to the sixty-plus participants. What I saw were heads nodding, smiles growing, and a twinkle in every eye with which I made contact. At a certain level of awareness, we all know this to be so.

In the first days of the gathering, oral presentations and written feedback were presented to the drafting committee. Very quickly I discovered what was common knowledge to the more experienced participants. When working with international multi-cultural organizations like the United Nations, to get a full paragraph adopted into a final draft is next to impossible. To get a few words or concepts accepted is a triumph.

In this instance I tasted success. I, along with two others, were able to get the words "reverence" and "mystery" and the concept "kinship with all life" into the draft text. Here is how the final document reads:

We are at once citizens of different nations and of one world in which the local and global are linked. Everyone shares responsibility for the present and future well-being of the human family and the larger living world. The spirit of human solidarity and kinship with all life is strengthened when we live with reverence for the mystery of being, gratitude for the gift of life, and humility regarding the human place in nature.

Emboldened by the fact that our contributions were making an impression and seeing them as actual text on the pages of the draft document, I, along with the few others who now had become colleagues-in-arms, went on to talk directly about dreams.

Unlike most methods of dreamwork which focus primarily on the human psyche, DreamTending sees into dream images from "nature's point of view." While most dreamworkers explore the historical associations which link the dream images to the personal developmental background of the dreamer, and most analysts delve into the realm of the collective human experience as they amplify archetypal patterns which resonate with the dream narrative, the DreamTender goes beyond these person-centered approaches to the dream. DreamTending sees the images in dreams as inextricably wedded to the psyche of nature, a psychic process that underpins the human psyche. Dreams are experienced as nature revealing herself in image and expressing herself in the dreams of persons. Traditional anthropocentric orientations to dreamwork are viewed as limited and give way to a broader approach which realizes the generative impulse of nature that fuses each dream image. DreamTending adds to traditional dreamwork methods those skills that are responsive to nature's dream.

To the small contingent of folk at the Earth Charter meeting—a single person—representing the indigenous peoples of the planet, this passage made some sense. Of course, to her sensibility it was overly intellectual and unnecessarily complicated. For her, put simply, nature and all of her inhabitants dream.

You might be wondering: how could we possibly get this concept into the Earth Charter? Well, the answer is, not easily. Yet, this central idea is so important. It is essential because if the creatures and things of the world dream, then the plea of the world's sick oceans, clear-cut forests, extinct species, mutilated mountains and forests appear as images in the dreams of humans. They present themselves on behalf of themselves, with their own story to tell. Dream images are experienced and valued as originating "out there," rooted essentially in the psyche of nature. Accordingly, each and every image in a dream does not refer to "me." My goodness, the prevailing attitude that all figures in dream represent aspects of ourselves separates us immediately from the voices, knowledge, and wisdom of the natural world. This familiar, (safe and secure), rational construct enables us to turn a blind eye to the continuing devastation of the others with whom we share our home, Earth.

After days of advocacy, and over a decade of dialog, here is what ultimately found its way into the final draft of the Earth Charter, Principle I:

> *Respect and Care for the Community of Life . . . in all its diversity. Recognize that all beings are interdependent and every form of life has value regardless of its worth to human beings.*

So many people contributed to the final drafting of this extraordinary declaration of fundamental principles for building a just, sustainable, and peaceful global society in the 21st century. To imagine that our work at The Hague, in some small way, helped shape the direction of this document is deeply fulfilling. It is a recognition that each thread in a tapestry is but a single element contributing to the beauty of the whole. And, too, with advocacy comes the responsibility to deepen our individual commitment. It is in this spirit that I offer the following orientation to the practice of DreamTending and tell of how this approach finds expression in the ongoing weaving of the Earth Charter.

The praxis of DreamTending is grounded in five ecopsychological principles, each implicating dream life with the deep psyche and the organicity of nature. These ideas are shaped by many who have walked the path long before I have. Healers, poets, and storytellers through the ages have lived these ideas. More recently, the work of James Hillman, Theodore Roszak, Marion Woodman, Thomas Berry, and Edward Casey inspire these considerations.

DREAMTENDING: FIVE ECOPSYCHOLOGICAL CONSIDERATIONS

I. The Psyche of Nature Animates the World

DreamTending starts with the idea that psyche is nature. The life force that permeates all being, that gives shape and texture to all creation, is psychic. This psychic process, which enlivens the phenomena of the world, is not limited to an interior feeling state of the human experience. The human species does not project psyche into the world, rather, it is the psyche of nature that ensouls human beings. DreamTending views the human psyche as a latter elaboration, grown out of the organicity of nature. As a community of beings, humans must develop new intimacies with what has been previously dismissed as soulless and dead. Through the portal of dream, access is opened to nature's animating display, a matrix that, in turn, mirrors the human soul.

DreamTending begins with this recognition—that the things and the creatures of the world exist with psychic presence, psychic depth. Each of the world's entities is experienced as an essential presence, containing a particular soul spark, a seminal image—all aspects of the *anima mundi*, a world alive, animated, and sourced by the psyche of nature. In tending a dream, images are experienced, most essentially, as expressions of nature's intent.

This finds expression in the Earth Charter, Principle I. Article 4:

Secure Earth's bounty and beauty for present and future generations.

a) Recognize that the freedom of action of each generation is qualified by the needs of future generations.

b) Transmit to future generations values, traditions, and institutions that support the long-term flourishing of Earth's human and ecological communities.

II. In an Animated World, Everything Dreams

DreamTending contends that dream images may not originate within the personal psyche of the dreamer. In an animated world, everything dreams. We humans live within an extended field of dreams. In this broader ecology of dream life, the earth's other beings express themselves, on behalf of themselves. Native peoples have long experienced the actuality of "the spirit that lives in the tree" or "the voice of the totem animal." These animating spirits are heard by native peoples through the images of dreams; they are valued as teachings, warnings, predictions of the future, and experienced as the dreams of the world.

To the DreamTender, a dream image of a tree is considered to be both as a reflection of the human psyche (representing the personal/ archetypal body of the dreamer) and of the world psyche (representing the actual body of a particular tree in the world). For example, imagine an old oak tree, one that literally has lived on the dreamer's property for well over 70 years. Imagine further that this old oak tree unexpectedly gets uprooted in a strong windstorm. That night, Old Oak Tree appears as a dream image of the dreamer.

DreamTending first considers, as most dream methodologies do, the emotional response of the dreamer to this image and, accordingly, associates to the surprise, grief, and horror of the day's discovery. DreamTending goes further, however, in that it acknowledges the voice of the actual tree—its grief, its decay, its sense of its own life and death and legacy. In tending a dream we would ask: "What is this tree expressing about itself through the dream image? What is the 'spirit' in the tree asking on behalf of itself?" These questions expand our relationship with the dream to include the voice of the particular oak felled in the windstorm, recognizing the tree as a living psychic phenomenon. Further, death of the oak does not occur overnight. The natural process of decomposition takes place over time, life gradually leaving the leaves, limbs, trunk, and roots. Dream images which reflect this process of dying may continue to present themselves to the dreamer as the felled oak in the world continues to dream.

On a larger scale, DreamTending views the planet as an entire ecosystem in various stages of transformation, speaking on behalf of itself through the dreams of humans. As the world expresses itself through dreams, the DreamTender becomes aware of many previously repressed images as they become more manifest. The repressed, the rejected, or neglected are the symptoms of the world condition. These dream images are the expressions of a world alive and always dreaming.

This sensibility is reflected in the Earth Charter, Principle II. Article 5:

Protect and restore the integrity of Earth's ecological systems, with special concern for biological diversity and the natural processes that sustain life.

a) Adopt at all levels sustainable development plans . . . that make environmental conservation and rehabilitation integral to all development initiatives.

b) Establish and safeguard viable nature and biosphere reserves . . . to protect Earth's life support systems, maintain biodiversity, and preserve our natural heritage.

c) Promote the recovery of endangered species and ecosystems.

III. Dream Images Are Alive and Embodied

DreamTending asserts that the images themselves are alive and embodied. "Living images" have enormous influence over that which is seen, imagined, experienced in the interior workings of the human psyche. In human beings, first, there is image; then, behavior. The animating image is *a priori*, and a deepened relationship with the world begins with an awareness of the primacy of the living image.

Living images are "tended" in a manner that honors their reality as imaginal beings. They are experienced as having body, presence, and pulse. It takes time to allow the dream figures to come back into their own lives, to walk about on their own legs. As embodied images, dream figures find immediate sympathy with the embodied dreamer. No longer is the dreamer only "in his/her head." The dreamer accesses the living image through the sensory awareness of his or her own body— touching, smelling, even tasting the embodied dream image. Through the body it becomes possible to feel into the other, to attune to the other, to breathe with the other, to be known by the other, to meet body-to-body. As images present themselves in their embodied autonomy, a relationship develops between the dreamer and the living dream image, and a new sense of "working the image" becomes possible.

In DreamTending, interpreting the meaning of images yields to noticing how images have an affecting presence, how a particular image touches, moves, or impresses us. In this way, it is not so much we who "work the image" as it is the images who work on us. The traditional psychological practice of reducing the image to a fixed explanation of meaning changes when tending the embodied image. Instead of the dreamworker taking the image to the place of a fixed explanation, it is the dreamer who follows the actual living image to where it would take him or her. To acknowledge the autonomy of the embodied image is to invite the generative intention of the image to be realized, the organicity of the image to emerge and develop. In this regard it is the images themselves that individuate. A world alive with living images is an evolving dreamscape, an animated topography that individuates through its images.

We see echoes of this in the Earth Charter, Principle II. Article 8:

Advance the study of ecological sustainability and promote the open exchange and wide application of the knowledge acquired.

a) Support international scientific and technical cooperation on sustainability, with special attention to the needs of developing countries.

b) Recognize and preserve the traditional knowledge and spiritual wisdom in all cultures that contribute to environmental protection and human well being.

IV. Mutual Regard Exists between Embodied Images

When the images of dreams are accepted as autonomous living figures with breath and pulse, a respectful, co-respondent relationship between the embodied dreamer and the image-body occurs. Dreamer and image are present to each other in the immediacy of the interaction, similar to the felt experience of an I-thou relationship. A kind of love often occurs, an elemental recognition that we are all living constituents of a dreaming psyche, a realm of existence that underpins the very nature of being itself.

For the DreamTender, psyche extends beyond the personal and collective domains of the human being to a broader realm which enfolds the world. The "world unconscious," referred to by some as an "ecological unconscious," is perceived as the dimension where all the earth's phenomena, not only human beings, are interrelated in a field of psychic mutuality. When dreams are tended from this perspective of a universal psyche, there is an inherent sense of reciprocity, a felt sense of mutual regard. People experience themselves as parts of the whole, caring for the world as they care for themselves. As the world expresses itself in myriad ways in the dreams of all dreamers, DreamTending provides the medium for intimate relationship between person and world.

From the Earth Charter, Principle VI. Articles 14 and 15:

Article 14:

Integrate into formal education and life-long learning the knowledge, values, and skills needed for a sustainable way of life.

a) Provide all, especially children and youth, with educational opportunities that empower them to contribute actively to sustainable development.

b) Promote the contribution of the arts and humanities as well as the sciences in sustainable development.

Article 15:

Treat all living beings with respect and consideration.

V. The City, too, Is Dreaming

DreamTending recognizes that the things of nature and the "human-made" things of the street are joined, most essentially, in the creative life-death forces of the psychic process. Nature is to be found not only in the wilderness landscape, but also in the psyche of the city, in the human-made. Contemporary society's tendency to place human-made and nature-made in opposition splits urban life from the natural world, in a way "orphaning" the city, tearing it from the life of Planet Earth. Too often, we leave the city to encounter "nature," imagining it only exists away from civilization, among the grasses and trees of the countryside. The city, too, is dreaming, and the pulse of nature beats strongly through its images.

DreamTending gives value to the process of nature rather than focusing only on the literal products of "wilderness places" found in natural landscapes. In tending dreams, one listens into the images of the city and the human-made to discover nature's harmonic at work. When the image of a building presents itself in a dream, the image is attended to as an imaginal structure of the city rather than simply labeled as a representation of the dreamer's personality structure. As a building of the cityscape, the "dream-image-as-building" has presence, purpose, soul. It belongs to the psyche of the city, and is experienced as one part of the unfolding rhythms of that place. The building is listened to for what it knows or needs, valued for its perspective, and regarded for its place in the living body of the city. Through DreamTending, the wisdom of nature is heard in the creative process that is inherent in the crafted steel and formed concrete that constitute the walls and the streets of the city. The dream of the city can be heard through its images.

From the Earth Charter, Principle III. Article 10:

Ensure that economic activities and institutions at all levels promote human development in an equitable and sustainable manner.

a) Promote the equitable distribution of wealth within nations and among nations . . .

CONCLUSION

In DreamTending the purpose is not to fix images in static explanations or to identify with them as aspects of ourselves. Instead, to tend a dream is to attend to the images by giving them time and place to present themselves on their own behalf. These visitations by the images, through their presence in the room, affect the dreamer and the dream therapist. It is the impact that they make on our experience which is noticed first, rather than the demands for meaning that we would impose on these images.

Dream images are not only representations of the neurotic complexes of the past, nor are they located only in our personal or collective human experience. Rather, these visitors of the night are the beautiful and the horrific beings of the world dreaming. To be in relationship with them offers each of us access to the life-affirming rhythm of the world psyche, a cadence rooted, most essentially, in the psyche of nature.

So many of us have split ourselves off from the timeless mosaic of nature's ecology. This harmonic is no longer active in our lives, and this creates illness. DreamTending as a psychological practice reconnects us to the universal pulse of life, uniting us with a broader ecology and, potentially, restoring health. The Earth Charter as well requires a change of mind and heart. In both instances we must imaginatively develop and apply the vision of a sustainable way of life locally, nationally, regionally, and globally.

DreamTending is an ecopsychological approach to the dream, offering something valuable to each of us. In DreamTending, we too are imaginal beings hosting the very images that in turn imagine us. In this ecological view of psychological life, DreamTending offers an approach to the dream that attends mindfully to the particularity of each image—discovering its nature, wondering about its activities, and listening to its experiences.

In an increasingly ego-centric, human-centered world, the well-being of the planet may depend on our ability to hear and respond to the many voices of nature's other beings. In adopting an Earth Charter, "let ours be a time remembered for the awakening of a new reverence for life, the firm resolve to achieve sustainability, the quickening of the struggle for justice and peace, and the joyful celebration of life and dream."

In tending the dream, we are tending the world.

For more information on the Earth Charter: www.earthcharter.org

For more information on DreamTending: www.DreamTending.com

CROSSING

Every stone is a doorway to the wilderness,
an ancient crossing point to another place,
through which I can sometimes pass
and sometimes not.
I imagine great rivers of time
once poured from them,
and what we now have left
are the prehistoric pieces
of a cosmic egg that cracked open
in some now long-forgotten,
Once-upon-a-time;
the fossilized shells
of a primeval wind and rain
that you can still feel
in your bones when you stand
naked in your own life,
a stranger in a strange land,
who lost part of himself
crossing between worlds,
and then one day, picking up a stone,
heard the sound
of his own breathing from within.

—*Michael Whan*

SOUL ON STONE

ROBERTO GAMBINI

There is a fundamental friendship found in the history of mankind between soul and stone. Two old friends indeed. One is all substance, the other immaterial. Stone has kept for us the record of soul's first images. Cave rock paintings and carved stone artifacts are the birth certificate of imagination.

Studies in evolutionist archaeology have recently demonstrated that the kind of intelligence that characterizes the species *homo sapiens* was fully developed at the end of the Paleolithic period. Around 100,000 years ago, four modalities of intelligence merged: a natural intelligence that enabled humans to understand and deal with the environment; a social intelligence, through which social relations, group life, and kinship were created; a technical intelligence, necessary for the invention and fabrication of tools; and, a linguistic intelligence, responsible for the creation of language, images, and symbols.[1] These four aspects of intelligence came together to form a whole, a cognitive flow. Our contemporary intelligence is by no means different, or better, than this primeval one. It was this pre-historic mind that, some 60,000 years ago, created culture when the skin of ritually buried corpses was painted with ochre. Dead skin was therefore the first

Roberto Gambini is a Jungian analyst in São Paulo, Brazil. His books include *Indian Mirror: The Making of the Brazilian Soul* and *Soul and Culture*.

canvas for art. Religion and art were born together, and they formed the matrix of culture.

The main purpose of this paper is to show that it was at this time, at the dawn of consciousness, that we see the first visual manifestation of the imagination as evidenced in cave rock paintings and carved stone artifacts. Thus, contrary to longstanding classical archaeological theories, rock paintings are not naïve attempts to copy the animals or people living in the sun, in the world outside the cave (to play with Plato), but are instead the fixation of inner images—soul on stone. They are psychic images, certainly not primitive photographs of outer realities. Each psychic—that is, inner—image painted on rock walls confirmed to the painter that he (or she too? Archaeology says nothing about the gender of artists) was beginning to discover what and who he was. As if saying, "I have inner images, therefore I am," the pre-historic germ of the Socratic dictum "Know thyself," or the Cartesian thinking that finally enabled Descartes to formulate his classical statement, "I think, therefore I am." This is what imaginal fossil philosophy consisted of: thoughts of the soul reflected in images that were forever fixed on stone. So we can assume that rock paintings and engravings are mankind's primordial psychological documents. Not a sketch of visible objects, but the dawning light of consciousness of the world, about the power of imagining inner realities.

When precisely is the historical moment when imagination appeared? It must have been when the four modalities of intelligence, discussed earlier, merged into one integrated tool of perception and reflection. When this happened, when the imagination revealed itself in depicted form, we see the birth of soul and its first contents—soul in its cradle is made visible. Crawling soul-making. Euro-centric theory has always maintained the idea that the first inhabitants of South America finally reached the Continent 9,000 years ago at most, after a long journey that started when the icy Behring Strait was crossed by humans pursuing game. But archaeological evidence in the Northeast of Brazil indicates that this vast land was impregnated by soul, quite probably, 50,000 years ago. If we were to try our hand at an archaeology of soul, we could imagine a stratigraphic cut of our collective psyche 50 meters deep, corresponding to these last 50,000 years. Let us then excavate 50 centimeters, corresponding to the last 500 years—beginning around 1492, when America was "discovered" by Columbus (although we know today that other explorers of the seas set foot on the Continent as early as the 10th century). At this rather superficial depth, our shovel would hit a rocky substratum, and we would conclude that this is the mother-rock, the beginning of historical time. But such a conclusion would be a total mistake. There is still much untapped depth beneath this rocky impediment. What exactly is this "rock"? What keeps us separated from our buried ancestral soul, unaware of its existence and its contents? I believe that this separation results from a failure to recognize new evidence, an adherence to narrow theories, a refusal to acknowledge soul as a psychological reality, and a depreciation of enigmatic obscurities that disturb modern certainties.

This "rock" has to be broken apart and we have to go beneath it if we are to discover that we have a very ancient soul, evidenced in images found on the mother-stone on Paleolithic walls which were created at a time when a true Big Bang of culture occurred—that is, when consciousness, intelligence, and imagination finally emerged from a shapeless and nocturnal pre-human mind hundreds of centuries old. Knowledge of this incommensurable past is fundamental to change our shallow emotions and the distorted mental representations we have of ourselves in the present. These stem from trying to understand the roots of our Latin American identity crisis and from all the historical and cultural tribulations our soul is going through to find its genuine character and individuality, renewed values, and a less hypocritical ethical standard. This is conceivably the only way to reach a more enlightened psychological position, knowing that the background of our soul consists not only of archaeological, historical, and artistic inheritances, but is mainly a *patrimony of sensibility* that is certainly more valuable than material monuments of times gone by. This sensibility is still alive in us, although not always—except in poetry and art—recognized as such. What was built in pre-historical Brazil, speaking of my own country, was a construction of feelings and meanings, modes of perceiving and understanding the world, and the sum of this immaterial wealth is our greatness richness and supreme achievement.

It is precisely this patrimony of sensibility that was negated in the 16th century with the arrival of both the Portuguese colonizers and the Jesuit missionaries, who had no qualms about enslaving the Indians and destroying their myths and religion, as if their soul, or lack of it, consisted of a despicable nothingness, since it was rooted in the dark world of the Indian mother that generated a whole new people. The white father's collective mind had neither the capacity to nor the political interest in valuing the ancestral soul of the land. Through catechization and cultural disruption, this phallic, rational European mind tried to annihilate all manifestations of the stone-age soul.

In my book *Indian Mirror—The Making of the Brazilian Soul*,[2] I analyzed some 200 letters written by the Jesuits in the 16th century working in Brazil to Ignatius Loyola, head of the Company of Jesus in Portugal, reporting their missionary efforts to convert to Catholicism the inhabitants of the newly conquered land. My main point in that book was to demonstrate that when they described the Indians and their alleged vices, they were projecting upon them a Christian shadow that they would never recognize was their own. Manoel da Nóbrega, head of the mission, at his arrival in Brazil in 1549 accompanying Tomé de Souza, the first General Governor appointed by the Portuguese Crown to launch a process of colonization that lasted almost three centuries, wrote the following words about the Indians:

> Amongst them there is no love or loyalty … They obey no one except their own will, and therefore they do whatever they please, inclining towards vices so dirty and so vile that I prefer to remain silent, not to reveal in writing such enormous wickedness." … It is amazing that God gave such a good land so long ago to such ignorant people who know Him so little, because they have no god for certain and they will believe anyone you tell them to.[3]

In 1551, in another letter, he went further:

> These gentiles worship nothing, nor do they know God, but only the thunder which they call Tupana, which is how they speak of something divine. So we do not have a more convenient word to bring them to the knowledge of God than to call him Father Tupana.[4]

In 1556, Nóbrega the missionary continues to write:

> These people were more forgotten by creation than brutal beasts, and more ingrate than the offspring of vipers which devour their mothers, they have no respect for the love and creation that one gives them.[5]

Brother Leonardo Nunes wrote, in 1550, a letter to the priests and brethren of Coimbra, Portugal, in which he made clear the eschatological images they projected onto the native inhabitants of Brazil

> … and they certainly looked like devils. All went around naked, as is their custom, some painted in black and others in red, and others covered with feathers, and they kept shooting arrows shouting loudly, and others shook some rattles which they use to make sounds in their wars, and it looked like Hell itself.[6]

In 1557, the missionary Antonio Blázquez wrote directly to Ignatius Loyola, presenting a completely prejudiced description of Indian dwellings:

> Their houses are dark, stinking and full of smoke, displaying in the middle pots that are like caldrons in hell. While some laugh, others weep through the night. Their beds are hammocks rotten with urine, because they are too lazy to do their needs elsewhere. And if that were not enough to imagine Hell… .[7]

After dozens of letters portraying the Indians in this style—as children of the Devil, strange soulless beings lost midway between animals and humans, whose only salvation was to be forcefully baptized in order to acquire a soul—in 1555 Manoel da Nóbrega, in his capacity of leader of the missionary team, announced his megalomaniac plan

> … to see the gentiles subjected in obedience to the Christians, so that we could do with them whatever we wanted … As they are brutal people, if they are left free one can do nothing with them.[8]

As a matter of fact, another Jesuit, friar José de Anchieta, who was eventually considered for sainthood due to alleged miracles he performed while converting thousands of Indians, wrote a dramatic letter urging that efforts be made by the Company to persuade the King of Portugal to dispatch armed forces to Brazil in order to

> put an end to all those evil ones who resist the preaching of the Gospel and to subject them to slavery, but also to honor those who come close to Christ. May our Lord give complete fulfillment to this hope of ours![9]

A century later, the great orator Priest Antonio Vieira, who in several of his inflamed sermons was a great defenders of the Indians, wrote a piece entitled *"Sermon of the Holy Spirit,"* in which he admonishes the missionaries that

> the only way to convert beasts into men is killing and eating them: for there is nothing more alike to teaching and indoctrinating than killing and eating. If a beast is to be converted into a man, it must no longer be what it was, and start being what it was not; and this is achieved through killing and eating it: by killing it, it ceases to be what it was, since dead it is no longer a beast; by eating it, it starts to be what it was not, because once eaten, it is already man. Since God wanted Saint Peter to convert into loyal men all those beasts that He showed him, so therefore the voice of the sky told him to kill and eat them, *'occide et manduca.'*[10]

This is Christian cannibalism in a nutshell. Jesuit missionaries killed the soul of the beasts they thought Indians were, and metaphorically ate their bodies, turning them into non-beings.

I would like now to turn to the ancient images produced by these beasts and the marks their soul left on stone. First and foremost, let us consider the widespread tracing of a hand on cave walls, just the empty shape of a hand delineated by patches of pigment contouring it. This image of the hand can be found in rock paintings in many archaeological sites around the world, and we could say it corresponds to this realization: "I am conscious of myself, this is my hand." It is a fantastic image conveying a tremendous evolutionary leap, reduced by abstract scientific terminology to *Homo Sapiens* and *Homo Faber*, without acknowledging that these images reflect a psychological, or inner process, taking place inside these predecessors. The capacity to know and fabricate things is recognized by science, but not the link between painted image and mental experience. This hand, more evolved that that of our anthropoid ancestors, is the sign of human perception of our own specific nature and our readiness to act in the world, transforming matter into new shapes and painting or carving artifacts such as a stone axe that even today can be appreciated as an achievement in harmony, smoothness, and symmetry (Fig. 1),[11] or a rock crystal spear arrow (Fig. 2)[12] that to our modern eyes can be appreciated as a sophisticated piece of avant-garde jewelry.

Along the coast of Brazil, covering some 4,000 kilometers, there is a series of artificial mounds made of sea shells, called "Sambaquis:" *Tamba* = shell, *ki* = mound. They were made by a people who lived near the ocean, where abundant nourishment could be found. This group lived around 6,000 years ago, and disappeared for reasons archaeologists cannot explain. The current hypothesis is that they may have been

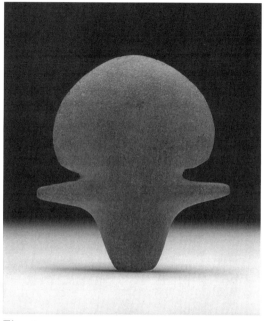

Fig. 1

Fig. 2

conquered and assimilated by agricultural and ceramist tribes coming from the West.[13] Until very recently, such shell mounds were believed to be just accumulations of litter without any archaeological significance. But recent excavations have conclusively established that they actually were funeral camps, since thousands of skeletons were found buried in the same way—in an upright position with ritual objects.

In the funeral rituals enacted in these mounds, the dead bodies were always surrounded by certain kinds of objects, from beads to sculpted bones or stone artifacts. From the several collections of such items that can be seen today in our museums, I have been especially impressed by a bird-like little sculpture, displaying a carved spoon in its belly (Fig. 3).[14] It probably served a ritual function having to do with the ingestion of some kind of beverage—that is as much as we know today, but from this single piece we can infer that this group of people had a religious conception of an

Fig. 3

Fig. 4

after-life. This is evidently not a naturalistic represen-tation of a bird, but rather a representation of a soul-bird, carrying in its entrails the power to promote a certain kind of psychological ex-perience to anyone who drank the beverage contained in its belly. This is not simply a sea-shore bird, but a magical one that takes imagination along in its flight.

Having already con-sidered the hand motif, let us now address the motif of the eyes (Fig. 4).[15] One could say this bas-relief depicts two spirals, which in themselves are highly representative of a newly acquired mental ability to conceive symbols; but the parallel arrangement of spirally lines above a vertical axis suggesting a nose, and therefore a facial structure, could as well allow us to identify a pair of eyes with a fixed gaze. Eye sight is an attribute of consciousness: not just looking outward and recognizing the external world in all its variety just waiting to be singled out, named, understood, and classified, but also looking inward and being aware of the images that appear on our mental screen, which is the imaginal world of which cave paintings are an expression.

If Paleolithic man had not become conscious of the power of his hands and eyes, maybe material culture would have been created anyway as a result of trial and error, like when chimpanzees quite unintentionally discovered that stones could be thrown, struck against a coconut to open it, or used as a mortar to soften edible hard roots. But symbolic or immaterial culture, as anthropologists call it, could only be created through the exercise of a certain modality of intelligence which is manifested by an awareness of hands and eyes as efficient media to create symbolic images—hands used to give the images visibility, and eyes to understand their meaning.

Several etchings on rocky walls in widespread areas of Brazil depict eyes duly placed on a head and a full body (Fig. 5).[16] In this type of

Fig. 5

Fig. 6

bas-relief a set of rays emanates from the head. Some archaeologists have suggested that these rays point to solar symbolism, representing a kind of "solar hero" (an interpretation which might be a retroactive projection of ulterior mythology on their part). Or, could the rays depict raised hair indicating fear of some threatening animal? Maybe. To my mind, though, they instead (Fig. 6)[17] indicate a conscious perception that thought-forms (rays) emanate from the head, or mind. This is in accordance with the current evolutionist theory that, in the period when this image was etched (some 15,000 years ago), different kinds of intelligence existed which complemented one another and created consciousness—that something that today we call mind, or psyche, was perceived as a source of mental products and, in other words, reflected a soul-making process.

We have already considered the image of the soul-bird. There is another image, this time found in a rock painting, in which a human figure bows, with raised arms, in what appears to be an act of reverence to a much larger bird standing on a slightly higher level, displaying wide-open wings (Fig. 7).[18] This is most probably a mythological bird, a spiritual power appearing physically to a man, a true epiphany of a supernatural being in the flesh.

The only possible way to access the meaning of images such as this is through "excavating" fossilized fragments of myths in our soul. Fragments that may still be alive in the psyche of our contemporary Indians, for instance, if analytical psychology paid a little more attention not simply to the vast array of stories they still tell, but to the temporal dimension they might suggest as remnants of a lost Paleolithic mythology. In any case, this awesome bird is certainly not perching on a tree "out there," at the back of the artist in the moment it is being painted. It is rather perched on the religious imagination of its author.

The first written mention of the existence of rock paintings in Brazil dates back to 1598, when a certain Brandônio (anonymous) published a book entitled *Diálogo das Grandezas do Brazil* (*Dialogue about Brazil's Greatness*).[19] Some Portuguese chroniclers were sure they could identify, engraved on stone, the footsteps of Saint Thomas, who was believed, in the 16th century, to have been in Brazil in remote times, but no one could explain why or how. It was again a Christian projection upon aboriginal images that were otherwise unexplainable to the conquerors' consciousness. The French Capuchins, alongside other European travelers (mainly German and French), looked at our prehistoric soul-images as vestiges of lost civilizations that had been in the country many centuries before its "discovery" by European travelers —for instance, Egyptians, Phoenicians, Hebrews, Greeks, Vikings. These paintings or etchings, chroniclers thought, must have been esoteric marks left by highly civilized peoples, since it was inconceivable that brute natives might have created them.

Fig. 7

Later, the paintings were considered to be no more than rustic scrawls, the meaningless pastime of a bunch of idle natives. Wilhelm Lundt, a Danish archaeologist, who did field research in the late 19th century and discovered a six-thousand-year-old human fossil in the State of Minas Gerais, had the following idea about rock art:

> The savage nomads of the Kaiapó tribe, in my view, took up residence and found shelter in the caves, beneath the arches of an immense crag. Full of enthusiasm for the beauty of the surrounding landscape, they tried to represent the objects which were most clearly visible. The foot of the crag is covered with their drawings, as primitive as the imagination which guided the hands of their authors. Yet this makes them no less interesting to the philosopher who wishes to know the products of the mind at its lowest level of development.[20]

This idea, shared by many other authors such as Saint-Hilaire, Spix and Martius, Alfred Russel Wallace, Charles Hartt, Germano Stradelli, Casper Branner, Max Schmidt and Henri Coudreau, among others,

was that visible objects were represented with very little skill and poor imagination, very much like children trying their hand at drawing a body, a tree, or a dog.

More recent authors, in the 19th and 20th centuries, dared to think that Brazilian rock art proved that aliens from other planets had left their enigmatic mark on our landscape. The scientist Alfredo de Carvalho, on the other hand, stated that these images were merely "the playful relief of idle savages."

Fig. 8

In the Amazonian State of Pará, in a vast fluvial area around the city of Santarém, archaeologists are presently discovering a wealth of anthropomorphic clay pots and figurines. When studying the literature, I was impressed by a small sculpture representing a mother and her child (Fig. 8),[21] generally taken as an image of the archetype of motherhood in most cultures. But this sculpture is much older than the myth of Isis holding Horus on her lap, yet still practically unknown by foreign researchers of archetypal imagery.

When I was preparing my book *Indian Mirror* for publication in 2000, I had the privilege of researching original pictures in the largest private collection of rare books ever assembled in São Paulo by Guita and José Mindlin, a treasure of invaluable images for the study of the Brazilian soul. For my book cover, I chose a 1856 engraving by the German naturalist Carl Friedrich von Martius which had been used as an illustration in a book about Brazilian flora: the image was of a colossal trunk of a native tree and its potent roots, surrounded by a ring of Indian men holding hands. Studying the archaeological literature to prepare this paper, I was astonished to find a similar image painted on the wall of a cave 10,000 years ago in the Capivara Sierra, located in the district of São Raimundo Nonato, in the Northern State of Piauí (Fig. 9).[22]

Fig. 9

In this tree scene, which is depicted in many variations in different caves scattered throughout this archaeological area, a group of ten men and women dance around a tree. There can be no doubt that this is a religious image, a representation of a ritual around a sacred tree whose meaning is forever lost for us. Perhaps this primordial tree had to do with a creation myth, since many cultures have creation stories in which men are born from a tree. Brazilian Indians still tell the story of the first men coming out of an underwater hole, climbing up the trunk of a tree until they reached firm ground on earth. (Jung wrote extensively about the tree in alchemy and made several references to and amplifications of this motif in his essays. I will not quote all this material, because it is already of general knowledge for readers familiar with symbolic interpretation of images, and, moreover, because I do not intend to leave the Brazilian context in which such images were painted.)

Piauí, the area where this image was found, is an arid region of Northern Brazil, and the less economically developed of all the Brazilian states. There is still little knowledge about geographical conditions in prehistoric times, but even before agriculture was introduced, when food had to be gathered wherever it might be found, trees were a source of life, due to their fruits, seeds, sap, timber, shelter, and the birds and insects they attracted. Paintings such as this, depicting humans honoring a tree, quite certainly suggest that trees were seen as a sacred entity connected with the maintenance, if not the origin, of life by these people portrayed by the Jesuits or foreign travelers as lacking sensibility and the capacity to conceive and represent transcendent powers.

The image of this ancient tree still reverberates today, when the media spreads the news that in the last ten years one billion trees have been destroyed in the Amazon rain forest, adding the dramatic image that, if all these trees were aligned close together they would form a ring long enough to encircle the planet Earth three times. The rock painting reminds us that trees are our ancestral gods, but we no longer have eyes to recognize their sacredness.

Bringing this short paper to a close, I want to make a few comments about the making of the modern Brazilian soul in the 16th century, when Portuguese men encountered the Indians and inaugurated a new historical process. Something valuable took place: the mixture of three races, Indian, African, and Portuguese, the white father and the Indian or black mother. Our genetic mixture is the greatest richness of Brazil, besides the fact that in this country two-thirds of the planet's biodiversity can be found. Racial mixture was seen as a sign of degradation until the end of the 19th century, but nowadays we are beginning to understand the value of plurality and difference. So we could say that Portuguese men, different from the Protestant colonizers of North America, had a strong Eros that attracted them to Indian women. But the tragic part of the story is that white men only mated with the bodies of these native women, not with their souls. They despised all that was not useful to them in their great task of conquest and colonization, including the accumulated knowledge of the Indians, their mythology, religion, and perception of the meaning of life. Instead the colonizers were mainly interested in Indian enforced labor and the artifacts that the Indians made, such as hammocks and baskets, pots and canoes, and in the Indians' hunting techniques and agricultural skills. At the same time that a new people was born, ancestral memory was lost. The offspring

of a white father and an Indian mother was a nobody. He did not know who he was, where he came from, or his own worth because he had lost a priceless link with a millenary patrimony of soul.

A rock painting found in the dark recesses of a cave shows a man and a woman kissing (Fig. 10).[23]

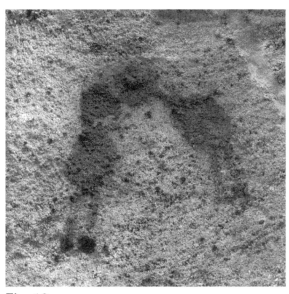

Fig. 10

A little sculpture discovered in a burial field in a Sambaqui gives shape to two swallows making love (Fig. 11).[24]

Fig. 11

To my mind, these two pieces are sublime. Our ancestors were no doubt able to feel the beauty of animals mating, the sweetness of sex, the joy of dancing and being together, and the taste of love. Two swallows making love: love on stone. To me, these two are the quintessential images of soul's lost memory.

ILLUSTRATION SOURCES

1. *Antes. Histórias da Pré-História*. Centro Cultural Banco do Brasil, 2005. Figures 1 (p. 221), 2 (p. 47), 3 (p. 51), 6 (p. 135), 8 (p. 105), and 11 (p. 25).

2. Anne-Marie Pessis, *Images from Pré-History*. FUMDHAM/PETROBRAS, 2003. Figures 7 (p. 161), 9 (p. 121) and 10 (p. 120).

3. Edithe Pereira, *Arte Rupestre na Amazônia* (São Paulo: UNESP Editora), Figures 4 (p. 38) and 5 (p. 84).

NOTES

1. Steven Mithen, *A Pré-História da Mente*, especially chapter 9, "O big bang da cultura humana: as origens da arte e da religião" (São Paulo: Editora Unesp, 2002), 247-303.

2. Roberto Gambini, *Indian Mirror: The Making of the Brazilian Soul* (São Paulo: Axis Mundi/Terceiro Nome, 2000).

3. *Ibid.*, 93. All translations of the Jesuit letters are mine.

4. *Ibid.*, 100.

5. *Ibid.*, 103.

6. *Ibid.*, 122-123.

7. *Ibid.*, 124.

8. *Ibid.*, 156.

9. *Ibid.*, 156.

10. Antonio Vieira, *Sermões, Vol. V* (Porto: Livraria Chardron, 1907), my translation.

11. Measuring 13 x 13.5 cm. Pernambuco State Museum.

12. Measuring 0.6 x 4.5 x 7.6 cm. Joinville Sambaqui Archaeological Museum.

13. Madu Gaspar, *Sambaqui: Arqueologia do Litoral Brasileiro* (Rio de Janeiro: Jorge Zahar Editor, 2004), 68.

14 Measuring 5.5 x 11 x 16.5 cm. Joinville Sambaqui Archaelogical Museum.

EARLY CELTIC ART

Of this motif
was written:

> '... a new pattern emerged
> that featured strings
> of triskles (three-limbed
> whirligigs)
> and wave tendrils.'

Where have I heard
all that before:
'strings of triskles
(three-limbed whirligigs)
and wave tendrills'?

It's a vision of wave-energy,
of spiral motion in a cosmic sea,
a Superstring Theory,
the kind you get
in a quantum leap
from standing on the shore
a long, long time, waiting
in wild contemplation,
your head as high
as a gull's.

—*Michael Whan*

REUNITING PSYCHE AND NATURE

DAVID KIDNER

INTRODUCTION: THE EMBODIED AND THE VIRTUAL

Herbert Simon, the great information theorist, stated in his "Travel Theorem" that "anything that can be learned by a normal American adult on a trip to a foreign country ... can be learned more quickly, cheaply, and easily by visiting the San Diego Public Library." Elaborating on this, he claimed that it

> is well known that one can circumnavigate the globe, penetrating deserts and jungles along the way, without ever venturing outside one's own Western, industrialized, air-conditioned culture, or learning that there is anything different from it. I have had a thrilling view of Ulan Bator and the Gobi Desert from 30,000 feet, in the business-class comfort of a B747.

Travelling to Europe with his wife in 1965, he visited many of the places depicted in Cezanne's paintings. However, they "learned nothing new; we had already seen the paintings."[1]

After a few years working as a chemical engineer in the petroleum industry, David Kidner moved into the social sciences with a Ph.D. in experimental personality research at London University. For the past three decades he has taught psychology, sociology, and environmental philosophy in England and the USA, and is currently at Nottingham Trent University. He is the author of *Nature and Psyche: Radical Environmentalism and the Politics of Subjectivity* (SUNY Press, 2001).

Edward Abbey provides an example of a fundamentally different kind of American pioneer. Lambasting those who would see the world only from behind a window, he argued that

> ... you can't see anything from a car; you've got to get out of the goddamned contraption and walk, better yet crawl, on hands and knees, over the sandstone and through the thornbush and cactus. When traces of blood begin to mark your trail you'll see something, maybe.[2]

These two accounts encapsulate a powerful, covert tension between an embodied, sensual perspective that is becoming an endangered species in the industrial world and a perspective based on cognition, language, and visual representation—almost a virtual world—that is in the ascendancy. In historical terms, the divergence between these perspectives reflects the underlying polarization between idealism and materialism which has plagued philosophy since Plato and Aristotle; and only rarely have social philosophers tried to understand us both as embodied creatures who participate in natural processes and as cultural beings who inhabit a symbolic realm. The same virulent trend can also be seen in our everyday lives, and is reflected in the increasing commodification of forms of individual subjectivity—often electronically amplified and manipulated by advertising—that are unanchored to external reality. The ethnobotanist Gary Nabhan has found that even indigenous children on the American continent "had seen more animals on television and in the movies than they had personally seen in the wild," and that direct knowledge of the natural world is rapidly being lost even among native groups such as the O'odham.[3] In this paper, I will argue that analytical psychology is, among other things, an attempt to address this tension, albeit one that is to some extent frustrated by the epistemological conditions of its birth. In particular, I will argue that analytical psychology and ecology are not two mutually incomprehensible realms, and that there are fruitful parallels and complementarities between them.

Jung, an enthusiastic traveller himself, was well aware of European philosophy's idealist slant. For example, in his discussion of the Mother archetype, he points out that with the Catholic doctrine of the assumption of the Virgin Mary, "the Mother of God was divested of all the essential qualities of materiality, [and] matter became completely de-souled."[4] Nevertheless, he was not immune to the same polarization of matter and spirit, and inconsistencies in his work are often symptomatic of a struggle between a view of the psyche which is rooted in a realm of pure human meaning and one in which meaning arises out of our embodiment and, ultimately, out of the earth. As Roger Brooke has noted, Jung's vacillation may have been partly due to the incompatibility between his insights and the available forms of language; and as a result his "intuitive understanding of psychological life far surpassed most of his theoretical formulations."[5] His view that there was a continuity between psyche and the biological world was one of his central "intuitive understandings," albeit one which is difficult to express given the reductionist and individualist connotations of the term "biology." Consequently, when Jung describes archetypes as "patterns of instinctual behaviour,"[6] he is not reverting to the reductive biologism of his day which viewed behavior as due to an array of internal "drives," expressed within a passive, featureless world. "Instinct," for Jung, is a far more flexible, intelligent, and structured entity than it is, say, for Freud.

Jung never entirely escaped the Cartesian emphasis on thought as the source of structure, however, and both his references to "withdrawing projections" from the world and his return to Europe following his visit to Mount Elgon can be viewed as strategic retreats back into the safety of prevailing assumptions.[7] But why were the Kenyan plains so captivating to Jung; and equally, why were they so threatening? I will argue that the absence of a dynamic conception of the world was the insuperable obstacle which made Jung's movement towards an embodied conception of psyche a dangerous one.

VANISHING RESONANCE

Is our only choice between a self defined through its safely dualistic separation from the world, on the one hand, and one in which we become so merged with the world within a larger psychic field that we lose all autonomy? Of course, both these types of experience are commonplace: we have all "withdrawn into ourselves" from time to time, and we have all "lost ourselves" in some larger field such as music, spiritual experience, or a natural landscape. But these experiences are not irreversible epistemological decisions which determine our character thereafter, but part of the ebb-and-flow of subjective experience, the spontaneous variation in resonance with whatever is outside ourselves. Like the homecoming traveller, we can return to our "individual" psychological boundaries, giving us the confidence to momentarily extend ourselves into the world as we empathize with another, whether human or non-human, or "lose ourselves" in a magnificent natural setting, or give ourselves to some cause; and it is this dynamic capacity of subjectivity to reach out into the world which is denied by most psychology. It is a capacity which is particularly endangered in a society which has become narcissistic through the cultivation of the individual, the loss of integrative cultural structures, and the shrivelling of our belief in a world which transcends our own lifetimes, individual powers, and spiritual capabilities.

Just as the self becomes ossified into the "individual" through this stilling of resonant relations with the outside world, something very similar happens to the world itself through our identification of "separate" items which are, in Alfred North Whitehead's terms, "fully describable apart from any reference to any other portion of matter." In the same way that the freezing of experiential spontaneity results from our definition as individuals, dynamism and structural spontaneity are drained from the world by its reduction to ecological fragments having only mechanical relations to each other. Whitehead goes on to note that this freezing of dynamism also applies to time: a stone, he remarks, is generally described "without any reference to past or future."[8] Tim Ingold's summary of the effects of such mappings of the world captures this well:

> ... all is still and silent. There is neither sunlight nor moonlight; there are no variations of light or shade; no clouds, no shadows or reflections. The wind does not blow, neither disturbing the trees nor whipping the water into waves. No birds fly in the sky, or sing in the woods; forests and pastures are devoid of animal life; houses and streets are empty of people and traffic. To dismiss all this ... is perverse, to say the least. For it is no less than the stuff of life itself ... .[9]

For present purposes, the main consequence of this dual freezing of self and world is that both can be "pinned down" and defined without reference to the other, fitting neatly into the industrialist conception of masterful, autonomous individuals acting within a world that is passive and devoid of spirit. Jung struggled against this conception; but his theory has nevertheless been portrayed in ways that he would be uneasy with. In various undergraduate texts, for example, I have seen the Jungian model of the personality portrayed in diagrammatic terms with consciousness at the top, "above" the personal unconscious, which is itself "above" a collective unconscious which spreads out into the earth. And of course such representations are not without a certain truth-value. However, what we gain in clarity and constancy through representing the psyche in such "geological" terms has to be balanced against the veiling of a sort of dynamic interpenetration which is as much a part of the world as any static structure.

Such resonant extensions of self are precisely what are lost in assumptions of "scientific objectivity" and in our everyday, common-sense experience of the urban, largely manufactured, "environments" we inhabit. This is a sort of vicious circle: in defining the self individualistically, we exclude the resonances that bring the world to life; and in constructing an environment with which resonance is difficult, we bring into being a psychically dead world. As a result, any other psychic organization than that of the contemporary narcissistic individual is extinguished, its possibility reawakened only by historical or anthropological accounts of ecstatic self-transcendence. So it is that we lose those properties of the world that have been seen as spiritual or even beautiful—or, in more prosaic ecosystemic terms, as emergent. For example, Nabhan recognizes that ecological relations are not *just* ecological, as the term is commonly used, but also imply something more ineffable. In pointing to the relation between the dwindling numbers of a desert flower, Kearney's Blue Star, in southern Arizona and the plummeting population of the species of bee that pollinates them, he remarks that "it was as if the Blue Stars' bodies were there, but their spirits had flown away."[10] One wonders whether something similar could be said about us: if, as Roger Brooke argues, we become spiritual beings not through the discovery of some capacity within ourselves, but through "the world's revelation as a temple,"[11] then the fragmentation and destruction of the natural world becomes a spiritual loss and, indeed, the loss of an essential dimension of humanity.

Representing the Resonant Self

Despite his cultural background, Jung clearly saw that psychic organization taps into the past and into the world itself, and he struggled throughout his life to represent this embeddedness. As he put it,

> the archetypes are as it were hidden foundations of the conscious mind, or, to use another comparison, the roots which the psyche has sunk not only in the earth in the narrower sense but in the world in general. ... [archetypes are that portion of the psyche] through which the psyche is attached to nature.[12]

But as he recognized, this metaphor of rootedness fails adequately to represent the *dynamism* of our relation to the rest of nature, as does his alternative image of a building with multiple floors, including a cellar and beneath the cellar "a choked-up cave with neolithic tools in the upper layer and remnants of fauna from the same period in the lower layers."[13] Pointing to the limitations of this metaphor, Jung argues that "[e]verything is alive, and our upper story, consciousness, is continually influenced by its living and active foundations."[14] Two decades later, he would suggest that "[i]ndividual consciousness is only the flower and the fruit of a season, sprung from the perennial rhizome beneath the earth."[15] Other remarks of his make it clear that he is striving toward a biology that is ahead of its time—one that is intelligent, self-organizing, and imbued with potentialities that transcend their present particular manifestations and the historically contingent splits between what is embodied and what is psychic. As Jung puts it, in "the world of the archetypes [we are] still a part of nature."[16]

In trying to express the dynamic spontaneous variations and fleeting mutual engagements of self and world, Jung converted *temporal* differences—in which the resonance of self with world varies from moment to moment—into *structural* differences between the conscious, egoic aspects of self and those which are collective and unconscious. If, during the course of our day, we are at times self-sufficient, self-absorbed, and inward looking, at other times empathic, engrossed in something outside ourselves, temporarily "forgetting ourselves," then we are both individual and transcendent of our individuality. These individual and self-transcendent moments are not easy to represent within a single model, and portraying the latter as "more deeply buried" inadequately conveys their *momentary* impact on some present situation. In other words, while the collective aspects of self are often represented as "older" or "deeper," they may also be expressed in terms of a fundamental resonance with the natural world, albeit one which is diminished today for reasons I have tried to express above. This "resonant" model better represents our collective aspects' continual influence on present functioning and avoids the implication that resonance with the natural world is somehow an outdated aspect of psychic functioning rather than an ever-present potentiality that is frustrated by the current political context.

THE ORDER OF NATURE

"The symbols of the self arise in the depths of the body and they express its materiality every bit as much as the structure of the perceiving consciousness," says Jung.[17] The "depths" Jung refers to are those of "chemical substances," since in his day there was little awareness of ecosystems or of the self-organizing tendencies of inorganic matter. It is surely likely that if Jung had had access to the ecological and biological knowledge we have today, he would have seen a relation between ecosystemic and psychological patterns.

As we have seen, Jung chose an image from the natural world— that of the rhizome—to illustrate certain properties of the psyche, since "both" realms embody temporal relations that are not simply linear and cannot be understood according to straightforward cause-effect paradigms, but rather contain circular and even more complex forms of relation.[18] According to this image, the past remains an active influence on the present, rather than simply "what happened before" and is now left behind. For example, ecological restorationists have found that simply reconstituting a system by bringing together the species that were originally present can result in any one of a variety of communities,[19] and that

> the order in which species attempt colonization tremendously influences final community composition and richness ... It is not possible to reassemble a particular community composition using only the species present in the final steady-state community.[20]

Furthermore, some ecosystems may be impossible to reproduce, since certain extinct ("ghost") species, while not part of the final, desired system, are vital to the evolution of the desired succession.[21] The *history* of an ecosystem, then, is an essential ingredient in its *current* functioning, as is the case with *psychological* functioning.

These dynamics are echoed in the cultures of many tribal peoples for whom the ancestors are living influences and presences rather than being cognitively relegated to the "past." In recognizing this, Ingold, like Jung, uses the image of the rhizome to convey relationships between thought and nature in terms of a "dense and tangled cluster of interlaced threads or filaments, any point in which can be connected to any other"[22] — a model that aims to "return [thinking] to the contexts of lived experience."[23]

There is thus a commonality between the analytical psychologist's awareness that the past is still a living influence on the present and the ecologist's recognition that the present state of an ecosystem depends on and embodies its history—that is, the order and pattern of its development, as well as its present constituents, affect its dynamics.[24] Clearly, human life is embedded in recursive natural patterns such as the orbit of the earth round the sun, the lunar phases, and so on; but there are more complex patterns than this in nature, such as the sometimes chaotic relations between predator and prey, most famously that of the Canadian lynx/snowshoe hare system.[25] The main characteristic of these chaotic systems is that they move between states in a deterministic and somewhat regular way, but never exactly reproduce the same conditions; and since tiny differences in initial conditions can result in major divergences a few cycles down the line, they are inherently unpredictable and cognitively opaque. Even apparently simple natural systems—such as the way a leaf floats to the ground, the behavior of eddies by a riverbank, or variations in a species' population can be dynamically enormously complex. There are even more rudimentary astronomical systems, exemplified by the "three body problem," which involves the behavior of three gravitationally-attracted bodies of roughly equivalent mass, which are also extraordinarily difficult to predict. Such cases alert us to the existence of patterns in the natural world which appear simple enough, but which cognition finds difficult to recognize or understand. As Jung argued, we refer to such things as "complicated, when in reality they are very simple and know nothing of our intellectual problems."[26] After all, the three bodies—supposedly made of "extended matter" and cognitively incapable, show no hesitation in deciding where to position themselves!

The lesson here—a very basic one which is usually evaded, since it directly challenges pivotal assumptions of industrial society—is that nature, like psyche, contains types of order and intelligence which are cognitively unmanageable, and that the varieties of order we are capable of conceptualizing are therefore a subset of natural orders. This lesson has been obscured by the view, particularly prevalent since Kant and now given added impetus by postmodernism, that cognition does not discover or recognize order *in* the world, but instead imposes its own order *on* the world—a view unfortunately echoed in Jung's statement that "it is my mind, with its store of images, that gives the world colour and sound."[27] In this way, the mind's incapacity to register the wholeness of nature is taken not as an indication of the limitations of cognition, but as an excuse to portray the world as structureless, as a blank screen onto which we project our mind-ful ideas and explanations and impose our industrialist structures. This in turn distances the (supposedly active) mind from the (supposedly passive) world.

While there is a certain amount of ironic truth in such a view, given our ongoing destruction of natural order and the emergence of a grossly simplified and artificial environment out of the resulting debris, this process needs to be understood in the historical context of our growing alienation from the natural order. We cannot take the industrially constructed world, including agriculture, simply as "reality," even— or particularly—if there is a close match between it and cognitive "rationality." Rather, what passes for "reality" in the contemporary world should be viewed as a special and reduced actuality compared to the diversity and multiple potentialities which are present in nature and which we can still sometimes sense through our embodied being; and equally, the "normal individual" should be viewed as a potentially whole person shorn of those resonant faculties that could bring both us and the world to life.

EMBODIED ECOLOGIES

Although cognition finds it difficult to recognize and respond to the complexities of nature, our bodies are often better equipped in this respect. Such taken-for-granted activities as walking, throwing a tennis ball, breathing, or maintaining a constant bodily temperature would overwhelm our cognitive faculties if they had to carry out all the necessary calculations. Non-human organisms, although lacking our cognitive equipment, are in many ways equally proficient. A tree "knows" how best to distribute its roots in order to ensure stability; and a prairie flower "knows" what colors will attract pollinators. These ecologically embedded forms of natural intelligence are usually ignored because of cognition's preoccupation with its own particular, abstract varieties of order.

Not all societies regard intelligence as necessarily disembodied. In a study of three Guatemalan forest dwelling groups, for example, Scott Atran found that although the Itzaj of the Petén Maya lowlands are better conservationists than other groups, they have little in the way of social organization that would encourage conservation, and seem rather individualistic. But a more intimate understanding of the Itzaj reveals that they embody an "emergent knowledge structure." As Atran explains,

> an emergent knowledge structure is not a set body of knowledge or tradition that is taught or learned as shared content. ... The general idea is that one's cultural upbringing primes one to pay attention to certain observable relationships ... [For Itzaj,] there is no 'principle of reciprocity' applied to forest entities, no 'rules for appropriate conduct' in the forest, and no 'controlled experimental determinations' of the fitness of ecological relationships. Yet reciprocity is all pervasive and fitness enduring.[28]

In other words, the Itzaj do not rely on conscious, rational algorithms in determining their behavior towards the forest. Rather, they exemplify Tim Ingold's view that among such indigenous peoples

> it is as entire persons, not as disembodied minds, that human beings engage with one another and, moreover, with non-human beings as well. They do so as beings in a world, not as minds which, excluded from a given reality, find themselves ... having to make sense of it.[29]

Such peoples illustrate Jung's view that "'at bottom,' psyche is simply 'world.'"[30] For example, *sila* is the root form of various Inuit words implying "intelligence;" and significantly, these words refer both to individual intelligence and intelligence that is "out there in the world."[31] Similarly, the language of the White Mountain Apache contains the root word *ni,'* which refers to both mind and land.[32] What such linguistic forms suggest is that for many indigenous groups, mind is in the world or—better—*mind is the world*; and that the landscape is also a *mindscape*. It is becoming increasingly difficult to dismiss such ecologically embedded epistemologies as involving "projection:" there is a wealth of anthropological material to counter such interpretations; and, in any case, in an environment such as the northern Greenland Arctic, mis-characterizing the natural environment is likely to result in an immediate and dire reduction in one's life expectancy.

The fact that such indigenous groups often have the utmost difficulty expressing their world-relatedness through language is only a problem for those who place the structures of language above those of the world and who are unsympathetic to Jung's recognition that "a great many archetypal images and associations are … absolutely incommunicable through language."[33] The questionable assumption we often make is that in order to "solve" a "problem," we first have to recode it into a form that can be consciously understood and communicated—a conceptual tyranny that has hampered the development of a grounded understanding of our relations with the earth. Conscious rationality is indeed a highly effective tool for certain purposes; but it is not effective for everything, and in particular it is not effective for grappling with environmental problems which, by their very nature, reflect the systemic types of interaction which consciousness finds difficult to recognize.

In industrial society, the polarization between a mentalistic realm and a physical realm of mere "matter" carries with it a tendency for entities to be ascribed to one or other of these realms. Some entities, however, are particularly difficult to fit into this dualistic scheme; and the "ecosystem" is one such entity. Some would claim that ecosystems have no existence outside thought, and that they are conceptual conveniences that bear no discernable relation to any physically-existing reality.[34] Others would claim that in talking about ecosystems, we are referring to objectively recognizable systems of trophic exchanges and physical interactions.[35] Like archetypes, ecosystems therefore belong to that class of epistemologically subversive entities which resist being viewed *either* as products of the human intellect *or* as pre-existing features of the world. In a society which seems to be rapidly abandoning the natural realm in favor of a manufactured world that is the product of human intelligence, the unsurprising notion that the fundamentals of our psychological and physiological functioning are rooted in the natural order is not a welcome one. To a greater extent than most societies, we rely on abstract systems of understanding which are only distantly related—if at all—to ecological and phenomenological realities and which are *imposed on* the world. This is in stark contrast to the many culturally and geographically diverse systems of understanding which are based on phenomenal *experience of* the world.[36] For those of us who inhabit a largely domesticated environment, the notion that the world is an amorphous cornucopia of "natural resources" is not obviously erroneous; but among peoples whose lives are more closely integrated with natural rhythms and processes, such a notion would seem baffling and unintelligent.

For example, the spawning behavior of fish in the Palau area of Micronesia is intricately related to the phases of the moon, and an understanding of the lunar calendar therefore becomes essential for survival in this fish-dependent society.[37] If the Palauans instead used the Western calendar, the behavior of fish would appear to vary unpredictably from year to year, and fishing would become more of a hit-or-miss affair. In assuming that nature has no structure, we *cover up* its structure beneath our imposed conceptual patterns, thereby furthering our alienation and blurring our awareness of natural patterns. While the fishermen of Palau, like the fish they catch, are embedded within natural processes, we often distance ourselves from these processes, from the other creatures that embody and express them, and from our own archetypal wisdom. Human behavior, we believe, is the outcome of cognitive calculation, and so is not comparable with "animal" behavior, which is supposedly lacking in rationality and more mechanistically determined. For example, Tim Ingold points out that while human tracking behavior tends to be viewed in terms of "cognitive strategies," almost identical tracking behavior among non-human species is seen as reflecting the mindless operation of "instinct."[38] As Jung noted, what we denigrate as "instinctual" may reflect patterns that are "common to man and animals alike."[39]

Mathematics, too, is frequently understood as a purely human pursuit; and yet it is often embodied in the behavior of other creatures. For example, cicadas emerge at intervals governed by prime numbers, thus minimizing the opportunities for attack by predators.[40] The arrangement of leaves and petals on plants, and the shapes of shells, often reflect the Fibonacci series, in which each term is the sum of the previous two terms. As Darwin showed, even the humble earthworm behaves in an intelligent way that is not reducible to instinct.[41] And the hunting capacities of the kingfisher or the hawk, and the navigational skills of the crane are highly sophisticated. Because these abilities are embodied rather than abstract, however, they tend to be excluded from our conception of "intelligence," thus fortifying our supposedly unique position in the animal kingdom at the price of denying part of our own identity and nature.

The Disembodied Society

Although the notion that physical being contains its own intelligence and order has often been dismissed as "mysticism," there is now a good deal of evidence to support this hypothesis, beginning with Stanley Miller's pioneering experiment demonstrating that under certain conditions resembling the early earth's atmosphere, basic components of living things such as amino acids spontaneously form from simple inorganic chemicals.[42] These and other results have been developed by biologists such as Stuart Kauffman to demonstrate that life is not due to some external (deistic or other) force imposing order on "extended matter," but rather that it stems from self-organizing qualities that are inherent in matter itself.[43] Such findings undermine the Cartesian attempt, which tacitly permeates much theorizing in the human sciences, to abstract a realm of intelligence or spirit from the rest of the world, including the human body.

If we are to advance beyond such dualistic splits, we need to reject the idealist notion that cognition imposes order on an otherwise amorphous world and to recognize, with Jung, that our embodied senses have evolved to recognize order that is already present in the world. Currently, the dominant view is that of Herbert Simon: learning necessarily comes from human symbolic representations, and direct experience of the world is merely a distraction. Such assumptions are often embodied in curriculum design and even in the physical infrastructure of learning: for example, in the academic institution where I teach, all the lecture theaters constructed in the past 20 years have been windowless and artificially lit so that no natural sound, sight, or smell is allowed to mingle with the information presented in lectures. The implied assumption is that learning involves shutting out the world rather than gaining access to it and that, as a recent postmodernist paper puts it, "language constitutes the human world and the human world constitutes the whole world."[44]

Not all Westerners, of course, commit this error. For example, Ted Strehlow, the important but largely ignored ethnographer of Australian aboriginal life, moved during the course of his career from a critical condescension toward the absence of rapid cultural "development" among Australian natives towards a dawning realization that the natural world *was* their cultural context, and that there was no reason for it to "develop."[45] This view sits so uncomfortably with contemporary assumptions about our necessary "progress" toward a "post natural" society that Strehlow's work has been largely buried since the 1930's. If, contrary to current academic convention, one finds meaning already present in the world so that culture is grounded in this meaning, then there is no particular need to develop independent realms of symbolism. For example, Morris Berman, discussing anthropologists' earnest attempts to find cultural meaning in the annual migration of the Basseri, dares voice a heretical possibility: "what if the meaning of the migration were ... the migration?"[46] All too often, the development of a complex symbolic realm is a first step towards the re-constitution of the world to accord with this realm, so that we forget the original world that the symbolism was supposed to be symbolic of.

As a child, I was puzzled why adults I knew were so captivated by paintings of landscapes or bowls of fruit. All I had to do was to look out of the window at the clouds or trees to see something incomparably more intricate and beautiful. Many indigenous peoples, too, value the natural over human representations, seeing the latter as expendable and temporary pointers to a more exalted realm. Karl Scheibe provides some examples:

> Alaskan Eskimo mask makers, ... having created a mask out of some inner impulse, use it once and then burn it. Similarly, Japanese and Tibetan Buddhists create paintings and images that are not to be seen, and Navaho sand paintings are to be destroyed almost as soon as they are finished.[47]

In contrast, our fetishization of manufactured things confines us within a narcissistic world of our own desires which, far from extending us into other realms of spirit and intelligence, dissipates psyche by consuming the natural world which is its, and our, home.

CONCLUSION

I am not suggesting that we can simply equate the archetypal and physiological dimensions of reality, or that we should rush into simplistic analogies or crude equivalencies. Roger Brooke rightly cautions us that although there

> are indeed loose analogies between certain archetypal experiences and physiological responses ... to situate one within the other is to confuse two radically different areas of discourse.[48]

Nevertheless, the radical difference to which Brooke refers is indeed a *discursive* one which does not reflect any corresponding divide in the natural world. "Psyche and body ... are one and the same," says Jung;[49] in which case discourse should strive to express this continuity. A key difference between the study of life at the molecular and cellular levels, on the one hand, and the study of archetypes, on the other, has traditionally been in the reductionist slant of the former and the systemic complexity of the latter, merging into the realms of culture and mythology. These divergent methodologies seemed justified so long as the biological sciences could not articulate the organizational intricacies of life; but given the contemporary awareness of natural complexity and ecological interactions, these divergences are much less justifiable today. Edward O. Wilson argues that our long experience of other creatures such as snakes inevitably led to their incorporation within culture:

> How could it be otherwise? The brain evolved into its present form over a period of about two million years ... during which people existed in hunter-gatherer bands in intimate contact with the natural environment. Snakes mattered. The smell of water, the hum of a bee, the directional bend of a plant stalk mattered. The naturalist's trance was adaptive: the glimpse of one small animal hidden in the grass could make the difference between eating and going hungry in the evening. And a sweet sense of horror, the shivery fascination with monsters and creeping forms

that so delight us today even in the sterile hearts of the cities,
could see you through to the next morning. Organisms are the
natural stuff of metaphor and ritual … We stay alert and alive in
the vanished forests of the world.[50]

Is it surprising, then, that our sense of otherness, even within
ourselves, resonates with our long experience of other natural beings?
Or that the "anima also has affinities with animals, which symbolize
her characteristics?"[51] Or that our own mothers carry "for us that inborn
image of the *mater natura* and *mater spiritualis*, of the totality of life of
which we are a small and helpless part?"[52] If, in "the world of the
archetypes, [man] is still a part of Nature and is connected with his
own roots,"[53] how can we justify the absence of a discourse which
articulates rather than obscures the unity of psyche and nature?

Of course, any single discourse or methodology will be unable to
capture the entirety of any natural structure; and so it is quite justifiable
that different discourses are used to describe the psychic and ecological
aspects of nature. The danger, however, is that the idealist and the
materialist, in developing their own paradigms and languages,
gradually lose touch with and suppress what they unknowingly share
—the unity of life—leading to the mistaken belief that these *discursive*
differences reflect *differences in reality*. To avoid this pitfall, we *also* need
to develop a connective language which articulates not the distinctions
suggested by the terms psyche and nature, but the often unrecognized
common realm to which they both refer.

NOTES

1. Herbert Simon, *Models of My Life* (San Francisco: Basic Books,
1991), 306, 308-9.
2. Edward Abbey, *Desert Solitaire* (New York: Ballantine, 1968),
xii.
3. Gary Nabhan, "Cultural parallax in viewing North American
habitats," in Michael E. Soulé and Gary Lease (eds.), *Reinventing
Nature?: Responses to Postmodern Deconstruction* (Washington, DC: Island
Press, 1995), 98.
4. C. G. Jung, *Collected Works of C. G. Jung,* Sir Herbert Read,
Michael Fordham, and Gerhard Adler (eds.) (London: Routledge and

Kegan Paul, 1959), vol. 9i § 108 [the *Collected Works* are hereinafter referenced as "*CW,*" followed by the volume number and the paragraph number.]

5. Medard Boss, quoted by Roger Brooke, *Jung and Phenomenology* (London: Routledge, 1991), 77.

6. Jung, *CW* 9i § 91.

7. Brooke, *Jung and Phenomenology,* chapter 4.

8 Alfred N. Whitehead, *Adventures of Ideas* (New York: Free Press, 1967 [1933]), 156.

9. Tim Ingold, *The Perception of the Environment* (London: Routledge, 2000), 242.

10. Gary P. Nabhan, *Cultures of Habitat: On Nature, Culture, and Story* (Washington DC: Counterpoint, 1997), 275.

11. Brooke, *Jung and Phenomenology,* 61.

12. Jung, *CW* 10 § 53.

13. Jung, *CW* 10 § 54.

14. Jung, *CW* 10 § 55.

15. Foreword to *Symbols of Transformation*, *CW* 5, p. xxiv.

16. Jung, *CW* 9i § 174.

17. Jung, *CW* 9i § 291.

18. See my "Industrialism and the fragmentation of temporal structure," *Environmental Ethics* 26(2), Summer 2004, 135–153.

19. E.g., J. Bastow Wilson, John B. Steel, Mike E. Dodd, Barbara J. Anderson, Isolde Ullman, and Peter Bannister, "Community reassembly using the exotic communities of New Zealand roadsides in comparison to British roadsides," *Journal of Ecology* 88 (2000), 757–764.

20. Julie L. Lockwood and Corey L. Samuels, "Assembly models and the practice of restoration," in Vicky M. Templeton, Richard J. Hobbs, Tim Nuttle, and Stefan Halle (eds.), *Assembly Rules and Restoration Ecology: Bridging the Gap between Theory and Practice* (Washington, DC: Island Press, 2004), 58.

21. H. K. Luh and S. L. Pimm, "The assembly of ecological communities: a minimalist approach," *Journal of Animal Ecology* 62 (1993): 749-765.

22. Ingold, *Perception of the Environment*, 140.

23. *Ibid.*, 426, n. 7.

24. Stuart Pimm, *The Balance of Nature?: Ecological Issues in the Conservation of Species and Communities* (Chicago: University of Chicago Press, 1991).

25. William M. Schaffer, "Stretching and folding in lynx returns: Evidence for a strange attractor in nature?," *American Naturalist* 124 (1984), No. 6, 798-820.

26. Jung, *CW* 8 § 269.

27. Jung, *CW* 8 § 623.

28. Scott Atran, "The vanishing landscape of the Petén Maya Lowlands," in Luisa Maffi (ed.), *On Biocultural Diversity* (Washington, DC: Smithsonian Institution Press, 2001), 166-7.

29. Ingold, *Perception of the Environment*, 47.

30. Jung, *CW* 9i § 291.

31. Edmund Carpenter, *Eskimo Realities* (New York: Holt, 1973), 44-45; Robert G. Williamson, "The Arctic habitat and the integrated self," in Michael Aleksiuk and Thomas Nelson (eds.), *Landscapes of the Heart* (Edmonton: NeWest Press, 2002), 177.

32. Jonathan Long, Aregai Tecle, and Benrita Burnette, "Cultural foundations for ecological restoration on the White Mountain Apache reservation,"*Conservation Ecology* 8(1), 2003: http://www.consecol.org/vol8/iss1/art4/

33. Jung, *CW* 9i § 136, footnote.

34. See, for example, John L. Harper, "The heuristic value of ecological restoration," in William R. Jordan III, Michael E. Gilpin, and John D. Aber (eds.), *Restoration Ecology: A Synthetic Approach to Ecological Research* (Cambridge: Cambridge University Press, 1987), 38.

35. Robert E. Ulanowicz, *Ecology: The Ascendent Perspective* (New York: Columbia University Press, 1997).

36. Michael E. Soulé, "The Social siege of nature," in Soulé and Lease (eds.), *Reinventing Nature?* A good example of this cultural divergence is that between modern systems of navigation based on satellite positioning and navigational systems based on observation of star positions, waves patterns, and the behavior of wildlife. See, for example, Thomas Gladwin, *East is a Big Bird: Navigation and Logic on Puluwat Atoll* (Cambridge, Mass.: Harvard University Press, 1970).

37. R. E. Johannes, *Words of the Lagoon: Fishing and Marine Lore in the Palau District of Micronesia* (Berkeley: University of California Press, 1992).

38. Tim Ingold, "The optimal forager and economic man," in Philippe Descola and Gísli Pálsson (eds.), *Nature and Society: Anthropological Perspectives* (London: Routledge, 1996), 26.

39. Jung, *CW* 9i § 291.

40. Eric Goles, Oliver Schulz, and Mario Markus, "A Biological Generator of Prime Numbers," *Nonlinear Phenomena in Complex Systems*, 3:2 (2000) 208–213.

41. Eileen Crist, "The inner life of earthworms: Darwin's argument and its implications," in Marc Bekoff, Colin Allen, and Gordon M. Burghardt (eds.), *The Cognitive Animal: Empirical and Theoretical Perspectives on Animal Cognition* (Cambridge, Mass., MIT Press, 2002).

42. Stanley Miller and G. Schlesinger, "Carbon and energy yields in prebiotic syntheses using atmospheres containing CH_4, CO, and CO_2," *Origins of Life* 14 (1984), 83–89.

43. Stuart A. Kauffman, *The Origins of Order: Self-Organisation and Selection in Evolution* (New York: Oxford University Press, 1993).

44. Steve De Shazer and I. K. Berg, "Doing therapy: A post-structural revision," *Journal of Marital and Family Therapy* 18 (1992), 73.

45. Ted G. H. Strehlow, *Songs of Central Australia* (Sydney: Angus and Robertson, 1971).

46. Morris Berman, *Wandering God: A Study in Nomadic Spirituality* (Albany: State University of New York Press, 2000), 168.

47. Karl E. Scheibe, "Replicas, imitations, and the question of authenticity," in Joseph de Rivera and Theodore R. Sarbin (eds.), *Believed-in Imaginings: The Narrative Construction of Reality* (Washington, DC: American Psychological Association, 1998), 59.

48. Brooke, *Jung and Phenomenology,* 68.

49. Jung, *CW* 7 § 194.

50. Edward O. Wilson, *Biophilia* (Cambridge, Mass.: Harvard University Press, 1984), 101.

51. Jung, *CW* 9i § 358.

52. Jung, *CW* 9i § 172.

53. Jung, *CW* 9i § 174.

CADENCE

I held my hand toward the late sun,
as if to catch the light, its lingering moments
of descent. The measure of this forest,
its orchestra of leaves sounding
in a time of waste, beyond the nearness of trees.
What then are the ways of language,
since we have been a conversation,*
since the hearing of words long renounced?
But listen to the green of ferns,
Theirs is another tempo, an adagio of evening.
In the wind's regret, I thought I heard your sigh;
a moment of presence, felt
like a leaf's influence upon the hand.

—*Michael Whan*

———————————

*Holderlin

CHARTING THE ECOLOGICAL IMAGINATION: BETWEEN LEAF AND HAND

LAURA H. MITCHELL

> With all its eyes the natural world looks out
> into the Open. Only our eyes are turned
> backward, and surround plant, animal, child
> like traps, as they emerge into their freedom.
> … for we take the very young
> child and force it around, so that it sees
> objects—not the Open …
> —Rilke, The Eighth Elegy[1]

To firstly see the Open instead of objects is a return to the world as intimate home. In his work on the primacy of perception, Merleau-Ponty describes the seamlessness of the Open in this way. There is no division between psyche and nature or the imaginal and the natural order: "I" and other, conscious and unconscious, all have their veracity from the "belongingness of each experience to the same world."[2] This reversal in thinking from appropriating the world to dwelling within its seamless unity sets up the needed orientation

Laura H. Mitchell is a practicing artist and director of the Expressive Arts Program at Sky Mountain Institute, California and is engaged in community and ecological fieldwork and participatory community artwork in the San Diego area. This article is based upon her dissertation on the ecological imagination.

for exploring the ecological imagination—the human mode of awareness for accessing the ongoing intersentient communication within the natural world, the shared *lingua franca* of intermundane experiencing. A return to the primacy of the body as the place where we directly engage our place-worlds allows us to get as close as possible to the Open, to the preobjective world, before we trap it into immobile meanings and objects.

Thus to return to the Open, to "see" with all our eyes, would be to return to our first-world of immediate embodied experience, to an *anima mundi* who communicates with us through her images speaking of the myriad presentation of things. This outlook would require us "to unthink this seemingly fundamental distinction between self and world, between subject and object"³ with its devastating outcomes to the natural world. Rather, we can see that these dichotomies are inconsistent with actual embodied experience and are in fact a late development in human history emerging slowly and bursting into distinct fluorescence during the modern period. One of the challenges of *unthinking* the world lies in facing the massive loss of place and diversity resulting from the objectification and consequent exploitation of nature due to industrialist policies and thinking. Coming to see the context one is in, gaining voice in relation to this context,⁴ and finding new concept-laden language—such as the ecological imagination— resonant with the natural order are steps toward re-engaging our place-worlds.

During my five years of advocacy and fieldwork in my home community of Harmony Grove valley, southern California—a rural environment now slated for large-scale development—I began a process of relearning to look at the valley place-world as a seamless unity. Out of this immersion came the exploration of what I came to call the ecological imagination. Harmony Grove, as part of the coastal watershed—itself a complex ecosystem of chaparral scrub, riparian woodlands, and richly diverse wildlife—is home to a small, agricultural community of dairy and chicken ranches spread out along the flat lands, flanked by clusters of residences and orchards here and there rising up along some of the more gentle slopes of the basin.

There was something particularly disheartening about the finality of the actual purchase of the farmlands of Harmony Grove valley by an out-of-town Los Angeles residential development corporation. The presentation of *their* plan for us interposed the stark reality that a historically established community can be objectified easily and exiled at the stroke of a real-estate pen. In general we all suffer from the slow incremental loss or degradation of place relations, like a slowly unraveling trauma punctuated by a vague nameless numbing. Yet sudden ruptures to place, as in Harmony Grove, also give a stark awakening to the ways that our identities are not only dependent on place but also profoundly and elegantly configured by place. This assault on physical places is accompanied by a more subtle and lethal disenfranchisement of our psychical implacement within the natural order.

Murray Bookchin's prophetic comments made in the 1980's concerning the erosion of an authentic ecological sensibility and the dislocation of the unity between nature and psyche seem even more relevant in the face of this escalating loss of place. "We have mobilized our human nature to embark upon a great social enterprise to disembed ourselves from external nature."[5] He believed that developing this sensibility with its inherent ethical, moral, and participatory orientation was the key to our times.

We are the ecological crisis and, as such, need to consciously generate language and modes of thinking, along with their revolutionary implications,[6] more consistent and resonant with the natural order and viable human-earth relations. The articulation of deep-seated primary place relationships is essential to the practice of community resiliency and advocacy. This sensibility, I came to believe, can be found in the private underbelly of community: in people's life styles and activities, in their gardens, in children's play, in relations with plants and animals, in the voice of the terrain, the flora and fauna, the landscape and the shape of the valley, and in places where small groups can cultivated the intimate practice-of-place.

The ecological imagination and its entwinement in psyche and place is one such aspect of our place-relations I wish to unfold here, along with other attendant structures such as intersentience, the lived body, and depth. In this discussion, Merleau-Ponty's phenomenology of the body-world unity, along with Edward S. Casey's work on place, are preeminently eco-imaginal terrain.

The Ecological Imagination

The ecological imagination is the shared interface, the commonality we share with all life: the Orphic principle of communion and transitivity between all things. Merleau-Ponty calls this primary elemental level the "flesh of the world"[7]— a participatory matrix in which psyche and nature, the imaginal and ecological, body and world are inextricably entwined. Because we are already part of the world's diversity and complexity, the preobjective world is directly knowable by way of the experiencing body. In this view, the world is already mapped onto our bodies and the imaginal is our specifically human analogue of this mapping. As such, images and metaphors are not just an intermediate reality, but also an actual borrowing from *anima mundi*, from the ensouled physicality and latent depth of nature, from her animals, plants, clouds, and invisible presences—a process of metaphoric reciprocity between nature and the human.

The eco-imaginal is the interface we share with nature that makes possible nature-human communion—a communication not measured exclusively in terms of the human mode of cognition but experienced at the more bio-centric and elemental level at which all life shares the same commonality. In this place, we access another mode of intelligibility arising from the shared condition of our interinvolvement—a participatory intelligence. We might call this our anonymous-self—a non-egoic state that is highly decentered, fluid, participatory, and diffuse. The foundational assumption to this way of thinking is that there is a unity and continuity between the lived body and the world. This self-body-world unity is much like Jung's third stage alchemy: the *unus mundus*.

The Body-World Unity

Because the world already exists as a living unity and because we are part of its diversity and complexity, says Merleau-Ponty, we have direct access to knowledge of this world. This preobjective world (which I refer to as our first-world)—that is the world that is already there before we interpret it through our cultural lenses and paradigms, (Rilke's "Open") is directly knowable by way of the experiencing body. Here he is not talking about the anatomical or mechanical body but the "lived body"— the body as sensed, felt, experienced, and imagined by the person at the immediate level of primary perception. The world and the perceptual body are continuous with each other and together form an inseparable unity—a reciprocal, two-way porous relation. Thus, the lived body has privy to another extensive mode of knowledge, more embedded and akin to the earthbody than to cultural contexts. Our second-world, including the analytic mode, is an abstracted overlay—a metaphysics—dependent on and fed by the massive foundation and depth of our first-world.

Merleau-Ponty describes this interweaving of body and our place-worlds as forming a common body so that each thing is bound to every other

> in such a way as to make up with them the experience of one sole body before one sole world . . . according to which the little private world of each is not juxtaposed to the world of all the others, but *surrounded by* it, *levied off from* it. (Italics mine)[8]

It is this sense of "surrounded by" and mutually "levied off from" that captures the essence of the implaced-community. Synergy exists among different organisms, he says, their landscapes interweave, their actions and passions fit together exactly. When applied to the living community in Harmony Grove, we can say that each human and nonhuman exchange, each encounter and presencing is bound to every other. All things are surrounded by and acquire their beingness from the others, and together this interpenetration of all occupants of the valley—their invisible coming into being, their tangible forms, their active processes—together form one sentient living, pulsing "body." Synergy exists between all occupants of the valley; their domains interweave; they constitute each other and are the mutual life of the community.

Our polycentrically located body is thus privy to another extensive mode of knowledge—a synesthesic direct knowing unedited by mental overlays or social lenses, a kind of fusion with the world. Because of the body's inclusion in the world, belonging to the world: "we are through and through compounded of relationships with the world."[9] The world is the natural field for all our thoughts and all our explicit perceptions and only in the world can we know ourselves.[10] This body-world unity sets the stage for intermundane experiencing and thus for the ecological self—the self that is embedded in, participates within the natural order.

RENEWING AN UNDERSTANDING OF PLACE

Because we have a body, we have the experience of place.[11] The bodily recognition that place *is* the primary ground of beingness is tied to a less obvious features of place: Harmony Grove valley is implaced by its watershed which is implaced by its region, and so also by the planet and ultimately the cosmos. Self, place, community, bioregion, planet, and cosmos are all telescopically nested within one another: place is an "intimate immensity,"[12] as Bachelard says. Place is thus specific and also every-where at the same time. The practical implications of place as simultaneously a particular locality and a global universal is that at-homeness in Harmony Grove is at the same time at-homeness within the planet and even the cosmos. Loss of place, then, is no simple thing and manifests often as disorientation, and psychic numbing—as was the case for my neighbors and myself in the valley.

Place seen as an animated presence in its own right is again a reversal of the normal way we think: we have been educated and acculturated to believe that our primary reference point is ourselves, that the modern ego—our privatized individualism—is a solid, reliable orienting center for existence in general. Place-relations reveal just the opposite: that we are constituted by our place-worlds and that it would be more accurate to say that our identity, in terms of Harmony Grove, is diffused throughout the valley and mutually constituted by the valley, its habitat, and nonhuman inhabitants. This condition does not limit our beingness but extends it by way of incorporating more and more of our place-worlds within ourselves and us in it.

Furthermore, objects do not stop at their visible boundaries but trespass and transcend beyond the edges of human sense perception. Let us take the sycamore that stands sentinel at the entrance to the woods in the valley creek bed. The sycamore captures the lightness and impressionistic beauty of its surround as a vibrating sturdiness in the canopied sunlight. The sycamore tree is more than its surface appearance. It "encroaches on" the frontiers of others: the sunlight, other plants, soil, insects, animals, microbes, biospheric conditions, and humans. It has rhythms consisting of sun, wind, and seasons registering as changing hues in scintillating pauses. Each of these many overlappings with the others summons whole new ranges of meanings. Seen in this way, the visible as a tangible thing is an "encompassing" rather than a fixed entity; it encompasses the moving field of its beingness and is thus a "field being" "presiding over a region,"[13] yet having a certain recognizable style of being of its own. We are all, in fact, field beings mutually encroaching on and penetrated by the organic and inorganic life around us. This is the way of the world as an ecology of interbeing.

It is this overlapping and mutual implication that leads into the concept of depth: depth being all the possible ways the sycamore can be experienced by all things—not just humans—and ultimately the cosmos. The visible tree, then, is but the surface presentation of an "inexhaustible depth."[14] Seen in this way, depth is the rhizomed dimension wherein everything is an overlapping interconnection: like the entangled roots of a stand of bamboo, no single stalk can be considered independent of all the rest, yet each stalk is uniquely configured, or like the rich microbial life of soil—our most complex living ecosystem—in which no single organism exists independently from the rest. Depth, then, is the condition in which all things interpenetrate and overlap, where the particular is simultaneously a universal,[15] where the diachronic and synchronic intersect.

Merleau-Ponty states it this way: depth is the "dimension of the simultaneous" and "the hidden."[16] Thus matter and depth, the sensory tangible thing and its invisible hidden depth are a continuum of each other wherein the surface sense data is as a sign signifying a more intensive and extensive meaning—the dimension of depth. This relation of matter and depth, the particular and universal is a living organic unity. Each part is torn up from the whole,[17] comes with coextensive roots, encroaches upon the whole, and transgresses the frontiers of the others.

Why is all this important? What does it look like to be in the continuum of the concrete surface and the synchronic depth of mutual envelopment? These are important, not abstracted issues, as the recovery of the ecological imagination is mute without a recovery of both particularized and universalized modes of experiencing. The splitting of these modes is a disconnected duality which has surfaced in modern times causing a loss of awareness of our fleshy cloaks of invisibility.

THE FLESH AS INTERSENTIENCE

With these primary place-relations laid out—the body-world unity, the primacy of place, the lived body, and depth—let us return to explore the nature of intersentience by way of Merleau Ponty's metaphor of the "flesh of the world." Ambivalence and confusion in regard to the nature of intersentience has haunted the Western mind since the Enlightenment debunked it with its obsessive abhorrence of animism. Novalis, in the midst of the Romantic revolt against the severance of the imagination from science, states the dilemma more delicately:

> Nature is a community of the marvelous into which we are
> initiated by our body ... The question arises, whether we can
> learn to understand nature and to what degree our ideas and the
> intensity of our attention are determined by it, or else determine
> it, thus snatching it away from nature and perhaps destroying
> its delicate flexibility.[18]

The modern era's unwiring of the human psyche from nature, its severance of the human from the earthbody, and its renting of the connective tissue of psyche and nature has fortunately not been fully accomplished. Mending the rent in this intersentient tissue is the task at hand.

THE WAY OF THE FLESH: BETWEEN LEAF AND HAND

It is late spring and the wind has torn off small branches, now strewn on the ground. I pick up one of the freshly grown, yet giant-fingered leaves. I notice that, really, it was the leaf that first touched me with its tactile presence and fuzzy textured underside, and I also notice I am touching the leaf.

Between the leaf touching me and my touching the leaf is a gap—like the pause between the in-breath and the out-breath where one is neither breathing in or out nor holding the breath, but just resting in a synchronic pause within this emptiness. An indeterminacy, a reversibility around who is touching whom, a perceptual bi-locatedness pervades this space. I am here in my body and there in the leaf at the same time, and so too for the sycamore: it is there in me and here in its own leaf-ness. In this gap, this chiasm, lies the fleshy medium of intersentience—a commonality that is neither it nor I but both of us in motion reverberating in and out and around each other. As I again feel the leaf touching me and my touching of the leaf, I notice we are knitted together as an inseparable unit.

Let us return to Merleau-Ponty's thinking around the "flesh of the world." As an intermundane medium or tissue contiguous with all life forms, like an intercellular fluid of the earth that acts as an intelligent transfer station between incoming forces and their distribution into the world of forms, this concept establishes a primary commonality making possible a natural and fluid exchange amongst all things: a kind of elemental intelligence, an intersentient presence that moves cross-species and cross-kingdoms. Because we are constituted through and through by the world of things, we also know and are known, at this foundational level, by all things. This is not a new idea within both ancient and postmodern traditions.

Lewis Thomas was inspired to write *The Lives of a Cell* when trying to think of the earth as a kind of organism. Suddenly the thought came to him that the earth is most like a single cell with a breathable atmospheric membrane.

> There is a tendency for living things to join up, establish linkages, live inside each other, return to earlier arrangements, get along, whenever possible. This is the way of the world.[19]

A deep pliable commonality, he says, inhabits all things. The commonality of the flesh of the world makes sense as soon as we no longer make human consciousness the only measure of awareness. In Harmony Grove valley, this intersentience, the commonality experienced by the total implaced-community, moves through the breezes in the trees, the cows grazing in the field, the twosome taking a brisk morning walk along the road, and the crows gathering in groups on the telephone lines.

In this way, the sycamore leaf belongs to its unique self and also to the world's flesh; likewise my body is uniquely mine and also belongs to the flesh of the world. Here is a principle of primordial kinship. My fleshy self is an anonymous communal event inhabiting me, it is a commonality I share with the world, a fluid transitivity that passes from one body to another—an unbounded beingness. I am this flux *and* I am also myself: the particular and universal interfuse. "It is not just I that sees and hears but also my flesh that belongs to the flesh of the world that sees and hears."[20] By way of my fleshy self, I am extended out into the larger world, and also, my anonymous interinvolvement establishes the primary ground of a participatory intelligence that makes me privy to the massive intelligence inherent in the world itself.

> Other eyes that phantom of ourselves of which we are not the titulars bring a vision that is not our own but that we participate in this larger, extensive vision of the flesh. A vision that goes beyond factual vision and communicates it to others through the shared flesh that others also participate in.[21]

The flesh as a prototype of intersentience is more like an "element" in the old sense of the word as was used to speak of water, air, earth, and fire. In the same way that fire has state-specific attributes such as burning, consuming, heat, and transmutation, the flesh has the features of reversibility, transitivity, and synergy. As an elemental event, the flesh moves in liminal space, in the chiasm between the invisible and visible—a place that is neither self nor other, neither explicate order nor implicate order, neither mind nor matter but both. It is thus a psychoidal event pregnant with interpenetrating possibilities.

The basis for kinship with the nonhuman environment is here laid down, given structure and metaphoric resonance. Nature and psyche, leaf and self are but two sides of the same world. And because of primal depth, there is fluidity between the self and the other: a bi-located metamorphosis, a co-habitation of the other while remaining oneself. These enfolded layerings allow for the presence of multiple permutations of lived meanings. Mineral, plant, animal, and human kingdoms mutually impinge and encroach on each other according to which a kinship of thinking takes place.

The Cloak of Invisibility

The flesh of the world and the ecological imagination are also mythemes—structures arising directly out of images of the earth and cosmos as dynamic archetypal energy sources of a timeless past and futurity.[22] Mythemes rise up as called forth by the collective needs of earth-human relations to create new possibilities, become activated for a period of time, and then collapse back into the latent field of potentiality. Presently, in this period of syncretic unrest and unprecedented human hubris, themes related to the participatory matrix of life and ecological viability counterpoise those of annihilation, homogenization, and domination.

Most of us have yearned at sometime in our growing up for a cape of invisibility. The longing to dissolve our humanness and blend indivisibly into the translucence of nature's abundant profusion is to become earth-bodied and understand all the living languages of bird, animal, plant, and rock. On the surface, this yearning may seem to be a desire to unmoor from the agonies of societal norms and their inevitable alienation from our indigenous knowing, or to escape from the dominance of the egoic self, with its insecure pompous-punitive swings. But the deeper hunger is to be rewoven back into the fabric of life, to be inextricably present in its primordial fecundity. This organismic, gravitational pull signals a return to the seamlessness of our origins, remembering, as rocks engraved with the striations of the millennium record the earth's movements, the cellular call of our original housing in Nature.

THE MYTH

The Mayan myth of the *Disobedience of the Daughter of the Sun*,[23] a pronouncedly eco-imaginal myth, relates the story of Tall Girl's elopement with Hummingbird Boy and their escape from the disapproval of her smoldering Father the Sun and her jealous mother, called Grandmother Moon. Trying to prevent their daughter's union with her lover, her parents barricade her in the compound. Tall Girl plots her flight by weaving on her back-strap loom a cloak of invisibility for her lover and herself. During the day, while her mother is away preparing lunch and her father tending the important business of the sky, Tall Girl—beloved and cherished by all the villagers and all of nature—weaves her sorrow and love into the beauty of the cloth. The warp and weft are made of the animated images of all of the living designs of the natural world, so that when the cloth is worn, the wearer blends indivisibly into the everyday activity of the life world, thereby hiding the wearer within. Every day she weaves and her tear-drenched tapestry takes on the beautiful wonderment of her great suffering, loss, and ardor for Hummingbird Boy. When the cloth is finished, Tall Girl and Hummingbird Boy don the cloaks and flee from the mountains toward the safety of the deep watery realm of his mother, Salty Woman

Ocean, and his Father, White Lord of Hurricane. Wearing their cloaks
of invisibility, Tall Girl and Hummingbird Boy become

> the devastating beauty of the natural world . . . in which moving
> animals, moving windy trees, creeping clouds, yawning animals,
> and lazy stones were all alive and each proceeding according to
> its nature. . . . And in all this the boy and girl, as unique particular
> beings, were utterly buried, lost in the complex foment and
> beauty of the world they now wore upon their backs. . . . Thus
> hidden, their identity became inseparable from the rest of nature
> and part of the moving kaleidoscopic play of life.[24]

The Cloak of Invisibility can be seen as a metaphor for intuiting
the sense of the "flesh of the world"— an elemental intelligence, an
awareness shared by all things, sentient and nonsentient: an ecological
commonality. "The Tzutujil Mayan shamans understand that every
individual human being carries the entire Earth within their skins."[25]
We long to live closely to our mutuality and participation in this skin.
We grieve at a cellular level the loss of a life lived deep within the
polytheistic web of life, one that also calls us into the tension of our
individuated particularity and consequent sense of alienation and
dismemberment from the earth-body.

Tall Girl's cloak of invisibility is analogous to Merleau-Ponty's flesh
of the world, and she herself, in her human-goddess form, is the
ecological imagination—the particular way that the human mode
participates in the commonality of the flesh. The cloak's invisibility is
like an implicate field replete with potentiality, dimensional levels, and
forces — "the streaming in of the universe"— to use Whitehead's term.

The invisible makes the visible possible, it "inhabits the world,
sustains it and renders it visible" and "the flesh is the place of emergence"
of the invisible into visibility.[26] When wearing the cloak, Tall Girl is
invisible, she has merged back into the indefinite, porous multiplicity
of life—into the flesh of the world that contains all possibilities but is
itself more like an element of intelligent invisibility. When Tall Girl
takes off the cloak, she is still woven into the cloak along with all other
things, but her particular mode of visibility as a human creature, her
individualized mode of imaginal and bodily presence is distinct. For
Merleau-Ponty, the imaginary is the way that the world is duplicated
hologramatically within the body, mapped into the body as a diagram
of the living earth, as something which allows us to incorporate more

and more of the world within our lived experience. Because of this cloak, we have access to a "speaking world:" an intersentience that makes us privy to all species and entities and to what Hillman refers to as an enduring intimate conversation with matter, a relationship with the sensuous as simultaneously a terrestrial thing and a psychic reality.[27]

The metaphor of the cloak of invisibility also helps to revision a human community such as Harmony Grove as an implaced community, that is, constituted not only by its human and built aspects but also inclusive of its environs. The implaced community is a term used here to indicate all the interdependent biotic and human-built aspects of a community, along with their ongoing interactivity and dimensionality constituting a specific place. The total environing surround of our communities interpenetrates and implaces us: we wear it like a cloak of invisibility and are infolded within it.

As we bring the locus of human experience out of the mind and into the experiencing body, we immediately gain new ground. By way of body knowing, the implaced community comes into focus in new ways, like binoculars clarifying a hazy scene only dimly apprehended. This bodily access to the massive intelligence of the world as a source of belonging and meaning is a firm ground to stand on: it clarifies our understandings as to the nature of our collective needs, gives us a sure-footed basis for advocating for our implaced communities, and generates new terminology with generative implications.

THE ECOLOGICAL IMAGINATION REVISITED

The eco-imaginal is the way we perceive and attune to our place-worlds, to *anima mundi*, and the earth body. It is the way the human enters into *anima mundi* as an ensouled being amongst other ensouled presences and ecological beings. The gods, says Hillman, are ecological relations.[28] The things of the earth arise in us as precise images of the world; they are thinking structures naturally intact. These images of earthly things and processes are already the archetypes. Because these living images are of the earth, they too are field beings—diffuse, ambiguous, autonomous—and as field beings they are particular universals.

This diffusion has a significant bearing on community identity. At the primary level, we sense ourselves distributed simultaneously out there in the outer place-world and also here within our own body. We are our selves and also our anonymous diffusion throughout the region of our awareness. I am my self *and* I am also the environing valley: self and valley mutually determine one another. This diffusion is the essence of eco-imaginal implacement.

Eco-imaginal awareness requires a profound shift in perspective—an *unthinking* of the world. It is this inversion, this return to the primacy of perception of the lived body and our first-world which can become a continuing practice offering a current that moves away from the commodification of daily life. Recovering from a deeply engrained inculcation into an objectified worldview, emptying one's thinking and writing of the language of mechanization, subject–object dualities, and viewpoints anchored in fixed, non-fluid containers is a mind-boggling learning arc. Nevertheless, a rethinking of our relationship with the natural world does *not* change the reality that these primary concepts are already experientially alive in the deeply lived commonality of our species existence. The simple and obvious premise of the *unity of the experiencing body and the body of the world* makes accessible the intrinsic continuity between nature and psyche, matter and spirit, and between community and place.

As I sit on the ridgeline overlooking Harmony Grove valley, the tyranny of seeing-as-appropriating gives way to a profound reversal in perspective. It is not my self-contained identity that holds claim to this vista but rather that this vista claims me as participant. The realization that the others—the bioregional features, the watershed and its unique inhabitants, the built community of Harmony Grove stretched out below my feet—all implace me and constitute parts of my identity registers as a gentle incorporative expansion, a diffusion of selfhood, a seeping into life: a *concrescence*.

The recovery of the ecological imagination requires this profound shift in perspective—an ecocentric presencing based in participatory awareness and a return to the contextualizing capacity of the embodied imagination. The eco-imaginal is geared into other primal structures: the body-world unity, a return to the primacy of perception with its proto-languages of movement, gesture, orientation, and expressiveness, to the lived body, and to the intimacy and immediacy of our first-world of direct experience. By listening for these primary voices of place, a new context is opened; different types of questions can be asked that in themselves open new terrain outside the standardized environmental dialogue. These questions call for new solutions and introduce alternate perspectives and practices, ones that can inform both immersion in and advocacy for our place-worlds.

The modern environmental crisis is also a crisis in thinking and identity. The loss of fluidity between modes of thinking, as between the imaginal and the analytic, between the mythic and the concrete, between first-world presencing and second-order thinking, between the sensory surface and the imaginal depth, between the local and the global, and between Rilke's Open and the literal object impairs the resiliency needed to respond to a realignment with the sustainable needs of the planet. As place-relations continue to become a more unacknowledged hinterland, the articulation and conceptualization of both the ecological and imaginal dimensions of individual and community identity are only all the more key to refinding our way back into an embodied relation within our communities.[29]

NOTES

1. R. M. Rilke, The Eighth Elegy, *The Selected Poetry of Rainer Maria Rilke,* trans. Stephen Mitchell (New York: Random House, 1980), 193.

2. Maurice Merleau-Ponty, *Phenomenology of Perception,* trans. Colin Smith (New York: Routledge 1945/1962), xxii.

3. Owen Barfield, *Poetic Diction: A Study in Meaning* (Middletown: Wesleyan University Press), 1973.

4. Helene Lorenz & Mary Watkins, "Depth Psychology and Colonialism: Individuation, Seeing-through, and Liberation," retrieved January 30, 2001 from http://mythinglinks.org/LorenzWatkins.html

5. Murray Bookchin, *The Ecology of Freedom* (Palo Alto, CA: Cheshire Books, 1982), 350.

6. See David Kidner for a critique of industrialist society, the language of the concealment of meaning, and the need for a conceptual language resonant with the natural order. David Kidner, *Nature and Psyche: Radical Environmentalism and the Politics of Subjectivity* (New York: State University of New York Press, 2001).

7. Maurice Merleau-Ponty, *The Visible and the Invisible,* trans. Alphonso Lingis (Evanston, IL: Northwestern University Press, 1968), 41. Hereafter cited as VI.

8. VI, 142.

9. Merleau-Ponty, *Phenomenology of Perception*, xiii.

10. *Ibid.*, xiii.

11. The following discussion of place and the body in place draws extensively on Edward S. Casey, *Getting Back into Place: Toward a Renewed Understanding of the Place-World* (Indianapolis: Indiana University Press, 1993), especially Part II, *The Body in Place*. For his discussion of the philosophy of Maurice Merleau-Ponty and place, refer to Edward S. Casey, *The Fate of Place: A Philosophical History* (Berkeley: University of California Press, 1997).

12. Gaston Bachelard, *The Poetics of Space* (Boston: Beacon Press, 1994).

13. VI, xlvii.

14. VI, 143.

15. See Casey, *Getting Back into Place*, 65-73, for a discussion of depth as global locality.

16. VI, 219.

17. VI, 162.

18. Friedrich von Hardenberg, Novalis, *The Novices of Sais: Sixty Drawings by Paul Klee,* trans. F. Ralph Manheim (New York: Curt Valentin, 1949). (Original work published 1798).

19. Lewis Thomas, *The Lives of a Cell* (New York: Bantam Books, Inc., 1974), 147.

20. VI, 142.

21. VI, 142.

22. James Hillman, "On Mythical Certitude," *Sphinx Journal,* 3, (1990): 224-243.

23. Martin Prechtel, *The Disobedience of the Daughter of the Sun: Ecstasy and Time* (Cambridge: Yellow Moon Press, 2001).

24. *Ibid.*, 44.

25. *Ibid.*, 109.

26. VI, lv.

27. James Hillman, *The Thought of the Heart and the Soul of the World,* (Woodstock, CT: Spring Publications, 1997).

28. Hillman, "On Mythical Certitude," 224-243.

29. For an in-depth study of the ecological imagination, see Laura H. Mitchell, *The Eco-imaginal Underpinnings of Community Identity in Harmony Grove Valley: Unbinding the Ecological Imagination,*

unpublished doctoral dissertation, Pacifica Graduate Institute, Carpinteria, CA., 2005.

On Reading the Zen Poet Ryokan
(or, The Great Transmission)

Reading the poetry of Ryokan, poems of a Great Loneliness
of soaring birds that disappear over distant mountains;

always an empty sky full of departure, and Ryokan himself
silently reading the poems of Kanzan and the ancients.

Within, a fire of burning leaves; outside, the autumn wind,
a light rain, and the rustle of reeds. Only the woodgatherer calls.

In his hermitage, the world is at a distance. Passing time
under a solitary pine: what is there to think, what is there to
doubt?

I can imagine a vast chain of reclusive poets, sitting
by themselves down through the long centuries, all reading

and writing each other poems of the Great Loneliness;
a conversation interrupted only by death,

and the arduous labor of translation across time and space—
Oh, and a little rice begging to fill our bowl—and all of us

trying to share the unshareable solitude, and all of us reading
in the other the Original Face of his Great Loneliness.

—*Michael Whan*

Developing a Jungian Ecopsychology

LIZ EVANS

INTRODUCTION

With our future survival on Earth now clearly under threat, we are living in critical times. The consequences of industrial activity are now impacting the planet in ways we apparently did not foresee, and climate change now poses a very real risk to the safe existence of our children and our children's children. In recent years we have witnessed environmental tragedy and disaster with the Boxing Day tsunami of 2004, the flooding of New Orleans, the devastating earthquakes in Pakistan and Indonesia, and the current melting of the Arctic ice caps, but this is just an indication of what is to come. Scientists have predicted that by the end of this century the impact of global warming will be somewhere between severe and catastrophic, causing unbearably hot summers, frequent forest fires, droughts, floods, and hurricanes.

In the face of such potential devastation, a common emotional response is, perhaps understandably, one of overwhelming despair and disempowerment. Confronted with the seemingly insurmountable problem of living on what appears to be a doomed planet and

Liz Evans has been a published author and journalist since 1988. She is currently conducting research for her Ph.D. in Jungian thought and ecopsychology at the University of Essex where she completed an M.A. in Jungian and Post-Jungian Studies in 2003.

confronted with the power of the governments and multinational corporations who perpetrate some of the worst crimes against nature, individuals tend to feel helpless, ineffective, and ultimately paralyzed as well as guilty of complicity. So how does one engage with the current ecological reality? How socially and politically conscious should one choose to become with regard to the environment? Indeed, what kind of consciousness does one need to develop if our species is to have a future?

We now have enough information about the causes of climate change to know that, on an individual level, we can make a difference to the future outcome of the planet. Small but significant changes in lifestyle, such as conserving energy, driving fuel-efficient vehicles, taking fewer trips abroad, and buying locally produced food, can all help to reduce our carbon emissions. Yet somehow, this rational, behavioral solution, relying on activism as the sole agent of change, fails to address the significant psychological impact of living within an endangered ecosystem. Social and political action are crucial if the planet is to remain fit for human habitation, but unless people feel themselves to be sufficiently connected to the planet on a deep, psychological level, the chances of this action taking place, or taking effect on the scale that is needed, are remote. In this paper, I will argue that a combination of ecopsychology and Jungian thought hold the potential to help provide that vital psychological re-connection.

Ecopsychology favors experiential reminders of our connection with the Earth, re-situating us as embodied creatures embedded within the ecosystem in the name of psychological well-being. Jungian psychology addresses us on a deeper, more unconscious level, both personally and collectively, enabling us to rediscover ourselves as part of nature, physically as well as psychologically, and consequently helping us to realize how deeply we are in relation with nature.

Without the benefit of Jungian thought, ecopsychology's efforts to identify human with nonhuman flounder on the shores of consciousness with its limited values and perspective. The depths of the unconscious remain unplumbed, incurring losses as great as those sustained by refusing to engage body, heart, and soul with nature. Yet without ecopsychology's essentially experiential methodology, much of what Jung says about humanity's connection with nature remains abstract and confined to the sphere of the intellect. However, I am less concerned here with a critical analysis of Jungian thought in the context of ecopsychology because of the field's overall reluctance to engage with Jung's ideas on nature, and I believe at this stage that it is more useful to focus on the benefits of integrating Jungian thought. Having said that, it is, in my view, the combination of these two approaches and the resulting holistic psychology that holds real potential for the kind of personal transformation needed for planetary change.

THE LIMITS OF EGO-CONSCIOUSNESS

Traditionally the western world (which deems itself "civilized") has opposed nature to culture, prioritizing humanity's physical requirements and material demands and emphasizing the development of the rational and conscious mind at the expense of more unconscious, uncultivated realms. Although some of the first Greek philosophers, including Aristotle and his pupil Theophrastus, have been described as forerunners of ecological thought,[1] the classical Greco-Roman era is better known for its cultivation of rationalism and logic.

As long ago as 500 BC, Parmenides of Elea prized human reason as the only legitimate basis of reality,[2] effectively initiating the notion of the superiority of the human intellect. This attitude is clearly echoed by Roman poet and philosopher Titus Lucretius' (99-55 BC) belief that human bodies belong to nature, while human minds afford the means by which to investigate the mechanics of nature, a position further emphasized by Judaeo-Christian religion, which awarded mankind stewardship over all living things.

Until now, the promise of fulfilling self interests through the negation of the nonhuman has proved more irresistible for humanity than gaining consciousness of, or concern for, nature. Having chosen to oppose and displace instinct, nature, and the unconscious with consciousness and culture, we now have little sense of ourselves as instinctive creatures. We have abandoned our connection with the guiding principle of nature, and the consciousness most of us are now encouraged to attain leaves us fundamentally alienated from the natural world as well as from our own inner natures. It is, as Jung says, "as if our consciousness had slipped from its natural foundations and no longer knew how to get along on nature's timing."[3]

Jung believes that isolation from the unconscious and nature brings insecurity, doubt, and uncertainty and that we now find ourselves facing "an all-too human fear that consciousness—our Promethean conquest—may in the end not be able to serve us as well as nature."[4] This amounts to what leading Australian ecophilosopher, Val Plumwood, refers to as an "ecological crisis of reason."[5] In other (psychological) words, we have become egocentric. While an intact, functioning ego is critical for psychic well-being, an unchecked ego-consciousness operating merely at the persona level is unbalanced, one-dimensional, and restrictive. According to Jung, an untended ego-consciousness is "merely the marionette that dances on the stage, moved by a concealed mechanism,"[6] leaving the egocentric individual confined to the limited values and perspective of his or her consciousness, controlled by his or her unconscious complexes, and ultimately liable to self destructiveness. Similarly, on a collective level, in separating from and appointing ourselves as superior to nature, we remain unconscious of our interdependence with the nonhuman world. In turn, this renders us more able to exploit it. However, now this exploitation has damaged the ecosystem to such a degree that our own survival as a species is currently under threat. For a culture that has supposedly built itself on a foundation of rationalism, this is not particularly rational.

There is clearly a need for a realistic, feasible alternative to a predominantly ego-driven anthropocentric consciousness. Ecologically speaking, consciousness should entail a keen awareness of our interconnection with nature, but given the predominance of humanity's assumed ascendancy over nature, we must ask ourselves if it is actually *possible* for such a consciousness to evolve.

Of course we cannot deny our hard-earned consciousness, but we can strive towards developing a more conscious relationship with nature. Ecopsychology, a relatively new, experientially-based means of bridging the psychological and the ecological, attempts to do just this.

ECOPSYCHOLOGY – A CRITICAL INTRODUCTION

In recent years, a growing number of western psychotherapists and psychologists have begun to realize the importance of developing a conscious relationship with nature, and together have started to mark out the beginnings of a field now known as ecopsychology. Rooted in radical ecology, a branch of environmental philosophy committed to the idea that all living things are interconnected, with each possessing the moral right to existence, ecopsychology is described by its founder, historian and cultural critic Theodore Roszak, as the "emerging convergence of psychological insight and environmental urgency."[7]

Built on the premise that humans have lost their sense of place within the ecosystem, ecopsychology questions the boundaries generally perceived to exist between the subjective self and the world by encouraging individuals to experience themselves in deep connection with the Earth through wilderness quests, solo treks, outdoor therapeutic workshops, and guided active meditations, among other exercises. In addition, it investigates the irrational forces that drive people to destroy their own environment and "seeks to redefine sanity within an environmental context,"[8] helping clients to develop awareness of their relationship to the world as an integral part of therapeutic treatment.

Concepts such as Sarah A. Conn's self-world connection, Stephen Aizenstat's world unconscious, James Hillman's ecological psyche, and Theodore Roszak's ecological unconscious illustrate ecopsychology's insistence on extending the traditionally self-contained subject of psychology into the world of all living things, both human and nonhuman. Conn emphasizes the relational nature of the self together with the "transpersonal, transhuman aspects of reality,"[9] stressing the importance of retaining individuality within a wider whole that stretches beyond psychology's usual limits to include the ecosystem. Aizenstat and Roszak draw on Jung's concept of the collective unconscious for their respective ideas concerning world and ecological unconscious, expanding the notion beyond human culture to open up a reality "in which all creatures and living things are animated by psyche."[10] And Hillman writes of "a psyche the size of the Earth,"[11] stipulating that where we draw a boundary between ourselves and the natural world matters less than the question of whether we draw the boundary at all.

Other factions of eco-oriented philosophy (known as ecophilosophy) and ecopsychology favor a full renouncement of human or personal concerns, which they seem to equate with anthropocentrism. Canadian psychotherapist Andy Fisher calls for the dissolution of ego;[12] Norwegian ecophilosopher Arne Naess urges solidarity with nature, encouraging his followers to "think like a mountain,"[13] Australian philosopher Warwick Fox strives to deny all human attachment in working towards a wholly transpersonal ecophilosophy;[14] and eco-activist Joanna Macy leads "Council of All Beings" workshops in which participants take on the personas of animals, rocks, and trees in an attempt to identify with the nonhuman world.[15]

Such an array of approaches inevitably opens up a myriad of questions concerning topics such as identity, subjectivity, consciousness, boundaries, relationship, the issue of anthropocentrism, the construction of concepts such as nature and culture, and what we mean by, or project onto, these concepts, as well as the more philosophical issue of environmental ethics. But while ecopsychology invites us into this rich arena, it fails to offer a close or critical analysis of any of the above. As Andy Fisher says, the field "has yet to demonstrate an adequate grasp of the intellectually complex and politically charged territory that ecopsychologists have entered into."[16]

Prioritizing the value of experience, ecopsychology is indeed very reluctant to explore theoretical measures. With the exception of Fisher's book, *Radical Ecopsychology*, which delves into phenomenology, existentialism, hermeneutics, humanistic psychology, nature writing and critical theory, ecopsychology concentrates on offering meaningful participation in nature rather than intellectual engagement. A recent proposal for a UK ecopsychology training suggested a mainly practical curriculum consisting of no more than eight to ten residential weekends during the course of a year, at the end of which there would be no formal assessment.[17]

Such an overwhelming aversion to theory may well mean that the ability to balance the experience of the body with a truly reflective process is sorely limited, and the results of this are often ironically human-centric and egotistical, as some of the literature demonstrates. Moreover, no effort is made to engage with unconscious processes, leaving much of ecopsychology stuck at the level of ego-consciousness rather than reaching the eco-consciousness it aspires to attain.

In her 1999 book, *Sight and Sensibility: The Ecopsychology of Perception*, visual psychologist Laura Sewall recounts taking a hike through Arizona's Prescott National Forest. Despite being warned against embarking on the trip alone, Sewall heads off on her trail only to find abundant evidence of mountain lions throughout her travels, yet rather than acknowledge the very real danger she is in, she chooses to imagine herself as undergoing a kind of shamanic initiation and implicitly presents herself as "Changing Woman receiving Sun as her lover."[18] Although in one sense she genuinely tries to address her fear of instinct, which she equates with a fear of becoming more conscious, in another she denies the reality of her situation which, coupled with her controversial, postcolonial show of indigenously oriented "enlightenment," ultimately suggests a real lack of consciousness.

Similarly, several tales of wilderness experience involving animal guides and initiation rites, as featured in Cass Adams' 1996 anthology, *The Soul Unearthed: Celebrating Wildness and Personal Renewal Through Nature,* reveal an unreflective eagerness to attain dizzy mental and emotional heights through supposedly sacred wilderness trips. For example, writer Gabriel Heilig spends a men's retreat feeling like the king of the forest. "Probably I'm inflated, right? … I don't give a sweet shit," he says, "These archetypes know how to have one helluva good time."[19] Wilderness guide John P. Milton explains the value of solo treks in terms of their ability to provide participants with "incredible, blissful, living energy and empowerment," "leadership roles," and "inner insight, wisdom and energy,"[20] and author Doug Elliott recalls a shamanic workshop during which a student interprets his encounter with a skunk as initiation into his "warrior path."[21]

In their attempts to be at one with nature, all of these writers focus on the empowerment they receive from being in nature. None of them take time to reflect on or consider how they impact nature, and why they, as humans, have had these responses in, or to, a natural environment. Aspiring towards recognition of continuity with and difference from nature enables humans to achieve a middle ground, where self and other exist in dynamic tension, but the failure to acknowledge nature's otherness and independence (while retaining a sense of deep interconnection with it) ultimately prevents effective communication with the nonhuman. Lack of reflection or critical thinking around the question of how we, as humans, situate ourselves in relation to the natural world will not help ecopsychology to manage these crucial issues.

Furthermore, the tendency to prioritize experience over intellectual engagement results in the kind of hierarchical binary opposition ecopsychology claims to want to transcend. The dualistic relationship of mind *versus* body, which has come to equate culture or consciousness *versus* nature or the unconscious, is merely inverted rather than resolved.

In his attempt to transcend the soma/psyche divide, Andy Fisher seeks an "approach in which critical analysis is allowed to coexist with talk of deer tracks, sunshine on tree trunks and heartfelt hugs."[22] He calls for new intellectual frameworks that can contain the human/nature relationship which would inevitably result in new kinds of practice. My question is: how can Jungian thought help to provide this kind of integrated approach?

Jung, fully aware that "the exaggerated rationalisation of consciousness" isolates humanity from its own nature by seeking to control nature as a whole, nevertheless suggests that a conscious relationship with nature is attained by "holding onto the level of reason we have successfully reached and enriching consciousness with a knowledge of man's psychic foundations."[23] In other words, intellectual life is as important as instinctive life in our attempts to become conscious of ourselves in relation to nature. I suggest that this key principle of integration holds great potential for the maturation of ecopsychology, which to date has failed to engage effectively with either the intellect or the unconscious aspect of the psyche.

INTEGRATING THE UNCONSCIOUS

Clearly, for Jung, the nature/culture divide is less a Cartesian issue of matter *versus* mind and more a question of how consciousness has evolved. If we choose to focus purely on attaining and refining our ego-consciousness, we must continue to forsake nature and refute our instincts.[24] If we would rather achieve a more balanced consciousness, however, we need to integrate our instincts, together with other aspects of ourselves, both personal and collective, which have been relegated to the unconscious. Without this integration of the unconscious, human consciousness can never hope to be fully attuned to nature, and humans can never hope to find true balance either within themselves or within the world.

Jung's collective unconscious, "the inherited psychic storehouse of the human species,"[25] forms part of the matrix of nature, it is "identical with Nature to the extent that Nature herself, including matter, is unknown to us."[26] We are always partly unknown to ourselves, just as nature is always partly unknown to us. As Jungian analyst Michael Whan notes, only when we turn away from nature and appreciate it as other can we experience ourselves as subjects and truly perceive nature as a force in itself, free from our anthropomorphic projections.[27] We therefore exist in dynamic relation to nature within our human location, but on a continuum, as Val Plumwood suggests,[28] although Jung's acknowledgment of the unconscious realm explores more complexities and opens up more possibilities for forging conscious connections between humanity and nature.

Developing the idea of fusion between psyche and matter, Jung sees the collective unconscious as constituting the "preconscious aspect of things on the 'animal' or instinctive level of the psyche."[29] It is "a quality of matter, or matter (as) the concrete aspect of the psyche,"[30] the deepest level of the unconscious where the psychological meets the physiological and which Jung referred to as the psychoid. "Life" he says "is really a continuum… one tissue in which things live by and through each other," and "the individual… is cut out of the tissue of the collective unconscious."[31] At this level, humans are "one with the animal" whether they experience themselves as such or not.[32] They are inherently somatically and psychologically bound up with nature on the most profound level; and, as we have seen, it is culture and civilization that are responsible for the scission that has emerged between the two.[33]

Jung's personal unconscious constitutes what he terms the shadow, and this is where cultured ego-consciousness has banished instinct with its instrumental connection to nature, along with every other unwanted, undesirable, unacceptable, inferior, shameful, and ultimately uncultivated—and therefore deeply feared—aspect of humanity. Obviously each individual has his or her own unique shadow aspects, but culture plays a key role in determining what is acceptable or what is to be encouraged and developed in a person. "The sinister darkness of the animal world of instinct" in traditional cultivated western society is, by and large, neither.[34]

Fear of instinct and nature in the west is a direct by-product of a culture balanced away from both. As Jung says, too much nature distorts civilization, while too much culture results in "sick animals,"[35] but there is no getting away from the animal nature at the foundation of all culture,[36] which explains why integration of the shadow is so significant. Without it, says Jung, originally speaking of war, the repression of instinct results in self destructiveness[37] because a narrow world view doesn't allow for this instinctive force to be given cultural form. Now, with our planet on the brink of catastrophe, we must literally widen our world view and integrate our instincts, remember that we are part of the animal realm, and put a stop to our destructiveness, or we shall be left without a home, along with countless other creatures.

As we have seen, ecopsychology has many practical suggestions for broadening our worldview and experiencing ourselves within the natural world where our instincts are heightened. Jung too suggests that we should project into the world around us because as true beings we are not confined to our bodies; and, without a meaningful relationship with our environment, we cease to be human.[38] Again, the issue of situating ourselves within the ecosystem *as humans* arises, although this notion of projecting into the world is not something automatically associated with Jung, who, throughout his writings, wavers between advocating the withdrawal of projections in the interests of becoming conscious[39] and warning against the dangers of heroic inflation which can result from the complete withdrawal of projections.[40] Yet in the context of what he calls primitive consciousness,[41] he is more supportive of the benefits of projection, or *participation mystique*, a term he borrows from anthropologist Lévy-Bruhl,[42] seeing it as an expression of the collective, rather than the personal unconscious. The projection Jung refers to in the above instance is "of a mythological content from the collective unconscious" rather than one arising from the personal unconscious.[43] This is where, for Jung's primitive, fusion between physical landscape and the "topography of the unconscious" manifests through symbol and metaphor as expressed in animistic belief and imagery.[44] Writing in 1945, Jung emphasizes that it is mythological, not elementary, literal belief, that underpins this kind of projection, reminding us that this is something we have lost to our detriment.[45]

It is Jung's contemplation of the possibility that projection has an objective power that results in his conclusion that the profound interconnection between human consciousness and nature, psyche and matter, exists on the physical plane as well as the psychological, hence his insistence that we need to project into the world around us. As philosopher David Abram says, reminding us of Whan's earlier observation concerning human subjectivity in relation to the otherness of nature, "We are human only in contact, and conviviality, with what is not human."[46]

If Jung and Abram are right, we are already barely human. As modern westerners we no longer appreciate the intrinsic bond between psyche and environment, and, having lost touch with our more unconscious levels of psyche and thus our interconnection point with nature, we no longer know that we are a part of nature.[47] This misconception is maintained by the artificially firm boundary we have created between ourselves and other life forms, which is what enables us to assume such a tenacious superiority over nature.[48]

Jung's answer to this hugely damaged and damaging relationship lies with the individuation process, the ultimate, albeit unattainable goal of his analytical psychology, which encourages us to regain contact with the unconscious, to reach deeply into all levels of our being, including the somatic,[49] and to re-establish our relationship with nature from the premise of reason we have reached culturally.[50] As we have seen, he is not in favor of attempting to regress to a previous state or stage of civilization, but rather recommends building from where we are, taking nature as our guide.[51] If we fail to take account of nature, he warns, it will undermine us and bring about our demise,[52] just as unconscious processes build up and take us by surprise when we refuse to bring them into consciousness. Aware of the delicacy of such a paradoxical procedure, Jung insists that "nature cannot win but she must not lose," indicating that nothing but a state of true balance will suffice.[53]

Individuation aims to achieve such a state of balance by moving towards a consciousness that acknowledges and integrates the role of the unconscious within the psyche, where egocentrism gives way to a more holistic sense of the self, or rather what Jung refers to as the Self. This is what I consider to be the development from ego-consciousness to eco-consciousness—a form of consciousness in which the part of our psyche which is conjoined with nature begins to move out of an unconscious into a more conscious state, thus rebalancing our relationship with our instinctual and what appear to be more irrational (or what Jung describes as our animal) selves and, in turn, our environment. As Jung says, "the self is an image born of nature's own workings, a natural symbol far removed from all conscious intention."[54] Put simply, the individuation process is growth towards nature.

If individuation is a process of self realization, as Jung claims it to be,[55] it must involve a discovery of oneself as part of an ecosystem, part of nature. Focusing on this possibility, taking into account some post-Jungian views of individuation, such as Hillman's idea of multiple individuation,[56] and looking more at the implications of collective as well as individual individuation, the process begins to resemble a powerful political as well as personal process. As Meredith Sabini says, "Individuation is compensatory for mass-mindedness of our era, — but rather than remove us from the social sphere, it enhances our interconnectedness."[57] So, while Jung's individuation process helps us to establish who we really are in all our uniqueness, it also serves to bring about a new consciousness of connection—to each other, to the nonhuman realm, and to nature. This is partly a re-discovery, partly an uncovering, and it holds much potential for both ecopsychology and Jungian thought. Finding out who we really are, no matter what our culture, involves an interconnectedness on the natural level that simultaneously celebrates difference. We can be in-dividual, while finding our place, our role, in the ecosystem.

CONCLUSION

Ecopsychology and Jungian thought offer significant possibilities for the forging of a new paradigm which offers possibilities for the future of Earth. But neither of them can offer it in isolation. Together, these theories, or positions, form an interdependent network of their own, an interdisciplinary site where the political, the spiritual, the psychological, the personal, and the collective can all be attended to and given new space for expression. Together, each illuminates the other, bringing about possibilities for transformation that could not occur without their synthesis. A natural born pluralist, Jung realized that one must extend into the world in this way—by making connections and links, by finding new ways of relating, and now, with our own species so sorely in need of healthy and supportive relationship with nature, we cannot afford to ignore this message.

Nature is said to have been de-psychized by the dualism of western thought and the withdrawal of projections,[58] but if we employ a phenomenological perspective, we realize that the psychological life is intrinsically bound up with the world and everything in it, that an experience involving what is known as projection "is no more a piece of poetry than the account of science."[59] Thus the world is seen through experience, and experience is seen through the world, and this has implications for both Jung's theories of consciousness and ecopsychology's insistence on connection with the nonhuman. (As Jung says, we know ourselves through the things around us.)[60] Jungian thought, together with ecopsychological ideas, constitutes a potential *re*-psychization of nature, where a conscious relationship allows for the human realm to see the nonhuman as having its own consciousness of which the human is a part—so there is difference, yet connection. We must learn to acknowledge our interdependent relationship with nature, to humble ourselves in the realization that nature can truly affect and heal us—maybe through dreams, which Jung claims to be the route to the instincts—before assuming we can effectively heal nature.

Our inflated sense of the superiority of our own human consciousness is where we have shown ourselves to be most unconscious, and now nature, which has never been this unashamedly unconscious, is reflecting this back to us through the slow but steady deterioration of our planet. It is up to us to open our eyes before the destruction of the Earth reaches a point where transformation has become impossible.

NOTES

1. David Macauley (ed.), *Minding Nature: The Philosophers of Ecology* (London and New York: Guilford Press, 1996).

2. Richard Tarnas, *The Passion of the Western Mind: Understanding the Ideas That Have Shaped Our World View* (New York: Harmony Books, 1991).

3. C. G. Jung, *The Collected Works of C. G. Jung* (Princeton: Princeton University Press, 1934), Vol. 8, para. 802. [the *Collected Works* are hereinafter referenced as "*CW*," followed by the volume number and the paragraph number].

4. *Ibid.*, § 750.

5. Val Plumwood, *Environmental Culture: The Ecological Crisis of Reason* (London and New York: Routledge, 2002).

6. Jung, *CW* 2 § 609.

7. Theodore Roszak, *Ecopsychology Online*, Number One, 1996.

8. Theodore Roszak, Mary E. Gomes, Allen D. Kanner (eds.), *Ecopsychology: Restoring the Earth, Healing the Mind* (San Francisco: Sierra Club Books, 1995), xvi.

9. *Ibid.*, 164.

10. *Ibid.*, 92.

11. *Ibid.*, viii.

12. Andy Fisher, *Radical Ecopsychology: Psychology in the Service of Life* (Albany: State University of New York Press, 2002).

13. Pat Fleming, Joanna Macy, Arne Naess, & John Seed, *Thinking Like a Mountain: Towards a Council of All Beings* (Vermont: New Society Publishers, 1988).

14. Warwick Fox, *Toward a Transpersonal Psychology: Developing New Foundations for Environmentalism* (London and Boston: Shambhala, 1990).

15. Joanna Macy and Molly Young Brown, *Coming Back to Life: Practices to Reconnect Our Lives, Our World* (Canada: New Society Publishers, 1998), 5.

16. Fisher, *Radical Ecopsychology*.

17. Personal correspondence, 2005.

18. Laura Sewall, *Sight and Sensibility: The Ecopsychology of Perception* (New York: Tarcher/Putnam, 1999), 190.

19. Cass Adams, *The Soul Unearthed: Celebrating Wildness and Personal Renewal Through Nature* (New York: Tarcher/Putnam, 1996), 81.

20. *Ibid.*, 32.

21. *Ibid.*, 112.

22. Fisher, *Radical Ecopsychology*, xv.

23. Jung, *CW* 8 § 739.

24. Jung, *CW* 8, 387-404.

25. Roszak, et al., *Ecopsychology*, 92.

26. G. Adler (ed.), *C. G. Jung Letters II* (Princeton, New Jersey: Princeton University Press, 1977), 540.

27. Michael Whan, "Jung, Nietzsche, and the Dehumanization of Nature: Psychological and Ecological Consciousness," *Harvest* 44: 2 (1998), 7-23.

28. Plumwood, *Environmental Culture*.

29. Adler, *Jung Letters II*, 540.

30. *Ibid.*

31. Claire Douglas, *Interpretation of Visions* (Princeton, New Jersey: Princeton University Press, 1997), 753-4.

32. *Ibid.*, 161.

33. William McGuire and R. F. C. Hull (eds.), *C. G. Jung Speaking: Interviews and Encounters* (Princeton, NJ: Princeton University Press, 1984), 396-7.

34. Jung, *CW* 14 § 602.

35. Jung, *CW* 7 § 32.

36. *Ibid.*, § 41.

37. Jung, *CW* 10 § 31.

38. McGuire and Hull, *C. G. Jung Speaking,* 201-203.

39. Jung, *CW* 11 § 85.

40. Jung, *CW* 7 § 110.

41. Although his use of the term "primitive" is arguably controversial, Jung said, "I use the term 'primitive' in the sense of 'primordial' and I do not imply any kind of value judgment. Also, when I speak of a 'vestige' of a primitive state, I do not necessarily mean that this state will sooner or later come to an end. On the contrary, I see no reason why it should not endure as long as humanity lasts." – *CW* 8 § 218.

42. After 1912 Jung employs this term to denote projective identification.

43. Jung, *CW* 10 § 43.

44. Jung, *CW* 10 § 44.

45. Jung, *CW* 18 § 1362.

46. David Abram, *The Spell of the Sensuous* (New York and Toronto: Vintage Books,1997).

47. Jung, *CW* 10 § 312.

48. McGuire and Hull, *C.G. Jung Speaking,* 220-223.

49. *Ibid.*

50. Jung, *CW* 8 § 739.

51. Jung, *CW* 10 § 34.

52. Jung, *CW* 16 § 227.

53. Jung, *CW* 13 § 229.

54. Jung, *CW* 16 § 474.

55. Jung, *CW* 7 § 266.

56. James Hillman, *The Myth of Analysis* (New York: HarperPerennial, 1992).

57. Meredith Sabini (ed.), *The Earth Has a Soul: The Nature Writings of C. G. Jung* (Berkeley, CA: North Atlantic Books, 2002), 57.

58. Whan, "Jung, Nietzsche, and the Dehumanization of Nature: Psychological and Ecological Consciousness."

59. Robert Romanyshyn, *Psychological Life: From Science to Metaphor* (Austin: University of Texas Press, 1982), 40.

60. McGuire and Hull, *C. G. Jung Speaking,* 201-203.

THE NAÏVE DREAM OF THE RETURN TO NATURE: A DEPTH PSYCHOLOGICAL PERSPECTIVE ON ENVIRONMENTALISM

LORI PYE

After a decade of working for environmental agencies, I have heard all possible variations of the oft-heard sermon to get back to nature and stop polluting. The problem with that kind of injunction is that it is about as useful as telling a drug addict to "just say no." Saying no to a destructive behavior is precisely what drug addicts cannot do, because they are psychologically incapable of moving out of their suicidal mindset. Ecologists use the word "ecosuicidal" for humans who are behaving in such a way as to destroy the resources they depend on for their survival. It is an admission that the connection to nature can be so neurotic that it becomes an unconscious ecocide. Suicidal or ecosuicidal behaviors have their source in unconscious factors playing out in a destructive way.

Ecologists are not necessarily familiar with or interested in the vocabulary of depth psychology. Environmentalists have their own set

Lori Pye, Ph.D., is the Executive Director of the Foundation for Mythological Studies and adjunct faculty at Pacifica Graduate Institute and Santa Barbara City College. She has worked in the environmental field for over 16 years with international marine conservation organizations, including the Jean-Michel Cousteau Ocean Futures Society, and formed a nonprofit corporation in Latin America to help develop the Eastern Tropical Pacific Seascape Corridor, a protected marine conservation area from Costa Rica to Ecuador.

of metaphors, most of them drawn from biology. Paul Shepard, for example, uses the metaphor of parasitic life forms to convey the idea that our survival, like that of a parasite, depends on the survival of the larger organism (the Earth). A parasitic relationship can work only as long as the parasite doesn't destroy the organism that acts as host. Analyzing the data about our parasitic relationship to the earth, he concludes that humans are demanding more than the eco-system can provide. In other words, the problem is not so much that we are parasites, but that we are suicidal parasites! His metaphor of suicidal parasites could work as a good enough definition of a neurotic relationship: one destroys the very love that one is begging for. Metaphors are only images that help us understand a complex reality. The fact that the field of environmentalism is dominated almost exclusively by scientists is responsible for a poverty of insights about the unconscious aspects of such ecosuicidal behaviors.

This lack of true interdisciplinarity in most environmentalist programs is extremely costly. The occasional so-called "interdisciplinary" approaches are not really interdisciplinary at all. They are comprised instead of clans, each of which claims its own turf: the specialists of water (either of ocean, lakes, or rivers), the experts on soil, the experts on food, the experts on air, and so on, a juxtaposition of specialties. Furthermore, there is rarely a professor who will dare look over the fence, for example, toward social sciences and the humanities.

As someone who was trained in depth psychology but has a professional history of working in environmentalism, I feel like a hybrid immersed in a sea of language where the theories of ecology are interchangeable with those of depth psychology. Let's take, for example, the theories about suicidal behaviors. The one common factor of all suicidal attitudes is a series of *disconnections*. In other words, the suicidal personality is disengaged from relationships, severed from the community of humans, cut off, detached, aloof, and deprived of all the connections that give meaning to life. Yet, the disconnection is not the main problem, as the challenge posed by a suicidal personality is that *the person lacks even the awareness of the disconnection. The disconnection has become the natural state.* Disconnection from fellow humans beings is an unbearable, unsustainable psychological state, and, as a result, one becomes destructive to self, but never grasps that it is because of this series of disconnections. The difficulty, from a therapeutic point of view, is that as long as the disconnection is unconscious, the patient will continue the suicidal behaviors.

Thus the depth psychological perspective suggests that, before anybody can "reconnect with nature," one has to first *feel* the disconnection, *feel* the threat it poses. The keyword here is *feel* as opposed to *think*. Environmental reports filled with alarming data stimulate thinking and logos. They don't translate into the kind of *emotion* that inspires change. The capacity to induce an emotion is not the concern of a scientist; in fact, it is disruptive to the scientific method. Evoking emotion is the task of the humanities and the arts.

Most ecologists are trained as scientists and lack even a basic education in the humanities. As a result, there is a psychological naïveté in the environmental movement. It is the naïveté of a scientist who heads a drug addiction program and believes that showing charts and statistics will convince addicts to stop abusing their body; or the well-intentioned doctor admonishing an overstressed man, "you better relax or you'll soon die of a heart failure." This is not only naïve, but it advocates a logical impossibility, as the addiction is a "desire" to abuse the body, and a patient's incapacity to get sober or to relax is precisely what helped cause his or her heart condition in the first place. Presenting data does not bring about change, but the well-intentioned community of ecologists overlooks the frustrating reality of the irrationally of human beings.

The scientific evidence that reveals our abuse of natural resources has been communicated in every possible journal, forum, and media, and has advanced research in all fields of environmentalism. Yet, scientific information, although crucial to research and restoration, does not have the power to *move*, to make a person or a community feel anything. For information to become education, and for education to become activism, something of a psychological nature needs to happen, a *feeling* that ignites passion for an ideal.

The Millennium Ecosystems Assessment Report to the United Nations General Assembly (March 2005)[1] offers one of the most comprehensive and integrated assessments of the ecological state of the world. An ecosystem, as defined by the MA report, is a "dynamic complex of plant, animal, and microorganism communities and the nonliving environment interacting as a functional unit, which humans are a part of."[1] This comprehensive report includes sociological and cultural aspects, even aesthetic and spiritual ones. Yet, it still leaves out the psychological, symbolic, or—to say it succinctly—the mythological aspect of our relationship with Earth.

A case example involves information from the the Millennium Assessment Report that was shared with fisherman to show them how their fishing practices (like overfishing, dynamite fishing, and shark finning)[2] negatively effected the fragile ecology of the ocean and led to the extinction of fish that they depend upon for their survival. One might think that once the fishermen were made aware of the causal link between their behavior and the damage it caused to the ocean environment, they would have stopped their detrimental practices. Yet, despite the effort and money that was spent to educate them about these things, their *feelings* did not change much nor did their practices. Being informed of all the good reasons to stop dumping pollutants on the coral reef, or to stop using dynamite or cyanide to catch fish around the reefs, or to stop shark finning has had very little impact. Imagine a good doctor explaining to a child to refuse the mother's breast because her milk has DDT in it. Only the dead corpse of the mother would convince a child to move away from her body. Only a dead ocean will convince the fishermen who depend on it for their survival to stop destroying it. Only lack of profit will convince the richest to stop their abusive methods. Scientific evidence is powerless to convince someone whose *emotion* has not been stirred.

Most fishermen have for many generations viewed the ocean as their ever-bountiful provider. They have a mythology in which the ocean, like Mother Nature, is so vast and generous that there will always be an infinite supply of the lifeforms, like fish, that live in it. Fishermen in the Philippines cannot entertain the image of a depleted ocean, even when confronted with the evidence. Their coral reef was once one of the richest sources of species diversity.[3] The use of dynamite, one of the most destructive fishing techniques, yields a large catch. A few sticks in the water and plenty of dead fish float to the top. Dynamite, in fact, supports their mythology of the inexhaustible generosity of Mother Nature. Their emotional experience of the abundance of fish floating to the top contradicts all the data from the scientists. That their practice is destroying the ecosystem goes contrary to their mythology of a plentiful ocean.

A mythology always defines what values are sacred. Environmentalism is asking anew the basic question at the core of all mythologies: What is sacred? What value are we to give to Nature and to Life itself? How are we to feel our interdependence with Nature? Indeed, each time someone brings up the topic of our relationship to nature, she or he is "mythologizing." A new ecological order is impossible without the courage to engage in a battle around religious values. In this aspect of the battle, the scientific approach is more an obstacle than ally.

The word "theology," whose original meaning was "a discourse about divinities," is now usually understood as referring to monotheistic dogmas. Theology has become, for many, synonymous with the word dogmatism. Thus, one can hear expressions like, "let's not be dogmatic about that" or "let's not make a theology of this" or "let's not be doctrinarian." Nevertheless, this restrictive definition leaves unexamined the fact that a new myth of nature cannot avoid a *theological* discussion, in the original sense of the word. The whole lexicon of religion has to be co-opted if ecology is really to permeate culture. The term *theophany,* which means manifestation of the divine, or the word *hierophany,* which also means an apparition of the sacred, can be redefined to liberate the sense of the sacred from monotheistic dogma and bring back a sense of the sacred to our relationship with nature. These incursions into religion are necessary to an ecological vision of the world. A new myth cannot appear without a rebuttal of the old monotheistic myth running in the background (domination over nature).[4] A myth may be compared to the system software that allows the computer to run one kind of software, but not another. It works in the background, yet determines the range of action. Without regular updates of our organizing myths, the possibility of change is limited.

Emile Durkheim argued that religiosity should not be reduced to what appears to be supernatural or mysterious. He reminded us that in so-called "primitive" religions the relationship to the divine, contrary to what we would consider supernatural, was perfectly natural and rational. He reached the conclusion that there are three basic components of religion.

1) Religion is a system.

2) Religion is about those realities that we perceive or value as sacred.

3) A religion is born and maintains itself through a moral community.

If one applies those three criteria to environmentalism, Durkheim's perspective takes on profound meaning for ecology because:

1) Ecology is the acknowledgment that we are all part of an organic "system." The discipline of ecology is itself a systemic knowledge.

2) Ecology is about realities perceived or valued as sacred: the protection or survival of animal and vegetable kingdoms, of the human race and its culture, and of life on this planet. Nature thus is reinvested with a value of sacredness, which means it has value *in itself,* in an unconditional and absolute way, not only as a resource to be exploited.

3) Ecological awareness is the result of growing a community of the like-minded.

It is, to take Durkheim's term; a *moral* community that appears to be planetary, ecumenical, polymorphous, one could say "polysacred," as one would say "polytheist" or "biodiversity."

The values held sacred by this ecological community, although they correspond to Durkheim's definition of religion, reveal a fundamental incompatibility with Christian theology. The ecological values are, in fact, closer to a polytheistic form of religiosity. For example, in terms of human ecology, the monotheistic notion of a chosen people or preferred race is contrary to the ecological principle of diversity and interdependence. In a polytheistic religion, each god or goddess has a limited role and function, all the different principles they embody functioning like ecological systems in which whales and worms, sharks and baby seals, all play their role in the drama of life.

The necessity for a "theological" move or, to say it more simply, for a new myth, is due to the critical importance of paying attention to the psychological aspect of the ecological revolution. Every member of the community has to be personally moved, emotionally involved, morally called into question, and personally and ethically impacted by the exhaustion of Mother Nature. Only a new mythology can do that, not the accumulation of scientific information. Research has amply demonstrated our eco-suicidal behaviors. Depth psychology and mythology demonstrate *how* we can change those destructive behaviors. By the deconstruction of the old monotheistic myth and the creation of new values, we can define sustainability in a more global context, one that takes into account the "emotional" nature of humans.

The knowledge accumulated by the science of ecology needs to include the psychology of ecology, in order to move from logos to mythos, to move from dialogue to action. Only then can it generate the kind of power that brings about revolution.

NOTES

1. Millennium Ecosystems Assessment Report to the United Nations General Assembly (March 2005), 3. The Millennium Ecosystem Assessment (MA) is an international work program designed to meet the needs of decision makers and the public for scientific information concerning the consequences of ecosystem change for human well-being and options for responding to those changes. The MA was launched by U.N. Secretary-General Kofi Annan in June 2001 and was completed in March 2005.

The MA focuses on ecosystem services (the benefits people obtain from ecosystems), how changes in ecosystem services have affected human well-being, how ecosystem changes may affect people in future decades, and response options that might be adopted on a local, national, or global scale to improve ecosystem management and thereby contribute to human well-being and poverty alleviation. The specific issues being addressed by the assessment have been defined through consultation with the MA users.

The MA synthesizes information from the scientific literature, datasets, and scientific models and includes knowledge held by the private sector, practitioners, local communities, and indigenous peoples. All of the MA findings undergo rigorous peer review. More than 1,300 authors from 95 countries have been involved in four expert working groups preparing the global assessment, and hundreds more continue to undertake more than 20 sub-global assessments.

2. Sharks are one of the main predators of the ocean. Their destruction results in overpopulation of other species of fish, severely destabilizing marine ecosystems. Shark finning entails catching a shark, cutting off its dorsal fin, and discarding the rest of the shark, which then cannot survive. This practice has been banned in the Atlantic

Ocean and the Gulf of Mexico since 1993, but it is still widely used in the Pacific Ocean, particularly in Hawaii, where fisherman can earn up to $40 for a pound of shark fins. In various parts of east Asia, shark fin soup is considered a delicacy and can sell for as much as $120 a bowl. The Ocean Wildlife Campaign reported that the number of sharks killed by Hawaiian fisheries has increased from 2,289 in 1991 to 60,857 in 1998.

3. To date, ten percent of the world's reefs have been completely destroyed. In the Philippines, where coral reef destruction is the worst, over 70% have been destroyed, and only 5% can be said to be in good condition (Texas A & M University, Ocean World 2006).

4. The Christian nature myth can be summarized in two often-quoted passages in the Bible. The first one is from Genesis I: 26: "Then God said, 'let us make humankind in our image, according to our likeness; and let them have dominion over the fish of the sea, and over the birds of the air, and over the cattle, and over all the wild animals of the earth, and over every creeping thing that creeps upon the earth.'"

The second is from Genesis I: 28: "God blessed them and God said to them, 'Be fruitful and multiply, and fill the earth and subdue it; and have dominion over the fish of the sea and over the birds of the air and over every living thing that moves upon the earth.'" (*The New Revised Standard Version Bible*, 1989)

To Praise Again: Phenomenology and the Project of Ecopsychology

ANDY FISHER

> This is the time for what can be said. *Here*
> is its country. Speak and testify. The things
> we can live with are falling away more
> than ever, replaced by an act without symbol.
> An act under crusts that will easily rip
> as soon as the energy inside outgrows
> them and seeks new limits.
> Our hearts survive between
> the hammers, just as the tongue between
> the teeth is still able to praise.
> —Rainer Maria Rilke[1]

Introduction: The Challenge of Ecopsychology

When eco-psychology stepped onto the cultural stage in the mid-1990s, one of its main spokespersons, Theodore Roszak, called it "a new beginning for environmentalism and a revolution in modern psychology."[2] Ecopsychology would place all

Andy Fisher is a psychotherapist in private practice and a wilderness guide. The author of *Radical Ecopsychology: Psychology in the Service of Life*, he lives in Perth, Canada.

This paper was originally published in *Renew the Face of the Earth: Phenomenology and Ecology: The 23rd Annual Symposium of the Simon Silverman Phenomenology Center*, edited by Melissa Geib (Pittsburgh: The Simon Silverman Phenomenology Center, 2006) (ISBN 0-9786572-4-1).

psychological and spiritual matters within the context of our membership in the natural world and foster a fruitful, if not radical, dialogue between environmentalists and psychologists. To put it bluntly, however: the revolution never came.[3] Despite the modest popularity today of various eco-therapies and earthen spiritualities, ecopsychology has produced little in the way of scholarly output and has yet to secure a place for itself within either the academy or the consulting room. Modern psychology remains unscathed.

So what went wrong? Why didn't ecopsychology fly? My own simple answer is that the conceptual, methodological, and political challenges facing ecopsychology are much greater than was originally imagined. This is a thesis I am developing elsewhere.[4] It is perhaps best exemplified, however, by the fact that the more mainstream field of environmental psychology has by now confidently moved into the general space that ecopsychology had hoped to occupy. And, to the extent that environmental psychologists acknowledge the existence of ecopsychology, they tend to do so with a dismissive wave, accusing it of being lightweight or flaky, of not even qualifying as psychology.[5] In a word, then, ecopsychology has a legitimacy crisis on its hands.

But this is to be expected. Ecopsychologists propose a radical revisioning of psychology, and it is therefore naïve to suppose that the birth of ecopsychology will be anything but difficult. As someone deeply committed to this difficult birth, I have assigned myself the task of describing the overall project of ecopsychology and identifying the challenges it faces in its psychological, philosophical, practical, and critical dimensions. I started this exercise in my book *Radical Ecopsychology*, but much work remains. What I intend to do in this article is to consider some of the advantages of adopting a phenomenological approach for meeting ecopsychology's developmental challenges.

Indeed, thinking about Martin Heidegger's famous line in *Being and Time*, I am tempted to say that *only as phenomenology is ecopsychology possible*. I say this because I was surprised when writing my doctoral dissertation by just how much I had to rely on the phenomenological writings of Maurice Merleau-Ponty. I had only a modest grasp of Merleau-Ponty's philosophy and so planned to use it sparingly. But when the time came, I found that there was just no other good way to get at a number of the points I wished to make. So the question arises:

why was Merleau-Ponty indispensable? Or more generally: what is it about phenomenology that makes it so well suited to building and legitimizing the project of ecopsychology?

ECOPSYCHOLOGY AND ENVIRONMENTAL PSYCHOLOGY:
A RADICAL DIFFERENCE

In order to clarify the nature of the task before us, I want to begin by distinguishing ecopsychology from environmental psychology. The most general distinction that can be made is that ecopsychology aligns itself primarily with the radical ecology movement whereas environmental psychology—insofar as it deals with the natural environment, and not just the built—aligns itself primarily with mainstream environmentalism. Radical ecology includes such schools of thought as deep ecology, eco-feminism, social ecology, and eco-socialism, all of which charge mainstream environmentalism with being, to greater or lesser extents, complicit in the social, cultural, and historical structures that are themselves responsible for the degradation of the earth—complicit, that is, in a human-centered, instrumental view of the natural world, in patriarchal institutions that operate according to a logic of domination, and in hierarchical and capitalist social relations that rationalize the control and exploitation of nature, whether human or nonhuman.[6] Ecopsychology takes its place among the radical ecologies by saying that there is a deep psychological and spiritual root to the ecological crisis, a profound estrangement of the human psyche from the larger psyche of nature, that is not accounted for or put into question by mainstream approaches.

Whereas ecopsychology therefore calls for a radical politics aimed at developing social and cultural forms that would reintegrate mind and nature, environmental psychology aims, for the most part, simply to promote mainstream environmentalism. Its vision is that of a kind of social engineering that would produce "environmentally responsible," "sustainable," or "pro-environmental" behavior.[7] Such behavior is not so much about developing a sense of kinship or intimate reciprocity with nonhuman beings but rather conserving energy and recycling your pop can. Thus, environmental psychology, with its managerial ethos, generally adopts a resourcist ontology. Even when the natural world is viewed as a "restorative environment" for relieving the stress of tired office workers, it is still a resource—now a psychological one.[8] For ecopsychologists, by contrast, nonhuman beings are not just resources but other forms of personhood. Everything, from a wounded bumblebee to a booming thunderclap, has its own voice, aliveness, and hold on the world. In short, then, this difference in politics and ontological starting point makes for a radical distinction between ecopsychology and environmental psychology.

It also has important methodological implications. Here, I take my cue from Hans-Georg Gadamer's description of hermeneutics as an exercise in letting "what is alienated by the character of the written word or by the character of being distantiated by cultural or historical distances speak again."[9] Following Gadamer, one of the ways I conceive of ecopsychology is as a hermeneutical effort to let the natural world come alive and speak again. Gadamer warns, furthermore, against allowing research to get trapped in an unreflective methodology that "flattens experience and leads to a betrayal of what is specifically other."[10] Consider, in this regard, the following passage from an interview with the archetypal psychologist James Hillman. Hillman is on a sailboat in the Alaskan wilderness, where he is conducting a dream seminar.

> I've talked about animal images in dreams for thirty years, and given seminars in many, many places, and this is the only place where it's really appropriate. Because the animals are right there. You have to be careful you don't say something stupid, because the animals are listening. You can't interpret them; you can't symbolize them; you can't do something that is only human about them. Their presence is felt.[11]

Notice Hillman's concern not to betray the animal others. What does it do to our research when we have to mind our manners in this way? When we have to refrain from resource-ifying other-than-human beings? When we have to think about the earthly place where we actually conduct our research?

And what about the methodological flattening of experience that Gadamer cautions against? I suggest that our everyday, shopping mall sense of alienation from the larger natural world requires just such a flattening. The research approach that ecopsychology adopts must therefore invite, and be adequate to, those full-bodied modes or regions of experience that explicitly link our own souls to the soul of the "more-than-human world," to use David Abram's phrase. We can point to such modes or regions of experience with words like: sensuous, intuitive, animistic, imaginal, dreaming, shamanistic, emotional, analogical, mythological, storied, oral, poetic, dramatic, sacred, spiritual, existential, singing, dancing, invisible, synchronistic, and so forth. Not surprisingly, these are precisely the areas of experience that mainstream, nature-estranged psychology has been most silent on or biased against. They do not lend themselves easily to conventional empiricism and rationalism. These modes or regions of experience do lend themselves, however, to a phenomenological approach—precisely because phenomenology is itself a radical mode of inquiry, as Husserl said right from the start.

In getting us back to the lifeworld, in ceaselessly striving to make better contact with reality, the practice of phenomenology aims to disclose the world and, correspondingly, ourselves in previously unimagined ways. Similarly, ecopsychology is an effort to suspend the ecologically and psychologically destructive reality principle of our current epoch in order to rediscover or recollect—in psychological terms—our embeddedness in the body of the earth, an embeddedness that our current economized and technologized understanding of being decisively obscures. Adopting a phenomenological ontology will allow ecopsychology to insist that we loosen our usual grip on reality and remain open to new experiential possibilities in our rediscovery of the earth and of the claims that it is making on us. Ecopsychologists ask: What is our rightful place here on this earth? What does it mean to be a human being as part of the natural world? What are our spiritual responsibilities toward this land we inhabit? In looking for answers, one might well turn to Heidegger, who tells us that to be human is to dwell poetically within the Fourfold of mortals, gods, earth, and sky,[12] to spare and preserve the earth, and to "safeguard each thing in its nature."[13] There may be some romanticism in all this that needs to be sorted out, but it is certainly better than saying that to be human is to selfishly consume the earth in order to meet unlimited wants or desires—which is what the economics text books would have us believe. There is a basic faith or intuition within ecopsychology that as we get closer to the meaning of human being, as we open ourselves to earthly suffering, as we attempt some kind of psychological reconciliation with the living world, then we will become less punishing and more revering of the earth. We will "praise again," as Rilke encourages us to do.

Given this apparent affinity between ecopsychology and phenomenology, it is worth mentioning a 1982 article by David Seamon, "The Phenomenological Contribution to Environmental Psychology." In this article, Seamon identified the prevailing positivism within environmental psychology and, as an alternative, outlined what he called a phenomenological environmental psychology. In the last two decades, however, there has been little change in philosophy within environmental psychology, and the kind of radical ecological view that Seamon endorsed has made little appearance.[14] At this stage, I therefore propose that the phenomenological approach that he was calling for would find a better home within ecopsychology than in environmental psychology. Indeed, the tradition of phenomenology may even be indispensable for building that home.

Having now made my initial case for a phenomenologically-oriented ecopsychology, I want for the rest of my presentation to discuss some of the ways that a marriage between or crossing of these two fields might produce something that is fruitful for both.

DISCURSIVE CHALLENGES:
ECOPSYCHOLOGY'S SEARCH FOR LANGUAGE

One of the challenges bedevilling ecopsychology is the lack of existing terminology for articulating its terrain. Most urgently, ecopsychology will fail as an intellectual exercise unless it can find concepts that avoid the philosophical dualism between the human mind and the natural world.[15] The human sciences talk about humans, the natural sciences talk about nature, and ecopsychology—which lies between these two sciences—has trouble talking at all. The grandfather of ecopsychology, Robert Greenway, has thus called ecopsychology, as much as anything else, "a search for a language."[16] And this is where Merleau-Ponty comes in. For perhaps more than any other Western philosopher, he offers a way out of our dualistic bind, thereby providing us with a philosophical basis for an ecopsychology.[17]

This is not the place to explicate Merleau-Ponty's ontology. I will, however, try to sketch some of its power for ecopsychology. Shortly before he died, Merleau-Ponty wrote the following note to himself:

> A philosophy of the flesh is the condition without which
> psychoanalysis remains anthropology.[18]

This one little line has become a sort of marching order for me. The way I read it, Merleau-Ponty is saying that a philosophy of the flesh is necessary if we are ever to build a psychology that goes beyond a narrow world of human projections. Such a trans-human psychology is of course what we mean by ecopsychology. But the question remains: what did Merleau-Ponty mean by flesh?

This is difficult to say in any kind of complete way, especially because Merleau-Ponty's writing was cut short by his untimely death. It is nonetheless clear that he meant this term to resolve the longstanding dualistic problems of mind and matter, inside and outside, subject and object, active and passive, identity and difference, humans and nature, and so on. He described flesh as an element that subtended all of these distinctions, as a common tissue, texture, or style in which all such terms overlap, encroach on, adhere to, or cross over and line one another. We make contact with the world only because our bodies and the world are made of the same general flesh. In other words, we touch and see things only because we are ourselves touchable and visible. Merleau-Ponty's favorite example for illustrating this was that of one of our hands touching the other, where our right hand not only touches our left, but by a sort of reversal we experience our left hand touching back. Thus, as we touch things from the inside so are we touched from the outside—and only because of this are we "in touch" at all. What Merleau-Ponty observed is that perception is always doubled in this way, always includes these corresponding counter-perceptions or alter-perceptions. We make contact, then, not only because we share a common flesh from the inside, but also because we are always in a sense outside ourselves, never identical with ourselves, but always finding ourselves in our interactions, as we are touched, mirrored, echoed, and completed by an otherness that transcends us.

So how does this philosophy of the flesh help set the stage for an ecopsychology?[19] The easiest answer is that Merleau-Ponty was not only describing how contact is possible between humans, but also how contact is possible *in general*, including that with the larger natural world. He spoke, for example, of a "kinship between the being of the earth and that of my body," noting that this kinship extended to other animals and even to stones.[20] Kinship, not surprisingly, is a central notion within ecopsychology. The human ecologist Paul Shepard, for example, built a kind of ecopsychology that traces how kinship with nonhuman nature develops through such processes as children imitating animals and adults telling stories that blur the boundaries between humans and animals, such as the famous tale of a woman who married a bear.[21] It is noteworthy that Shepard described kinship as a sense of likeness-within-difference, for this characterization fits exactly with Merleau-Ponty's ontology of the flesh, wherein beings overlap and touch yet never completely coincide. We could even say that Merleau-Ponty gives Shepard's work some philosophical legs— and that we are now in a position to run. Merleau-Ponty conceives of the mind in terms of mirroring, resemblance, kinship, intertwining, "flesh responding to flesh."[22] It makes perfect sense, then, when naturalist Loren Eisley, making an essentially ecopsychological point, writes that: "One does not meet oneself until one catches the reflection from an eye other than human."[23]

While Merleau-Ponty in a sense comes to the rescue of ecopsychology, simply adopting his terms—or those of any other phenomenologist—will of course not completely solve our discursive problems. As ecopsychologists, we have trouble talking, not just because of the division of the sciences, but also because we have relatively little direct experience of the territory we hope to talk about. Ecopsychology cannot be done through perceptual studies of tables and chairs, but only through opening ourselves to, and disclosing, one little step at a time, a larger than human reality that is hidden from us by modern society. This anthropocentric occlusion of the earth in Western history has been dealt with at length by the likes of Heidegger, and more recently David Abram, so I will not dwell on the topic here. What this historical situation means for ecopsychology, however, is that we must actively seek out new, trans-human kinds of experience from which we can then let original thinking and language come. It is not enough to pour over psychological and philosophical texts in search of their ecological relevance. As I put it in my book: "the leading edge of our theory will be the leading edge of our experience."[24] This demand for new experience in turn raises the matter of practice, so I will discuss that topic next.

PUTTING PHENOMENOLOGY INTO PRACTICE:
THE CASE OF VISION QUESTING

In an article on the state of phenomenology in America, David Levin laments the fact that so much work in phenomenology remains programmatic and lost in seemingly endless methodological self-reflection. Sharing his own impatience with this situation, Levin calls for a more worldly, pragmatic phenomenology that would instead concentrate on putting itself into practice.[25] Taking a cue from Levin, what I want to explore here is how phenomenology might put itself into practice through ecopsychology. More specifically, I want to consider how certain phenomenological principles and findings could inform one particular practice that is popular among ecopsychologists, and that has the potential to give it a strong experiential base, namely, vision questing.

Briefly, a vision quest is a trans-cultural rite in which a quester spends solo time in the wilderness in order to seek spiritual renewal or guidance at a time of transition or crisis. The vision quests of Black Elk, Jesus, Moses, and other spiritual leaders are well known, though the archetypal vision quest is probably that undertaken by adolescents at the time of their transition into adulthood. Questers prepare for their solo in the company of elders, and when they return their new status and social place is ceremonially honored. One seeks vision and empowerment, then, not so much as an act of individual therapy, but so that one may better serve one's people and maintain a personal relationship with the natural world. Because vision questing deliberately locates itself in this way within community and earthly life, it offers a radical alternative to office-bound psychotherapy, which, as James Wright notes, "leaves us stewing in our fluorescent-hued inner sanctums, divorced from the teachings of animals, plants, rocks, and rivers."[26] Indeed, many of the Euroamericans currently reviving this practice dream of a distant day when we will not even need therapists—because they have been replaced by elders.[27]

So what role could phenomenology play in informing the practice of vision questing? Consider, first of all, the instructions given to questers in the preparation time prior to the wilderness solo. One common piece of instruction is for the quester to develop what the poet John Keats called "negative capability," which he described as the ability to remain in a state of "uncertainties, mysteries, doubts, without any irritable reaching after fact and reason."[28] The quester is asked to formulate a question or an intention for their quest, but then to let go of any further control over the process and allow themselves to be taken by the experience and surprised by what they discover. What we need to recognize is that this entering into a state of negative capability can, as psychologist Robert Romanyshyn tells us, be likened to the procedure of phenomenological bracketing.[29] In a sense, then, the quester is being instructed in phenomenological seeing. It is not that the vision quester will become a philosopher. But I do think that this negative capability instruction, as well as other instructions aimed at loosening up the quester's perceptual sediments, do constitute a kind of giving away of phenomenology. If, moreover, these instructions were given with more deliberate attention to phenomenological method, then the parallels with phenomenology would become even greater.[30]

I will offer an example from my own experience as a quester in order to illustrate how vision questing can act as a kind of phenomenological experiment. In my own questing I have intentionally avoided adopting beliefs and ritual forms that go beyond a necessary minimum. On my first vision quest, I was therefore indeed surprised, shocked even, when I received unmistakable messages, first from a series of grasshoppers and later from a bird. The choreography of the interaction with the animals or the synchronicity of the event generates a strong personal resonance and the message intuitively comes through, like a window opening. On subsequent quests I have again had this experience of animal communication, even being visited by the same species of bird. The experience for me at these moments is that of somehow being known by the animals and also of feeling an amazed gratitude for their demonstration of kindness. I was delighted, then, to read that:

> According to a Pawnee account, a great council of all the animals (*Nahurac*) meets in perpetual session in a cave under a round mountain (*Pahok*) (actually located, it is believed, near the Missouri River). These animals monitor the affairs of humans wherever they may be on the earth, and if a man or a woman is in need or in trouble and seeks aid in humility, perhaps through the vision quest, the council will choose one of the appropriate members—whether winged, four-legged, or crawling—who will

then appear to the man or woman and give something of its
own power, or present advice that should thereafter guide the
person's life.[31]

Although this is a story from a culture different than my own, from a
land distant from my own, it rings perfectly true for me. While I do
not know anything about a cave near the Missouri River, I have
discovered this dimension of knowingness and kindness—one might
even say godliness—in the animal world. What astonished me is that,
after all the violence that human societies have perpetrated against the
living world, this kindness is *still* being offered to us. But kindness is
of course not the only dimension in the natural world, for there is
cruelness there too.[32] There is also what I call a fierce kindness, where
we get stung by a bee or bitten by a snake when we are being arrogant
or inattentive—where the kindness has a bite to it.[33] If ecopsychologists
can phenomenologically describe these and other such experiences,
then I think the practice will in turn help to build the theory.

At the same time, I believe that certain phenomenological findings
might be fed into, or help guide, the practice of vision questing. I am
again thinking of Merleau-Ponty and his notion of intertwining.
Borrowing an anatomical term for the crossing over of the optic nerve,
Merleau-Ponty also called this perceptual intertwining or reversing
the *chiasm*. The phenomenologist Samuel Mallin calls chiasm "the
deepest universal mode of relation or binding," yet also notes that it
"is a ground that, as Heidegger might say, is withdrawn and shallow
because it is a trait of our epoch to actively repress it."[34] Mallin has
therefore attempted to release his thinking from the regularized, external
mode of relating that characterizes this epoch by philosophizing in an
actively chiasmic way, by letting his own thought be displaced and
shaped by others, in a process of mutual enrichment. Now, if our
concern is to put phenomenology into practice, how might these ideas
be translated into vision questing?

I will answer this by mentioning one chiasm that is often
emphasized on vision quests, namely, the chiasm between dreaming
and waking worlds.[35] There are today a small number of dream workers,
such as Hillman, who promote acknowledging the otherness of the
dream image—allowing it to transcend us, to have a life of its own—
rather than merely reducing it to a symbol of our own personal

unconscious. The depth psychologist Stephen Aizenstat has, for example, developed an approach he calls dream tending, in which all dream images are regarded as the dreaming of the world itself, and in which the goal of dream work is to let these images unfold, speak, and place worldly demands on us. This then opens up a dialogue with the soul or inner life of the creatures and things of the world itself.[36] In my experience, practicing such dream work in a wilderness setting allows the psychological life discovered in the dreaming to spill back out into the larger natural world, so that even when awake one now senses the world as a living presence, with its own psyche and agency. Such dream work, in other words, fosters the ability to perceive animistically. When in my waking life I suddenly have the felt sense that I am in a dream, I now know that I need to pay careful attention because I am about to receive a message, whether from Tree, River, or Bear. Conversely, the more I experience a dream sense while awake, the more awake or lucid I am while dreaming. The more I tend to my dreams, the more they tend to me. In this way, by actively working this particular chiasm, one comes to experience an inter-presencing[37] of dreaming and waking worlds that lends one's life a unique meaningfulness and depth.

THE INTELLIGENCE OF THE ORGANISM:
LETTING THE BODY TALK BACK TO HISTORY

I want to turn now to a theme that no ecopsychology or ecophenomenology can avoid, namely, our belonging to the natural world by virtue of our embodiment. I have been speaking so far about the need to let nonhuman nature speak again, but we also need to let human nature speak again, by allowing our bodies to have a voice. This is a vast topic that can go in any number of directions. As an example of one particular avenue, though, I wish to consider the topic of the inherent intelligence of the human organism, and the implications that acknowledging this intelligence has both for the conduct of our research and for the way we address the problem of historicity.

What do I mean, first of all, by the intelligence of the organism? In coming to this topic, I draw almost exclusively from my background in humanistic psychology, especially the work of the psychologist and philosopher Eugene Gendlin. One of the main ways that humanistic psychology differs from other schools is that it considers the body to be wise. In contrast to the Freudian body of chaotic drives, the humanist's body is itself meaning seeking, being intricately ordered from the inside as a sensitive, knowing relationship with its environment. In Gestalt psychotherapy, for example, we say that the organism regulates our experience in completing need-fulfilling gestalts or experiential wholes within the organism/environment field. Or as Gendlin says, the body is always implying further steps of living that will carry our experiencing forward, even if the actual steps have a certain indeterminacy about them, never being completely specified in advance. Gendlin is quick to point out that he is not arguing for a body unaffected by language, culture, and history, but only that these do not wholly encompass the body. There is always a moment within our lived experience in which the body can talk back.[38]

My point in raising this matter is that ecopsychology and eco-phenomenology, of all fields, surely must acknowledge and respect this deep organismic wisdom at the center of our experience. Indeed, our thinking and researching can itself be seen as an instance of bodily living, as an organism coping with an environment, or creatively adjusting to its situations, as it seeks to meaningfully resolve tensions in the field of its experience. I am myself attracted to the tradition of phenomenology precisely because I find its concepts so satisfying; they are good food for my intellectual hunger. Merleau-Ponty, of course, made a major turn in this organismic direction when he called the body itself the subject of perception. He spoke of a pre-given harmony between body and world, such that our bodies are always engaged in a "communication with the world more ancient than thought."[39] Abram's work has, moreover, extended Merleau-Ponty's thinking into the domain of the body's relationship with the earthly surround. Beyond these moves, however, what I would like to stress is that in allowing the body to speak we can also discover this crucial *life-forwarding* directionality. When we drop down into our body's silent conversation with the world and join with it, what we find there is nothing arbitrary but rather implied steps of living that move in the direction of an increase in vitality, a resolving of conflicts, a forming of satisfying new meanings, a healing of old emotional wounds, a softening of frozen or structure-bound experiencing, an increase in awareness and feelings of wholeness, and many other possibilities that feel right.

By deliberately bringing attention to the meaningfulness of our bodily felt experience in this way we allow ourselves to align with the wisdom of the body and to experience these kind of therapeutic steps. If our scholarly inquiry were itself more explicitly guided by such bodily felt sensing, then it too would take on a therapeutic character.[40] In any event, this is the approach I am personally taking with ecopsychology, seeing it as an attempt to therapeutically link this bodily intelligence with the intelligence of that vaster body of the more-than-human natural world.[41]

The idea here is not to assert the possibility of some ahistorical knowing, for we clearly live within historically sedimented meanings. I am interested only in finding a way to give the earthly places we inhabit, and the human bodies we live through, a challenging voice in a dialogue *with* history. Indeed, rather than surrender to a strict historicism, we may work with the life process in order to develop better interpretations that then alter our historical horizons. One of my interests, in this respect, is in making interpretations of human nature in order to build my own version of ecopsychology, which I am calling naturalistic psychology. I sometimes call my approach the "method of pain," in that by inquiring into our suffering we gradually deepen our understanding of human nature as we are naturally guided through a hermeneutic process that progressively releases us from that suffering. This is also the principle behind Buddhist practice and other experiential therapies.[42] I am simply applying it to the terrain of ecopsychology as a kind of research method.

As an example, now, of the body's ability to talk back to history through the experience of pain, consider the phenomenon of emotional trauma. Medical film clips from World War I show "shell-shocked" soldiers in states of paralysis, violent trembling, spasmodic movements, facial grimaces, and zombie-like behavior. One man, for instance, "lies almost naked on the bare floor, his back rigidly arched, his arms and hands clawing the air, as he tries, spasmodically and without success, to clamber onto his side and stand up."[43] What is striking about these images is that they bear so little resemblance to how post-traumatic distress shows up in our own times. Trauma survivors today often look unperturbed on the surface but are meanwhile living in a private hell of nightmares, flashbacks, suicidal preoccupations, crippling shame, gastrointestinal difficulties, chronic illnesses, and so on. Their distress is less visible and more interiorized.[44] Post-traumatic experience, in other words, has steadily lost its place in the public world, resulting in a compacting of the experience into the private life of the individual, where it rebounds and intensifies in its concealment.

Not surprisingly, the therapy for trauma survivors entails a reversal of this concealing of the traumatic distress, bringing it into contact with the world in a supportive environment. Against the historical interiorizing of the psyche, our bodies call for a re-establishment of safe and loving world-relations. Only when the traumatic event has been publicly named, witnessed, and acknowledged does a life-forwarding, healing process really begin to unfold. The healing process is also assisted when trauma survivors adopt spiritual frameworks that allow them to make sense of their horrifying experience and hold it in their bodies in a less personal, and so less painful, way. While these and other elements of the healing process are by now well known, our historical situation in many ways continues to work against them. The sexual abuse of males, for example, is so denied and stigmatized, so shrouded in shame, that many men will go to their grave without mentioning to a single soul that they were abused in childhood— although they may engage along the way in much road rage, substance abuse, and high-risk behavior. Because we live in such a de-spiritualized age, moreover, many abuse survivors simply cannot find their way to a spiritual practice (such as vision questing) that would place their experience in a larger mythological, natural, or cosmic context.[45] The voice of traumatic pain in our own time is thus asking for a more loving, human, spiritualized world. That's the body talking.

It is not true, then, as many believe, that human nature simply changes across historical epochs. Rather, certain aspects of our nature can be recollected and put into conversation with the epoch. The principle here is to reconnect through experiential work with the life still beating beneath the crusts of our age —"Our hearts survive between/ the hammers," says Rilke—and to let this life talk back. I must take issue with Hubert Dreyfus, then, when he says that in an age of computers "human beings may become progressively like machines."[46] Although he seems unhappy about this, Dreyfus regards human nature as so malleable that he leaves it at that. What is missing from his account is the notion that to be dehumanized to the point of becoming a machine can only be accomplished at the price of depression, repressed fury, panic attacks, chronic fatigue, back pain, and so on—a natural revolt that can be put down only through all our powers of denial, addiction, medication, numbing, workaholism, mystification, and all the rest of it. Rather than put this revolution down, I would rather we join it.

All of this discussion is leading up to a final point about the intelligence of the organism that I can make only suggestively. If the method here is to listen to our pain through experiential work and to take organismic directions from it in changing our lives, then what about the pain of being thoroughly alienated from our earth-home and from the life process within us? This pain is so pervasive and so little symbolized that it is difficult even to name. Bringing this pain to light, then, and letting it guide us back to the earth, is exactly the task of ecopsychology.

CONCLUSION: LOOSE ENDS

To conclude, now, I want to tie up two loose ends.

First, ecopsychology, as I fashion it, is not only a recollective project but also a critical one. If ecopsychologists wish to foster "ecological consciousness" and if our society fosters narcissistic consciousness instead, then the social order simply cannot be bypassed. Ecologizing our therapy practices will not be enough. Rather, we must ask how psyche, nature, and society all intertwine, and then produce a body of critical theory that shows how our pervasive psychospiritual problems and our exhausting of the earth are inherently linked in our nature-punishing social order. Although space does not allow me to pursue it here, I believe that a phenomenological approach is suited for developing a critical theory that appeals more directly to lived experience than other theories, and that supports experiential practices that counter the life-negating aspects of modern society.[47] Finally, although I have attempted to show how a phenomenological approach might lend some scholarly weight to ecopsychology, it would of course be a mistake to say that ecopsychology *must* be phenomenological. It is safer to say that ecopsychology will in some broad sense be hermeneutical: a reinterpretation of humans, nature, and society. But different ecopsychologists will rightly find a variety of ways to undertake the project.

NOTES

1. From the "Ninth Elegy" of Rainer Maria Rilke, *Duino Elegies and The Sonnets to Orpheus*, trans. A. Poulin, Jr. (Boston: Houghton Mifflin, 1975), 63-64.

2. Theodore Roszak, interviewed on the videotape, *Ecopsychology: Restoring the Earth, Healing the Self* (Baylands Production, 1995).

3. As Roszak admits in the afterword to the second edition of his *The Voice of the Earth: An Exploration of Ecopsychology* (Grand Rapids, MI: Phanes, 2001).

4. "The Challenge of Ecopsychology," article in progress.

5. As discussed by Almut Beringer in his "A Conservation Psychology with Heart," *Human Ecology Review* 10.2 (Winter 2003), 150. See also, Joseph P. Reser, "Whither Environmental Psychology? The Transpersonal Ecopsychology Crossroads," *Journal of Environmental Psychology* 15 (1995), 235-257.

6. See Carolyn Merchant, *Radical Ecology: The Search for a Livable World* (New York: Routledge, 1992).

7. The special issue, "Promoting Environmentalism," *Journal of Social Issues* 56.3 (Fall 2000), contains a good sampling of environmental psychology writings in this respect.

8. The psychologists Rachel and Steven Kaplan, who have developed the notion of the "restorative environment," are explicit on this point. For example, they call the natural environment a "resource for enhancing health, happiness, and wholeness" (*The Experience of Nature* [Cambridge: Cambridge University Press, 1989], 198).

9. Hans-Georg Gadamer, "Practical Philosophy as a Model of the Human Sciences," *Research in Phenomenology* 9 (1979), 83.

10. Hans-Georg Gadamer, "The Problem of Historical Consciousness," in *Interpretive Social Science*, ed. Paul Rabinow and William M. Sullivan (Berkeley, Calif.: University of California Press, 1987), 133. Instead of method, Gadamer promoted the idea of research as "the praxis of life itself" and viewed understanding as a "form of community" (Hans-Georg Gadamer, Foreword to Jean Grodin, *Introduction to Philosophical Hermeneutics* [New Haven and London: Yale University Press, 1994], x). From this view, the understanding sought by ecopsychologists must include well-mannered dialogue within the more-than-human community.

11. James Hillman, "Animal Presence" (interview by Jonathon White), in Jonathon White, *Talking on the Water: Conversations About Nature and Creativity* (San Francisco: Sierra Club, 1994), 123.

12. The Fourfold is Heidegger's term for the worldly intertwining of mortals, gods, earth, and sky, as they are gathered together by things, such as a wine jug (see "The Thing," in *Poetry, Language, Thought* [New York: Harper & Row, 1971]). Although some regard the Fourfold as Heidegger's personal mythology, it finds a remarkable echo in the words of a Lakota medicine man, John (Fire) Lame Deer: "I think about ordinary common things like this pot. The bubbling water comes from the rain cloud. It represents the sky. The fire comes from the sun which warms us all—men, animals, trees. The meat stands for the four-legged creatures, our animal brothers, who gave of themselves so that we should live. The steam is living breath. It was water, now it goes up to the sky, becomes a cloud again. These things are sacred. Looking at that pot full of good soup, I am thinking how, in this simple manner, Wakan Tanka takes care of me" (John [Fire] Lame Deer and Richard Erdoes, *Lame Deer, Seeker of Visions* [New York: Washington Square, 1972], 107).

13. Martin Heidegger, "Building Dwelling Thinking," in *Poetry, Language, Thought* (New York: Harper & Row, 1971), 149.

14. In his article Seamon spoke favorably of Joseph Grange's "foundational ecology," saying that it is "a more authentic alternative because it fosters a mode of thinking and action grounded in care and reverence" ("The Phenomenological Contribution to Environmental Psychology," *The Journal of Environmental Psychology* 2 [1982], 135). Grange contrasted his foundational ecology with what he called "dividend ecology." Today, we would recognize this as a form of contrast between radical ecology and mainstream or reformist environmentalism.

15. The technical, instrumentalist, positivist language of environmental psychology offers no help in this regard.

16. Robert Greenway, "The Wilderness Effect and Ecopsychology," in *Ecopsychology: Restoring the Earth, Healing the Mind*, ed. Theodore Roszak, Mary Gomes, and Allen Kanner (San Francisco: Sierra Club, 1995), 123.

17. It is possible, of course, to draw on non-Western sources of non-dualistic thinking, such as Buddhist psychology. I do so in my own work to some extent, but I think it is most important to employ

thinkers whose terms help us carry forward the tradition we are actually living.

18. Maurice Merleau-Ponty, *The Visible and the Invisible*, trans. Alphonso Lingus (Evanston: Northwestern University Press), 267, hereafter cited as *The Visible*. In the same note, Merleau-Ponty also wrote: "Do a psychoanalysis of Nature: it is the flesh, the mother." Elsewhere he uses the term anthropology to refer to a kind of activity that describes "a world covered over with our own projections, leaving aside what it can be under the human mask" (136).

19. I hasten to say that Merleau-Ponty's philosophy offers conceptual assistance not only for ecopsychology, but also for psychology in general. Within the world of psychotherapy, for example, people empathize, role reverse, and re-enter dreams in order to shape shift into various dream figures, and defend themselves through such "mechanisms" as "projective identification" (as we clumsily call it). Yet none of this is intelligible within a dualistic framework. Noteworthy here is Sue Cataldi's effort to develop a theory of emotion from a philosophy of the flesh, *Emotion, Depth, and Flesh: A Study of Sensitive Space* (Albany: State University of New York Press, 1993).

20. His exact words: "This kinship extends to others, who appear to me as other bodies, to animals whom I understand as variants of my embodiment, and finally even to terrestrial bodies, since I introduce them to the society of living bodies when saying, for example, that a stone 'flies'" (Maurice Merleau-Ponty, "Husserl at the Limits of Phenomenology," in *Themes from the Lectures at the Collège de France, 1952-1960*, trans. John O'Neill [Evanston: Northwestern University Press, 1970], 122). In his later philosophy, Merleau-Ponty made much of the notion of kinship, even suggesting that we have "access to objectivity" only because we can experience that "point of intersection and overlapping where families of facts inscribe their generality, their kinship, group themselves about the dimensions and the site of our own existence" (*The Visible*, 116).

21. See, for example, Paul Shepard, *Nature and Madness* (San Francisco: Sierra Club, 1982).

22. Merleau-Ponty, *The Visible*, 209.

23. Cited by W. H. Auden in his introduction to Loren Eiseley, *The Star Thrower* (San Diego: Harcourt Brace, 1978), 16.

24. Andy Fisher, *Radical Ecopsychology: Psychology in the Service of Life* (Albany: State University of New York Press, 2002), 42.

25 David Michael Levin, "Phenomenology in America," *Philosophy and Social Criticism* 17.2 (1991), 103-119. As an example of a worldly application of phenomenology, Levin mentions Eugene Gendlin's Focusing practice. Often used in psychotherapeutic settings, Focusing involves making direct reference to implicit, bodily felt meanings and then allowing explicit words and other symbols to form from this felt sense of some situation. There is now a worldwide Focusing community that uses this practice in a large variety of settings.

26. James M. Wright, "A Cauldron-Born Quest: Speculations on European Vision Quest Rituals," *Shaman's Drum* 46 (1997), 58.

27. I first heard this thought from the wilderness guide Rhona Trotter.

28. Cited in Linda K. Loos, "Sitting in Council: An Ecopsychological Approach to Working with Stories in Wilderness Rites," Ph.D. dissertation, Institute of Transpersonal Psychology, 1997, 435.

29. Robert Romanyshyn, "Psychology Is Useless; Or, It Should Be," *Janus Head* 3.2 (2000), 2. Romanyshyn calls phenomenologists "witnesses of epiphanies."

30. The point I am making in this paragraph was partly inspired by my reading of Erazim Kohák's book *The Embers and the Stars: A Philosophical Inquiry Into the Moral Sense of Nature* (Chicago: University of Chicago Press, 1984). Kohák's book is an inquiry into the moral sense of nature, based on his solitary experience at a New Hampshire homestead over a period of seven years. In addition to the usual bracketing of prior concepts, Kohák undertook what he called a bracketing of artifacts. In other words, he believed that in order to do a phenomenology of nature, he had to remove himself from the bright lights and noisy machinery of the city, had to perform a double bracketing. There is a parallel here with vision questing. In contrast to Kohák's experiment, however, which was that of an individual philosopher, I see the vision quest as an opportunity for large numbers of people, with proper instruction, to undertake their own "inquiries" in the wilderness.

31. Joseph Epes Brown, *The Spiritual Legacy of the American Indian* (New York: Crossroad, 1982), 124.

32. "Life in the wild is not just eating berries in the sunlight. I like to imagine a 'depth ecology' that would go into the dark side of nature—the ball of crunched bones in scat, the feathers in the snow, the tales of insatiable appetite. Wild systems are in one elevated sense above criticism, but they can also be seen as irrational, moldy, cruel, parasitic" (Gary Snyder, "Blue Mountains Constantly Walking," in *Practice of the Wild* [San Francisco: North Point, 1990], 110).

33. I coined the phrase "fierce kindness" after reading Ram Dass describe a massive stroke he experienced as an act of "fierce grace" (Ram Dass, *Still Here* [New York: Riverhead, 2000]).

34. Samuel B. Mallin, "Chiasm, Line, Art," in *Merleau-Ponty: Critical Essays*, ed. Henry Pietersma (Washington, D.C.: University Press of America and The Centre for Advanced Research in Phenomenology, 1989), 219-220.

35. There are other notable chiasms from vision questing practice that could be mentioned, e.g., that between death and life or, to overlap these two chiasms themselves, dreaming and death.

36. Stephen Aizenstat, "Nature Dreaming: Depth Psychology and Ecology," (2003), 4. Available at www.dreamtending.com/resources.html. See, also, Robert Bosnak, *Tracks in the Wilderness of Dreaming* (New York: Delacorte, 1996).

37. Gary Brent Madison suggests that Merleau-Ponty's term "flesh" refers primarily to "the presence of the other in the same" ("Flesh as Otherness," in *Ontology and Alterity in Merleau-Ponty*, ed. Galen A. Johnson and Michael B. Smith [Evanston: Northwestern University Press, 1990], 31).

38. For a discussion of Levin's philosophical work, see David Levin, ed., *Language Beyond Postmodernism: Saying and Thinking in Gendlin's Philosophy* (Evanston: Northwestern University Press, 1997).

39. Maurice Merleau-Ponty, *Phenomenology of Perception*, trans. Colin Smith (London: Routledge, 1962), 254.

40. Indeed, phenomenological practice is always potentially therapeutic. Working carefully with one's experience, mending dichotomies, increasing one's awareness, and making better contact with reality are all both phenomenological and therapeutic activities. The experiential psychotherapies all share in this phenomenological character. While the therapeutic dimension of phenomenology may at times be more latent than actual, or play only a minor role for the

text-bound researcher, I am suggesting here that it be deliberately brought out and emphasized. Gendlin's approach to theory building, which he calls "Thinking At the Edge," does just this. The method of his phenomenology is to make direct reference to a bodily felt sense of some situation or of some knowing that one has, and then to let new words form from this felt place of implicit knowing. See the special issues, "Thinking at the Edge: A New Philosophical Practice," of *The Folio: A Journal for Focusing and Experiential Therapy* 19.1 (2000-2004).

41. I would mention here, in particular, Merleau-Ponty's characterization of the body as an *exemplar sensible* in its exceptional ability to sense and make contact with the manifold things of the world (*The Visible*, 135). It is as if the body contains the entire world within itself. I have in mind here, then, a style of inquiry that therapeutically connects the body's deep worldly intelligence with the intelligence of the world itself.

42. It is present, moreover, in Gendlin's work. He writes, for example, that "The bad feeling is the body knowing and pushing toward what good would be. ... The very existence of bad feelings within you is evidence that your body knows what is wrong and what is right. ... the life process has its own direction and this is not relative" (Eugene Gendlin, *Focusing* [New York: Bantam, 1978], 76).

43. Another man, "who once bayoneted an enemy in the face, now opens his mouth wide into a gaping yaw and then closes it, and opens it and closes it, over and over again" (Mary Sykes Wylie, "The Limits of Talk: Bessel van der Kolk Wants to Transform the Treatment of Trauma," *Psychotherapy Networker* 28.1 [2004], 30).

44. Writing in the early 1960s, the Daseinsanalyst Medard Boss observed that for some time the anxiety and guilt of his patients had been "creeping into the obscurity of the bodily organs" due to a lack of loving or supportive world-relationships ("Anxiety, Guilt and Psychotherapeutic Liberation," *Review of Existential Psychology and Psychiatry* 2 [1962], 174).

45. On this, see James Hillman's remarks in James Hillman and Michael Ventura, *We've Had a Hundred Years of Psychotherapy, And the World's Getting Worse* (New York: Harper Collins, 1992), 26.

46. Hubert Dreyfus, *What Computers Can't Do: The Limits of Artificial Intelligence*, Rev. ed. (New York: Harper & Row, 1979), 280.

47. As I attempted to demonstrate in my book *Radical Ecopsychology*.

Phenomenon and Place: Toward a Renewed Ethics of the Environment

EDWARD S. CASEY

> Nature is a personality so vast and universal that we have never seen one of her features.
> — Henry David Thoreau, "Walking"

> What binds us morally has to do with
> how we are addressed by others in ways that we cannot avert or avoid.
> — Judith Butler, *Precarious Life*, p. 130

I

The "phenomena" of phenomenology are what show themselves—"let themselves be seen from themselves in the very way in which they show themselves from themselves."[1] Heidegger's famous formula attempts to capture phenomena in their manifestness—

Edward S. Casey is Distinguished Professor at the State University of New York at Stony Brook, and also teaches at the New School for Social Research and at Pacifica Graduate Institute. His books include *Spirit and Soul: Essays in Philosophical Psychology; Imagining; Remembering; Getting Back into Place; Representing Place in Landscape Painting and Maps*; and (most recently) *Earth-Mapping: Artists Reshaping Landscape*. He has just completed a new book, to appear in 2007: *The World at a Glance*.

in their very appearing in the light of disclosure. Phenomena in this inaugural sense—which Heidegger traces back to Greek roots in *phainesthai* ("to bring to light") and *phos* ("light")—are the self-revealing par excellence, "that wherein something can become manifest, visible in itself."[2] Heidegger here reconfigures what Husserl had sought in the ideal of *Evidenz*, the moment of eidetic insight untrammeled by the shadows of the natural attitude. This is an insight taking place, asserted Husserl, in "the brightly lit circle of pure presentation,"[3] an epistemic disclosure space wherein "the things themselves" show themselves as they are in their essential structure, their sheer noematic sense.

Heidegger and Husserl both insisted on qualifying their pure photology—as we may call any doctrine that emphasizes showingness as such: truth as light or at least coming into the light, whether light is conceived as the visual rays that so fascinated the Greeks or as the "natural light" to which Descartes appealed. For his part, Husserl emphasized that the evidence proper to things of the perceived world is never more than "adequate," that is to say, partial in its very disclosure; Heidegger took the further step of underlining the factor of concealment, of untruth, as part of phenomenal self-disclosure itself: by 1935, eight years after *Being and Time* was published, he could say that "the clearing in which beings stand is in itself at the same time concealment... Truth, in its nature, is un-truth."[4] But in both cases we have to do with complications of models that remain photocentric in their basic gesture: Heidegger's clearing, aptly named *Lichtung*, may not be as "brightly lit" as Husserl's circle of presentation; but it remains a disclosure space wherein the link between *lux* and *veritas* is indissoluble.

The subsequent history of phenomenology can be read as a series of ever more radical critiques of the photocentric model of insight and truth—to the point where the very idea of "phenomenon" is put into question. Merleau-Ponty's *Phenomenology of Perception* pointed to the ingredient of the pre-reflective and anonymous subject in the activity of perception—a hidden subject who never comes fully to the light of day and who never grasps things in all lucidity: "obscurity spreads to the perceived world in its entirety,"[5] as Merleau-Ponty put it in his great text of 1945. By the same token, Sartre's for-itself is unavailable to ordinary perceptual inspection, being a creature of its own action of nihilation, which is as spontaneous as it is non-phenomenal. Derrida proposes in *Voice and Phenomena* that the Western ideal of epistemic transparency no longer obtains—the perceptual given itself not only withdraws from our grasp, it was never given in the first place and is as much of a "myth" as Wilfrid Sellars argued was the case for the supposed direct deliverances of the senses: in Derrida's words, "contrary to what phenomenology...has tried to make us believe, contrary to what our desire cannot fail to be tempted into believing, the thing itself always escapes."[6] For Derrida, there is no pure phenomenon, just as there is no pure voice; each is invaded by the unsettling traces of indicative signs, which spoil the scene of pure presentation, contaminating it from within by adumbrating what is *not* there—and never can be.

Still more radical is Levinas's move in *Totality and Infinity*, a book that sets out expressly to eliminate the very idea of "phenomenon" from the discourse of ethics. Just as he will have no truck with any photocentric theory of truth, so Levinas forcefully rejects the notion of totality with which it is associated on Heidegger's initial description.[7] Ethical action takes us into the heart of darkness where nothing shines, nothing is illuminated, all is disintegrated. The other human being, ethically regarded, is for me an essentially invisible entity who has permanently withdrawn from the light. Even if I take in this Other from his or her face, this face is no phenomenal surface, no *facies* that my look encounters, notes, or remembers (*that* would be a "countenance," which is nowise ethical in its bearing). Rather, the face of the Other is permanently precluded from showing itself as a phenomenon available in the light of perception. Being in an ethical relation with the Other is responding to his or her call to me to be responsible to and for that Other—infinitely so, without qualifications or reservations. Such an Other is not a knowable, totalizable phenomenon. No full presence, perceptual or otherwise, is here given; only "the trace of the Other" and an evasive, fugitive trace at that.[8]

I would like to propose in this essay that yet another and quite different step needs to be taken—a step as radical as that taken by Levinas but now with respect to an entirely different realm from that of interhuman ethics: that of the natural environment. For this realm is non-phenomenal and non-photocentric, and it resists totalization as fiercely as does the human face; yet all this happens in a very disparate way and to very different effect.

II

But wait? Isn't the natural world just what presents itself most manifestly to human beings and to other living creatures—thrusting itself upon us with considerable force and irrecusable visibility? Is it not as such a paradigm of that which "lets itself be seen from itself in the very way in which it shows itself from itself"? What more evident phenomena are there than the blue sky above and the monumental hills beyond? What is more unquestionable than the ruddy soil underneath my feet and the air I breathe? What is more visible than the open field in which I stand at high noon, the wind coursing through my hair and my body feeling the warmth of the sun? As matters of sheer impingement, these sensed phenomena are surely real. Only an extreme skeptic would attempt to deny them. But we need to consider further. What is real at the level of felt impingement is not necessarily the same as what occurs in the zone between the lived body and the material thing or element. This is particularly true for those aspects of the natural world that are too subtle to discern consciously or forthrightly. The blue sky above may be filled with portents of a storm to come which I have not yet suspected—certain cloud patterns, certain shifts in wind vector and speed, a faint rumbling in the distance to which my eyes are not equal, though other animals may pick up all these things. The soil beneath me may look and seem healthy—green, herbaceous, and flowering—and yet in fact it may be laced with pesticides and herbicides, invisible to the eye and unknown to any one but the farmer who put them there. The effects of these noxious chemicals may not be felt directly by those living in the region in which they figure—say, in Kansas, where I might now be standing— and yet thousands of miles away they are accumulating in the Dead Zone of the Gulf of Mexico, created by their massive buildup in underground streams and overground rivers that empty into the Mississippi, whence they are swept to the Gulf. So, too, the warmth I feel in the same field may be part of a global warming trend which my isolated body is incapable of discerning as such: even if I know that such warming is happening from what I have read, my body may seem to be telling me something very different: as happened in Chicago two winters ago. Judging from the temperatures alone—it was the coldest December since 1871 in the Windy City—how could we conclude, indeed even suspect, global warming?

This last example is far from casual. It is part and parcel of the natural world in which we live today—on any part of the earth, not just in Kansas or Chicago or in New York City. Complicating its perception as a single coherent phenomenon is the fact that this massive warming is consistent with certain effects of cooling in a given place or in a given season or among certain ocean currents. To experience these effects is not spurious—it is correct and genuine for the place and time in which it occurs—but it fails to tell the deeper story. This story is at once too extensive in space (spreading across the entire globe from the upper stratosphere) and too displaced in time (its origins lie in the industrialization of the West two hundred years ago) for us to be able to assess the larger picture that underlies what my skin registers and my body experiences. The issue is not that of sensory deception but of global perception—where the latter is not available to human beings or other animals in their individual life-worlds, some of whom do suffer from such warming (for instance, those polar bears who must now stray from familiar territory to find food) and some of whom do not (some may even thrive in warmer air or water). Perhaps for the first time in planetary life, we cannot trust the truth of our own senses. What is happening here?

Global warming is something so subtle that the supervalent event is difficult to detect as such: meterologists tell us, for example, that there is not so much an increase in the literal number of tropical storms and hurricanes but rather an augmentation in the degree of their severity in recent times. Moreover, a storm like Katrina may not seem so alarming in Houston, located at the outer edge of its path of destruction, and in New Orleans itself its full force was difficult to discern even on the ground: we learned of its extreme severity only months later, by a form of deferred knowledge in the form of unsuspected damage, lives lost, and life disrupted. For those trapped in New Orleans at the time, there was no doubt as to its seriousness as experienced close-up; yet this experience as such does not link to anything existing on a global scale. Even for those suffering directly from its effects, global warming did not exist as a "phenomenon:" it did not come into any clearing, any light—not even for those who know of global warming as a matter of serious scientific postulation.

This is not to deny that the reality of global warming may be indeed measurable—but only over a span of years that exceed any individual or even generational life-time and by methods that make reference to changes that fall outside the range of human or animal experience. For example, in November 2005 the journal *Science* published a study that analyzed air bubbles trapped in Antarctic ice for the last 650,000 years: a striking case of vast removes in space and time which no group of contemporary sentient beings could possibly detect. The study showed definitively that levels of global warming caused by the retention of greenhouse gases has increased from 280 parts per million two hundred years ago to 380 such parts today. This is an amount and rate of increase for which there is no precedent in the entire preceding 649, 800 years. Otherwise put, the rising level of carbon dioxide alone is 27 percent higher than any previous peak during all the preceding millenia—a rate of accumulation more than one hundred times faster than at any other time in the overall period in question. Edward Brook, geoscientist at Oregon State University, remarks that "There's no natural condition that we know about in a really longtime [way] where the greenhouse gas levels were anywhere near what they are now."[9] Not only is any such long-term trend not noticeable by higher organisms, the exact level of the very greenhouse gases themselves that have caused the increase—most notably, carbon dioxide and methane—are not discernible as such by the human sensory system, which is attuned only to such overtly perceptible things and events as melting ice, rising ocean levels, and salient weather patterns.

Of course, the *results* of such changes of *longue durée* are being felt, and will be felt further, by living beings, not only humans but many other species of animal and plant life, especially in the later stages when the changes begin to become manifest; but the thin transverse section of the larger pattern, the current screen through which we "see" it as through a glass darkly, does not announce these changes, confined to one lifetime as our sensings are or, at best, to the several lifetimes of those who benefit from the transmission of knowledge by prior generations. Here we see Nature at work beyond the pale of our habitual sensing—even if it is humans themselves, and only five or six generations of them that have brought on this impending disaster.

It is this very inaccessibility to ordinary experience that has made it all too easy for our nation to refuse to sign the Kyoto Accords and to fail to co-operate in the recent discussions on ways to address global warming—quite beyond the economic costs of the Accords which President Bush has invoked. But to claim that the scientific evidence is moot regarding the contribution of the burning of fossil fuels to global warming—as this administration has also proposed—is no longer defensible in the wake of such a study as I here cite and others like it that are based on indisputable long-term trends whose definitive evidence is locked in the frozen ice of polar ice or found too high in the sky above to see with the naked eye.

III

"Nature loves to hide," said Heraclitus at the dawn of the classical Greek era: *phusis kruptesthai philei*. The natural world is not fully apparent in its own appearances, nor is it transparent in whatever evidence it manages to offer. It does not wear its secrets on its sleeve. This is not to say that it misleads in any systematic way; when it disguises itself in an explicit way, as in animal or plant camouflage, it is in order to enhance or prolong the life of the organism. We need to distinguish such cases of partial hiding—which also include the occlusions afforded in refuges of many kinds (dens, nests, burrows)—from the more radical hiding at stake in the extremes situated at the ends of particular experiential scales. These more extreme cases include what is literally invisible to the eye or untouchable by the hand or unsmellable by the nose: in any case, out of the range of human (and often other animal or plant) sensing. Here I have in mind such mega-things as supernovae and unseen galaxies, or gravity and electromagnetic forces on the one hand and such micro-entities as viruses and bacteria on the other. Since none of these is detectable with the unaided eye, they require the assistance of advanced technologies, starting with the construction of the microscope and teloscope in the seventeenth century and eventually including many forms of radiography, electron microscopy, MRI scans, and the like. We say routinely that such prosthetic devices extend the range of human perception, but we do not mean that by their means we are looking directly into the enormous and the miniscule; instead, we are gaining a readable *image* of such macro- and micro-things—an image that is, strictly speaking, an effect or product of their interaction with our instruments. It is this image, not the thing itself, which we can be said properly to *see*, for only *it* lies within our normal sensory range.

Thus it would be mistaken to speak of invisible stars, or of equally invisible microbes, as "phenomena" — not because they are unreal (in certain respects, they figure among the ultimate realities) but because they are situated outside the range of unaided human perception, even if they are trackable and traceable in their instrumentally mediated images. These images, however, *are* genuine phenomena and must be accorded the full respect which we pay to any other full-fledged appearings. When I stare at the moving image of my own beating heart in an echocardiogram following a stress test, I am not seeing what is normally invisible to me, I am seeing its image—in this case, a visual image that is itself constructed from inaudible ultrasounds sent through my heart region: the action of an unseen organ captured by unheard sounds. This redoubled inaccessibility does not prevent the conveyance of this action in the image at which I look in astonishment! Even here, in the presence of what I take to be a reliable icon of my moving heart, I need guidance to know exactly what I am "seeing," and it takes a cardiologist to spot a thickened heart muscle in the left ventricle of my heart that is evidence of high blood pressure.

IV

When it comes to nature's cryptic ways, its proclivity for withdrawing from full phenomenality, we need to distinguish between two orders of things: *peri-phenomenality* and *para-phenomenality*.[10] By "peri-phenomena," I refer to those things that exist on or beyond the outer edge of unaided sensing—like invisible nebulae or clusters of atoms—and that, as I've just been insisting, require technological intervention to reach them, and then only through the intermediacy of readable images or other traces. But they may also reach us by their sheer effects, as when an imploding star produces a certain luminescence in the night-time sky, even though it has happened untold milllions of years before I register it. In this case, the image is the effect of the event; it is its trace in a percept. All such entities or events circle around the outer limits of my perceptual powers, at their periphery as it were: hence the prefix peri-, meaning 'around' or 'about,' existing at an external edge (such as a perimeter).

By "para-phenomena," I make reference to those things or happenings that stand *alongside* manifest phenomena, contiguous to them and attendant upon them so to speak. Less cosmic or microcosmic in scope than peri-phenomena, such para-phenomena are indispensable constituents of ordinary human perceiving. They include such things as unseen sides—sides that are "adumbrated" by the seen sides and that can be seen in turn by circumambulating the object—as well as what lies just beyond an inner or outer horizon. The outer horizon, one of Husserl's most important contributions to the philosophy of perception, withdraws from us as we move toward it. We never attain it as such, yet it accompanies all that we do attain in everyday perception—hence the prefix *para-*, connoting 'beside,' 'next-to:' contiguous. Instances of natural disguise such as changing skin color and configuration fit here, since the coloration or patterning of the skin allows the disguised animal to fit into its natural surroundings in a virtually indistinguishable manner: to appear inconspicuously and unsuspiciously next to other natural things as if one of their own kind.

Further reinforcing the differences between para- and peri-phenomena is the fact that whereas the invocation of scientific investigation is virtually indispensable in the latter case, it is only optional in the former. When a citizen of the Adirondack region is subjected to acid rain, he or she may well witness the effects of such rain in the damage done to tree life and growth but cannot *in experiencing such rain itself* detect the acidity that is the cause of such damage. As a straightforward *phenomenon*, the rain presents no qualitative difference from ordinary "clean" rain—nothing at least which the human sensory system is able to discern in its untutored state. It requires the expertise of ecologists and meteorologists to determine the chemical composition of the rain as well as the geographic source of the detrimentality: in this case, to know that the unfiltered emissions from midwestern power plants end up in rain that falls in upper New York state. The acidity itself is a peri-phenomenon, and to grasp it calls for intermediate sciences that trace out the causal sequence from the original emissions to the noxious effects that emerge elsewhere. Just as *ta mathemata* connect the realm of the Forms to the domain of perception in Plato's epistemology, so here too we require the equivalent intermediaries (now in the form of geosciences) to bring source and effect together in something we can decipher and understand.

The situation is quite different with para-phenomena. In their case, the scientifically naive subject can be trusted to give an adequate, if not a complete, interpretation of the corresponding hiddenness. If I am in a semi-tropical rain forest, I may at first miss the presence of a chameleon who has effectively blended in with the plants around him: rather than a phenomenon that stands out as such, this animal has become a concealed para-phenomenon at the edge of the flora that surround him. But as I look in his direction, I suddenly note his body moving, a displacement of mass that catches my eye and allows me to disambiguate the scene before me. I do this with comparative ease, and certainly without invoking any detailed knowledge of the pertinent ecology or biology. I realize that I was momentarily misled and engaged in a literal oversight of the creature without having to know just how or why chameleons have evolved into their contemporary forms or why they inhabit this particular rainforest. I know what is happening in my immediate surveillance of the scene—know it sufficiently well to grasp the situation as it unfolds on its surface—whereas I do not know what is happening in the experience of acid rain, whose origins and toxic effects cannot be grasped without appealing to what I might learn, on another occasion, from knowledgeable third parties.

Together, peri-phenomena and para-phenomena constitute two major regions of that which is not presented, and thus not recognized, on its face—on its own sur-face. If it is true that "the surface is where most of the action is,"[11] this holds only for *phenomena* in the strict sense, the manifest faces of things and events. It does not hold for that which lies so deeply under the surface as to be buried entirely, or for that which is so high and far above it as to be beyond perception. In each of these latter two cases, that of the sub- and the super-sensory—which I have identified with peri-phenomenal macro-cosmic and micro-cosmic worlds—there is no proper surface at all, nothing to be perceived as such. In the case of para-phenomena, however, the surface continues to be in play, only now as disguised, adumbrated, or horizoned. In their instance, it is a matter of shifting or slippery surfaces, off from which we slide toward something else, whether this be the form of a moving animal or another side of an object or an adjacent region with its own configuration of surfaces.

An important caveat: in pursuing Heraclitus's apothegm, I am not (and I think he was not) claiming that nature is somehow *intending* or *trying* to hide itself. That would be unduly anthropocentric, and here I follow Kant's strictures in *The Critique of Teleological Judgment*: any intentionality of the natural world has to be regarded as imputed to it by human reflective judgments, posited in it without being considered actually constitutive of it.[12] We need not assume that nature expressly *aims* to hide itself to recognize that it consists in many layers and modes of hiddenness. It is to two of the most important of these varieties of the hidden that I have been pointing in talking of peri-phenomena and para-phenomena: two ways of not coming into the lighted clearing of truth.

Even if the attendant obscurities of para- and peri-phenomena do yield to eventual understanding, it remains the case that drawing back one veil often reveals only yet another veil, now at a new and deeper level. For it is not as if Nature will be laid bare by one grand unified theory that is equally able to clarify and explain everything at once—whether within a single species, or between species, or beyond any speciation. More, and still other, things will be hidden; the otherness of Nature is intransigient—at least as much so as, and very likely more than, the otherness of human beings to one another. This is a very basic challenge to any phenomenology that would claim it can describe all things, natural and human, as manifest and fully lit "phenomena."

V

Instead of keeping within the confines of earlier usages of "phenomenon" by first and second generation phenomenologists—or chucking it out altogether, as does Levinas—I am in effect proposing that we consider expanding this very notion to include peri- and para-phenomena, so as to respect the undeniable fact that there are several significant sorts of hiddenness in and of nature. This has the advantage of securing for phenomenology new dimensions of present and future work—especially as phenomenology engages more fully with the environment in the wake of piecemeal efforts made by Husserl and Merleau-Ponty in their very last writings.[13] Such an approach has the further advantage of not merely waving toward a mystery before which one lays down one's philosophical arms. Nature does work in mysterious ways, but this does not mean that we cannot make important inroads into these workings, whether in science or in philosophy, including a philosophy of a distinctly phenomenological cast as it takes in the natural world, as well as creative cross-overs between phenomenology and science. Goethe's *Farbenlehre*, meant as a serious contribution to the scientific understanding of the human experience of colors, was in effect a phenomenological project *avant la lettre*. Similarly, J. J. Gibson's ecological model of perception is equally an advance in perceptual psychology and in descriptive phenomenology: both at once. Science and philosophy constructively converge in the very idea of phenomenon, so long as we are willing to acknowledge the remarkable range of this latter term, its full family escutcheon as it were.

In much the same cross-over spirit, but moving in the reverse direction, I want also to propose that we *restrict* the very meaning of the term "environment"— narrow it down to more manageable proportions than it has come to assume in recent decades. "Phenomenology" and "environment" can only meet meaningfully if the term "phenomenon" is opened out beyond its traditional employment, while "environment," in contrast, is reined in considerably from its ordinary acceptation, wherein it is referred to as "the environment" — as in the title of this essay. The truth is that "*the* environment" is an impossibly broad term precisely because it is so abstract: as if to say that there is only *one* environment, and as if the very meaning of "environment" were already clear to us. In its very abstraction and amorphousness, it can stand for things as different as "urban environment" and "natural environment" — or even for "educational environment" and "political environment."

Nevertheless, most speakers of English favor "natural environment," which I have presumed to be the case throughout this essay. But this first narrowing down is still not sufficient. We still have to ask: is there such a single thing—entity, event, or region—as "*the natural* environment"? I do not think so. The most plausible single candidate for this generic term is the "biosphere," which encircles the earth but does not occupy all of it: it is not found within tectonic plates, or in the many forms of vulcanism rising from the earth's core. Even with "biosphere," therefore, we are still dealing with a term of high generality, and we need to look for a more delimited model if we are to build any effective bridges between "phenomenology" and "[natural] environment."

The important step we must take is to admit that *every* environment, natural or contrived, presents itself only in a concrete place-world—in its terms and within its limits. For it is only in a given place that we can be said to *experience* an environment—such that it surrounds us closely and is a proximal presence to humans, other animals, plants, soil, and even to stones, water, and air. How is this so? Here phenomenology can be of specific assistance, perhaps more so than any standing science, whether foundational or intermediate. For it is well situated to describe the detailed infra-structures of the local environments that cling to particular places. Although these local-environments are clearly and closely related to each other, each becomes highly singular in a given instance—just *this* environment as it obtains for *these* organisms, uniquely configured for them, both *between* them and often *within* them.

It is not surprising, then, to find that working ecologists have proliferated terms that capture different aspects of such environmental place-worlds: "eco-niches," "ecotones," "eco-systems," "ecological communities," "bioregions," and the like. Even though these overlap —with a bioregion being the most inclusive; so that a single place, like a lake, is linked to the watershed of which is it a part[14] — each of them reflects a very particular set of related parts, forming a unique ecological profile as it were. We may understand them as features of different natural place-worlds, each of which is distinctive but all of which are ultimately, at some level, connected with one another. Doubtless it is the interconnectivity that is meant when we speak grandly of "the environment," which is no given thing or place or event but a pastiche of particular place-worlds that interact while remaining distinctively different in each case. As a consequence, the interconnectivity itself will differ in accordance with which place-worlds are brought together: which watersheds, which eco-systems, which eco-niches.

What makes up a particular place-world is not only its literal, material constituents, organic and inorganic, and their shared history, but the characteristic *edge* of such a world—by which edge it is defined not only geographically but also environmentally. An environmental edge is not some mere demarcation and is rarely linear, much less rectilinear. It is, instead, a porous boundary through which many things pass: leaves along with dust and various microbes, the wind that carries the leaves, water, various species of animals and plants, sunlight and darkness. However porous it may be, however difficult to detect, it acts to surround a given eco-place (as we can call this most basic environmental unit: a place-world in its environmental specificity). It is a remarkable fact that many of the most important environmental events occur in and through the edges of eco-places— say, the edge of the savanah in central Africa, where crucial events in human evolution occurred, or the edges of the earliest settlements, where (as Darwin speculated in *The Origin of Species*) innovations happened that led to fundamental adaptive mutations in the early hominids. So indispensable and powerful is the edge of any place-world that I am tempted to say (varying the Gibsonian formula for surface) that an edge is "where most of the action occurs." For it is by responding to the challenges of an edge that feats of adaptation arise and deep-level change occurs: "change comes from the edge," as Rebecca Solnit has said.[15]

The edge of an eco-place is itself an instance, a particularly telling one, of a para-phenomenon: an environmental edge is, after all, an enclosure that acts to contain a particular eco-system, however loosely it may do so. The decisive difference from previous kinds of para-phenomena I have considered is that in this case the role of lived bodies—animal and floral—is especially prominent in their constitution and emergence. An eco-place is animated by such bodies, which are acutely aware of the edges of the circumstance, often acting and moving in relation to them. There are, of course, eco-places that do not seem to contain any living, much less lived, bodies—e.g., mountains above a certain height, or Antarctica in some especially barren stretches, though even here microbial bodies may well be in play, as they are at the bottom of the deepest seas. Nevertheless, robust place-worlds do characteristically feature lived bodies in various forms of intimate interaction. Think only of an ordinary freshwater lake, where the bodies of fishermen, fish, zooplankton, and plant life such as reeds and spartina grass all form a nexus of close relationships—in effect, a world of para-phenomena bound together and dependent on each other. In this world, the locus of a lived body vis-à-vis an edge (whether that of the lake itself, or of its upper and lower surfaces) is not merely a matter of exact location or general orientation but often an issue of life vs. death. Where an organism is in relation to a given edge will determine its very existence, since both nutrition and predation typically occur at or near a particular edge, which is both recognized and respected by the organism (here is the root of "territoriality"). There is a veritable ecological community of diverse kinds of living (and dying) bodies to be found in this circumstance—as Thoreau already grasped so discerningly in *Walden*.[16]

Edges and bodies together make up the inner dynamic of an enviromentally specified place (and every place, including an urban place, is so specified). They are the active epicenters of any such place —as well as the more capacious bio-regions that such places make up in their complex interactions and mutual influences. The phrase "any such place" refers to the singularity of the circumstance, and edges and bodies contribute immensely to the generation and maintenance of ecologically significant place-worlds (and there are no such worlds that are *not* without ecological significance). Without them, these worlds would be lost worlds, adrift in an indifferent space that lacks telling boundaries for the intense centers of energy that all organisms embody. Bodies and edges are the singularizing forces within a given place-world, whose other parameters exist at a much more abstract level: e.g., biochemical composition, physical and electromagnetic forces, molecular structure, etc. An environmental phenomenology must not only take these parameters into account; it must re-think "environment" itself in their terms. In this way "the environment" is brought down to earth and is given a much-needed concretion—a local habitation and a name: "Lake Louise," "the Hudson River," "the Mohave Desert," "the Adirondacks."

VI

As my own description risks becoming abstract in its own way— e.g., by speaking of "edges" and "bodies" as if these were neutral collective terms—let me give a concrete example from the heart of New York City: Central Park. This is not just a landmark place, unique to the world's great cities in its accessibility and sheer size. The Park is a considerably complex ecological community of its own. It brings together, in one ecologically multiplex place, many things that would be classified separately as "natural" and "cultural:" hills and lakes and birds and trees and shrubs on the one hand, strolling human beings, landscape architects, police, concessions and playgrounds, restaurants, a swimming pool, outdoor theaters, and one major museum on the other. These all co-exist equably to form a continuous place-world that contains elements of human history and politics as well as many non-human entities situated in the same space. Especially remarkable is the fact that this teeming world is set within a strict rectilinear shape bounded by 57th St. and 110th St. on the south and north, and by Central Park West and Fifth Ave. on the west and east, and that it is traversed by roadways that carry cars and taxis every which way. These incursions of civilization do not spoil the always resurgent eco-place; they are incorporated into it as surely as are the gates and walls and monuments that are situated throughout. There is a rare sense of ecological equipoise throughout—an equipoise whose precise constituents change from hour to hour but which perdures through many intervening changes. Whole ethnicities have come and gone through the Park; diverse flora and fauna have populated the pathways and hilltops and open fields; yet a sense of persistent identity has been nurtured and maintained for almost 150 years now, ever since Olmstead and Vaux became the primary architects in 1858.

In this exemplary place-world, bodies and edges figure prominently. Any living body, save for birds and burrowing beasts, enters through gates and other openings—one gate on the west side is significantly entitled "Strangers Gate," since every body entering from without is a stranger to the scene until incorporated into the life of the Park: at which point everyone and everything becomes a co-inhabitant, however briefly and even if unknown to (and unseen by) each other. The collective moving bodies activate the Park's many pathways, those that are informal and barely marked as well as those more conspicuous and clearly indicated. These bodies move in relation to various sets of edges—edges of the paths themselves, the contours of the natural features (rocks and lakes and trees), the outer sidewalks and streets. None of these bodies loses track entirely of these edges even when they are out of sight: the sound of traffic also adumbrates an external edge. Between bodies and edges there is a continuously affirmed bond— a pact of sorts, a literal com-pact, a form of "natural contract" you could say, spontaneously realized and just as spontaneously undone and then redone. The result is an ongoing pageant, rarely programmed or planned, one that is happening at its own pace and in its own place.

I shall not belabor this example. It is quite unique. But so is every place-world of ecological import. And every such world bears such import. It carries it with it, not just on its surface but as part of its deep material identity. This is true even of the most civilized circumstance: for example, in the plaza before St. Peter's in Rome, where fountains course and spout, doves and seagulls fly overhead, and many human bodies make their way on various kinds of pilgrimage, all in the shadow of monumental architecture. Framed by Bernini's colonnade and Michelangelo's dome, this is a place alive at all times of the day and night. It is an instance not just of the mathematical sublime—as Kant claims expressly of St. Peter's[17] — but of a dynamic sublime that is as natural as it is constructed. The Romantic credo "Nature Alive" is as true of heavily built St. Peter's as it is of the hills outside Rome. There is no place on the earth's surface that is not thus alive to some degree, and the aliveness itself is due to the interplay between bodies and edges, constituting every successive place-world as a distinctive eco-place that combines factors of the natural and the contrived, rendering them coeval in the generation of a local environment.

VII

My approach in this essay has been two-fold: to distend the meaning of "phenomenon," while constricting that of "environment." On the one hand, I have rejoined Levinas and Derrida in their skepticism toward the photocentrism that privileges illuminationist models of evidence and truth as they are presumed to manifest themselves in the pure phenomenon. Instead of invoking a non-phenomenal human Other or an ever-deferred appearance of the trace, however, I have suggested a strategy of proliferating the senses of "phenomenon" itself, identifying two main varieties of the phenomenal in environmental experience—neither of which is perfectly self-revealing, a matter of sheer show. These less than fully transparent phenomenalities implicate the invisible extremes, first, of peri-phenomena located outside the range of human sensing, constituting a vertical *axis mundi* that extends from galactic proportions to the nano-sphere; then of para-phenomena of the contiguous in the mode of concealment (whether as disguise or occlusion), and more generally anything lying on a horizontal axis of displacement. These two basic forms of less than evident phenomenality (and doubtless others that I would designate as "pre-" and "sub-phenomenal") fall short of Heidegger's criterion of being seen "from themselves in the very way in which they show themselves from themselves," just as they fall outside (or are concealed within) Husserl's "brightly lit circle of pure presentation." To invoke them begins to do better descriptive justice to the polyform hiddenness of the natural world, its evasion of direct capture in unblinkered observation, including the telling fact that it is more likely to be caught in a perspicuous glance than in a prolonged gaze.[18]

On the other hand, I have proposed a narrowing-down of the term "environment," including the idea that there is such a thing as "the" or "one" "natural environment." Rather than the unity or totality which such terminology implies—as if there were only a single such thing—a nuanced phenomenology of the environment holds that what is genuinely environmental occurs, and is experienced, solely in its unique concretions in particular place-worlds, arising and appearing differently in each such world in the form of a singular "eco-place." I have advocated this latter term not to replace the technical language of ecology—with its admittedly more precise terms such as "ecological niche," "bioregion," "watershed," and the like—but to supplement this language with notions that are more sensitive to the felt character of a given place, whether located in wilderness or in the city: felt specifically by human and other animal and plant bodies as they exist in that place. The work of scientific ecology is indispensable in helping us to understand the larger workings of the natural world. It is only by its rigorous investigations (aided by other geosciences, and by medicine) that we shall be able to grasp fully what is happening in the emergence of global warming, or in the relationship between chemical pollution and nuclear radiation of soil and food and various kinds of cancer. But in every actual instance of exposure to the effects of warming, or of pollution or radiation, it is always a lived body in a particular place that is at risk. Even if that body cannot consciously detect the deeper danger on a given occasion—and I have emphasized how often it cannot: how the danger does not appear as a discrete phenomenon —its felt experience on that occasion is overlooked with peril.

What counts phenomenologically is that this body, my body or yours or that of the racoon who visits my house at night or that of the tree that stands sentinel in my yard, apprehends what is happening to it within a coherent world: even if this "what" may be withdrawn from view. Phenomenological description singles out the salients in this world—above all, those salients I have called "bodies" and "edges" —while allowing for their immense variation in experiential modalities across different place-worlds. Such description of such things need not be inimical, or indifferent, to ecological science. It offers an important addition to the explanatory urge of such science: namely, a detailed testimony of what it is like to be a lived body living within the edges of a given place. If place-worlds are indeed the concrete ways in which any natural or cultivated environment (and their very frequent combination: as in Central Park) occurs for earth's inhabitants, then the experience of these inhabitants cannot be left out of account: for there are no such worlds without such experience.

There is an underlying premise common to both of the moves I have made in this essay. This is that the natural world, the so-called environment, is not just around us, arranged at some safe distance, arrayed in its own separate splendor, but it is also *with us* and *within us*, both at once. Because it is so intimately located in relation to us— as it is in regard to any animal, plant, and mineral body—it cannot be some single gigantic Thing or Space, that sails straight over our finite saliencies. Nor can it be a pure blazing Phenomenon, utterly self-disclosed and indeed unclothed (as Bacon wished Nature, considered as a woman's body, to become in the hands of modern science). As a nexus of particular place-worlds, the natural world is not right in the light, it does not dazzle in a perpetual high noon. Instead, it has always already found its way into the innermost crevices, the hidden interstices, of the myriad places and regions inhabited by all the creatures of the earth, each in its own idiosyncratic way. It has gone, if not altogether underground, then into the dense and dank bodies on the ground itself, into their sense organs and gullets, their animal and plant and mineral bodies—there to reside in a darkness that is altogether dynamic. This is why I have had to emphasize hiddenness in the face of photocentric models spawned from an excessive theoretical optimism doubtless inherited from the Enlightenment, and it is also why I have underscored the particularity of the places, the discrete eco-places, in which Nature locates itself in its cryptomania, its preference for veiling the truth rather than for outright revealing it. To recognize the polyvalence of phenomenal appearance—the many ways of *not* being altogether apparent—is to recognize the indefinite plurality of place-worlds and their organic and inorganic constituents. To embrace one is tantamount to embracing the other; it is to have polyvalence and pluralism alike.

VIII

In drawing to a close, I would like to consider certain consequences for ethics. This is called for on two grounds. For one thing, the word "ethics" itself can be traced back to *ethea*, the Greek word for the place where wild horses go to rest at night: the imbrication of ethics and place has a long history. For another, I sense that we are still waiting for a more convincing ethics of the environment than has so far been achieved in more than half a century of discussion of this timely but elusive project. I do not mean to belittle accomplishments to date in this burgeoning area of philosophical work: they are genuine and significant, ranging from Aldo Leopold's "land ethic" and Holmes Rolston III's idea of the "intrinsic value" of nature to many more recent notions, including important work on animal rights on the part of Tom Regan and Peter Singer. But I am convinced that something has been missing.

Missing is something analogous to what Levinas found lacking in existential, and more broadly humanistic, ethics: recognition of the sheer otherness of the human Other. Not only is this Other invisible qua phenomenon, but it possesses a sheer alterity that Levinas labels "absolute" in that it is never merely a function or reflection of human needs and interests, however altruistic or admirable these may be. The Other presents her/himself to me as absolutely destitute, a sheer vulnerability commanding me to respond to him, to be deeply hospitable toward her. Such an ethical demand as the Other here places upon me is bottomless—it is nothing short of "a traumatism of astonishment"[19] — and Levinas conveys my undilutable responsibility for the Other by the image of bread being seized from my mouth by the Other's call to me. I must be prepared to give up my own nourishment to answer this call: a call that issues from the Other's face as I relate to it in my very separation from this Other.

I am not the only one to believe that that this model of ethics, however exacting and extreme it is, is a path that merits pursuit as we rethink ethics in the interhuman realm. But I have begun to believe that we also need to open a trail in the non-human domain that is analogous, if not precisely parallel, to it. Elsewhere, I have suggested how we might take the first few steps along this trail, guided by the activity of the human glance as it takes in the natural world with a special discernment that is freed from the burden of belabored observation.[20] Throughout, the guiding principle is that articulated by Levinas in *Totality and Infinity*: "the absolutely foreign alone can instruct us."[21] If this is true in the domain of human ethics, I take it to be all the more compelling in regard to a renewed environmental ethics, where we must cope with the still more intensive and extensive foreignness of the natural world in its endemic hiddenness.

The dilemma for any such ethics is this: beyond Nature's massive non-manifestness, there is the disturbing fact that it gives us no obvious clues as to how to act toward it ethically on our part. If there are any such clues, they are themselves hidden from our perception. The human Other signals its destitution in expressive signs: *the face speaks*, as Levinas insists.[22] In the natural realm, in contrast, we are at a double loss: we have no full accessibility to its hidden modalities, nor is there any effective or intelligible conveyance of imperatives to act on its behalf.

Confronted with this dilemma, I shall limit myself to the following line of thought. Nature's proclivity for concealment is not some cat and mouse game of flight and pursuit but is essential to the natural world itself, which is such that, as Thoreau says, "[humans] have never seen [even] one of her features." This gets it just right: Nature does not parade itself before us in a series of pure phenomena, transparently displaying its deepest needs. All that we receive from it are epiphenomena (I have called these peri- and para-phenomena) and then highly ambiguous ones when it comes to indicating how we should behave toward it. Part and parcel of its concealment is a lack of forthright directives to which we humans can straightforwardly respond. At best, we can be moved by environmental damage and distress and try to heal the most obvious wounds such as strip-mining and clear-cutting—and to prevent future injury.[23] More important, we must recognize that environing place-worlds are worthy of our respect as much, if not more, than other human beings. "If not more"

—well, really, *more*. Not just because the non-human world is so *injurable* and *precarious* (as is any human being)[24] but because it is in fact so *resourceful,* an undelimited reservoir from which we and other species of plant and animal take our rise; in this latter capacity, it possesses a sheer *abundance* that elicits an astonishment comparable to that attributed by Levinas to the ethical encounter with the human Other and that is also akin to the Greek experience of "wonder"(*thaumazein*): the "sense of wonder is the mark of the philosopher," as Plato says in the *Theatetus*.[25]

Such abundance, occasioning such wonder, is to be contrasted precisely with the destitution of the human Other. It is not as destitute or lacking but as overflowing that the otherness of Nature calls me, wordlessly, to a new form of ethicality. This abundance takes many forms—for example, that found in the insect world, which has managed to proliferate through millenia at an amazing rate. From an awkward wingless six-legged creature that first crawled out of water onto dry land some 400 million years ago, insects now number over five million living species, far more than those of all other animals combined. They are more essential to the ecology of the earth than any other group of living beings.[26] The story of the evolution of their delicate and effective wings and of their versatile powers of vision is a tale of ever-increasing adaptive ingenuity. Even though it is true that 99% of all species of any kind have vanished from the earth—and that many species are now disappearing at an alarming rate which is due in considerable measure to human depredation such as the devastation of rain forests in the Amazon basin—the insect world itself is continually evolving new species in an awesome abundance.

This kind of abundance, once fully appreciated, occasions not only astonishment at its coping power and sheer productivity; it calls for a form of respect that is ethical in character and that suggests, even if it does not declare, an imperative to this effect: "Do not undermine this abundance when you can avoid doing so." Understood as forbidding the knowing (or just careless) extinction of species, this would be the equivalent of the First Commandment among humans: "Thou shalt not kill," a commandment that Levinas re-affirms by speaking of the "impossibility" of murdering the Other in his or her face.[27] It may be true that members of the non-human environment "have no face,"[28] but it does not follow that they do not make ethical demands upon us and present their own imperatives.

Wonder at natural abundance is a close cousin of Schweizerian "reverence for life," but this famous formula rings of a certain biologism that may mislead us. It is not life as such that is the primary instigator of wonder-induced respect for Nature; to be "pro-life," as we know from contemporary debates, lends itself to tendentious argumentation and outright polemic. Instead, we need a more capacious vessel for the respect we owe to natural things, which certainly include the non-living as well as the living. I take this vessel to be none other than the place-world within which all earthly entities, living or not, reside. Even if these entities may change place-worlds from time to time—as in winged and non-winged migrations of many sorts—and even if the place-worlds themselves alter considerably in composition and character (i.e., from era to era as well as season to season), such worlds nevertheless retain enough material identity to allow us to recognize them as the matrices of the eco-systems that provide indispensable support for the diverse denizens of this planet. Toward these systems along with their constituents we owe a respect that prohibits undue and thoughtless human intervention in their midst.

I would agree with Gary Snyder when he writes that

> the ethics or morality of [being part of the natural world] is far more subtle than merely being nice to squirrels... [It involves] feeling gratitude to it all; taking responsibility for your own acts; keeping contact with the sources of the energy that flow into your own life (namely dirt, water, flesh).[29]

Yet it entails something else as well. This is respect for the place in it all: not just for the very place you now occupy (that way lies lococentrism) but for all the places on earth, each as having its own integrity, its own edges, its own habitat and inhabitants, its own stake in the biosphere, its own place in the sun (however dimly lit it may be, as in the interior of a rain forest). Such places are not pure phenomena in the sense posited by the pioneers of phenomenology, and their putative totalization should not lead us to think that there exists something called "the environment;" but in their sheer superfetation, their teeming abundance, and in their often absolute strangeness, they call for our collective respect.

Our ethical task is not to preserve place-worlds as they are or were (though we can assist in making them as hospitable as possible to their endemic life-forms by enhancing their habitat), much less to change them for the better in ways that we humans would presume to stipulate. We need to regard them as the primary constituent elements of that natural Other, that Other-as-Nature, which calls us to be responsible in a radically new fashion: not only "taking responsibility for [our] own acts," but also being as sensitive to such places as we humans can possibly be in responding to their quietly (and sometimes urgently) demanding presence—so as to attend to the continuing command performance in which all members of the Earth, all earth bodies, have an approximately equal, albeit infinitely diversified, part to play.[30] If we could do this, we would have made a major move toward devising an environmental ethics worthy of its name—one that does justice to the many place-worlds in which we live and breathe, move and have our being: and in which they have theirs as well in exhibiting the equivalents of these same basic actions.[31]

NOTES

1. Martin Heidegger, *Being and Time*, trans. J. Macquarrie & E. Robinson (New York: Harper & Row, 1962), 58; I have changed the nouns to the plural form.

2. *Ibid.*, 51.

3. Edmund Husserl, *Ideas I*, trans. W. R. Boyce Gibson (New York: Macmillan, 1975), 181 (section 69).

4. Heidegger, "The Origin of the Work of Art," trans. A. Hofstadter, in *Poetry, Language, Thought* (New York: Harper, 1971), 53-4.

5. Maurice Merleau-Ponty, *Phenomenology of Perception*, trans. C. Wilson (New York: Routledge, 1996), 199: "l'obscurité gagne le monde perçu tout entier."

6. Jacques Derrida, *Speech and Phenomena*, trans. David B. Allison (Evanston: Northwestern University Press, 1973), 104.

7. "'Phenomena' are the totality of what lies in the light of day or can be brought to the light" (*Being and Time*, 51).

8. See the essay by this title as translated by Al Lingis in *Philosophy Today* (1972); and my commentary in "Levinas on the Trace," in *Papers*

from the Collegium Phaenomenologicum: The First Ten Years (Nijhof: The Hague, 1987). For further discussion of "phenomenon" by Levinas, see his essay, "Phenomenon and Enigma," in *Collected Philosophical Papers*, trans. A. Lingis (Pittsburgh: Duquesne University Press, 1987), 109–126.

9. Edward Brook, cited in "Scientists Track Disturbing Rise in Greenhouse Gases," *Santa Barbara News-Press* (November 25, 2005, B6).

10. I here set aside a third: pre-phenomenality, by which I mean what is coming to phenomenal presence but has not yet reached such presence; as well as a fourth: sub-phenomenality, that is, what lies just under the surface of a given phenomenon.

11. J. J. Gibson, *The Ecological Approach to Visual Perception* (Hillsdale, N. J.: Erlbaum, 1986), 23.

12. Immanuel Kant, *Critique of Judgment*, trans. W. Pluhar (Indianapolis: Hackett, 1987), sections 61-68, esp. 263: "when in telelogy we speak of nature as if [its] purposiveness were intentional, we do so in such a way that we attribute this intention to nature, i.e., to matter. This serves to indicate that this term refers here only to a principle of reflective, rather than of determinative, judgment."

13. I have in mind Husserl's late essays, "Foundational Investigations of the Phenomenological Origin of the Spatiality of Nature" and "The World of the Living Present and the Constitution of the Surrounding World External to the Organism," in Edmund Husserl, *Shorter Works*, eds. P. McCormick & F. Elliston (Notre Dame: University of Notre Dame Press, 1981), 222-34 and 238-50 respectively. See also Maurice Merleau-Ponty, *Nature: Course Notes from the Collège de France*, trans. Robert Vallier (Evanston: Northwestern University Press, 2003), *passim*.

14. "Lakes take in a great deal of material from their watershed— leaves, pieces of wood, and a miscellany of organic garbage. This exogenous material may be eaten by bacteria, which are in turn prey for microzooplankton, which feed larger zooplankton, which in turn feed fish." (Lawrence B. Slobodkin, *A Citizen's Guide to Ecology* [Oxford: Oxford University Press, 2003], 96).

15. Lecture at a conference on Spiritual Activism, Berkeley, California, October, 2005.

16. On Thoreau as a pioneer of modern ecology, see Slobodkin, *op. cit.*, 95.

17. Kant, *The Critique of Judgment*, section 26, "On Estimating the Magnitude of Natural Things, as we must for the Idea of the Sublime."

18. For a more sustained statement of the virtues of the glance vs. the gaze, see *The World at a Glance* (forthcoming 2007, Indiana University Press), chapter two and Afterword.

19. Emmanuel Levinas, *Totality and Infinity: An Essay on Exteriority*, trans. A. Lingis (Pittsburgh: Duquesne University Press, 1969), 73.

20. See the chapter "Glancing at the Environment," in *The World at a Glance*.

21. *Totality and Infinity*, 73.

22. "The manifestation of the face is already discourse," *Totality and Infinity*, 66.

23. I develop this point further in "Glancing at the Environment," *op.cit.*

24. On "the extreme precariousness of the Other," see Levinas's essay, "Peace and Proximity," 163, as discussed in Judith Butler, *Precarious Life* (London: Verso, 2004), chapter five. Butler also remarks, commenting on Levinas, that "the [human] face bespeaks an agony, an injurability" (*ibid.*, 135).

25. Plato, *Theatetus* 155 d (Cornford translation).

26. See "A Pair of Wings Took Evolving Insects on a Nonstop Flight to Domination," article by Carl Zimmer, *New York Times*, November 29, 2005, section D3.

27. On the ethical impossibility of murder, see *Totality and Infinity*, 198, 232-3, 236.

28. *Ibid.*, 140.

29. Gary Snyder, "Reinhabitation," in *A Place in Space: Ethics, Aesthetics, and Watersheds* (New York: Counterpoint, 1995), 188.

30. On earth bodies, see the remarkable study of Glen A. Mazis, *Earthbodies: Rediscovering Our Planetary Senses* (Albany: SUNY Press, 2002).

31. An earlier version of this essay was presented as an invited address to the American Philosophical Association, Eastern Division, New York City, December 29, 2005.

Touching Earth, Finding Spirit:
A Passage into the Symbolic Landscape

BETSY PERLUSS

> That the world inside and outside us rests on a transcendental
> background is as certain as our own existence, but it is equally
> certain that the direct perception of the archetypal world inside
> us is just as doubtfully correct as that of the physical world
> outside us.[1]

About once a month, I travel from my urban home in Southern
California north along Highway 395 and into the heart of the
Owens Valley. The Owens Valley, also known as the "Deepest
Valley," is surrounded by towering mountains. Most notably stands
Mount Whitney at 14,494 feet, saw-toothed and shadowing the small
town below. And, situated across the valley, it is easy to make out
White Mountain Peak at 14, 246 feet, weathered and bald, presiding
over the populace like an old saturnine god. The word "mountain" is
related to the Latin root, *ē-minēre,* which means to stand out, to project,
and to be eminent. Emphatically, mountains bend our heads back

Betsy Perluss, Ph.D., has a doctoral degree in depth psychology from Pacifica
Graduate Institute. Her dissertation on landscape archetypes weaves together insights
from Jungian depth psychology, nature literature, and wilderness experiences. She is
Director of Education and Outreach at the School of Lost Borders
(www.schooloflostborders.com), a training center for wilderness rites of passage located
in Big Pine, CA. She is also Assistant Professor of Counseling at California State University,
Los Angeles.

and turn our gaze toward heaven. One *has* to look up to a mountain. Mountains *insist* on being seen and yet, like God, they cannot be fully apprehended. One must walk *around* the mountain to see the mountain, and in doing so the mountain becomes the center.

From the beginning of history, people from around the world have revered mountains as cosmic centers, or the Center of the World. While the base of the mountain outlines the circumference of sacred space, the axis acts as a medium between the upper, middle, and lower regions of existence. This demonstrates that the bright white peaks are inseparable from the shadowy ground below; sky is inseparable from earth, spirit is inseparable from matter, consciousness is inseparable from the unconscious. Essentially, the mountain and its valley below mirror the Self in its most starlit and sultry existence.

> Heaven above
> Heaven below
> Stars above
> Stars below
> All that is above
> Also is below
> Grasp this
> And rejoice.

— "The Emerald Tablet"[2]

How could we possibly comprehend this alchemical treatise if it were not for shimmering mountains and the sultry valleys? How could we differentiate above from below? How could we feel the palpability of the Holy Other, which exists both within and outside of ourselves, if we could not approach and climb the mountain? I dare speculate that it is the landscape that gave us this very archetypal structure in the first place.

By paying attention to the sensations manifest by the landscape, whether it is mountains or valleys, oceans or deserts, I have come to learn that it is nearly impossible to speak about archetypes without making reference to the natural world. Although archetypal motifs are found in myths, fairytales, legends, and dreams, most of these motifs can be traced to the shapes and patterns found in the natural landscape. Thus, *in addition* to being a mass of rock, the archetypal mountain is also the *cosmic* mountain, linking heaven and earth and fastening the four cardinal directions. Similarly, in addition to being an eroded crevice in the earth's surface, the archetypal valley is the valley of shadow and death or, in other cases, a paradisiacal recess flowing with milk and honey. The archetypal motifs that emerge from the natural landscape are as diverse as the landscape itself, and throughout all cultures and locations we find a vast range of archetypes that take on the appearance of mountains, rivers, trees, oceans, caves, and canyons. Archetypes symbolize the union of soul and earth, and from this union is the birth of a world that is living and sensual, full of character and meaning.

The relationship between archetypes and landscape is most evident in the beliefs and practices of traditional and contemporary land-based cultures where psyche and nature have not yet been split asunder. For instance, Gregory Cajete, a Native American writer and educator from the Tewa tribe, speaks of archetypes as being born from the earth. He writes:

> The archetypes—being born from the earth of a place, and the participation of earth spirits in human conception—are universal among Indigenous people. This perception is reflected throughout the myth, ritual, art, and spiritual tradition of Indigenous people because, in reality, our development is predicated on our interaction with the soil, the air, the climate, the plants, and the animals of the places in which we live.[3]

Cajete uses the term *geopsyche* to describe the landscape's imprint upon the human psyche. He claims that when people live in a particular place for long periods of time, they physically and psychically mimic the characteristics of the landscape. Different landscapes, therefore, produce varied geopsyches. That is, "The development of mountain people as distinct from desert people and as distinct from plains people begins to unfold."[4] Although the concept of species adaptation is not new to biological science, Cajete is addressing something more here. The term *geopsyche* implies that the psyche, as well as the physical body, shifts and shapes according to the landscape, and that it is from this movement that the archetypes emerge.

Jung makes a similar case when he discusses his observations of how the physical world imprints the psyche with mythic images and archetypes. He writes,

> Just as the living body with its special characteristics is a system
> of functions for adapting to environmental conditions, so the
> psyche must exhibit organs or functional systems that correspond
> to regular physical events.[5]

Jung was deeply moved by his experiences among the land-based
cultures of the Taos Pueblo Indians in New Mexico and the Elgonyis
in East Africa, and these experiences led to his interest in the
relationship between soul and Earth. Jung makes the case that the
natural landscape has a conditioning effect on the psyche, and that
particular landscapes give shape to the personality as well as the
physique of their inhabitants.

The interaction between the human psyche and the physical
landscape is a multifaceted one. Although notions such as
projection, *participation mystique,* personification, animism, and
anthropomorphism have been used to explain this relationship, I
believe that it is far more complex and meaningful than such
theories could ever articulate. Taken from a personal experience, the
following is a portrait of a common event, which in all its
ordinariness reveals the intricacy of interaction between the physical
world and the human psyche.

*I am in a coffee shop staring out the window. It is a clear day in Los
Angeles—a rarity—and I can see the mountains far off in the distance. As
I am watching the cumulus clouds forming over the L.A. basin, I drift into
reverie. I am completely caught up in the clouds and the sun's rays streaming
over the sparkling mountaintops. At this moment, a man walks past the
coffee shop window, briefly smiles at me, and continues walking. As his
smile catches my eye, I instinctively smile back. Something about his smile,
perhaps the simplicity of it, fills me with delight. I muse about how my
presence triggered his smile which, in turn, induced mine. He obviously
noticed my daydreaming stance and I wonder what, if any, feelings, thoughts,
or images my reverie induced in him. Then, I remember the clouds. They,
too, provoke a response from me, and I imagine that my presence also has
an effect on the clouds, which they mirror back to me, and I to them, and so
on.*

The above account is simple and mundane, and yet so much
occurred between the clouds, the smiling man, and me. Even the
coffee shop seemed transformed in that brief moment. What filled

the spaces between us? What *drew* me to the clouds, the mountains, and the man's smile? Hillman suggests that the *anima mundi*—the world soul—is the intermediary from which this interaction transpires. He writes:

> Then we realize that what psychology has had to call "projection" is simply animation, as this thing or that spontaneously comes alive, arrests our attention, draws us to it. This sudden illumination of the thing does not, however, depend on its formal, aesthetic proportion which makes it "beautiful;" it depends rather upon the movements of the *anima mundi* animating her images and affecting our imagination. The soul of the thing corresponds or coalesces with ours.[6]

When the soul of one thing corresponds with the soul of another, there is more involved than "meets the eye." My unconscious, the smiling man's unconscious, and the world's unconscious interact with each other in ways that are largely imperceptible to human consciousness. This is to suggest that psyche is not restricted to the human realm but extends to all phenomena, including the landscape.

Jung, who spent his life observing the movements of psyche, also gives credence to the inner subjectivity of the external world. To fully engage the world, according to Jung, is no less than to delve into the unconscious realm of the human psyche. In the final analysis, the two are the same. Thus, it is impossible to conceptualize the physical landscape apart from the viewpoint of the unconscious. Conversely, we cannot ascertain the unconscious apart from its mirror image upon the physical world. For this reason, Jung writes,

> All the mythologized processes of nature, such as summer and winter, the phases of the moon, the rainy seasons, and so forth, are in no sense allegories of these objective occurrences; rather they are symbolic expressions of the inner, unconscious drama of the psyche which becomes accessible to man's consciousness by way of projection—that is, mirrored in the events of nature.[7]

In addition to the statement above, I suggest that the external world is not only a mirror for psychic events, but is also the ground—the *terra firma*—of the soul. Does not psyche need a place for her feet, a mountain to climb, a river to drink from, and a garden to tend? Furthermore, from psyche's viewpoint, is not the unconscious more than simply imprinted by the physical world but also a participant in its creation? "The psyche is the world's pivot," writes Jung, "not only is it the one great condition for the existence of a world at all, it is also an intervention in the existing natural order."[8]

DEPTH PSYCHOLOGY AND LAND-BASED PRACTICES

I do not intend to promote a sentimental revisit to the premodern world. That would be nothing more than a nostalgic yearning for an irretrievable past—a new age version of *participation mystique*. Secondly, although I've lived in Southern California all of my life, my heritage is not indigenous to this landscape. My family immigrated to North America in the early nineteenth century. To assume that my consciousness is related to this landscape in the same manner as the Native Americans would be to replicate acts of colonization, albeit under a friendlier guise. On the other hand, I do follow the lead of poet Gary Snyder, who admonishes those of us who are not native to act and be reborn as inhabitants of this place, as mindful citizens of the land: "Please get to know these rivers and mountains, and be welcome here. Euro-Americans, Asian Americans, African Americans can—if they wish—become 'born-again' natives of Turtle Island."[9] By being conscious of where we live, of our landscape, says Snyder, we cultivate a deeper understanding of who we are. The two aspects, self and place, are inseparable. "Thus, knowing who we are and knowing where we are are intimately linked."[10]

In the tradition of depth psychology, I adopt the metaphor of going *down* and *below* to unearth a new understanding of psyche and nature. Jung writes:

> Its [the unconscious's] contents, the archetypes are as it were the hidden foundations of the conscious mind, or, to use another comparison, the roots which the psyche has sunk not only in the earth in the narrower sense but in the world in general.[11]

To consider landscape from a depth psychological perspective involves a downward movement toward the roots of our being and the wellsprings of our soul. Without a living connection to these roots, we are left only with a dried up and withered perspective of nature and of ourselves. The dig begins in the human psyche, through unpleasant complexes, unruly projections, irrational dreams, and finally reaches down to archetypes and the collective unconscious, to the place where the psyche and the world are the same.

GODS OR COMPLEXES?

> It is time for all the heroes to go home
> if they have any, time for all of us common ones
> to locate ourselves by the real things
> we live by.
>
> Far to the north, or indeed in any direction,
> strange mountains and creatures have always lurked:
> elves, goblins, trolls, and spiders—we
> encounter them in dread and wonder,
>
> But once we have tasted far streams, touched the gold,
> found some limit beyond the waterfall,
> a season changes, and we come back, changed
> but safe, quiet, grateful.
>
> — William Stafford, "Allegiances"[12]

Many ancient myths provide portraits of the natural world filled with living beings such as elves, fairies, giants, goblins, ghouls, gnomes, nymphs, trolls, Leprechauns, and a host of earth spirits of all kinds. These creatures are often regarded as strange or frightful beings that lurk in mountains, dark forests, beneath bridges, or murky seas. But they also evoke a sense of wonder and reverence, for such mythic beings connect us to the land, which, in the ancient world was animated by spirits, gods, goddesses, and creatures of every kind. Many of these divine and supernatural beings have continued to live on as characters in our most treasured folktales and stories. For instance, the Green Man, the ancient deity of the natural vegetative world, evolved into the 14th century, post-Christian Celtic figure of the Green Knight. More recently, J. R. R. Tolkien, in his beloved book, *The Lord of the Rings*, has recaptured elements of the Green Man in the form of the Ents, a race of giant, tree-like people whose sole purpose was to protect the forests of Middle-Earth. Even today, we find characteristics of the Green Man in the garden statues and decor of modern homes.

Some ancient philosophers and architects have referred to the notion of *genius loci,* meaning the spirit of place, or a place that contains spirits. They argued that "divine providence, the gods, had filled the earth with an animating presence," which bestows places with their unique characteristics and virtues.[13] If we maintain the perspective that spirits inhabit the land, then it seems likely that where we are born and the landscapes in which we live call us into participation with these spirits. In the tradition of depth psychology, it is when we forget the gods that they become cultural, environmental, and personal pathologies, or as Jung often pointed out, "The gods have becomes our diseases."[14] In this respect, the land spirits never die. Rather, they transform into symptoms and pathologies crying out for our attention. Whether a physical or psychological malady, a cultural or environmental crisis, nothing sharpens our attention more than a painful symptom— a warning from the gods.

Marie-Louise von Franz also speaks about the spirits of the land, which inhabit animals and plants and play a decisive role in the life of indigenous communities. She writes:

> The spirits that rule over animals and plants are probably the oldest forms in which archetypal contents were imagined; among the Bushmen and the Australian aborigines—that is, in cultures that have remained especially close to their origins—they are actual gods.[15]

In these cultures, it is often the tribal shamans who are responsible for maintaining contact with the spirits of the land. Having undergone a powerful initiatory ordeal, which involves a confrontation with these powerful spirits, the shaman is now able to maintain contact with the spirits without becoming possessed by them. The shaman is the chosen mediator between the human community and the larger community of animals, plants, and the land, ensuring that the two retain a sustaining and reciprocal relationship.

As much as modern culture has succeeded in demythologizing the natural world, mythic and spiritual beings continue to crop up in our fantasies, dreams, and imaginations. And, we need to create and practice our own rituals of initiation for maintaining and nourishing ways of entering into living relationship with these nature spirits. This has become evident to me during my work with the School of Lost Borders, a training center for wilderness rites of passage located in Big Pine, California. It is not uncommon to hear participants describe their fears in terms of the mountain lion, scorpion, or rattlesnake waiting to devour, sting, or bite them during the night. Fears such as these can grip, possess, and freeze a person, leaving him or her feeling helpless. Such fears often take on a larger, mythic quality. They are the psychological demons and dragons which must be confronted before one can be initiated into the next stage of life.

Although wilderness rites of passage, or the "vision quest," have been most commonly associated with Native American traditions, similar land-based practices are found throughout cultures worldwide. Anthropologists have identified a three-phase archetypal structure in the rite of passage, which includes severance, threshold, and incorporation.[16] The *severance* entails leaving behind the roles and personas held within one's home and community. Even more so, the severance is a symbolic preparation for death, including the acceptance of loss that heralds the promise of transformation. At the School of Lost Borders, this involves preparing oneself to leave the security of the group and to go into the wilderness without food or shelter for four consecutive days and nights. If this sounds extreme, it is only because in modern society we have become deeply suspicious and mistrustful of the natural world. But throughout Western history, spiritual seekers commonly used solitude in nature as a means for finding connection to God, for confronting demons, and for gaining spiritual direction. Furthermore, fasting as a spiritual practice has been used as a means for radically shifting consciousness and for breaking down the ego barriers that inhibit connection to the more-than-human world.

The *threshold* stage of initiation involves stepping into the wilderness and into the liminal space where the boundaries between psyche and nature, inner and outer, become less defined. Here, birds, animals, plants, and rocks appear like characters in a dream, and all of nature speaks to those who are willing to listen. Steven Foster and Meredith Little, founders of the School of Lost Borders, write:

> Maintenance of the relationship between 'natural' and 'human' (as in the term 'human nature') is a basic function of the threshold ceremony. Mother nature needs the ceremonies of humans if she is to reveal her sacred face to us.[17]

Finally, when it is time for the initiates to return from their solitude and from the liminality of the threshold, they begin the stage of *incorporation* (literally, to "take on the body"), and return to their communities with a new and deeper vision of self and their relationship to nature. At this stage, the great task is to *embody* this new vision—to make it *real*. In doing so, the initiates become mediators between the human and more-than-human realms, between psyche and nature, and thus play a role in the health and sustainability of the larger world.

As a depth psychologist, I have been keen to observe the unconscious processes that take place during this wilderness rite of passage. In many cases, the spirits, gods, demons, and dragons encountered can be compared to what Jung termed "feeling-toned complexes." Jung defines complexes as "splinter psyches" that appear most often as unacceptable bits and pieces of our selves that have become dissociated from consciousness:

> The aetiology of their origin is frequently a so-called trauma, an emotional shock or some such thing, that splits off a bit of the psyche. Certainly one of the commonest causes is a moral conflict, which ultimately derives from the apparent impossibility of affirming the whole of one's nature.[18]

When complexes remain unconscious, they can have an enormous effect on our feelings and behaviors—interfering with intentions, blocking memory, and cutting off the flow of creativity. Like the spirits of the natural world, complexes can seize us and make us feel powerless. Complexes, like the gods of antiquity, operate as living and autonomous entities within the psyche. For this reason, Jung writes,

> Everyone knows nowadays that people 'have complexes.' What is not so well known, though far more important theoretically, is that complexes can *have us.*[19]

Essentially, complexes are ancient spirits in modern dress seeking our attention. Hillman succinctly captures this idea when he writes:

> Archetypal psychology can put its idea of psychopathology into a series of nutshells, one inside the other: within the affliction is a complex, within the complex an archetype, which in turn refers to a God. Afflictions point to Gods; Gods reach us through afflictions.[20]

In this respect, just as the shamans must survive a grueling and dangerous initiation ordeal with the spiritual forces of the natural world, so too do modern people face the task of integrating their complexes (i.e., archetypal and spiritual forces) into consciousness. Through suffering our afflictions we give complexes form, and in doing so, we outlast their possession and gain access to the gods, which, in turn, guide us back to our archetypal roots buried within and also manifested by the natural landscape. To attune one's heart and mind to the spontaneous manifestations of the unconscious in both psyche and nature, is no less than what Jung called "the individuation process." "We need a relationship with nature …. Individuation is not only an upward but also a downward process."[21] Rituals and ceremonies in nature, such as wilderness rites of passage, can serve as a portal to our psychic depths.

I can see how these compelling psychic forces, such as complexes, have guided me into the wilderness. Over the last decade, I have developed an annual practice of going out into the desert, usually someplace near Death Valley or the Inyo Mountain Range in California. I go out alone for four days and nights with only a sleeping bag, a tarp, and four gallons of water. I enter into the slow and mysterious pace of desert time. My perceptions twist and turn as large things begin to appear small and small things become large. I begin to see images of myself in the animals, bugs, and plants around me. Often powerful thunderstorms pass over just to remind me of my human fragility. At night I see demons and shadows in the form of mountain lions and scorpions. During the day I muse, paying careful attention to slow movements of the desert. The following is an excerpt from my journal written during one of these occasions. This was a particularly difficult trip, given that three days before I left my father was diagnosed with heart disease.

On the third day I wake up feeling weak and dizzy. I can't go for a walk as planned. The sun is already high, but time seems nonexistent. All the small things look big—the spider webs, each stalk of Mormon tea, and the lizard that visits me. I feel a primordial and instinctual longing. The lizard looks at me and moves closer. I feel a time when we were inseparably one. The lizard is me. I am the lizard. The longing for that oneness hurts deeply. I have flashbacks of camping in the desert with my father. I recognize it as the same longing. The warm breeze, the smell of pinion pine, and the lizard make me ache for my childhood. I realize that my attachment to my father is this yearning to return to the place of wholeness.

My complexes, exemplified by my childhood memories of being in the desert with my father, certainly added the emotional fuel that made this experience so remarkable, but I am also inclined to think that the lizard actually came to me, and that the desert herself spoke to my ancestral soul. This is the living, fully autonomous characteristic of the complexes. When we allow complexes to become personified, whether in the form of a lizard, plant, or a human figure, the complex no longer remains unconscious, but becomes a living being with which we can relate. This process of active imagination is what enables us to integrate our complexes and, in the context of nature, rediscover our inherent connection to the psyche of the land.

Although complexes are fragments of the unconscious projected upon the external world, they can also serve as guides into the archetypal realm of the collective unconscious. Furthermore, having traced a complex through the labyrinth of the collective unconscious, we may catch a glimpse of that most primordial state of existence, which ancient alchemists referred to as the *unus mundus,* the in-between realm where psyche and matter are one and the same. If we can learn to sharpen our focus to observe the subtle movements of psyche, both within and without, momentary glimpses of the *unus mundus* begin to appear to the conscious ego, often in the form of synchronistic events, but, more subtly, through a shift in consciousness which gives equal weight to both psychic and natural events. Within the *unus mundus,* psyche and nature are woven together; psyche glides along mountaintops, and rivers flow deep within the valley of the soul. In this union, psyche speaks to us in the form of desert breeze, lizard, pinion pine, mountain lion, and scorpion. "In our soul everything moves guided by a mysterious hand," writes the poet Antonio Machado,

> The deepest words
> of the wise men teach us
> the same as the whistle of the wind when it blows,
> or the sound of the water when it is flowing.

> — "Rebirth"[22]

The Transcendent Function as Mediator
between Psyche and Nature

When Adam and Eve were cast out of the Garden of Eden, they were separated on the earth, and met only afterwards at a mountain near Mecca called by the Arabs Arafat, or The Recognition.

— "Moslem Legend"[23]

Jung refers to the transcendent function as the mediating force between oppositions within the psyche. The transcendent function arises out of intense and concentrated conflicts within the individual. Like the koan of the Zen masters, extreme and painful paradoxes can lead us to a place where we must transcend the ego so that our perception of reality is no longer split into two opposing forces. Jung says that holding the tension of the opposites is essential to bridging the gap between ego-consciousness and the unconscious. If the tension between the opposites can be held long enough without succumbing to the urge to identify with one side or the other, the *third*, a completely unexpected image, one that unites the two in a creative new way, comes into view.

The transcendent function has important implications for an ecological psychology because it can serve as a bridge between rational thinking and archetypal sensibility, thus facilitating a renewed connection between the human psyche and the natural world. The privileging of rational thinking in modern culture characteristically diminishes or rejects the irrational unconscious, hence the archetypal realm, as inferior. The same dismissive attitude prevails in relation to the landscape. The archetypal characteristics of the landscape, such as the *genius loci,* are no longer taken seriously, and therefore remain unconscious. On the other hand, if one can hold the tension between the unconscious psyche and the rational ego, eventually consciousness will expand to accommodate the previously unconscious content. Furthermore, the natural landscape, and all that it contains, will begin to reveal its own psychic nature—its *genius loci.*

Perhaps, the transcendent function is best understood by way of illustration. The following is a story told by a woman who had just returned from a modern day "vision quest," a four-day-and-night solo in the wilderness without food, shelter, or company. Prior to this event, she had been engaged in psychotherapy for many years, working through difficult complexes and coming to new realizations about herself. She had been diligent, paying careful attention to her dreams and tending to her spiritual and psychological development. Nonetheless, she was frustrated because no matter how much she worked on herself she felt that no real progress was being made. When it came down to it, she still experienced the conflicts, struggles, and disappointments that had plagued her prior to beginning analysis. After three days in the desert, she had the following vision.

> *Today I wake up before sunrise. It's a remarkably clear morning. I am enjoying the naturalness of the birds singing, the fresh spring air, and the butterflies that flutter around my sleeping bag. In a state of reverie, I watch the sun slowly rise over the mountains. I'll get out of my sleeping bag when the sun is in full view and I am fully saturated with warmth. But, just as the sun crests the surface of the mountains, I see a monstrous creature, black as the night, attached to the rising sun. He looks like a giant cockroach, dressed in armor with a shield. He flies out of the sun and lands right on my ceremonial circle of stones.*

This woman had been carrying great tension between her innate driving force toward individuation and her inability to escape the struggles of her daily life. Essentially, her dilemma exemplified the tension between spirit and matter, between the desire to move upward and skyward (i.e., psychological development) and the powerlessness to escape her earth-bound humanness. She accentuated this tension by embarking on a vision quest, which required her to be alone for four days and nights in the wilderness without the distractions of modern day life. What she received in return was a gift from psyche, the symbolic image of the black bug, which initially left her perplexed. At first sight, symbols are always cryptic and arcane for they point to something that cannot be directly known by ego-consciousness. Jung admonishes us not to jump to interpretation of symbols too quickly, but to first take the time to pay careful attention to the pure image itself. To interpret a symbol prematurely is to deflate it of its feeling tone and mystifying nature; the tension is alleviated and the process is suspended. On the other hand, to pay attention to the image, despite the frustration of not yet knowing what it represents, is an essential aspect of holding the tension of the opposites.

Fortunately, this woman had learned that images are not to be dismissed as trivial, and so she stuck with the image. She drew pictures of the black bug, engaged it through active imagination, and allowed herself to feel its creepy black bug essence until she was no longer so repulsed by it. It wasn't until much later that she realized the dark cockroach resembled the ancient Egyptian scarab which, according to Egyptian mythology, pushes the sun up from the depths of the underworld. At first sight, the scarab is hardly romantic; it is a disgusting black bug! But, as the myth informs us, the rising scarab also symbolizes the shadowy, instinctual forces that lie beneath consciousness. As Jung has pointed out, the development of consciousness is driven by natural instinctual forces. This woman's vision of the scarab indicated a new rising consciousness that integrates both the light and dark aspects of the Self. Not perfection, but wholeness. She then realized that her painful complexes and worldly struggles are a natural aspect of a developing consciousness; just as black bugs and other grubby creatures are an essential aspect of nature. Furthermore, throughout this process, she developed a new appreciation for her own unique humanness, which in turn expanded her capacity to appreciate, and thus connect with, the larger, natural world.

Marie-Louise von Franz writes, "the symbol helps us over."[24] Holding the tension of the opposites requires paying careful attention to the symbolic expressions of the unconscious as they appear in dreams, symbols, fantasies, and active imaginations. In terms of psyche in relationship to nature, the practice entails attending to the details presented in the landscape—the highs and lows, rocks and trees—while simultaneously noticing the movements of psyche— dreams, feelings, fantasies, and imaginations. What emerges is a symbolic *and* sensual relationship with the living landscape. By holding the tension between the inner and outer worlds of psyche and nature, one is led to an intermediate space—an imaginal place that Sufi scholar Henry Corbin refers to as the *mundus imaginalis* and describes as

> both intermediary and intermediate … a world that is
> ontologically as real as the world of the senses and that of the
> intellect. This world requires its own faculty of perception,
> namely, imaginative power, a faculty with a cognitive function,

a *noetic* value which is as real as that of sense perceptions or intellectual intuition.[25]

The *mundus imaginalis* is the soul's terrain, where the countless voices of the living landscape are heard once again by the human heart. It is a liminal space that is spirit and nature, personal and transpersonal, neither side opting for precedence. According to ecologist David Abram,

> By acknowledging such links between the inner, psychological world and the perceptual terrain that surrounds us, we begin to turn inside-out, loosening the psyche from its confinement within a strictly human sphere, freeing sentience to return to the sensible world that contains us. Intelligence is no longer ours alone but is a property of the earth; we are in it, of it, immersed in its depths. And indeed each terrain, each ecology, seems to have its own particular intelligence, its unique vernacular of soil and leaf and sky.[26]

Holding the tension of the opposites is certainly no easy undertaking. To truly experience the split, to acknowledge it and feel its intensity, can be like trying to cross the Grand Canyon on a tight rope—not only is it nearly impossible to see the other side, but the canyon itself is too deep, dark, and terrifying to fathom. Many of us may experience a very uncomfortable paradox in the realization that, despite the desire to obtain an archetypal and ecological sensibility, we find it impossible to tear ourselves from our dualistic roots. And, even more painfully, despite our desire to heal the wounds that have been inflicted upon the Earth, we are inevitably, and by the very fact of being alive, participants in its destruction. Such is the tension. To reject this indisputable paradox would be nothing less than a wish-fantasy to return to a Garden of Eden. But in contrast with the original garden, this one would be isolated and fenced off from the rest of creation. It is no wonder that in our culture we have resorted to notions of "wilderness preserve" or "wildlife refuge," as if it were possible to manage and organize the wilderness according to our own perceptions of what nature should be. Although preserving our natural resources is an essential undertaking, these metaphors imply nothing less than our attempt to control the wild unconscious, to fence it in, and protect it from outside forces, namely, from *ourselves.* Perhaps the better we come to know our own inner wild natures—i.e., powerful unconscious forces—the less we will destructively manipulate the outer wilderness.

Prior to commencing my doctoral studies, I had the following dream: *I am working on constructing a bridge over a gulch. After a lot of hard work, I manage to build a very nice, solid bridge. I am pleased with my accomplishment.* And so, during my studies, while striving to learn and understand the complexities of depth psychology—which, no doubt, has been essential to my quest—I am having dreams, which each week I quietly take to the therapy room where I discuss the seemingly insignificant events of my life. And each year, I go into the desert for four days and nights to seek visions, and while I sleep at night, I have nonsensical dreams and I ask myself, "How could these dreams have anything to do with anything significant?" These are just dreams and have nothing to do with the important stuff; the big stuff, like saving the world from ecological destruction!

But, as time moves on, I begin to notice patterns in my dreams, and as a result I gradually become more interested in them. I begin to engage in dialogue with a lot of things, such as rocks and trees, and although at times I feel foolish, eventually, quietly, like a faint voice crying in the wilderness, I begin to hear something resonant from deep inside the canyon.

In other words, initially I thought there were only two sides to the canyon needing a bridge, but the depths of the canyon itself were going unseen.

In this respect, the bridge doesn't simply cross from one way of knowing to another; it represents more than just coming to agreement with the other side or finding new remedies to old problems. Rather, this "third space" is totally new. Like a bridge, it is a place on which we can stand and view the wild unconscious that exists both in us and in nature.

THE SYMBOLIC LANDSCAPE

> We need new stories, new terms and conditions that are relevant to the love of land, a new narrative that would imagine another way, to learn the infinite mystery and movement at work in the world.
>
> —Linda Hogan[27]

Any attempt to explain this larger vision of the world through rational language will always result in a partial and inadequate understanding. How can we articulate the depth and width of the soul? To do so is like trying to slide the universe through the eye of a needle. Our rational egos cannot contain the immensity of the world. For this reason, the symbol provides a fundamental form of expression for the collective unconscious. A symbol is the best possible expression of something that cannot be known directly. And because the relationship between psyche and nature cannot be known directly, this relationship is expressed symbolically. Symbols defy reason. They do not succumb to reductive interpretations but instead point to something greater than themselves. The word symbol originates from the Greek word, *sym-bolon,* meaning *to throw together.* Thus, a symbol is a mixture that is neither purely rational nor purely irrational. Jung writes: "The symbol is neither abstract nor concrete, neither rational nor irrational, neither real nor unreal. It is always both."[28]

The creation of symbols is going on all the time within the psyche; symbols appear spontaneously in fantasies and dreams, but we need to adopt a *symbolic attitude* to value them. Jung describes the symbolic attitude as one that "assigns meaning to events, whether great or small, and attaches to this meaning a greater value than to bare facts."[29] From this perspective, everything *matters*—the small lizard, the pungent sage, the faint desert breeze, and dreams.

When we adopt a symbolic attitude, we become more than just the product of our egos, and the natural landscape becomes more than just the inconsequential background to our lives. The symbolic attitude allows for the personal and collective to coexist, creating a sense of "me-ness, personal importance, soul sense, that is not an ego inflation, and at the same time there is an awareness of one's subjectivity being fluid, airy, fiery, earthy, made of many components, shifting, ungraspable, now close and intimate."[30] This way of being enables us to loosen our sole identification with the heroic ego and embrace a reality that is all-inclusive without losing a sense of individuality. Psyche, like the wilderness, is full of living entities, and the ego is just one character among many. From this perspective, we are not just concerned about saving the rainforest, but at this greater level of awareness we are the rainforest, we are the canyons, we are the oceans and rivers. And we are the buildings and cities. Things no longer exist just *out there,* but they resonate deeply in our bodies and souls. They exist in our bones.

To unite psyche and nature within a symbolic consciousness opens the door to a new awareness of self in nature. This became clear to me during a recent solo excursion into the desert regions surrounding Death Valley. Shortly before the trip, I had a discussion with a friend of mine about the disparity between irrational and rational ways of perceiving the world. According to my friend, to converse with non-human things, such as rocks and trees, is irrational and thus intolerable. I couldn't agree with her logic. I have endeavored to listen to psyche's voice through the world around me via active imagination, dream tending, and wilderness experiences. And, because of psyche's presence in such things, I know quite well that it is possible to listen to and discern the language of stone, tree, river, and wind. Nonetheless, I began my quest with a great debate going on in my head: is there a psychic realm where the world is animated with soul, or am I just fooling myself?

And thus, on this early spring morning, I embark upon a walk within the desert landscape of Eureka Valley. My only intent is to walk as freely and openly as I can, and to pay attention to the sounds and sensations that unfold around me. But, perhaps my intent is not so simple. I want to see what lies beyond the exterior of things. I want to know the spirits that inhabit this land. I meander up the wash, which is sweetly in bloom with creosote and little golden poppies. Eventually, the wash leads me to a great pile of stones, a hundred feet high. Each stone looks like an old face, aged, hardy, and wise, carved out by millions of years of erosion. I sit beneath the stones and listen to the wind that is blowing through the crevices in the rocks. The sound and motion of the wind lulls me. I sit and listen for a long time, intermittently dozing off, falling into dreams, and re-awaking to the sound of wind stirring the creosote. Suddenly, I hear voices, deep and resonate, emanating from the canyon. The sound startles me. I turn to look up the wash, but I don't see anyone. My heart begins to beat hard as if the voices are vibrating within me. I sit and listen for a long time. Eventually, the voices cease, the wind stops, and a great stillness saturates the wash. I feel incredibly calm. I look upward and see the full moon cresting the canyon wall, illuminating the place where I sit.

My experience in the desert wash left me a little perplexed. Did I really hear voices coming from the canyon? Or was I tricked by the sounds of the wind? Certainly, the way wind moves along the rocks and plants could produce auditory sensations of all kinds. But what made this experience so remarkable was that it did not matter to me whether the voices were "real" or not. The truth of the matter is, I heard what I heard. The sounds came from the wind, but they were *heard* by psyche. Thus, at this moment, the argument between what is real and not real ceases to matter because, as Jung writes, we just don't know. "Whether that is our own psyche or the psyche of the universe we don't know, but if one touches the earth one cannot avoid the spirit."[31]

> But you have been listening to me
> for some time now
> from the very beginning in fact
> and you are alone in this canyon of stillness
> not even cedar birds flutter.
> See, the sun is going down now
> the sandrock is washed in its colors
> Don't be afraid
>   we love you
> we've been calling you
> all this time
>
> —Leslie Silko, "Story from Bear Country"[32]

NOTES

1. C. G. Jung, *Collected Works of C. G. Jung* (Princeton: Princeton University Press, 1960), Vol. 14, para. 787. [the *Collected Works* are hereinafter referenced as "*CW*," followed by the volume number and the paragraph number.]

2. Quoted in Jung, *CW* 16 § 384.

3. Gregory Cajete, *Look to the Mountain: An Ecology of Indigenous Education* (Durango: Kivaki' Press, 1994), 83.

4. *Ibid.*, 83.

5. Jung, *CW* 8 § 326.

6. James Hillman, *The Thought of the Heart and the Soul of the World* (Woodstock, CT: Spring Publications, 1981), 102.

7. Jung, *CW* 9i § 7.

8. Jung, *CW* 8 § 423.

9. Gary Snyder, *A Place in Space* (Washington, D.C.: Counter Point Press. 1995), 234.

10. *Ibid.*, 189.

11. Jung, *CW* 10 § 53.

12. William Stafford, *The Way It Is: New and Selected Poems* (Saint Paul, MN: Greywolf Press, 1998), 128-9.

13. Edward Relph, "Modernity and the Reclamation of Place," in *Dwelling, Seeing and Designing: Toward a Phenomenological Ecology*, D. Seamon (ed.) (New York: State University of New York Press, 1993), 27.

14. Jung, *CW* 13 § 54.

15. Marie-Louise von Franz, *Projection and Recollection in Jungian Psychology* (La Salle & London: Open Court, 1980), 104.

16. See Arnold Van Gennep, *The Rites of Passage* (Chicago: University of Chicago Press, 1960).

17. Steven Foster & Meredith Little, *The Roaring of the Sacred River: The Wilderness Quest for Vision and Self-Healing* (Big Pine: Lost Borders Press, 1997), 99.

18. Jung, *CW* 8 § 204.

19. *Ibid.*, 200.

20. James Hillman, *Re-visioning Psychology* (New York: Harper Perennial, 1975), 104.

21. C. G. Jung, "Man and his environment," *C. G. Jung Speaking*, William McGuire and R. F. C. Hull (eds.)(Princeton: Princeton University Press, 1950), 202.

22. Antonio Machado, "Rebirth," *News of the Universe: Poems of Twofold Consciousness,* ed. R. Bly (San Francisco: Sierra Club Books, 1995), 108.

23. Quoted in Thomas Frick, *The Sacred Theory of the Earth* (Berkeley: North Atlantic Books, 1986), 37.

24. Marie-Louise von Franz, *The Golden Ass of Apuleius* (Boston: Shambhala, 1997), 127.

25. Henry Corbin, "Mundis Imaginalis, or the Imaginary and the Imaginal," *Spring 1972*, 1-19.

26. David Abram, *The Spell of the Sensuous* (New York: Vintage, 1996), 262.

27. Linda Hogan, *Dwellings: A Spiritual History of the Living World* (New York: Touchstone, 1995), 94.

28. Jung, *CW* 12 § 400.

29. Jung, *CW* 6 § 819.

30. James Hillman, "Peaks and Vales," *Puer Papers* (Dallas: Spring Publications, 1991), 54-74.

31. Jung, *The Vision Seminars I* (Zurich: Spring Publications, 1976), 164-5.

32. Leslie Silko, "Story from Bear Country," in *Intimate Nature*, eds. L. Hogan, D. Metzger, & B. Peterson (New York: Fawcett, 1998), 5.

TERRAPSYCHOLOGY:
REENGAGING THE SOUL OF PLACE
—AN INTRODUCTION—

CRAIG CHALQUIST

SUMMONED BY THE VOICE OF PLACE

I walk out; I see something, some event that would otherwise
have been utterly missed and lost; or something sees me, some
enormous power brushes me with its clean wing, and I resound
like a beaten bell. — Annie Dillard, *A Pilgrim at Tinker Creek*

Six years ago you could have found me under the glassy spires of
downtown San Diego, the city of my birth, interviewing street
artists, meeting with community activists in search of funding,
and holding free psychology classes for parents on welfare. For my first
year of doctoral fieldwork at Pacifica Graduate Institute, I had been
advised to reacquaint myself with the margins, the edges, the shadows

Craig Chalquist, M.S., Ph.D., teaches depth psychology, ecopsychology, myth, and
research at Sonoma State University, JFK University, New College of California, and the
Institute of Imaginal Studies. He lives and works in the San Francisco Bay Area.
    The following excerpt introduces his new book, *Terrapsychology: Reengaging the Soul
of Place* (Spring Journal Books, 2007), which calls for a new perspective of deep encounter,
terrapsychology, for listening into the presence, voice, or "soul" of the land and its features
as sites of earthly animation.

of my home town while monitoring my moods and dreams for clues about its psychic underside. "From out of the consulting room and into the world" read my psychological brief to myself.

With the growing sense I was overlooking something important, a depression moved in like fog along the coast. It was not the fieldwork; I had undertaken similar activities previously. I was depressed because of a relationship, or so I thought, but I didn't understand why. The surface harmony in which my partner and I talked and listened to each other was strained again and again by a caginess, a guardedness, that continually marched back and forth in the psychological demilitarized zone between us like a frontier soldier on patrol. No amount of probing for unanalyzed trauma or unconscious motivations healed it. From my end it felt like being haunted by a demon whose names might have been Defense, Fortification, Outpost, Citadel. Reaching out came to feel more and more like daring some risky border crossing.

Meanwhile, "something is missing," I kept thinking as I wrote about my fieldwork for school. During this time, I had toured the Gaslamp, traversed the Silver Gate, picked up sand dollars from the shoreline near the Del, spoken with artists and street people. I had stood under a statue of Cabrillo and looked out of a summer day onto endless sheets of shimmering blue on either side of North Island. I knew the wet touch of fool's gold at La Jolla Shores, the cold sting of seawater pounding the cliffs there, the moist snuffle of a giraffe eating from my hand at the Wild Animal Park in Escondido. San Diego, named for the flagship of Captain Vizcaino, who in turn was named after a saint who fought to protect a militarized border: my home, even though I chose to ignore the top gunners' jets screaming over Miramar, the aircraft carriers in the bay, the congested traffic, the smog, the flag-waving, squads of young Marines on leave, submarines at Point Loma, the SEALs, and Camp Pendleton where the Border Patrol remained on the lookout just above the base for unwanted migrants surfacing from the south.

Two weeks after my relationship finally imploded from excessive guardedness, a feminine figure visited me one night in a dream. Thinking she was my former lover, I called her by name. But, *No*, she shook her head; and, as I stared, I began to see that indeed the figure before me was not the woman I had loved. *That is not my name,* confirmed her look and frown. I knew that frown, and the gloomy sense of presence she exuded, but somehow could not place them.

Then who are you? I asked her.

San Diego, she said with a look the color of battleship steel. *My name is San Diego.*

I woke in shock, the cartographic image of a downward-turning bay clear in my mind's eye and a question to which I had no answer forming in my heart: How could a place self-personify and speak to me from inside a dream? For most psychological schools and perspectives that take dreams seriously (not all do), dream figures function as symbols of various aspects of the dreamer's mind, body, or immediate situation. A Freudian analyst hearing my dream might inquire about a mother problem, and a Jungian traditionalist might wonder about the state of my *anima*, the feminine side of a man, or his "woman within." Other analysts might wonder about split-off fragments—"introjects"— of internalized "good mom" and "bad mom" impressions stored up over time, or, at a more transpersonal level, look keenly for the mythological Great Mother archetype. (By now the reader might well wonder whether psychotherapy sometimes finds *itself* saddled with a mother problem.) A medical doctor might ask what I had for dinner, a psychiatrist which medication might be most effective in silencing that figure whose deeply frowning mouth recalled the San Diego Bay. Few would be the experts willing to risk taking the dream figure at her word—staying *with* her, as the more daring of phenomenologists would recommend—even after the usual explanations I tried on had utterly failed to resonate. In fact, as I worked with this feminine image, my attempt to think of her as part of myself gave way to an uncomfortable certainty that instead I was somehow a part of her, not as child to mother, but as witness become the witnessed by something (or someone) far larger than any unresolved object relation or failed relationship through which she might beckon my attention.

In the end, there was simply no gainsaying what had happened. Because my focus on the social sphere had actively repressed the roused presence, or "voice," of San Diego, its ignored defensiveness, naturally sheltered, ever on guard, claimed and named after frontier troopers, site of the first military fortifications in California, and dredged and reshaped into the largest and best-armed naval port in the world, had fallen down into and permeated my relationship with my partner and, because I would not listen, had finally blown it apart, the unacknowledged presence of the place thundering into the foreground like cannonfire echoing over an unexpecting household.

This discovery of the inner power of place opened a passageway into five years of qualitative research up and down El Camino Real, the old Mission Trail connecting San Diego with Sonoma along the coast of Alta, or Upper, California; the reading of histories written about Alta and her various Mission cities and counties; an intensive study of *ecopsychology*, the discipline that deals with our psychological connection to the environment; a foray into *psychohistory*, the analysis of how psychological life shapes historical events, and, eventually to the assembly of a new methodology for listening to what I now thought of as the resonant "voice," or trauma, of place. My primary question was: if I put aside the anti-terrestrial biases of my culture and regarded coastal California as a psychically active being, viewing her with eyes and ears sensitized by therapy training to hunt for recurrent motifs, what would present itself to me?

Initial research supported the impression of parallels between shadowy key motifs alive in heavily developed geographical locales and those at work in human psychic life. Themes of San Diegan defendedness, caginess, and paranoia run all the way back to the Mission days, when padres and soldiers packed Indians into adobe conversion centers, fought off attacking warriors protesting this invasion, and guarded the coast from behind the walls of a Rome-style fort. Klan activity, the aggressive conservatism of city founder Alonzo Horton, the Naval presence and hardware, Air Forces over North Island, Marines in desert training near Oceanside, the police and patrols along the international border, the barricade itself: these are not simple, solid facts of politics or geography, but long-standing expressions of defense and attack, splitting and control. *Features of the landscape cross through the frontiers of consciousness to image themselves as psychic beings, but without relinquishing their environmental qualities. Repress the manifestations of this lively interactivity and they return with symptomatic force, over and over, until they receive a place in a more extended, more ecological, sense of self.*

A careful examination of California's twenty-one Mission towns and all fourteen of her Mission counties uncovered repeating themes, images, and echoes roaring and bleeding like feverish, unhealed syndromes shared by people and places alike. In Los Angeles, for example, with its frankly Babylonian collisions and mutual contaminations of nature and spirit, prehistoric bones and teeth emerged from the tarry ooze at La Brea at the dawn of the 1900s in the very center of the enormous cross of asphalt spreading over the face of the future metropolis. Given this showy infiltration (one of countless examples) of cruciform urban progress by the chthonic depths of nature, no wonder the horizontal crosspiece was named the Miracle Mile. It is possible to imagine the most outlandish spiritual cults springing up in the City of Angels as saber-toothed wingbeats or well-oiled flights of fancy.

Idealism, mood, aspiration, and economy in hilly, bipolar San Francisco go to historical extremes and always have, swinging up and down like a peninsular manic depression; gold and silver work on divisive Market Street like lithium medication. Drops from the heights into the depths, from suicides at early Carmel and Big Sur to John Denver's tragic Icarian plunge, predominate in Monterey, its Bay, and its underwater canyons, the deepest to be found off the coast of California. In Sonoma, where an American band of invaders charged in and raised their Bear Flag above the outpost plaza, railroad tycoons and grape-growing industrialists have been bear-flagging real estate ever since.

The state as a whole is not immune to such metaphorically suggestive concatenations. It is as though Alta, portrayed as an island on European maps for centuries after explorers knew otherwise, were some wary, sensitive organism determined to shield itself from human invasion. Adobes and bell towers have dissolved over and over in sudden storms, or fallen to pieces in relentless earthquakes. (The shaker that greeted conquistadors entering Orange County rumbled "for about the length of an Ave Maria.") Spanish sailors up "The Crotch" in the Gulf lost ships to sudden maelstroms; up and down California, more than thirty submerged galleons collect barnacles near the sea cliffs they strove to mount.

A few more examples from a growing list of how what happens in, or to, a given geographical location can become thematic for those nearby:

- A woman working in a conflict-ridden institution, whose employees stage a baffling attempt to push a popular leader downhill, realizes that she and her coworkers unknowingly repeat a 150-old drama in which a charismatic key player was likewise unseated. Underlining the persistence of this highly localized echo, the institution bears the name of that earlier leader and sits on property once owned by him.

- A graduate student, researching the designs of petroglyphs scattered around a present-day bombing range, discovers carved images shaped like bombs, jets, and explosions— images carved hundreds of years before the invention of missiles or aircraft. Indigenous locals attributed these images to the presence of the Thunderbird deity known for centuries to fly over the area.
- Another student preparing to visit a country he's never been to dreams about it the night before his trip. The word "contaminated" occurs throughout the dream. When he arrives at the place, he finds this motif everywhere, from polluted bays and streams to invading species and underground oil spills.
- In a small sample of interviewees asked to describe their experience of a sacred or meaningful place, all describe it as though it were a soothing, healing mentor or spiritual presence.
- A dreamer awakens in a sweat from images of towers of burning flame. A week later he sees them again on television as the largest brushfire in the history of his homeland consumes an area the size of Rhode Island.
- Shortly before a tsunami strikes, five tribes move inland to avoid a flood that destroys their villages. One medicine leader claims that the god responsible for the deluge warned him in a dream.

What qualities distinguish these uncanny connections between dwellers and the land? They are deeply symbolic. They are local. They persist through time, even over many human lifespans. They are registered internally. They tend to organize themselves into discernible syndromes. They resist reduction to either human interiors or environmental externals. And they are often spectacularly interactive, even to the point of showing up as human styles of perception and modes of discourse. In short, what C. G. Jung wrote about the unconscious seems true of the presence of place: *it turns toward us the face that we turn toward it.* Psychologically, shouting down the inner critic who fills fearful minds with doubts and self-loathing only strengthens it; repressing sexuality guarantees its later return in bizarre actings out; reducing spiritual yearnings to the status of childhood longings enlarges them unconsciously into creeds, oughts, and isms. Cover a place's history and vitality in asphalt, concrete, or forgetfulness, and it returns an episode at a time in symptoms, dreams, and folklore as well as in crime, public politics, and private fights until brought fully into the present through conscious reflection.

A premise to explore, then: *When people inhabit a particular place, its features inhabit their psychological field, in effect becoming extended facets of their selfhood. The more they repress this local, multifaceted sense of environmental presence, the likelier its features will reappear unconsciously as symbolic, animated forces seething from within and from without.*

As the methods evolved for tracking the pain found in folklore, nightmare, romantic conflict, or historical reenactment back to the "pain" of place with a view to eventually healing it at the root, the question arose of what to make of healthier locales, like holy sites and relatively unspoiled expanses of land. The method clearly wanted widening beyond its initial preoccupation with pathology. A newly reengaging perspective on the world was needed, a standpoint wide enough to welcome in the reconnective paradigms of psychology, psychohistory, and ecopsychology, yet flexible enough to try out its assumptions anywhere on our highly reactive planet. It should also make way for a deepened understanding of "place" as a nexus of symbolic animated forces, from the actions of animals and the gestures of storms to the fascinations gleaming forth from everyday objects: gemstone facets, shards of glass, ripples across a pristine pond.

This new framework for viewing "human-humus" interactivity offers a reverent outlook on a sentient cosmos as well as a more formal set of practices for minding matter and tending the matter of mind. Its mythopoetic (or "geopoetic") eye envisions the cosmos as nested spheres of animation from intimate quanta to distant quarks: a natural world of emplaced beings beckoning our attention through their deep connections with the human interior. Its name is *terrapsychology*, the study of the presence, or soul, of place.

"Animism! Human projection!" Thus resounds the habitual explaining away of any apparent reactivity we observe in the places we inhabit. If places seem to be alive, goes this self-congratulatory logic, it is only because we anthropomorphically endow them with life as self-certain humanism and literal-minded fundamentalism shake hands over an increasingly desolate globe. We, the supposed peak of creation, rose as living beings from a dead world, turned around, and gave it back its sense of liveliness in a kind of animation-at-one-remove before we became Enlightened. A civilization of intelligent robots might well argue one day that they similarly endowed their mysterious human creators with life.

Touted as self-evidently objective, the convenient belief in a lifeless, soulless Earth carries a heavy religious charge because it requires one. Otherwise, polluting, strip-mining, and warming the globe would feel like sacrilegious acts of violence. It is no coincidence that a civilization whose economies depend on such violence is *the only one in history* to regard the planet as a heap of insensible material or, in line with this grandiose creed, to misinterpret its faces and voices in dreams, art, folklore, and fantasy as purely human expressions. The real wonder is in how we promoted ourselves to the center of all things as bipedal bestowers of truth upon the universe in the first place. Imagine the astonishment were astronauts to discover a civilization from a Milky Way backwater, one hardly out of the trees, visualizing itself as the very justification of cosmic being—despite its suicidal unwillingness to refrain from desecrating its own tiny corner of the galaxy. Behind the rush to label animistic cosmologies "regressive" hides a habit of displacing the spaces of deadness in our mechanistic worldview into the world rather than locating them in ourselves. The true regression is in objectifying the environment to an ecocidal extent undreamed of in the wildest flights of archaic totemism.

Centuries of looking at matter and nature, and even people, from the outside, as quantitative sciences inevitably must, even when focused on psychodynamics, has blurred the crucial distinction between *literalized animism*—explaining meteorology or other natural events as being caused by a spirit or arcane force—and the *inner* experience of these events as responsive, ensouled, and full of significance. The first conflicts with Western notions of science, but the second need not; in fact, it could complement them while resurrecting a sense of connection to the world. Inwardly, a molting dream monster named "Babushka" chases a dreamer out of a building; outwardly, the polluted Russian River floods communities out of their homes and towns a month or two after the dream. How we experience this conjunction of inner and outer depends on the mode of consciousness available: literalistic and externalized, or symbolic and interpretive. Could not disciplined inquiry finally make room for both? Could it not accept the persistent psychological experience of feeling projected *into* by the surround?

This book opens up the question of whether the uncanny aliveness of the locations we inhabit may well be the rule rather than the exception. It's as though *what the conscious mind is trained to see as nonliving places and things, the unconscious reacts to as animated presences and metaphors.* Borderlines and borderlands, sludgy bays and constricted moods, personal complexes and apartment complexes seem to resonate together as events in the world symbolize aspects of the human self, and those aspects, in turn, point back to the features of the world that evolved our remarkable minds.

Does this sense of psychic animation come from us or from the terrain? Does the nonhuman and even the inorganic possess a rudimentary subjectivity? These inquiries have a long cultural, intellectual, and spiritual history. For now, a few points to consider. First, quantitative research cannot directly observe a subjectivity, even in us: all it sees are firing neurons and complex circuits. No inner homunculus, no ghost in the machine, nothing detectable from the outside. Naturally: subjectivity is an *interiority* of matter, not a measurable secretion of it. The more complex the matter, the richer the expression of its inner nature.

Second, if the working model of the psychological (or "transferential") field as identified by psychoanalysis is widened beyond groups of people to include impactful features of the environment, then parallels between ecological and human wounding and well-being need not be causally reduced to one or the other. Our method can honor them as interactive, multidimensional, interdependent, and symbolically connective and meaningful. In fact, we can interpret them much like the images of dreams, where even the most literal facts display a symbolic character. Instead of a psyche confined to human heads, we behold an ecology of the heart, where verdant landscapes moisten verdant souls. Perhaps we are all "animists" in the unconscious.

To a careful "ear," places can "sound" like animated beings. Why not assume for once that they *do* exhibit qualities of animation in the field that dances between them and us? Why not approach them over the bridges of symbol and dream they extend, listening *into* them for images and meanings instead of learning *about* them only from outside? Rather than simply representing pieces of ourselves piled up at some random location, couldn't a chipped street corner, a leaning tree, a spindly arbor each open a doorway into a fuller sense of belonging, emplacement, and consciousness?

Terrapsychology is the study of how the currents of this aliveness, reactivity, interiority, or psychic animation of a geographical location and its creatures and features interact deeply with our own. It offers descriptions of this interaction, methods for registering it, and practices for managing it. Because we assume a confluence of sensitivities—namely, ours, with the places we wish to tend—*qualitative* methods of direct encounter receive more space in this book than *quantitative* strategies that regard a living presence as an object to measure or control. Our endeavor is not merely to pinpoint matter from an "objective," impersonal distance, but to reengage it more fully, heart and soul.

Here your investigator is happy to report that such forays into intersubjective animism, or *interanimism*, have not deprived him of his ability to juggle equations, understand new scientific discoveries, or operate the computer on which he types these words. The working assumption that the world is reactively sensitive in ways not measured but open to demonstration has not packed him off to medievalism or, even farther back, left him stranded in archaic superstition or banished him from the artificially brilliant world of the empirical, never again to enjoy the benefits of medicine, automation, or the Periodic Table.

To an ear tuned to place, the fear of regressing into hopeless "primitivism" and the fear of falling off the world's flat edge grate like different chants playing in the same dreary key. It is long past time to change our tune. A perspective worthy of its subjects (not objects) of inquiry would require the sophistication to "put away childish things" and leave the clacking billiard balls of causality and reductionism on the table where they belong. We have played enough dangerous games with matter. Our willingness to risk it reflects an institutionalized failure to connect two great traditions of knowledge: the empirically scientific and the richly animistic. What after all is relentless reductionism but a defense against the numinous power of the world's animation?

A primary goal of terrapsychology is to find out more about the depths of relations between people and places, the human soul and the soul of locale (*genius loci*). By doing so, it strives to play a meaningful part in ending the war against nature that is poisoning the ecosphere while mutating lethally into suicidal antiworlds like isms and ideologies, spreading states of exile and warfare, and displacing what remains of collective human sanity.

It is impossible to ignore the context of global deterioration in which this new perspective of terrapsychology makes its appearance. With pandemics, ecological destruction, and the largest mass extinctions ever accelerating on every side, leaders of the "free" world play at politics as though business as usual were still compatible with survival—human survival or anything else's. Ordinary environmentalism having proved ineffectual in halting this satanic machinery, a case must now be made for indigenous ecological values carried into an interanimistic concern for places as presences impacting our survival and psychological well-being just as ours impact their remaining integrity. Only that level of urgency has given me the boldness to publish such new but potentially transformative work.

My hope is that this new terrapsychological primer will encourage "world therapists" to explore how the cracks in stones and the veins of leaves parallel the lineaments of the human soul.

WATERCOURSE

The water's swirl,
translucent like liquid glass,
too many directions all at once.
The river is seeking its way,
trying to find itself
amidst commotion;
at the water's edge, a heron,
meditating, balancing
on its thin axis of leg;
holding the still point
in this chaotic sublime.

—*Michael Whan*

THE SOUL OF THE TIETE RIVER: REFLECTIONS ON THE ECOLOGICAL CRISES IN SÃO PAULO, BRAZIL

"The important thing is the question that nobody ever asks:
What happens to those figures and phantoms, those gods,
demons, magicians, those messengers from heaven and monsters
from the abyss, when we see that there is no mercurial serpent in
the caverns of the earth, that there are no dryads in the forest
and no undines in the water, and that the mysteries of faith have
shrunk to articles in a creed?"

—C. G. Jung [1]

INTRODUCTION

There is no vaccine for the ecological crisis. Global warming,
scarcity of drinkable water, and overpopulation cannot be
isolated and introduced into an organism to produce antibodies.
Environmental strategies drawn up by engineers, agriculturists, and
geographers hardly ever consider the psychodynamics of anti-ecological
behavior. The positivist-Cartesian paradigm inherent in unilateral,

Ricardo A. Hirata (ricardoahirata@yahoo.com.br) is a Jungian psychotherapist with
a private practice in São Paulo, Brazil. He is a doctoral candidate in clinical psychology
at Pontifícia Universidade Católica in São Paulo, and is writing his thesis on the
contributions of analytical psychology to the teaching of a Psychology and Nature course
in undergraduate and postgraduate programs.

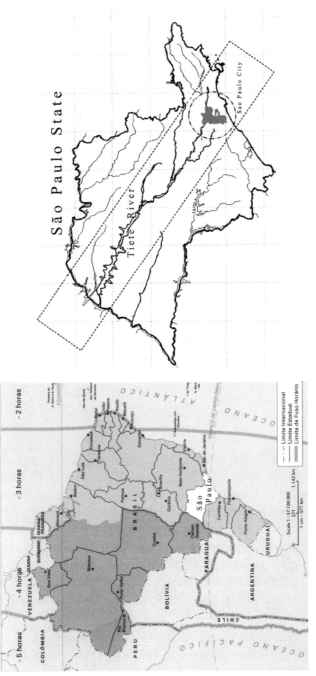

Fig. 1: Brazil, São Paulo State, the city of São Paulo and the Tiete River

reductionist medicine and the natural sciences does not encompass the complexity of environmental phenomena, because it ignores the psyche. Religions exert little counterforce on behalf of the environment, and schools seldom teach children about the environment in such a way that includes soul, the human soul as well as the soul of the world. The environmental problem demands a new paradigm, one which relinks nature and psyche. It is my belief that Jungian psychology provides a means to accomplish this relinkage through which our ecological crises can be understood as a symptom of a sick collective soul.

In a much larger work, I have employed a Jungian approach to explore aspects of the ecological crisis in São Paulo, Brazil, focusing upon the Tiete River, the largest and most important river in São Paulo.[2] The purpose of this shorter paper is to describe the history and mythology of the Tiete River and how, as the river has become more and more polluted—thus changing from a river of life to a river of death—its mythology and symbols have changed along with it. I further explore how the river and the psyche of the Paulistano (the people of São Paulo) are interconnected, each mirroring the other. My search for the identity of the river has been also a search for a deeper understanding of the metropolis itself with the hope that both the river and the city might one day soon regain their essential vitality.

THE RECENT HISTORY OF SÃO PAULO AND THE TIETE RIVER: A BRIEF SUMMARY

The city of São Paulo, the capital of the State of São Paulo, is the largest city in the Southern hemisphere and the fourth-largest city in the world, with 19 million inhabitants (see Fig. 1). The motto of the city is a Latin phrase, "*Non Ducor, Duco*," which means, "I am not led, I lead." São Paulo City's GNP was $78 billion in 2005.

The São Paulo region is located at the far end of an extensive valley formed over millions of years from a sedimentary basin containing great flat areas and an extensive network of waterways, with the great Tiete River flowing into the city of São Paulo. If each city has an "ecological identity," São Paulo may be said to have, to a large extent, a water, or fluvial, identity.

Going against the norm, the Tiete River springs from close to the sea, and then runs inland towards São Paulo. (Consequently, as will be discussed more fully later, the river played an important role in

Fig.2: The Tiete River and São Paulo

Brazilian colonization by providing the means through which colonizers traveled from the sea inland.) The area's geological composition, combined with historic events, resulted in very impressive economic development of the metropolis (see Fig. 2).

Some important natural features of the São Paulo region that contributed to its development are: (1) high quality water sources (many now polluted); (2) the presence of basalt in the red earth, which enhanced the fertility of coffee plantations; (3) the availability of rock plates from the Crystalline Foundation for coating and street paving, and to provide the necessary materials for building the city of São Paulo; (4) river rapids, waterfalls, and rock formations, which are tourist attractions; (5) water-generated power. (In 1990, the hydroelectric potential generated by the 19 plants constructed in the Tiete basin represented 88% of the electricity generated in São Paulo and 28% of that generated nationally. [3])

During the 20th century, the city of São Paulo experienced a population "explosion."[4] In 1900, there were 239,820 inhabitants; in 1940, 1,326,261; in 1970, 5,924,615; and in 1996, 9,839,436. The city's growth was accompanied by the degradation of the Tiete River. In the Industrial Period, during the first half of the 20th century, a sewage disposal system was built to take care of industrial and domestic waste. It fed into a hydroelectric station to generate power for the metropolis. In a very short time, pollution became such a problem that even the water in the reservoirs that provided the city's water supply became polluted. During the second half of the 20th century, an intensive period of industrialization, great amounts of raw industrial and residential sewage were dumped into the Tiete River. This caused the annihilation of all river life. Studies showed that by 1960, there was no more oxygen in the water. Towards the end of the 90s, only 24% of the inhabitants of the metropolitan area of São Paulo had treated sewage and the city's main reservoirs were increasingly contaminated.

The crisis reached alarming proportions in 1999, with river pollution affecting an area of 350 kilometers. The polluted river caused contagious diseases —"70% of the diseases in São Paulo are water related"[5]— and was not even fit to generate electric power. In 2001, water contamination together with little rainfall and increased power demand resulted in the country's first great modern energy crisis— the famous "*apagão*" blackout.

Over the past ten years the Brazilian government, with financial support, has spent $ 1.7 billion dollars on engineering projects to widen and deepen the river and build sewage treatment stations. Flooding has diminished somewhat and the level of oxygen will probably rise. However, specialists warn that as long as people go on dumping trash on the streets and the houses on the outskirts of the city remain unconnected to the public sewage system, pollution and flooding will continue to present serious problems.

In this way, then, during the 20th century, the Tiete River changed from a river of life to a river of death. This picture is part of the cultural complex of São Paulo, which has deep roots in Brazil's colonization, the massacres of Indians and disrespect for nature, the Catholic influence over the educational process, and the stress on the economy over culture and the environment. Surely, this is not just a Brazilian problem, it is a world crisis. But for Brazilian people, who live in a country with some of the greatest natural resources and the largest biodiversity in plants and animals in the world, it is tragic that this has happened, and it is imperative that our people begin to show respect once again for nature.

A Journey through the Mythology and Imagery of the River

Bearing in mind this background information, I invite you to imagine now with me the Tiete from its beginnings. Let me take you along the stream of the river as we envision São Paulo's development from its origins as an Indian settlement, on to a Jesuit village, and finally to the great metropolis we know today. On the trip, we will adopt the perspective of the river. Its source, its rapids and lakes, its spirits and entities, from the real to the imaginary, from life to death. The river will be character and scene, stage and actor, subject and object.

The Tiete survives despite São Paulo. It is not the liquid that runs straight, imprisoned in the skeletal margins of the city's avenues. This dark, fetid, pestilent, foul muck is not the river. The Tiete cannot be seen from the outside. It must be gone into. To feel it, a glance from a car stopped in heavy traffic does not suffice. More is necessary. Allow the density of the liquid to drag you within. To empathize with the Tiete, now the sewage depository of São Paulo, demands deepening. There can be no resistance if we are to reach the place the river reserves for us. It is necessary to look at death to find where life resides. The

Tiete subsists in the shadow of the Paulistano's gaze, but the inhabitants of this great metropolis would rather not look at their river.

> I've seen everything. There are always dead animals. But what struck me was to see a baby floating, once. … It was shocking! … I've seen, over the 10 years I worked on the Tiete, four human bodies in addition to large dead animals. [6]

We start off as a trickle of water springing from the mountainsides of the *Serra do Mar* (Ocean Mountains), close to the coast. Added to other trickles from other springs we form a small stream that soon transforms itself into a rivulet. Increasingly more voluminous, the river defies nature, running inland for 1,200 kilometers into the mighty Paraná River. Our time precedes the arrival of European colonizers. The Indians who lived on the Paulista Plateau (the plateau that encompasses the State of São Paulo) called this plateau the *Tiete*, meaning "mother of the river," because after the floods you could catch with your bare hands the fish stranded in pools in the fields left behind by the receding waters. It is curious to think that a place that was once called "mother" provokes so much repulsion or indifference today.

Water, food, and vast expanses of open forest attracted various indigenous groups to the region of the Paulista Plateau. (Later, it was precisely these features, coupled with a colder climate than that of the coast, that attracted Jesuits in search of natives to catechize.)

In Guarani mythology, *water* is seen as a symbol of life, wisdom and moderation.[7] The Tupi group of Indians, the first inhabitants of São Paulo, which include the Tupinambá, Tupinikim, and Guarani, had strong symbolic and affective links with the water. Their settlements were always constructed near rivers. Fishing, daily bathing in the river, and the rich presence of water in their mythology and rituals are some aspects of this connection.

In the mythology of the Kamaiurá Indians, also part of the Tupi-Guarani group, water and its elements appear in the creation of man, as a symbol of the origin and end of life.

> *Mavutsinim*, the First Man, transformed a lake shell into a beautiful woman and married her. In the *Kuarup* ceremony of the dead, tree trunks that come to life are, at the end, taken out of the earth and flung deep into the waters, where they will remain forever. In yet another myth, an enchanted canoe, on

touching water, is covered with many fish of the most varied sorts. And also the ancient women-spirits *Iamuricumá* flung their children in the river and they became fish.[8]

During this early time, various entities inhabited the river and waters. These included (1) *Boitatás,* described in indigenous myths as a serpent of fire with two large eyes, or as a bull that breathes fire through its nostrils, associated with hidden treasure and with protecting fields against fire; (2) *Boiúnas* (serpent / big worm/ *"minhocão"*), an enormous, greedy, dark serpent, a water mother, who reigned over dark stretches of the river, drawing in vessels to the bottom of the waters, and who also had the ability to shape-shift—sometimes taking the form of a ship or, more rarely, that of a woman. "Each river, each lake, has its Mother, which appears only as an immense serpent. She has no mercy and nothing satisfies her hunger. She kills and devours whom she finds;" (3) *Ipupiaras,* a ferocious monster who lived in the waters in the form of a marine man. This figure mixed with the European mermaids in the imagination of the colonizers and was later associated with African orixas, or deities, especially Oxum; (4) *Mães-d'água* (water mothers), also influenced by European mermaids, was a creature that was half woman, half fish, who inhabited the rivers and lakes.

> Iara, the queen of the waters, was the most famous woman of the tribe. A great friend of nature, she liked to spend her days on the white sands of the river. One afternoon, while she bathed in the river, strange men with beards, heavy clothes, boots and hats assailed her. She fainted and, even so, was violated and abused. In the end, they threw her in the river, where the water spirit transformed her into a double being—half human, half fish. She continued living in the rivers, beautiful, but deadly.

Another legend, related to the fury of the waters, tells that in some stretches of water there are bewitched water mothers, who caused great waves to make terrible noises, killing some men. They were always described as horrible monsters, which inhabited fishy wells. According to Câmara Cascudo,[9] the water mothers originated partly from *Cobra Grande* (Big Snake), and partly from Ipupiara: "*Ipupiara* became the Water Mother." In other Paulista folklore there are helpful and good water mothers who can love and show you treasure.

From the first Paulista settlements, the Tiete provided water and, especially, food—concrete and symbolic—to the plateau's inhabitants.

> Mara, the daughter of the chief, became pregnant during a dream
> and her daughter Mandi died while still very young. As her tears
> and milk fell over the tomb of her daughter, wishing that she be
> reborn, she caused the sprouting of a manioc plant, originating
> thus, the main Indian food.

The Tiete also served as a means of traveling to various parts of Brazil. The *Bandeirantes* set out further into the hinterlands guided by the river. From its banks colonizing movements of all of the South, Midwest, and West of Brazil traveled and spread their influence across the Northern dry lands. In the 16th, 17th, and 18th centuries, during a period of great expeditions and colonizing in search of precious stones, the São Paulo rivers, including the Tiete, were objects of veneration, especially because of the dangers encountered in river crossings. Expedition diaries from this period richly document the striking biodiversity and teeming life in the waters and banks of the Tiete.

> There are lions, tigers, great packs of wild pigs that you hear from
> afar for the noise they make with their teeth. These rivers have
> their great dourado and pacu fishes. They also have ducks, many
> otters, many alligators that along the banks of the rivers bask in
> the sun, some of such extraordinary size that when shot at with
> bullets are not in the least hurt for the thickness of their skins.[10]

During the 18th century, with the discovery of gold and precious stones in the region of Minas Gerais, huge expeditions left São Paulo in canoes on the Tiete River. Even if the Portuguese Court sought, above all, to extract raw materials and take riches away from Brazil, the Tiete favored, as well, a contrary movement, providing a means of transporting food to the migrants and miners in the backlands of the country.

Later, with the development of agriculture, fertile land and clean water from the Tiete offered ideal conditions for the green gold of coffee plantations. Around 1890, the State of São Paulo was the most important coffee production center in the world. Coffee prompted the development of railroads and attracted even more foreign colonizers. Profits from coffee were invested in modernizing great plantations and at the same time brought changes in the habits of the local inhabitants. During the Industrial Revolution, it was the waters of the Tiete that generated the power to move the machines that set off the prosperity of the future metropolis of the 19th and 20th centuries.

São Paulo's inhabitants had a strong, positive emotional link with the Tiete up to the beginning of the 20th century. During the second half of the 19th century, the life of the river blended with that of the Paulistano on the bridges that crossed the river, in the activities of fishermen, and in the floodings of the floodplains. "Who doesn't remember the great floods of the Tiete? All of São Paulo used to go see the floods, gathering together all classes of people."[11] In 1919, a considerable part of the Paulistano cultural activities was still concentrated along the Tiete. Besides being the grand sports arena of the epoch, the river invited Paulistanos to walk on its banks, and it inspired songs, paintings, and poems. Despite the hardships occasioned by the floods, such as those of 1906 and 1929, the banks of the river were festive sites: "… [S]occer matches, romantic serenades, picnics. Its waters were the stage for water sports and fishing."[12] *The Tiete was the heart of the city.*

> Today I hear so much talk about stress, fatigue, depression. …
> The Tiete, with its tame waters, really helped many people deal
> with and forget all of this.[13]

THE DISTORTION OF THE IMAGES AND
MYTHS OF THE RIVER

Yet the biological and cultural diversity of the Tiete did not remain unscathed by progress. Little was left after the clearing of land for the cultivation of sugarcane, coffee, and other agricultural products. The enormous amount of garbage and sewage from the greatest populace-attracting center in Brazil brought about the death of the river in the city of São Paulo. While the ecological devastation in the Tiete region became critical in the 20th century, already in the 18th century, with the development of sugarcane cultivation and the clearing the riverbanks, the river's ecosystem was in peril.

After the decline in inland colonizing movements, and more specifically, the prohibition of sports and leisure activities on account of the pollution, the Tiete and its waters assumed a new, highly destructive and morbid representation in the Paulista imagination. "With time, it took on a reversed prestige: it acquired an alarming level of pollution and its image became associated with something bad and destructive."[14] Although the level of pollution surpassed the limit of zero oxygen circa 1960, already at the start of the 19th century the floodplains of the Paulistano rivers served as garbage and dead animal dumps, leaving the air infested and the waters contaminated.

At the time of the founding of São Paulo, various rivers and streams crossed the plateau. Over the years, these were canalized, straightened, diverted, or became extinct. With landfills and asphalt, the excess water previously received by the floodplains no longer had anywhere to flow. All the liquid that might have been contained as groundwater was used to generate electricity.

> … [E]ven the dirt and devastation in a way helped. … [E]very drop of urine poured in the toilets of the metropolis ended up going to the turbines at the foot of the Serra do Mar: the water that no longer infiltrated naturally in the soil swelled up the rivers and produced more kilowatts.[15]

In addition to causing the loss of a vast leisure and sports area, the pollution of the Tiete also drove away religious celebrations. The sanctuary of Pirapora de Bom Jesus, located a few kilometers from the metropolis, was the most affected by the river's pollution.

> There were river processions brightened by firework spectacles, and in accord with an old tradition, animals that arrived in cavalcades of the devout were bathed in the river. At dawn, the "curing baths" took place, with the immersing of the sick in the waters of the river. Many leprous people were part of the procession. But as of the mid 80s, the degradation of the river in Pirapora, today known as the ocean of foam from industrial detergents mixed with foul-smelling sewage, put an end to this practice.[16]

In 2004, on the day of the Holy Mother, Mary, a mass was celebrated on the Tiete River and the holy water, collected at the source of the river, was distributed in small glass containers to the devout.

> The passage [of the image of the Holy Mother] moved many of the devout. Some asked themselves whether it would be easier to repeat the miracle of Jesus, who transformed water into wine at the Cana of Galilee marriage, or make the liquid that runs in the Tiete become drinkable one day.[17]

Between 2001 and 2004, the main São Paulo newspapers (OESP and FOLHA) ran various articles on the Tiete. The terms and expressions most generally used were: "dead river," " forgotten," "filthy," "bad-smelling," "oily," "dead world of organisms that cause diseases," "garbage and sewage," "floods," "neglect," "lack of care," "cemetery," "toxic foam." The river is 300 kilometers of death. Eight thousand tons of waste per day. When we look at the river, we see a "thick oily layer," empty soda bottles and plastic bags accumulated on the banks, which have no vegetation.[18] All types of garbage can be found "from chemical waste to sofas, cadavers, body pieces, sandals and the incredible mark of 120,000 tires."[19]

Slowly, the city began to look at the river, looking for an opportunity to do something about the results of years of neglect. During São Paulo's 450th anniversary celebrations in 2004, a few "brave" souls went rowing on the fetid waters of the Tiete. For the children who went on a boat ride on the river, the worry: "If I die, you can keep my Nintendo."[20]

THE SUPPOSED REBIRTH

In 2004, as a result of efforts to depollute the river, floods decreased and the imagery of the river began to show themes linked with purification, rebirth, rescue, resurgence, and salvation. The São Paulo newspapers ran headlines such as: "Tiete: 16 years to 'resuscitate' a dead river" and "The Tiete River is the main character in São Paulo's 450 years." Trees and flowers were planted along the banks of the river. Specialists forecast an improved scenario by 2030. Recently, a theater company chose the river as the setting for a floating stage. Another headline declared: "The Tiete begins to revive." For the present governor of the State, a clean river and embankments filled with greenery will change the self-esteem of the people: "In São Paulo, I have no doubt that the Tiete River is amongst our most important symbols, for what it represents to the Paulista people and the very country."

> For the Jurunas, Sinaá, the most powerful shaman, in the face of the great rains and the threat of floods, built an immense canoe where he preserved a seedling of every plant species. "In a few days the river overflowed the banks and the flood covered the entire region, but the great chief saved his people from hunger."[21] As he got older, Sinaá rejuvenated with each waterfall bath, so he could live until the end of his people.

A project to make the river navigable is being studied as an alternative means of transport and environmental education. Others believe in the tourism potential of the river. In sum, for those who know the importance of the river in the history of the city, revitalization and depollution are the payment of a debt to the river, the "key to restore the pride of Paulistas." However, doubt about such rebirth remains. Diverse factors suggest that the physical cleaning of the Tiete may not be sufficient to eliminate the ecological problems: (1) the municipal problem of garbage collection—"nearly 40% of the garbage that reaches the river, today, comes from garbage not collected or badly handled;"[22] (2) the destination of toxic mud removed from the river; (3) the quantity of chemical pollutants that reached the river over the years is unknown, cannot be fully determined, nor removed safely; (4) with control of the discharge of industrial pollutants in the river, there is the risk of proliferation of pathogens coming from domestic sewage; (5) the resistance of people to connecting their houses to a sewage system; (6) the distrust of some people towards depollution measures; (7) the lack of education among people who persist in throwing garbage in the streets. "Unfortunately, 20% of the refuse in the river is not from sewage. It comes from garbage dumped into the river. It's a matter of education;"[23] (8) the political thinking that "what is buried does not bring votes;"[24] (9) the river as scapegoat: the Paulista places on "the Tiete the blame for a large part of the ills that encumber the city, especially since 1900."[25]

The River as a Symbolic Mirror

From a Jungian perspective, the pollution of the river is more than biological death. It also represents a morbid spiritual condition—a pathology of the cultural soul. According to the geographer Mário Mantovani, "The river is a thermometer of society. If the river has sewage, that's a sign of a sick society. If it has garbage, of a piggish society."[26] If the river is a mirror that reflects our society, the Tiete River shows us that we are not doing well. As a journalist once said, "In São Paulo, the rivers and streams became symbols of pollution. And because of this, people run away from it and don't feel guilty about disposing of their sewage directly into the river or using the streets as garbage cans."[27]

The Tiete shows the destructive, dark side of the city, which, surely, no one wants to see. Is this perhaps why we remained alienated from the morbid condition of the river for so long? The Tiete died and we have not mourned. We did not know how to deal with the death of the river and would rather ignore it, provoking a veiled aggression and unconscious *acting out*. Concomitantly with the pollution and the physical distancing of the population from the Tiete, there occurred a traumatic inner or psychic distancing. The modern Paulistano "withdrew" from the animic river and "polluted" the inner river, the "river of the soul." The ecological devastation of the Tiete and the pollution of the psyche are simultaneous processes. The river and its waters lost their original symbolic meaning, passing from a "live" symbol to a "dead" or "dark" symbol.

Returning to the opening quote by Jung at the beginning of this article, we can ask ourselves: Where have the entities gone that once inhabited the waters of the Tiete? Given a culture that is split, where religion and economic development do not include the preservation of nature, what is the destiny of these psychic figures? I believe that the Paulistanos' anti-ecological behavior, such as throwing trash in the streets and rivers, are perverse manifestations of these psychic images. Furthermore, when we consider the body of the city, we discover a curious relationship between the mythical figures of Tietê, particularly Boiúna and Iara, in the way in which the city was constructed.

The ecological crisis evidenced in the Tiete River marks the body of the city. The main viaduct of São Paulo was nicknamed after the mythic serpent that once lived in the Tiete River, the *minhocão,* or "big worm.*"* Surrounding the viaduct are billboards, mostly of semi-naked women advertising lingerie, clothes, and sex shops. The street under the viaduct has become a place where prostitutes work at night. Aggressiveness towards nature runs together with repression and reification of the Feminine.

The Tiete appears concretized in the form of a viaduct, which is one of the ugliest architectural constructions in the city. Its proximity to the buildings in the region, and the incredible noise and pollution produced by the vehicles driving by it has affected the value of property and also the health of the people who live there. This situation is worsened by the visual pollution created by the immense billboards, and the presence of beggars, prostitutes, and transvestites along the viaduct. Like the Tiete, the "minhocão" is a great eyesore for the inhabitants of São Paulo, a shadowy reflection of the concretization of the contents of the Paulistano cultural complex—

and the split existing therein. Symbolically, the river has been concretized in the horrendous form of this viaduct, and the mythical images of its entities have been perverted and distorted into instruments of mass-consumerist culture, oblivious to environmental degradation and the ecological crisis.

I'd like to share a poem that came to me while I was writing about this topic:

> The great serpent Boiúna that once lived in the Tiete waters
> lies grey and concrete, cemented in the viaduct Costa e Silva,
> the "Big Worm Minhocão."
> Of Indian Ipupiaras and country folk Iaras of the old
> Anhembi,
> rest only the song that echoes from the viaduct billboards.
> From
> the lingerie, shoe, clothing, and sex shop ads, the song of these
> mermaids seduces into consuming the ephemeral and
> disposable,
> While under the viaduct, beggars and garbage collectors,
> transvestites and prostitutes build their abodes of cardboard
> and their illusions of silicone.
> We are all agonizing prisoners inside the stomach of the
> concrete monster.

—R. A. H.

Unfortunately, today, very few people know about the myths and legends of the old indigenous people from the São Paulo region that I have described in this paper. Almost no one knows who Iara, Boiúna, Maraí, Ponaim, Mandi, etc. are. The earlier positive mythology and imagery associated with the river has been distorted and converted into ghosts and shadows that haunt our cityscape. The serpent that once imaginally animated the river now appears concretized in a viaduct. The bountiful river is paralyzed. The image of the concrete viaduct, in contrast to the flowing and sinuous river of the past, points to a transformation of the "river of life" into a "river of death," in which pollution stifles the flow of energy.

The sinuous fluidity of the river has become a straightened skeleton which the cars of the metropolis—cars that cannot stop—rush by daily. The modern Paulistano rhythm is marked by hurry. The city sapped energy from the river and polluted the river in return. The river is

Fig. 3: Iara (*top left*), Boiúna (*bottom left*), and the Costa e Silva viaduct (*top & bottom right*)

stopped, the city dissociated. From Jung: "They still have no notion of what it means to live in a de-psychized world"[28] (see Fig. 3).

SOULLESS DEVELOPMENT

Symbolically, the rivers and waters of São Paulo represent an important part of the city's soul. The drama surrounding the Tiete River reflects the history of a marvelously rich, strong city that did not know how to grow in harmony with nature. The periodic flooding of the river and the life of the river's imagination worked as a pacemaker for the original peoples, connecting the rhythms of the environment with the archetypal dynamics and consciousness of the Paulistanos. Now, devoid of flux, the "cement" river no longer provides this regulating rhythmic pace. As the river stopped flowing, the daily rhythm of the metropolis quickened in a disconnected way, dissociated from the natural rhythms that the river had previously provided—a dissociation seen in the frenzy of automobiles stuck on viaducts, or in diseases linked to stress, anxiety, panic, and depression.

As a means of escaping from the monster of concrete and the song of the mermaids, we resign ourselves to the comfort of emotions restricted to adrenergic, fast, ephemeral release. The ego wanes from lack of Eros. The feminine principle violated (as expressed in the *Iara* myth) is actuated in addiction to drugs, games, eating disturbances, violence, rupture, and madness. An excess of adrenergic emotions is the fruit of a life lived in dissociation and vice-versa. When we do not feed on symbolic life, on deep food, and yield to the bountiful table of ephemeral, poor, adrenergic food, we pay a high price: the accumulation in the organism of cortisol, the stress hormone.

I call the temporal aspect of the cultural complex of São Paulo, *the Chronos complex*.[28] The lack of harmony between the rhythms of consciousness, the unconscious, the body, nature, the economic model, emotions, and the self-other relationship makes way for increased disturbances and pathologies linked to excess production, runaway consumerism, disposable affections, absence of mourning, anxiety prompted by the feeling of "little time," among others.

We overvalue innovation, style, youthful looks, speed, full agendas, and predictability. The rapid changing of partners, channels, fashions, and technologies is a trigger for adrenergic emotions and volatile, transitory pleasures. On the other hand, the time for resting, mourning, symbolic work, natural recycling, physiological metabolism, old age, the memory of a people and its traditions is confined to the cultural unconscious. These repressed contents are actuated, resulting in actions that are contrary to our survival as a species. As long as we do not deal with the deeper meaning of the serpent of concrete, the serpent will continue to devour us.

The mermaids of the *"minhocão"* (big-worm) viaduct entice us into looking at old age as an odd intruder that consumes youth, which we cannot let go of. We are incapable of accepting any part in finiteness, death, and suffering, and we undergo plastic surgery in defense. Rather than embracing a new aesthetics integrating the wisdom of age, we seek refuge in an illusory, edenic childhood.

We strive to buy a piece of Paradise with each new style of car, clothes, cell phone, high-resolution technology. What is the cost to the planet's ecosystem and to future generations? The global economy and the media together impose an imagery in which old age is ugly, passé, out of style. We fear an apocalyptic scenario, in which our children will grow amidst violence and poverty. On the other hand, the Paradise promised by the present economic paradigm is for no one, not even those who control capital and the means of production.

It is possible to accelerate the information processing activity of the ego, but when there is *no meaning*, or all is *meaningless*, the complex is fed, and the psyche is polluted; there is no recycling. Contact with the garbage we produce, within and without, is avoided. The linking of the feeling that there is no time with the need to consume the ephemeral is the great shadow aspect of our moment in history. Pleasure hooked up with the adrenalin rush of buying and risking is a destructive way of making ourselves feel alive when the symbols of the self are powerless to feed a polarized and dissociated ego.

CONCLUSIONS

As aspects of our social shadow which must be brought to consciousness, the dark history of colonization, the dissociated educational system, the important history of the Tiete River, the problem of overuse of water, and improper garbage disposal, all need to be addressed.

In environmental terms, the river of the soul of the inhabitants of São Paulo is as polluted as the river Tiete. As a result, *acting out,* concretizing, and perverting mythic and symbolic contents emerge as impediments to the development of a sustained ecological awareness. Jungian psychology provides a unique theoretical prism through which to analyze ecological questions, since it enables a symbolic reading that ranges from the contents of myths and cultural imagery to quantitative and qualitative historical data. As a result, a new form of "archetypal teaching" could develop as an instrument of awareness that encourages the preservation of nature through empathy and the re-valuing of forgotten cultural contents, rather than through a unilateral and utilitarian conservationist notion that teaches to "preserve so we don't go without." This may consecrate a new baptism, a new flow of the "water of life," which awakens the serpent imprisoned in the concrete of the viaduct and allows for the restoration of peace. In return, she might give us more life, more *numen,* and re-establish a new parental relationship with the Great-Mother, *Patchamama, Anima Mundi.*

In closing, I would like to quote the words of the beautiful song *"Canto em Qualquer Canto"* (I Sing in Any Corner) by Ná Ozzetti and the black genius Itamar Assumpção, one of the main musical innovators in São Paulo (born in the Paulista town of Tiete!, on September 13, 1949): "If this street were mine / the Ypê tree would be alive." Inspired by these words, I would say: "If this city were mine, the Tiete River would be alive." I hope that the fluvial voice of the river may also be mine. And that the song of Maraí, Ponaim, Mandi, Mavutsinim, Sinaá, Mumuru, Jacy, Anhurawi, Oxum, Iara, and Boiúna, amongst so many others, may once again be sung and heard. "I sing because it's necessary / because life isn't easy / so I don't lose my head." May these words raise their silenced, violated voices to other countries and peoples, and may the *aesthetic* union of compassion bring truth, matter, and spirit back to life.

NOTES

1. C. G. Jung, *The Collected Works of C. G. Jung*, Vol. 18: *The Symbolic Life*, trans. R. F. C. Hull (Princeton, NJ: Princeton University Press, 1964) § 1362 (hereafter referred to as *CW*).

2. Ricardo Alvarenga Hirata, "O Rio da Alma: Contribuições do simbolismo religioso e da psicologia analítica para uma reflexão sobre a crise ecológica no rio Tiete (uma proposta da Ecologia Arquetípica)"

[The River of the Soul: The Contribution of Religious Symbolism and Analytical Psychology to Reflections on the Ecological Crisis in the Tiete River]. Master's dissertation for the post-graduate degree in the Science of Religion at the Catholic Pontifical University of São Paulo (PUC-SP), 2005.

3. Ricardo Ohtake, ed., *O Livro do Rio Tietê* [The Book of the Tiete River] (São Paulo: Estúdio Ro, 1991).

4. Vicente Adorno, *Tiete: Uma Promessa de Futuro para as Águas do Passado* [Tiete: A Promise of the Future for the Waters of the Past] (São Paulo: Texto Art Gráfica e Editora Ltda., 1999).

5. Mário Mantovani, "Livro conta histórias sobre o rio Tietê" [Book tells stories to save the Tiete River]. *O Estado de São Paulo* (OESP), March 22, 2004: C02. [*Editor's note:* This translation from the Portuguese original into English and all subsequent translations from Portuguese sources are by Ricardo Hirata].

6. "Uma missão quase impossível: salvar o Tietê" [An almost impossible mission: To save the Tiete], *O Estado de São Paulo* (OESP), September 2, 2002: A02.

7. Benedito A. Prezia, *Os Indígenas do Planalto Paulista: nas Crônicas Quinhentistas e Seiscentistas* [The Aboriginals of the São Paulo Plateau: In the Chronicles of the 15th and 16th Centuries] (São Paulo: Humanitas/FFLCH/USP, 2000), 144.

8. Waldemar Andrade e Silva, *Lendas e Mitos dos Indios Brasileiros* [Legends and Myths of the Brazilian Indians] (São Paulo: Pancrom Indústria Gráfica, 1990).

9. Luís da Câmara Cascudo, *Geografia dos Mitos Brasileiros* [Geography of the Brazilian Myths] (Rio de Janeiro: José Olympio, 1976), 141.

10. Jonas Soares Souza and Miyoko Mikino, eds., *Diário da Navegação* [Ship's Log] (São Paulo: Editora da Universidade de São Paulo, Imprensa Oficial do Estado, 2000).

11. Adorno, 60.

12. *Ibid.*, 58.

13. *Ibid.*, 63.

14. Ohtake, 10.

15. Adorno, 49.

16. *Ibid.*, 66.

17. "Devotos homenageiam santa no Tietê" [Devotees honor Holy Mother image at the Tiete], *O Estado de São Paulo* (OESP), Dec. 7, 2003: C04.

18. "Tietê ainda muito longe de comemorações" [Tiete River Day celebrations still a long way off], *O Estado de São Paulo* (OESP), Sept. 23, 2003.

19. "Polêmica nas obras do Tietê" [Controversy over the goings-on on the Tiete River], *O Estado de São Paulo* (OESP), Jan. 28, 2004: C02.

20. Rosa Bastos, "Excursão da escola pelo Rio Tietê" [A school tour on the Tiete River], *O Estado de São Paulo* (OESP), Nov. 10, 2004: C03.

21. Andrade e Silva, 22.

22. "A problemática do esgoto e do lixo nas ruas de São Paulo" [Sewage and garbage problems in the streets of São Paulo], *O Estado de São Paulo* (OESP), Feb. 2, 2001: C02.

23. Gilberto Amendola, "A limpeza gradual do Tietê" [Cleaning of the Tiete comes gradually], *O Estado de São Paulo* (OESP), Sept. 22, 2004: A03.

24. "Lixo e esgoto em São Paulo" [Garbage and sewage in São Paulo], *O Estado de São Paulo* (OESP), February, 02, 2001: C02.

25. Adorno, 39.

26. Rita Magalhães, "Um presente paro o Tietê: nível zero de oxigênio" [A gift to the Tiete: Zero-level oxygen], *O Estado de São Paulo* (OESP), September 23, 2002: C03.

27. Benedito Lima de Toledo, "A reconquista do rio Pinheiros" [The re-conqest of the Pinheiros River], *O Estado de São Paulo* (OESP), January 21, 2001: C02.

28. Jung, *CW* 18 § 1366.

29. Ricardo Alvarenga Hirata, "O Complexo de Chronos e o Descompasso Emocional" [The Chronos Complex and Emotional Disharmony], *Junguiana* 23 (2005): 67-77.

THOREAU'S BEQUEST

In the autumn trees, a handful of crows.
The season of mists returns,
of ploughed fields, where starlight
seeds beneath the furrowed soil.
I step through a landscape of sacrament,
hearing in the wind, the wilder sorrow
of a birdcry; the last shimmer of evening
spinning its gossamer in the purple grass.
I have a leaf-harvest to gather,
for the pages of a book
I will never write,
but bequeath to posterity
these lines on solitude,
written for where and what I live,
this touchstone of woodland earth.

—*Michael Whan*

Travel and the Soul's Geography of Yearning

SHIRLEY FRANCES MCNEIL

> To know oneself in the garden of the world requires being
> physically in the world. Where you are reveals who you are.
> —James Hillman

Psyche yearns for new landscapes, to explore what lies just beyond the horizon. At times we catch a glimpse of the soul's yearnings in our dreams, in paintings, or in literary images conjured up by poets, novelists, and travel writers. Edward Casey has proposed that images "are places of psyche—its place-holders."[1] This study examines the experience of travelers who seek to discover and understand the affective connection between psyche and world. It considers travelers as phenomenologists, who set out on a journey to experience a city or landscape to which they are drawn, but find themselves in the imaginal space of a depth image.

Shirley Frances McNeil, Ph.D., has an undergraduate degree in philosophy and religion from Reed College and a doctorate in mythological studies with an emphasis in depth psychology from Pacifica Graduate Institute. Her dissertation, *The Memory of an Emotion: Travel and Reverie*, is an interpretive study of travel and imagination and draws on twenty years experience in the travel industry. She is an avid traveler, writer, and teacher, focusing on personal myth, imagination, psyche and nature, and the transformative value of travel. Her website is: www.mythiclandscapes.com.

Why do we go? How does the "where" of our travels influence "who" we become? Travel, like active imagination, taps into an archetypal depth that can have a significant effect on the restructuring of psyche. The soul embraces the "royal moments" that result from meeting an unconscious psychic structure, an archetypal form that enters time and space in the material world. Both are modes of imagination that interweave the imaginal with the real, the novel with a sense of déjà vu, the mythic with the mundane. The soul's geography, created through imagination and memory, has a continuous terrain, a coalescence of diverse landscapes, cultures, and images we have experienced through art, literary works, and physical travel where the common boundaries are not the limits of time or space but emotional resonance. It is a poetic world, to borrow a phrase from French philosopher Gaston Bachelard, of "a soul which is discovering its world, the world where it would like to live and where it deserves to live."[2]

TRAVEL AND THE EXPERIENCE OF PLACE

"Why do we travel?" asks travel writer Pico Iyer, whose insatiable curiosity about people and places has led him to far corners of the world. Why do people put themselves through the rigors of travel? He concludes: "Travel is like love: It cracks you open, and so pushes you over all the walls and low horizons that habits and defensiveness set up." Like love, "it quickens a sense of vulnerability and so admits us to states of mind, or areas of knowledge, that we didn't know we had …."[3]

Travel is like love in many aspects, among them the mysterious eros of attraction, surrender to the heart's desire, immersion in the sensuous impressions of place, the joy of discovery, and the imaginative complexity of projection onto the material world. As Iyer notes, like love, travel has that porous quality that can admit us to places within, previously unknown or forgotten, that can have a transformational influence.

Australian sociologist Peter Bishop remarks that a geographical site is transformed into a place when it takes on meaning for the traveler, when its contours are shaped by fantasies and stories.[4] This is the soul's terrain, the comprehension of place as inner and outer landscape. Bishop relates places to memories and to the heart; places can become soul images, and the fascination with place, a form of eros. Accordingly, "anima fascination," as he terms it, is with the "*display* of the landscape, of the art, the architecture, the colors and the light," which often has a mysterious quality.[5]

Travelogues and travel advertising exploit the eros of place with photographs of white crescent beaches or a rustic village high on a hilltop, inviting us to imagine ourselves there. In recent years, bookstore travel sections have continued to expand with titles promising "traveler's tales," "adventures," and "journeys." The immediate appeal of these stories appears to be escapism and fantasy, but closer examination reveals that much travel literature has an almost redemptive tone, as if the narrator encountered an unexpected divinity on his or her path. At times one's imagination is captivated by a particular image or a story set in a place that beckons to the traveler, as if psyche has recognized some aspect of herself and yearns to explore her own depths through interaction with it.

Artist Alan Gussow muses on the difference between an abstract "environment" and a specific place in his book, *A Sense of Place*:

> The catalyst that converts any physical location—any environment if you will—into a place, is the process of experiencing deeply. A place is a piece of the whole environment that has been claimed by feelings.[6]

Although one may visit places in images, literary or visual, the sensuous encounter with place imprints memorable details that can have far-reaching effects. In fact, nature preservation organizations urge influential leaders and potential donors to visit areas involved in preservation battles because, once psyche has encountered the living presence of the place, the *genius loci*, the place is no longer just an abstraction.

The phenomenological experience of place links it to ontology. Casey points to the archetypal human condition: "To be is to be bounded by place, limited by it."[7] Imagination, memory, and place are phenomena that have a complementary character because place is integral to both imagination and memory. "If imagination projects us out beyond ourselves," suggests Casey, "while memory takes us back behind ourselves, place subtends and enfolds us, lying perpetually under and around us."[8]

In his scheme, place is "the bedrock of our being-in-the-world."[9] For a culture like the traditional Navajo of the Southwest, the landscape figures prominently in their cosmology and mythology. Each topographical feature plays a fundamental role in a sacred story, literally and symbolically the "bedrock" of a meaningful existence. Modern Western cultures have developed a sense of independence from place in an attempt to transcend the human condition, but we might then ask what is lost when we cut ourselves off from the lifeworld that enfolds us. C. G. Jung believed that the sense of sacred landscape was essential to psyche's well-being:

> As scientific understanding has grown, so our world has become dehumanized. Man feels himself isolated in the cosmos, because he is no longer involved in nature. . . . No river contains a spirit, no tree is the life principle of man. . . . No voices now speak to man from stones, plants, and animals. . . . His contact with nature has gone, and with it has gone the profound emotional energy that this symbolic connection supplied.[10]

Archetypal psychology seeks the reanimation of the world that Jung feared was lost to modern consciousness. Psyche still responds to the spirit of place whether we consciously acknowledge it or not; the soul seeks "the place where it would like to live," seeks symbolic touchstones in the material world. A place that has affected us deeply can become the "bedrock of our being-in-the-world" and continue to influence us in consequential life decisions. We can deliberately recognize and cultivate our response to the spirit of place or shut it away for fear of the transformational possibilities.

Even when they have an unusually powerful response to place, the experience may seem too much like a romantic fantasy to travelers who then return to their "real" lives. Author Claire Krulikowski, who wrote about how a trip to India changed the direction of her life, was interviewed by a journalist who seemed somewhat skeptical. The journalist challenged the truth of the author's story, and shared a story of her own with the author. The journalist revealed that three years earlier she had gone on a vacation trip to Thailand. It was very beautiful, the people very good, and life very different from her life back at home. It was such a wonderful experience that she had not wanted to leave, and on the flight back she had cried all the way home.[11]

The journalist, though, then commented: "It was tough coming back, I'll admit, but after a while I got back into the swing of things."[12] Although she had been exposed in Thailand to a way of life her soul craved, the journalist was unable, or unwilling, to allow some of these new elements into her everyday life once she returned; whereas the author Krulikowski had made significant changes after her trip to India to honor her soul's needs. Nevertheless, the memory evoked by the journalist's trip to Thailand resonated in some deeply felt place, for as she related her traveler's tale to Krulikowski tears welled up in her eyes.[13]

The reporter's experience in Thailand could be described as an awakening of the psyche, the recognition of a sacramental way of living with nature, an aesthetic response engaging her in a harmonious state of flow. Returning to her normally time-driven "fragmented" world, she was not able to sustain this awakening consciously, but her psyche would not let her forget it either. Thailand became a soul image, the place her soul yearned to live and where it dwelled whether the reporter consciously acknowledged it or not. If images "are places of psyche— its place-holders," and places are soul images, as Bishop believes, we might ask how psyche inhabits images and what attraction to images of place can tell us about the soul's yearning.

TRAVEL AND IMAGINAL WORLDS

In *Healing Fiction*, James Hillman writes that word-images conjure up imaginal worlds unique to each individual. Each reader imagines a fictional character or a novel's setting differently from another, whereas one usually recalls a cinematic story in the filmmaker's vision: the setting, faces, colors, and lighting having been first perceived on the screen rather than in our imagination.[14]

In oral tradition, children learn from stories, and the culture's history is recalled through storytelling. The individual who is told stories or who reads them at an early age develops an active imagination, one that can "*imagine life*" and realize that "imagination is a place where one can be, a kind of being."[15] Dream images have a similar sense of being and place. Hillman contends that dreams are attempts to gain a different vantage-point from the customary perspective of daily life, to which I would add that travel also serves this purpose in many respects. In dreams, one travels far distances in seconds, converses in nonsensical terms (like trying to converse in foreign languages), trades puns with archetypal figures, and views astonishing images inconceivable in waking life. In fact, the dream image offers an opportunity for "the psychological moment, a moment of reflection, wonder, puzzlement."[16]

To psychologize, according to Hillman, we need to change position, to "move closer," or "back off." There are several motifs that give shape to the reflective moment; changes of physical position and attitude can be metaphors for seeing through. Other motifs, like entering, descending, and traveling to a foreign land or a different period of history, are all "concrete images for shifting one's attitude to events, scenes, and persons."[17] Stories are set in particular places, and successful stories invite us into the place-world where the story occurs. In this manner imaginative people can travel through history, cultures, and the geography of the world, not to mention the inner workings of countless characters in novels. By Hillman's definition they are psychologizing as they move through the inner and outer landscape of the narrative.

For the inquiring traveler, fantasy images created by the descriptions of diverse cultures and wondrous places so unlike one's comfortably familiar home stimulate an intense desire to go to see these places for themselves. British travel writer Freya Stark recalls one of her earliest childhood memories when "the joy of running away became conscious," and she set out with only a toothbrush and a penny in her pocket. "Running away," she suggests, is not the right term for such an adventure, for it is not to escape but to seek that we go.

> The beckoning counts, and not the clicking latch behind you:
> and all through life the actual moment of emancipation still holds
> that delight, of the whole world coming to meet you like a wave.[18]

The beckoning world waiting to envelop us just over the threshold is the subject of Eric Overmyer's play, *On the Verge*, a fantasy about three Victorian lady explorers on safari. The title was inspired by Andre Breton's comment, "Perhaps the imagination is on the verge of recovering its rights."[19] Subtitled "The Geography of Yearning," the play takes three women, proper in their Victorian expedition wear, to "darkest Africa," "highest Himalaya," and to *Terra Incognita*, a terrain of shifting time and place. Throughout the piece the trio tell stories of intrepid past adventures as they encounter characters, music, and gadgets in cultural glimpses of the future. Mary, the eldest and the leader, picks up images and messages about Burma Shave, cream cheese, Red Chinese, and Teddy Roosevelt, puzzling over these nonsensical dream-like phantoms. The audience is privy to her reverie as she writes in her journal:

> I feel the rare air of *Terra Incognita* working its way upon me like
> acid on an old coin, the tarnish of the past dissolving in a solvent
> of iridescent light. I tingle. Objects shimmer on the horizon. At
> sunset, a tantalizing mist, a web, a membrane envelops us.[20]

Mary the explorer leaves behind the mundane Victorian world, entering the *mundus imaginalis*. Every traveler can identify with this tingling sensation that amplifies Iyer's statement about travel which, like love, "admits us to states of mind we didn't know we had." The irreverent Overmyer supplies a tongue-in-cheek word-image for the connection between travel and imagination via his youngest character, Alexandra, who writes in her journal after an evening of fireside stories about "natives:" "Funny word, native. Native. Native. (She Kodaks an imaginary native.) Image. Native. Image-native. Imaginative. I am a native of the image. An indigene of the imagination."[21]

Overmyer's wordplay makes us smile because, of course, she is a fictional character in his play, but a "native of the image" or an "indigene of the imagination" might also describe active imagination with a dream image or immersion in the setting and characters of a novel. Like Alexandra, travelers may use the same terms to describe the immediate impressions of the experiencing body while traveling. We may feel as if we have stepped into a dynamic image where everything is going on at once and we can't quite get our bearings. The effects of jet lag intensify the overlapping events and sounds, the cadence of unfamiliar languages, the change of light, perhaps the vivid colors and scents of a marketplace. If it is too much to process consciously, the unconscious may be activated to absorb the overload. In retrospect, these chaotic sensory impressions are reflected upon, edited, and shaped into a pattern to form a holographic sense of place, a moving image that we can revisit as we do with dream images and word-images.

PSYCHE IN THE GARDEN

In her study of the imagination, Eva Brann, like Casey, connects imagination with place and concludes, "the imagination is essentially spatial rather than temporal."[22] One can dwell in images, as I learned while designing and creating a garden. In preparation I studied garden design books and magazine layouts, visited plant nurseries and local gardens, and immersed myself in horticultural lore. When scent became a significant feature of my ideal garden, the images in the books began to take on a three-dimensional, sensuous reality. Visits to actual gardens and the first steps of the physical landscaping of the garden space led me to translate the printed images into holographic experiences. While looking at a garden design diagram, I could imagine turning and moving around within the image to view different perspectives. When I was introduced to the Jungian style of active imagination with dream images, the process seemed familiar from my imaginal landscape work. Both had a similar type of psychic reality to that of literary characters moving about in their landscapes.

An imaginal space can become quite as real to us as a physical place. For a landscape designer, the joy lies in seeing one's imaginal space manifest into a material place that has visible pattern, touchable textures, and scent that one can inhale. The understanding of form and relationship is intellectual; the sensate impressions are physical, yet psyche is able to grasp both in a transcendent moment, at once immediate and eternal. Place, regarded as a dynamic image of interrelated parts, can suddenly shift into an archetypal configuration, like a kaleidoscope falling into a dazzling pattern. It can evoke an emotional response that overwhelms the psyche with a sense of wholeness we rarely experience in our daily lives. The sudden intake of breath at the wonder of the image observed was named *aesthesis* by the Greeks, for whom the heart was the organ of sensation as well as the seat of the imagination. For the Renaissance philosopher Marsilio Ficino, the heart translated sensory impressions as an aesthetic function.[23] Learning to translate sensory impressions, the spirit of place, into psyche's language is not entirely a lost art, as American landscape designer Julie Moir Messervy learned when she apprenticed with a master Japanese gardener. The first assignment in her apprenticeship was to visit eighty gardens and "open my heart to their beauty and spirit," observing, noticing, feeling their presence.[24] In this way Messervy practiced what Hillman calls *notitia,* the soul's capacity to "form true notions of things from attentive noticing."[25]

One of the goals of archetypal psychology is to reanimate the world by paying attention, by observing and appreciating the particulars of the "things" around us. Hillman's essay, "In the Gardens—A Psychological Memoir," considers the garden as psyche; the style of a garden can reveal much about the psyche of an individual or culture.

The interiority of the garden, he says, "is wholly objective and displayed. We are in it, moving inside it, much as when we dream we move inside the dream which embraces and includes us in its images."[26] A successful garden has an almost imperceptible boundary in the mediation between nature and human shaping. Many places in the world have been shaped and reshaped by humans for so long, the boundaries are equally obscured. The most beloved cities in the world, like Rome and Paris, are time-deep places where layer upon layer has been added over the ages, yet somehow the whole achieves an aesthetically pleasing effect.

Walking in the Japanese garden, Hillman notices that instead of a central viewpoint of the whole, "there is perspective and eachness." There are constant shifts in focus as the body moves through the garden. Like the garden, the world is on self-display; its insights and teachings available to anyone who pays attention.[27] Contemporary Americans face the dulling standardization of place in housing developments and identical strip malls. We don't look because it all appears to be the same; mundane familiarity is the goal of the designer. When we encounter the "eachness" of a Tuscan hilltown, walking the narrow winding streets that continually change direction piques psyche's interest. We enter the archetypal field of the particular place, moving about, observing as we go, "performing an activity of psychic reflection in correspondence to our surroundings." In fact, Hillman proposes that the site itself in all its physical particulars—setting, weather, season —"'displaces the subject' by precisely placing its subjectivity."[28] This phenomenological effect could account for the distinctive intensity of the memory or soul image of place that is experienced by artists and occasionally by travelers.

The First Time World

Art historian Kenneth Clark once observed that Italian art expert Bernard Berenson's imaginative ability to inhabit the landscape of a painting became so identical to that of physical reality he would occasionally find himself critiquing a natural view framed by a window.[29] In his "Moments of Vision" lecture at Oxford in 1954, Clark spoke of the sense of wonder and the "illumination" of the world that is "the commonplace experience of childhood."[30] He argues that this sense of wonder can only be synthesized in adult imagination by exposure to and interaction with literature or art, and to these I would add the experience of travel. A more explicit title of his lecture, writes Clark, might have been "the moment of intensified physical perception."[31] Gaston Bachelard refers to this "intensified perception" as the first time world of childhood, recalled through the poetic imagination.

Bachelard had a celebrated career as a philosopher of science at the Sorbonne, but his later studies led him beyond the philosophical problems raised by the nature of scientific knowledge to the philosophy of art and aesthetics and to the phenomenology of the imagination. Schooled in French rationalism, but influenced by the rhythms of nature and the language of poetry, Bachelard's later works explore the material imagination and its reverberations in the human soul.[32]

In his essay, "Reveries Towards Childhood," Bachelard speaks of the *once-upon-a-time* ("*autrefois*" in French), that is, the childhood world of the *first time*.[33] The young child experiences places and "things" of the world in this first time participative mode of perception. In effect, the child is involved in the process of *poiesis*, from the Greek, meaning "to make," "shape," or "give form to." Here it indicates the making of a world by moving through it, by how he or she encounters and learns about the material "objects." All the first time memories are images with the timeless quality of Clark's intense physical perception. Brann calls these exceptional moments "moments of being," when the imagination "gathers the mundane appearances into an imaginative world dense with meaning."[34]

Bachelard observes that the first time world, dense with meaning, is what the poet struggles to express, the "union of the poetry of memory and the truth of illusions," the qualities of the perceived world, using poetic imagination in creative combinations of words, structures, and rhythms.[35] Accordingly, in the "Poetics of Reverie," he states that poetic "reverie gives us the world of a soul" and the "poetic image bears witness to a soul which is discovering its world, the world where it would like to live and where it deserves to live."[36]

SHAPING A LIFE

Travelers who explore a new place also create a world by combining immediate sensory data with the mythos of the place that drew them there. The soul re-imagines itself, shapes, and is shaped by, these two aspects of place. Brann describes the middle space of the soul:

> In the middle, between our appearance in the world and the
> invisible ground of our being, there is . . . a space of place, an
> inner world . . . the quasi-visible topography of our individual,
> unique soul. Here . . . where we are no longer quite individual
> and not yet quite essence, the soul takes shape and appears as a
> manifold panorama of memory and imagination.[37]

In this middle space, the "quasi-visible topography" of our soul forms
a contiguous landscape of childhood memories, places we have visited
in word-images, places that live in our imagination, and places to which
we have traveled in the physical world. These place images are the
placeholders of psyche and their presence is vital for psyche's resilience.

Literary place images can be the call to action for the travelers who
yearn for poetic landscapes that feed their souls. Novelist and
screenwriter Jessamyn West made her first trip to Europe in 1929, a
journey with unexpected consequences. Some fifty years later she finds
a box of her journals and letters home, saved in her mother's attic. West
opens the box "more to discover who I had then been than to remember
where I had gone."[38] In one entry written on a dusty train crossing the
country to New York, she reflects on the motivation for her trip. She is
recently married and dislikes the inconvenience of traveling, especially
by the cheapest transport she is forced to take: crowded trains and
"school teacher" quad cabins on a steamer ship. She asks, "Why do I
go?" and muses:

> I was going to England, not to see the houses, or even the rooms
> where these writers had worked. All I wanted to do was to walk
> about in their world, the world they had written of: a world where
> heather and bracken *grew* and nightingales and cuckoos could
> be *heard*. This reason for going to England I knew.[39]

The imaginal world of her favorite English writers calls to West,
a place so exotic to one raised in the dry California desert; just "to
walk about in their world" is reason enough to endure the hardships
of getting there. The poetic imagination is awakened not only by the
poet's description of place but through the emotional value of the
image, for as West acknowledged in her memoir, she had a secret desire
to become a writer. To walk about in the territory of the writers' world
helped her to re-imagine herself as a writer and take the first step
toward her vocation.

Bachelard, writing about the poetic imagination of place and the contemplation of aesthetic emotion, claims that material reveries precede contemplation. "Any landscape is an oneiric experience before becoming a conscious spectacle. We look with aesthetic passion only at those places we have first seen in dreams."[40] West dreamed of Britain where her favorite writers had walked. Travel writer Stark was so fascinated by Alexander the Great that she learned Arabic to follow his path through the Middle East during the early twentieth century. She writes, "This is a great moment, when you see, however distant, the goal of your wandering. The thing which has been living in your imagination suddenly becomes a part of the tangible world."[41] At times it becomes difficult to distinguish the boundary between the dream and the material world as travelers, like the Victorian explorers, find themselves in liminal space.

TRAVEL AS LIMINAL SPACE

Inspired by a London exhibition of art and artifacts from British colonies, C. G. Jung set out for Africa in 1925. During this trip, he often felt himself in a dreamlike state, transported to some eternal time by new images that evoked intense feelings. Traveling by train from Mombassa into the interior, Jung describes awakening at dawn to such an image:

> The train swathed in a red cloud of dust, was just making a turn around a steep red cliff. On a jagged rock above us a slim brownish-black figure stood motionless, leaning on a long spear, looking down at the train. Beside him towered a gigantic candelabrum cactus.[42]

The scene was both "alien," never before experienced, and at the same time, "a most intense sentiment of *déjà vu*."[43] He goes on to say that the "feeling-tone" of this experience accompanied him throughout his entire journey. Trained as he was to observe the unconscious, Jung was aware that throughout his trip his psyche was unusually active.[44]

Though postmodern critics might criticize Jung for his colonial psyche, it is the "feeling-tone" of the image that I want to consider. The image has a mysterious combination of the "alien," or novel, and a *déjà vu* quality; the anamnesis of place offers a clue to the soul's embrace of an aspect of herself.

Like Jung, I have at times found myself captivated by certain natural configurations or by a landscape that had a peculiarly familiar feel about it, though I had never physically been there before. An especially vivid experience happened on my first visit to the Big Island of Hawaii, a sojourn that felt like a homecoming. For the first time in years, I relaxed into a slower pace, into what is known as "island time." Although, as usual, I had an ambitious list of places to see on the island, I found myself frequently sitting on the porch swing, daydreaming. The view from the cabin's porch enthralled me, my gaze resting on the timeless scene in the meadow.

The meadow landscape was not beautiful in the tropical lushness we associate with Hawaii, but was very distinctive: several overlapping umbrella-shaped monkeypod trees stood amid overgrown dry grass and scrubby undergrowth. It seemed familiar, like an African savanna, although I had never been to Africa except in my imagination. Time lost any meaning, for this meadow presented itself as it might have hundreds or even thousands of years earlier, with few hints of human habitation. Robert Romanyshyn describes the effect it had on me: "In reverie we slip into that place where the eternal quality of the world shines through the veil of the here and now."[45]

As Jung's unconscious was highly stimulated by his trip to Africa, mine had become active in Hawaii. One day towards the end of our stay as I was in deep reverie on the porch, I quite distinctly heard a voice tell me that life could be different. Startled, I looked around, but found no one nearby. The event had a powerful impact, but seemed so inexplicable that I did not reveal the details to anyone for years. Though I have never been back to that particular place, the archetypal image of that landscape is very clear in my memory, and I have often thought that it had a healing effect on my psyche. I began to examine the mythic power of place, asking how hours quietly observing this particular configuration could change my sense of self and begin the process of reshaping my life.

One explanation lies in the encounter with an unconscious psychic structure, an archetypal form that enters time and space in the material world. But which arises from which? The psychic image from the landscape, or the landscape shaped as a result of our psychic perception? Bachelard suggests that the imaginal realm is the meeting of the two spheres, and would call this image a "depth image," a dreamlike image that reflects back to us our own depth.[46] As Hillman remarks about the garden/psyche experience, the place displaced the subject. "Where you are reveals who you are."[47]

Clark notes the importance of emotion in an encounter, and comments that in some way we are able to possess the gestalt, the image, and are simultaneously possessed by it, a two-way communication. "In the moment of vision we are both participating with our whole being and at the same time contemplating our externalized selves with possessive delight."[48] It is a perfect description of a depth image. Certain places may trigger such an emotion, or even possess our imagination, as Jung learned on his trip to the Sahara.

Jung traveled a great deal to "find a psychic observation post" from which he could discover the lost or repressed parts of his modern European consciousness.[49] During his first trip to northern Africa, he could feel himself responding to the slower pace and the emotional intensity of the people going about their traditional and religious rituals. He recognized a certain timelessness in the Sahara and observed that "the deeper we penetrated into the Sahara, the more time slowed down for me: it even threatened to move backward."[50] He commented on the archetypal memory awakened in him by North Africa:

> Just as a childhood memory can suddenly take possession of
> consciousness with so lively an emotion that we feel wholly
> transported back to the original situation, so these seemingly alien
> and wholly different Arab surroundings awaken an archetypal
> memory of an only too well known prehistoric past which
> apparently we have entirely forgotten. We are remembering a
> potentiality of life which has been overgrown by civilization, but
> which in certain places is still existent.[51]

When psyche encounters the spirit of place, a "potentiality of life" may be activated, as my own experience suggests, for soon after my trip I had a series of numinous dreams set in gardens.

"Our dreams and symbols," says Michael Conforti, "as well as the patterns of our behavior are shaped by the fact that we are creatures of a material universe."[52] In his book, *Field, Form, and Fate: Patterns in Mind, Nature, and Psyche*, Conforti compares Jung's theory of archetypes as underlying patterns with "fields" described in the theories of dynamical systems. One of the most influential fields, or archetypal patterns, is the landscape, or the power of a particular place.[53] The presence and existence of the archetype is felt through its effects,[54] and its restructuring effect often "occurs outside the domain of conscious perception and becomes available to conscious awareness only in retrospect on the basis of its results."[55]

The restructuring effect on the psyche through an encounter with a place that holds a powerful resonance for the traveler is one of the many wonders and joys of travel. Indeed, it is one of the tenets for pilgrimage and, in many ways, every journey is a *theoria*. In ancient Greek practice, humans made pilgrimages to sacred sites such as Delphi, site of Apollo's victory over the Pythos. The ritual of going to meet the divinity was called a *theoria*. When the Greeks substituted mandatory attendance at the theatre, the early Greek myth-inspired plays were performed in verse with the strophe and antistrophe rhythmic movement of the chorus across the stage, a holdover from early forms of ritual.[56]

The movement of travel is a ritual, a *theoria,* even though we may not know which god or goddess we seek and must depend on Hermes, the god of travelers, to direct us to a chance meeting with the deity required at the moment. The movement in a travel narrative can be as effective as the movement across a stage; in effect, all the world's a stage. Iyer reminds us of the etymology of *ecstasy,* from *ex-stasis,* and proposes "that our highest moments come when we are not stationary." In fact, he writes, "epiphany can follow movement as much as it precipitates it."[57]

Extraordinary travel experiences often involve the timeless suddenly breaking through into the present time, a numinous experience the soul yearns for and duly preserves in memory. In leisure travel and during odd moments in business travel, we enter *kairos* time rather than *chronos,* or clock time, a condition for the reflective state Bachelard names reverie. Phenomenologically, reverie feels like wasting time, useless in a practical sense, like the daydreaming we were warned against as children. Romanyshyn points out that we can only be present to the world when we are not useful, when our focus softens and we breathe together (con-spire) with the world. Reverie, he says, positions us to be able to respond to our surroundings.[58] If I had not sat daydreaming on the porch swing for hours, my Hawaii experience might never have happened.

Like Bachelard, Romanyshyn thinks of reverie as a way of knowing the *mundus imaginalis,* the imaginal world. He writes about an

illuminating encounter in a tiny village in the Luberon valley of
southern France where the ancient and alien surroundings "opened a
portal to another world that I once knew but had forgotten, a world
that does and does not belong to my biographical history."[59] He writes:

> To linger as a phenomenologist in the moment is to open oneself
> to these breakthroughs of the timeless into the timebound,
> breakthroughs that are experienced as ontological surprises, that
> is, as breakdowns of our usual and familiar ways of knowing the
> world and being in it.[60]

Reverie dissolves the separation between the spectator and world
or between the reader and poetic image; instead one suddenly finds
oneself in the midst of things. Often we are unprepared for the
overpowering emotional affect of being present to the "aesthetic depths
of the world."[61]

"Topographical correspondences can . . . exist between the sensible
world and the *mundus imaginalis*, one symbolizing with the other,"
writes Henry Corbin.[62] However, "it is not possible to pass from one
to the other without a break." One may start out with a geographical
location in mind, but at some point, the map's geographical coordinates
break down and the traveler enters the imaginal world. The traveler
only realizes what has happened after the event, comments Corbin,
"either with dismay or amazement." Active imagination plays the
mediating role in this "topographical inversion," a movement from the
outside to the inside.[63]

LANDSCAPES OF THE HEART

Lawrence Durrell has written extensively about the *genius loci*, the
spirit of place. In the essay, "Landscape and Character," he comments
that a "friendly" critic once noted that he writes "as if the landscape
were more important than the characters," to which Durrell replies
that he sees characters "almost as functions of a landscape." A place
will "express" itself through the people and culture, just as much as it
does through its flowers, and the task of the travel-writer is to "isolate
the germ in the people which is expressed by their landscape."[64] He
urges the traveler take the time to look and listen; to breathe in the
atmosphere; to quietly absorb the particulars of one's surroundings.
Once you have gotten the "essential sense of landscape values," Durrell

says, this "inner identification," you will get all the rest, for it is the key to the culture.[65]

Writers (and, I believe, all people) seem to have a "personal landscape of the heart which beckons them," writes Durrell. When they find a place where their soul comes alive with inspiration, they have found their "'correspondences.'" Perhaps this is why, when we are drawn to a particular landscape or location, we find that we easily fit into the lifestyle of the culture there. A contemporary example of this phenomenon is Frances Mayes, who found the place where her poetic soul thrived in a small village in Tuscany. Mayes's Tuscan *topophilia*, to use Yi-Fu Tuan's word for the human attraction to place,[66] was made famous by her book *Under the Tuscan Sun*, recently made into a popular film. Judging by the wild success of both book and film, millions of people around the world resonated with her discovery of a time-deep place where she could re-imagine her life as she restored an abandoned old house into a beautiful home.[67] Every year, thousands travel to Tuscany, hoping to be inspired by the beauty and culture of the area, dreaming that just for a few days they too will find the soul connection Mayes found there.

A Continuous Terrain

Proust observed that our imagination takes us to places we desire; the miracle is that it makes "psychically contiguous" places that are separate on earth.[68] Places we have known as children and collected in our travels can be transformed into a singularly personal map of the world in which the common boundaries are not the limits of time or space but emotional resonance. Brann proposes that the interplay of perception, imagination, and memory makes an "imaginative" rather than an "imaginary" world. The difference is that there is not a separate encapsulated world but one that is a "humanly coherent environment," neither "exclusively internal nor external."[69] Whether roaming physically or in reverie, the imaginative traveler's map is shaped by aesthetic values and desire. It is a world distinct from the busyness of our daily routine, separated by the sense of a "festive heightening of human existence."[70]

The "festive" occasion for the archaic Greeks meant that the gods would be present in eating, drinking, and the recital of mythic poetry. At festival time, the world of the gods and the human world were intermeshed and co-dependent. In his study of the Greek gods, Kerenyi describes *theoria* as going to meet the gods, traveling to a place where a god has been "seen."[71] Like West, who wanted to walk in the world of her literary gods, we go to enter the liminal space of the soul-image.

The essence of travel, writes Stark, is what lies beyond, "its symbol is the horizon, and its interest always lies over that edge in the unseen."[72] Psyche will always yearn to know more of herself through her circuitous exploration of the *anima mundi* and the heightened experience of the depth image. We can reframe travel in the service of the soul, not as escapism from our mundane lives but as going to meet the world waiting to enfold us, a world on self-display waiting to be noticed. Imaginative travel, like dreaming, is always a *theoria*.

NOTES

1. Edward S. Casey, *Spirit and Soul: Essays in Philosophical Psychology* (Dallas: Spring Publications, 1991), xx.

2. Gaston Bachelard, *The Poetics of Reverie: Childhood, Language and the Cosmos*, trans. Daniel Russell (Boston: Beacon, 1971), 15.

3. Pico Iyer, "Why We Travel," *Salon.com's Wanderlust: Real Life Tales of Adventure and Romance* (New York: Random House, 2000), H.

4. Peter Bishop, "The Imagination of Place: Tibet," *Spring 1984*: 196.

5. *Ibid.*, 202-203.

6. Alan Gussow, *A Sense of Place: The Artist and the American Land* (Washington, DC: Island Press, 1971), 27.

7. Edward S. Casey, *Getting Back into Place: Toward a Renewed Understanding of the Place-World* (Bloomington: Indiana UP, 1993), 15.

8. *Ibid.*, xvi-xvii.

9. *Ibid.*, xvii.

10. C. G. Jung, *Man and His Symbols* (Garden City: Doubleday, 1964), 95.

11. Claire Krulikowski, "The Blueprint of the Soul," *The New Times* 18.2 (July 2001): 20.

12. *Ibid.*, 21.

13. *Ibid.*

14. James Hillman, *Healing Fiction* (Barrytown: Station Hill Press, 1983), 46-47.

15. *Ibid.*, 47.

16. James Hillman, *Re-Visioning Psychology* (New York: HarperCollins, 1992), 141.

17. *Ibid.*, 142.

18. Freya Stark, *The Freya Stark Story: A Condensation in One Volume of Traveller's Prelude, Beyond Euphrates,* and *The Coast of Incense* (New York: Coward-McCann, 1953), 31.

19. Eric Overmyer, *On the Verge or the Geography of Yearning* (New York: Broadway Play Publishing, 1986), iii.

20. *Ibid.*, 22.

21. *Ibid.*, 27.

22. Eva T. H. Brann, *The World of the Imagination: Sum and Substance* (Savage: Rowman & Littlefield, 1991), 748.

23. James Hillman, *The Thought of the Heart and the Soul of the World* (Dallas: Spring Publications, 1992), 80.

24. Julie Moir Messervy, *The Inward Garden: Creating a Place of Beauty and Meaning* (Boston: Little, Brown, 1995), 12.

25. Hillman, *Thought of the Heart*, 82.

26. James Hillman, "In the Gardens—A Psychological Memoir," in *Consciousness and Reality: Studies in Memory of Toshihiko Izutzu* (Tokyo: Iwanami Shoten, 1998), 178.

27. *Ibid.*, 176-77.

28. *Ibid.*

29. Kenneth Clark, *Moments of Vision and Other Essays* (New York: Harper & Row, 1981), 9.

30. *Ibid.*, 2.

31. *Ibid.*, 1.

32. Gaston Bachelard, *The Poetics of Space*, trans. Maria Jolas (Boston: Beacon, 1994), xvi.

33. Bachelard, *Poetics of Reverie*, 116.

34. Brann, *World of the Imagination*, 4.

35. Bachelard, *Poetics of Reverie*, 119.

36. *Ibid.*, 15.

37. Brann, *World of the Imagination*, 770.

38. Jessamyn West, *Double Discovery: A Journey* (New York: Harcourt Brace Jovanovich, 1980), 3-4.

39. *Ibid.*, 7.

40. Gaston Bachelard, *Water and Dreams: An Essay on the Imagination of Matter,* trans. Edith R. Farrell (Dallas: Dallas Institute, 1983), 36).

41. Freya Stark, qtd. in Phil Cousineau, *The Art of Pilgrimage: The Seekers' Guide to Making Travel Sacred* (Berkeley: Conari Press, 1998), 159.

42. C. G. Jung, *Memories, Dreams, Reflections*, recorded and edited by Aniela Jaffe, trans. Richard and Clara Winston (New York: Vintage, 1989), 254.

43. *Ibid.,* 254.

44. *Ibid.,* 264.

45. Robert Romanyshyn, *Ways of the Heart: Essays Toward an Imaginal Psychology* (Pittsburgh: Trivium, 2002), 134.

46. Gaston Bachelard, *On Poetic Imagination and Reverie,* selected, translated, and introduced by Colette Gaudin (Dallas: Spring Publications, 1971), 54.

47. Hillman, "In the Gardens—A Psychological Memoir," 178.

48. Clark, *Moments of Vision and Other Essays,* 11.

49. *Memories, Dreams, Reflections,* 244.

50. *Ibid.,* 240.

51. *Ibid.,* 245-46.

52. Michael Conforti, "History of Assisi Conferences and Seminars." 12 December 2001. <http://www.assisiconferences.com/about/history.html>

53. Michael Conforti, *Field, Form, and Fate: Patterns in Mind, Nature, and Psyche* (Woodstock: Spring Publications, 1999), 37.

54. *Ibid.,* 22.

55. *Ibid.,* xv.

56. Karl Kerenyi, *The Religion of the Greeks and Romans* (New York: E. P. Dutton, 1962), 152.

57. Iyer, "Why We Travel," Hvii.

58. Romanyshyn, *Ways of the Heart,* 136-7.

59. *Ibid.,* 142.

60. *Ibid.*

61. *Ibid.,* 136.

62. Henry Corbin, "Mundus Imaginalis: Or The Imaginary and the Imaginal," in *Working with Images,* ed. Benjamin Sells (Woodstock: Spring, 2000), 82.

63. All quotes in this paragraph, *ibid.*

64. Lawrence Durrell, *Spirit of Place,* ed. Alan G. Thomas (London: E. P. Dutton & Co., 1969), 156.

65. *Ibid.*, 158.

66. Yi-Fu Tuan, *Topophilia: A Study of Environmental Perception, Attitudes, and Values* (New York: Columbia UP, 1990).

67. Frances Mayes, *Under the Tuscan Sun* (San Francisco: Chronicle Books, 1996).

68. Brann, *World of the Imagination*, 745.

69. *Ibid.*, 753.

70. *Ibid.*, Dilthey, as qtd. 753.

71. Kerenyi, *The Religion of the Greeks and Romans*, 152.

72. Freya Stark, *The Zodiac Arch* (London: Cox & Wyman, 1968), 139.

'ENVIRONMENTAL ART'

That day, the stone shone in the mountain air;
the sky held clear, a crystal of far-off blue.

Thought fluttered between us like crows,
austere in the harsh winds, as we clutched

our word-hoard tightly in our hands;
memories abiding of that terrain of solitudes.

Ice had formed an exquisite geometry
in the shaping wind; bird feathers delicate

as a sacrament or the beginning of water,
frozen forever in their winged moments.

And after, our return to lower ground,
to the valley of ordinary lives;

what each bore with him to the hearth, cold
mountain poems, told in the borderland of his eye.

—*Michael Whan*

THE ARCHIVE OF SOLES:
WALKING IN THE SOULSCAPE OF HISTORY

RUTH MEYER

WALKING AND THE HISTORICAL IMAGINATION

Walking is something I am having problems with in California, where I now live. I should perhaps explain first what I mean by walking. I do not mean hiking, which Californians are definitely very keen on and which a whole leisure industry has grown up to promote, complete with high-tech boots and trail guides. I certainly do not mean jogging, with all of its speed and intensity. Rather, I mean ambling along a country lane or city street, taking your time, walking in a natural rhythm, enjoying your surroundings, unmindful about time taken or calories burned or miles per hour. California is just not designed for this. If I want to walk, I need to get into my car and find a trail. This is not the case in Europe and was not the case for Sigmund Freud or C. G. Jung.

Ruth Meyer, Ph.D., studied and taught history in England before moving to America in 1999 to pursue her doctoral degree in depth psychology at Pacifica Graduate Institute. She now teaches world history in a college preparatory school in San Jose, California. Her forthcoming book, *Clio's Circle: Entering the Imaginal World of Historians*, will be published by Spring Journal Books in 2007.

Even if I were able to gently stroll along a Californian country lane or city street, I would rarely find myself opened to the layer of history available to me in Europe. Dissociated from Native American history due to social amnesia about the genocide perpetrated upon Native Americans to advance European colonization of the continent, most Americans find themselves surrounded by the present, with a door locked to the past. In many of the hotter parts of the United States, mall walking has become the most popular form of walking. In these air-conditioned corridors of pleasure, how many of us ever pause to wonder about the lives and deaths of the people who once walked on the earth where our feet now tread? The white polished marbled floors of the malls only reflect the shapes of today's consumers. Even the air is artificial.

The European historians whose moments of inspiration are the basis of this article walked in ways which may be very alien to many Americans. They walked along footpaths (much more informal and smaller than Californian trails) and country lanes (hard to find here as American automobiles are so big and consequently roads tend to be much bigger too), bridle paths made by horses, and the shores of lakes and riverbanks. Sometimes they walked in places of great historical importance, such as along Offa's dyke, which marks the border between Anglo-Saxon England and the north. Sometimes they walked with friends and chatted about the old houses and churches which they passed. Sometimes they took off for days on end, tramping around Greece and Italy. Sometimes, like the ancient Greek muses, they roamed on midnight mountain walks. Sometimes it was the city which attracted them, and they would walk regularly every day, like clockwork, yet paradoxically out of time, lost in thought, observing the people going about their business and pondering how they were the same and how they were different across the centuries. But however they walked and wherever they walked, it was not done with the intention of burning calories.

The hope was more to gain inspiration than to get fit. But inspiration is elusive and can't be forced. Each of these historians had their own particular preferences. Some, like G. M. Trevelyan, would revel in plunging into the hillside surrounding Rome, enjoying the uncertainty of the agenda when anything could happen and nothing was predictable. Some, like Richard Cobb, preferred a more rigid itinerary and, once established in a city, would follow set routes at set times to observe its rhythms. Both ways of walking seemed to have worked their magic as eventually both men produced their best works by nurturing imaginal seeds planted when walking.

In the western tradition, we usually credit the Greek historian Herodotus as the founding father of history. A romp through his works is like an exotic whirlwind tour of ancient cultures and their customs. He tells great stories, but admits that he cannot always be sure of their veracity. Herodotus embodies the archetype of the storyteller, one who can narrate great events of the past and make us feel as if we are reliving them through the powerful imagery of the narrative.

Four heirs of Herodotus are the British historians G. M. Trevelyan (1876-1962), A. L. Rowse (1903-1997), Richard Cobb (1917-1996), and Simon Schama (1941—). All in their own way argue passionately in favor of literary rather than scientific history, and of good narrative, which grips the reader, rather than rigid and dry dissection of historical sources. Perhaps because of their preference for literary history, all reveal something of their search for historical inspiration in their autobiographical writings. Although they spent thousands of hours of valuable research time inside the traditional building of historical inspiration, the archive, they also believed in setting foot outside the library and walking into nature's landscape of collective memory. All speak of the inspirational moment when history comes alive and when a vision of the past appears to them after walking in nature.

WALKING, WORDSWORTH, AND SPOTS OF TIME

The British poet William Wordsworth (1770-1850) is a good starting place for our discussion about walking and historical imagination. His writings greatly influenced G. M. Trevelyan (1876-1962) and A. L. Rowse (1903-1997). Both of these historians share with Wordsworth an almost mystical belief in the power of walking as a way of putting the historian in touch with the imagination. A. L. Rowse wrote poetry as well as history, stating in his autobiography that Wordsworth was his "creed."[1] G. M. Trevelyan read Wordsworth as a boy and loved to walk in the Lake District. His daughter, Mary Moorman, actually wrote a biography of the lakeside poet. Furthermore, Wordsworth's ideas about spots of time or special places of memory and imagination to be found by walking in nature influenced the writings of these two historians.

Wordsworth habitually walked in the beautiful English countryside around his home in the Lake District while composing. Even when bad weather made walking and composing difficult, he would seek out a sheltered grove of trees under which to write. His long autobiographical poem, *The Prelude,*[2] records a long solitary walk on Salisbury Plain near the Neolithic stone circle at Stonehenge. It was here that he had frightening visions of ancient Britons at war and druids engaged in human sacrifice, and it is here that we can observe the phenomenon of walking at a historical site bringing the poet/historian in contact with the past in such a way that inspires his creativity and enhances his historical vision. Wordsworth writes of the ancient warriors:

> While through those vestiges of ancient times
> I ranged, and by the solitude o'ercome,
> I had a reverie and saw the past,
> Saw multitudes of men, and here and there,
> A single Briton in his wolf-skin vest
>
> With shield and stone-axe, stride across the Wold.[3]

Later in the same passage he sees human sacrifices taking place on an altar stone and mysterious druid teachers pointing towards the sky with their wands:

> Albeit with an antiquarian's dream;
> I saw the bearded Teachers, with white wands
> Uplifted, pointing to the starry sky.[4]

Wordsworth also discusses in *The Prelude*[5] his theory of spots of time in the poet's imagination. When our minds are worn down by the ordinary trivialities of life, Wordsworth believed that walking in nature could become a source of nourishment and repair. When we enter this deeply contemplative state brought on by walking in nature, we are more receptive to experiencing a timeless moment or a spot in time where the normal boundaries of chronological time break down and the moment takes on a vertical dimension as it puts the walker in touch with the landscape of history, the natural world, and with the archetypal realm.

Wordsworth's descriptions of these timeless moments have much in common with the experiences of Freud and Jung. When Jung was traveling in Ravenna[6] and in North Africa,[7] for example, he felt the regular dimensions of time and space dissolve, and he felt himself taken back in time to a deep, ancestral memory. When Freud visited Athens and stood on the Acropolis, he had a similar feeling of the break down of time and was taken back in memory to his childhood, feeling overcome by sad, gloomy thoughts.[8] Freud's descriptions of the fictional Norbert in Jensen's *Gradiva,*[9] walking at noon amongst the ruins of Pompeii and suddenly overcome by emotional turmoil as he sees his childhood sweetheart, also illustrates the timeless historical moment at work in the literary imagination. In all of these cases, a boundary is somehow crossed in the process of walking, and the writer is put in touch with an unconscious memory.

G. M. TREVELYAN AND C. G. JUNG
WALK INTO HISTORY

George Macaulay Trevelyan (1876-1962) is well known in Great Britain for his passionate defense of literary history over scientific history. He championed great writing over a scientific approach to history and poetry over unbiased treatment of historical sources; consequently, he was a great storyteller rather than a rigorous analyst. He is also remembered as a supporter of the Whig view of history. Whig historians see history as a march towards freedom and progress. Consequently religious freedom and personal liberty are important themes in Trevelyan's work. Some of his most famous works include a trio of books about the 19th century Italian freedom fighter, Garibaldi, his *English Social History*, and his essay defending literary history, entitled *Clio, a Muse.*[10]

Even in his own lifetime, Trevelyan was aware of the objections which could be leveled at his work by professional historians. As early as 1913, Trevelyan felt compelled to defend himself against the professional elite of historians who preferred to treat history as a science and to concentrate on evidence, techniques, and statistics, even if the general public found their work unreadable. Consequently, Trevelyan and his literary heirs, such as A. L. Rowse, Richard Cobb, and Simon Schama, focus more in their writing on the poetic, imaginal, and mystical dimensions of history, and herein lies their interest for the depth psychologist.

G. M. Trevelyan (1876-1962) was a contemporary of Jung (1875-1961). Their life spans form an almost perfect match. Although I have been unable to find any evidence that they met or even read one another's work, they share a special sensitivity towards historical places. They are open and receptive to the *genius loci* (the spirit of the place), and they allow the past to enter their bodies through walking on sacred ground.

Trevelyan's greatest delight was solitary country walking, but he was neither a road walker nor a mountaineer, preferring to walk off the beaten track. He walked in Italy, where his wanderings laid the foundation for his books on the 19th century Italian liberator, Garibaldi. Like Wordsworth, he walked in the Lake District. Northumberland, however, was his favorite place to walk—the melancholy borderland between England and Scotland, at the site of his family home.

The way in which Trevelyan walked gives us clues as to how unconscious experiences were allowed to enter the process of history making. Trevelyan liked to walk alone, away from the road, in places where many generations of historical activity lay in sedimentary layers under the ground. This is important for, like Jung, he believed that modern man was in danger of losing his connection with nature and his ancestral family. Walking was a way of restoring this lost connection to the past. Walking alone, perhaps at night as he did in Italy, or allowing himself to go off the well-trodden path, to drift off course, and to get lost, meant the ancestral memories could act upon his psyche.[11]

Trevelyan devoted an entire essay to the subject of walking. In it, he compares his wanderings to falling in love, where a man can "drift" in a "half-conscious process," opening himself up to the magic in the landscape.[12] By walking for long hours in a regular rhythm, the body naturally enters an altered state, but by deliberately plunging himself into a remote area and by surrendering ego control and losing his way, he allows history though nature to speak to him. It is also significant that Trevelyan chooses to walk in a very remote spot, away from the roads, off the map, which no surveyor could find. He is now in an environment where the chimes of the town clock, the school bell, or the factory siren cannot be heard, so his psyche is free to enter into a different time zone. Perhaps for an historian who is seeking to develop a closer relationship to the historical time patterns of different eras, it is a helpful practice to move deliberately away from the sounds and sights of the modern world, and to plunge for a time into the most remote areas of the countryside, although sadly of course this is much harder to achieve in 2006 than it was in Trevelyan's era.

Trevelyan wrote his playful essay on walking in nature in 1913 at the same time that Jung was attempting to confront the forces of the unconscious on the lakeshore at Bollingen in Switzerland by playing in the sand and constructing a model stone village from pebbles by the water's edge. By comparing the experiences of the depth psychologist and the historian, we can see something more of how the transcendent function, or the meeting of the conscious ego with unconscious psychic material, works. In Jung's psychology, the transcendent function emerges when unconscious psychic material is raised to consciousness and one actively engages with it. If one is depressed, this can result in a release from depression and a renewal of the life force. If an historian is stuck and searching for inspiration, then the transcendent function can bring new insight.

With Jung, we get a feel for the out-of-time experience in his walking along the shore of the lake and picking up pebbles. When we read Jung's autobiography and when we view pictures of Jung by the lakeshore, we see absolutely no evidence of modern man in the lakeside environment. Sometimes Jung is barefoot in the pictures taken during this time, as if he is deliberately trying to get into direct physical contact with the ground and the ancestral forces dwelling under it. Jung's account of playing on the shores of the Swiss lake at Bollingen in 1913 illustrates a surrendering of ego consciousness in his activities, which is similar to Trevelyan's half-conscious state when roaming. In order to allow the unconscious forces of creativity to surface, we must move out of ego consciousness: out of the concerns of here and now and into an altered state where psyche is receptive to unconscious insights, to the natural world that surrounds us, and to the layers of human history behind the present moment.

When Trevelyan searched for historical inspiration, he invoked Clio, the muse of history. This was in keeping with his view of himself as a poet-historian. Clio is one of the nine Greek muses of art and inspiration. The muses were the daughters of Zeus and the goddess

Mnemosyne (Memory). They dwelled on Mount Olympus, dancing, singing, and bequeathing poetic inspiration to those they favored. They also inhabited Mount Helicon where mountain springs held the promise of conferring poetic inspiration upon those who drank from their waters.[13] Those who drank from these special pools were said to be filled with divine vision, and this is the origin of our phrase "well springs of creativity."[14] By walking in the Lake District close to the mountain peaks or by wandering the shores of the lake at Bollingen, Trevelyan and Jung were in muse country, and they were inviting inspiration into their lives.

There are certain similarities between the figure of the muse and Jung's concept of *anima*, a man's soul image or his inner feminine side. Both Jung and Trevelyan encountered these feminine soul images at a time when they were in personal crisis, being forced to stand up for what they believed in. Jung encountered the *anima* after his break with Freud in 1913, and Trevelyan summoned the image of the muse Clio in that same year in a passionate essay defending literary history against its scientific critics.[15] It is possible to see Clio as a manifestation of the anima. (Hillman views *anima* as the archetypal image of the soul and sees imaginal figures such as nymphs and muses reflecting this archetypal image.[16] He also emphasizes the historical character of the *anima*. She appears in historical dress and is always associated with the past, not the future.)[17]

Walking, for Trevelyan, could evoke a "Clio state" where time suddenly slipped away and the historian received a moment of inspiration. Trevelyan acknowledges that after long, solitary 25-mile walks, he often experienced moments of strange, vivid feeling where regular time seemed to break down and where a new inner vision came into being. One such spot of time or vertical moment of special historical vision is described in the essay *Clio, a Muse*.[18] In this instance Trevelyan was in the mountains of England's Lake District, looking up at the mountain called Hellvellyn on Wordsworth's home turf, when linear time stood still:

> For half-a-minute I stood in thoughtless enjoyment of this new range (of mountains), noting upon it forms of beauty and qualities of romance, until suddenly I remembered that I was looking at the top of Helvellyn! Instantly, as if by magic, its shape seemed to change under my eyes, and the qualities with

which I had endowed the unknown mountain to fall away, because I now knew what like were its hidden base and its averted side, what names and memories clung round it. The change taking place in its aspect seemed physical, but I suppose it was only a trick of my mind. Even so, if we could forget for a while all that had happened since the Battle of Waterloo we should see it, not as we see it now, with all its time-honored associations and its conventionalized place in history, but as our ancestors saw it first when they did not know whether the "Hundred Days," as we call them, would not stretch out for a hundred years. Every true history must, by its human and vital presentation of events, force us to remember that the past was once real as the present and uncertain as the future.[19]

Somehow walking in the Lake District close to the mountain Helvellyn—which, like Mount Olympus, is rich in mythological associations for the English—gives Trevelyan this out-of-time experience where he is able to imagine England before the Napoleonic Wars and the Battle of Waterloo. The timelessness of the mountain, the home of the muses and pathway to the gods in Greek mythology, helps to put him back in time to an important crossroads in English history and to consider what it must have been like for his ancestors to be facing possible French invasion and defeat in battle. Now, with hindsight, Napoleon's defeat in the Battle of Waterloo seems inevitable, but at the time our ancestors did not know whether Napoleon's comeback would last a hundred days or a hundred years: things were much less certain. Perhaps, Trevelyan was also musing on the dangerous European situation in 1913, the year he wrote this essay, when England was once more at a great crossroads, facing the prospect of the First World War with tension mounting and rival alliances in place. Perhaps Trevelyan's walk in the mountains gave him a sense of reassurance, that although his country was in great danger, it had survived similar tough times, and the mountain, too, was still standing in all its timeless natural beauty.

His experience of walking in the Lake District and remembering his ancestor's real thoughts and feelings is so important to Trevelyan that he tries to hold on to it, but it is as elusive as a dream. It is fleeting, like a deja-vu moment when we know on some deep level we have been here before. But, try as we might, we can't quite hold onto the feeling. We sense this in Trevelyan's commentary on the Helvellyn experience. He swoops like a butterfly catcher trying desperately to capture it, but usually he can't. Only when the guards of ego consciousness slip down is he permitted glimpses of it.

> Normally I cannot recollect what I then felt. It comes back to me only at chance moments when my mind has let slip all forms and pressures stamped on it in later days .... I have forgotten most of it, but I remember some of it sometimes, as in a dream.[20]

TREVELYAN'S MIDNIGHT WALKS IN ITALY AND THE EFFECTS OF THE JOURNEY SOUTH ON THE PSYCHE

The imaginal therapist and writer, Nor Hall,[21] reminds us that midnight mountain walking is a favored activity of the muses. The Greek poet Hesiod describes the muses walking and singing on Mount Helicon at night, their soft feet stepping lively in time,[22] and somehow leading the historian to step out of time and into history and mythology. Although the muses' first home was in Greece, neighboring Italy gave the young Trevelyan one of his earliest experiences of the inspirational benefit of walking at night in countryside where classical history lies thick on the ground. Italy also birthed powerful experiences of the unconscious forces of history for Jung and Freud.

Trevelyan describes his first visit to Italy with his parents in 1897 in his *Autobiography*.[23] It was through this early journey south that Trevelyan's young body absorbed the Italian landscape through night walking, eight years before he ever thought about writing books about the Italian freedom fighter, Garibaldi. Trevelyan began his solitary walking practice, preferring the wilder paths away from the cities. He writes,

> I used to prolong my walks till late into the charmed Italian night ... at the right time of year I could walk after dark, mile after mile, to the continuous song of innumerable nightingales.[24]

It is as if these Italian wanderings were preparing the historian's psyche, well in advance, for the years of writing about Garibaldi and Italian liberation that were to come.

In his *Autobiography,* Trevelyan describes the exact moment of inspiration when his unconscious preparations in Italy with his father came together with the conscious desire to write a book about Garibaldi. Eight years after Trevelyan's trip to Italy, a friend gave him several books about Garibaldi as a wedding present.

> I began one day to turn over their pages, and was suddenly enthralled by the story of the retreat from Rome to the Adriatic, over the mountains which I had traversed in my solitary walks: the scene and spirit of that desperate venture, led by that unique man, flashed upon my mind's eye. Here was a subject made to my hand: if ever I could write a 'literary history,' this was the golden chance.[25]

This sense of place, combined with the effect of long solitary walks amidst the landscape of his chosen field of study, was to prove one of the main ways in which Trevelyan sought inspiration for his historical writing. Trevelyan's biographer, David Cannadine, comments:

> Often in Trevelyan's case, the springs of his historical imagination were released by visiting the scenes of past events: "*This* was the railway station where Garibaldi was arrested, amid *this* ruined cloister living monks once walked and talked, in *this* dark passage William the Silent was murdered."[26]

Trevelyan shared with Freud and Jung a desire to walk in the footsteps of his historical heroes. Trevelyan visited Italy with his parents in 1897, and he walked in Garibaldi's footsteps in the same year that Freud walked in the footsteps of his childhood hero, Hannibal. Later Jung would feel at Ravenna that he was reliving something of the experience of the Roman Empress Galla Placidia. The sensual Mediterranean climate of Italy seems to have opened up the unconscious minds of fellow travelers—Jung, Freud, and Trevelyan.

Coming from northern Europe myself, I can well imagine the effects of a journey south on the psyche. Sometimes in the winter months when the days are short and darkness and damp weather blanket the British Isles in a huge wet shroud, one longs to escape to a hotter, sunnier climate to dry out and feel warm and sensuous once more. According to James Hillman, who as a young man lived for a time in northern Europe, the journey south has profound effects on the northern European psyche.[27] The northern European climate, he suggests, where Freud, Jung, and Trevelyan spent most of their working lives, favors cool, rational observation, but the journey south to the hot, sensuous Mediterranean feeds the senses and opens up the emotions. Hillman tells us, "Venturing South is a journey for the explorer. It is the direction down into depth."[28] So by traveling south and walking at night in the footsteps of his Italian heroes, Trevelyan was re-enacting the ancient Greek prescription for muse visitation. Somehow it seems fitting that the historian who called Clio his mistress and who wrote so passionately to defend her virtue should be participating in a ritualistic type of walking, almost designed to awaken the muse within, in lands so close to Clio's mythological birthplace.

A. L. Rowse and Wordsworth

A. L. Rowse (1903-1997) is another British historian who admired Wordsworth and who experienced historical inspiration when walking. Rowse was a prolific writer, leaving behind a rich and varied legacy, which includes several volumes of poetry as well as numerous scholarly articles, short stories, and history books. He is perhaps most famous for his work on Shakespeare and the Elizabethan Age. He wrote poetry throughout his life as well as history, and much of his autobiographical work evokes a poet's sensibility to time, place, smells, sound, color, and light.[29] Rowse acknowledges the influence of Wordsworth in his best-selling autobiography, *A Cornish Childhood*.[30]

Rowse shared with Trevelyan a love of Wordsworth, a passion for walking, and an appreciation for the poetic nature of history together with a firm belief in the power of historical imagination. In *A Cornish Childhood*, Rowse records his earliest memories of walking to school, daydreaming, and discovering the magic of Wordsworth. When Rowse was still a schoolboy, he read Wordsworth's *Tintern Abbey* and *Intimations of Immortality*. Rowse's reading of Wordsworth gave him a feeling of recognition and understanding, which became a type of creed for his life.[31]

Rowse describes an early moment of power and beauty: He was walking to school in his Cornish village when he was struck by the beauty of a group of thatched cottages set against the spring sky. This memory of the cottages with apple blossoms in the gardens and of seeing the blue sky through the blossoms etched itself indelibly on the young historian's psyche. He writes:

> In that very moment it seemed that time stood still, that for a
> moment time was held up and one saw the experience as through
> a rift across the flow of it, a shaft into the universe.[32]

When Rowse read Wordsworth, he discovered a mirror for his core experience. He hugged the moment, recognizing its power and prescience. It became "a secret touchstone of experience," "an inner resource and consolation."[33] Everything of value seemed expressed in this déjà vu moment, and Rowse spent his life blending country walks with writing history and writing poetry.

When asked to write a book for history students on *The Use of History* in 1946, Rowse likened the moment of illumination for the historian to the moment of illumination in Wordsworth's poetry. He believed the moment of illumination, which Wordsworth expressed in *Tintern Abbey* in the ode on *Intimations of Immortality,* and again and again in the *Prelude*, is "at the core of the historian's experience."[34] He agreed with Trevelyan that the appeal of history was imaginative and "its impelling motive is poetic."[35]

Just as Trevelyan found inspiration in walking across the wild Northumberland countryside surrounding his family home, so Rowse found poetic inspiration and renewal in walking through his native Cornish countryside. Here he could feel the poetry of history in his body as well as in his mind; he was in touch with what he called his "subconscious," his "deepest part."[36]

In *The Use of History*,[37] Rowse spends several pages extolling the pleasures of walking before addressing the pleasures of reading history. He describes sauntering through old villages, lingering in churches, eating sandwiches by a ford which was important during the Wars of the Roses, resting at a spot where he could look down at the outlines of a Roman villa in the valley below, stepping into a stone circle like the Rollright stones in the northern Cotswolds, and having tea in a Devonshire Inn where the Cavalier poet Sidney Godolphin died. With Rowse, we always feel that memories are just below the surface, living on in the fabric of the building and the land to be rediscovered by the ambulatory historian. As Rowse writes, "Every parish has its church, usually an old one, with its memorials left behind by the tides and currents of life that have flowed through it."[38]

In an interview towards the end of his life, Rowse said he didn't think many people were aware of the importance of the "subconscious."[39] He explained that he learned to trust ideas which suddenly entered his mind like imps from another world. Rowse, like his fellow historian Trevelyan, was fortunate. He didn't need to mine his dreams and dialogue with historical figures to gain historical insight or, if he did, he has left no trace of such practices in his memoirs. The world, which was all around him in the English countryside, was enough. By developing a profound reverence and understanding of the Wordworthian timeless moment so early in life, Rowse knew what he needed to do. To saunter through the English countryside and to sit in a pew of an old parish church, looking at the sun playing with the patterns in the stained-glass windows, was enough for him to feel the tides of time moving through his body. It was all there just below the surface of ordinary consciousness.

ROWSE'S CORNISH BORDERLANDS

Entering the Cornish peninsula on England's southwestern tip is like entering a foreign country. Although it is dying out, Cornwall has its own dialect, and it is easy to get lost amidst its winding country lanes. Disused tin mines and ruined farmhouses litter the countryside, and the evocative place names, such as the mournful Lostwithiel and the magical Tintagel, suggest a closeness of the past which is yearning to be rediscovered.

Rowse's autobiography, *A Cornish Childhood*,[40] describes "Lost House," where he played as a child. This was a green, shady place on the edge of the village, where once perhaps there had been a house and a family. Rowse would take his books there and sit on the edge of the site against a tree trunk. Here is a real borderlands place where the past is so close that you can sense its immediacy. Rowse was drawn to this spot again and again, and he imagined that in some way his own name and family history were connected to the site. Perhaps his ancestors had once lived in this place. An investigation into Cornish place names did reveal a link between the name Rowse and "Lost House."

The place clearly seemed to cast a spell upon the young historian. The house was full of potent memories. It suggested a once crowded life with children playing in its rooms. Rowse felt slightly uneasy in this place, as if the former inhabitants of the house were watching him. He remembers,

> I always had the feeling that the place was waiting and watching—not that it was unfriendly, but that there were so many eyes looking out at me among the myriad tongues of the leaves. What did it mean?[41]

Rowse believed that one day when he was much older he would be rich enough to buy the land and build his own house in this special place. But when the time came, he found a house on the seacoast. "Lost House," however, continued to exert a strange power over his imagination. Since he read some of his first history books in this special childhood place, we can observe a potent cocktail in the making: walking to a special place and then reading history in that spot. The historian Richard Cobb remembers fondly the same walks into the landscape of the past, accompanied by a favorite history book, in Tunbridge Wells.[42] Are these early solitary experiences part of a rite of passage in the making of an imaginative historian?

THE BORDERLANDS OF MY CHILDHOOD

Rowse's description of "Lost House" reminds me of my own secret childhood places. When I was 8 or 9, my family visited a tiny fishing village on the Scottish coast called Garlieston. The first line of houses and stores faced the seafront promenade, but hidden behind this façade lay a mysterious row of ruined houses, which I called "Secret Street." Some houses were mere shells with ferns growing through the floor. Others were uninhabited, but the windows were intact, and one could peer into the gloomy interior, searching for clues about the owners. Like Rowse, I felt the houses were somehow watching me and, like Rowse, I would make up stories about the people who once lived there.

Ruined places, like the shell of Tintern Abbey which inspired Wordsworth, the tribal mounds and Border Towers in Northumberland which inspired Trevelyan, and "Lost House" which inspired Rowse, are places where the unconscious, ripped remains of history seem to erupt into the landscape. The incompleteness of the ruin is a powerful magnet to the historical imagination, which naturally desires to reconstruct the building and place it in the correct historical context. Walking in these ruined places often seems to evoke an historical calling: a desire to investigate more deeply how the people of the past lived, loved, and died.

Certainly this was my experience. I grew up walking and playing in Coventry, England, where the ruins of the medieval cathedral laid waste by the Nazis lie next to the new cathedral, a symbol of hope, peace, and reconciliation. The woods at the back of our house, where I played Tarzan on a rope swing, contain clay pits dug steeply into the red/brown earth. This place is known as Devil's Dungeon, and a short walk away is Gibbet Hill, marking the city boundary where criminals were once hung and their corpses left to rot in irons as a warning to citizens and visitors alike. Here past crosses over into present: conscious memory into dreams and nightmares—these are my historical borderlands.

THE CHILDHOOD WALKS OF RICHARD COBB

A poetic sense of place pervades the writings of post-war British historian, Richard Cobb (1917-1996). Cobb was sent to France at the age of 18 to study the language and became a committed Francophile. His most famous historical works, such as *The Police and the People*[43] and *Death in Paris, 1795-1801*,[44] give vivid accounts of life in France during the revolutionary period. He also leaves behind several autobiographical volumes, including *Still Life, Sketches from a Tunbridge Wells Childhood*,[45] and *A Second Identity, Essays on France and French History*,[46] which give us insight into Cobb's love affair with France and his ability to recreate the memory of the country and its people in his historical writings.

I have found another powerful mirror for my childhood memories of walking in ruined landscapes in the work of Richard Cobb. In his poignant memoir of inter-war England, Cobb[47] remembers walking, reading, and sketching amidst the ruined castles surrounding his native Tunbridge Wells. He says he liked to sketch ruins best as they offered him "the greatest opportunities for vigorous cross-hatching."[48] His "boy's paradise"[49] was a secret hole in the ruins of "a mysterious, nameless zone" of old houses, scheduled for demolition, on the outskirts of Tunbridge Wells.[50]

Like Rowse, Cobb[51] describes how he would take off on solitary walks around Tunbridge Wells in South East England from an early age. Sometimes, like Rowse, he would take along a history book to read. Cobb recalls reading different history books in different evocative locations. Thus history and childhood memory blend together, bound with a strong sense of place. He read the plays of George Bernard Shaw in a little thatched shelter on the Common, but he saved his favorite historical scene, the death of William the Silent from Motley's *The Rise of the Dutch Republic*, for his favorite place "among the ferns that edged the eastern curve of the Old Race Course."[52] Like a cat with its favorite toy in its secret hidey-hole, Cobb relishes the drama and emotion of the historical scene in his special place. He re-experiences the grief of the Dutch children at the death of their hero and blends their grief with his own. If he had read the book in a library, a schoolroom, or at any ordinary location, the imaginative impact would not have been the same.

RICHARD COBB'S PARIS WALKS

Just as Trevelyan loved the sensuality of Italy, Cobb drank in the sensuality of Paris, with its rich aromas of cheeses and cooked chestnuts, coffee and croissants. Living and working in France, he said, was like living double, and crossing the English Channel was a metaphor for crossing over into the sensual world of French history. France gave Cobb a new identity into which he slipped, almost unconsciously, as soon as he crossed to the other side of La Manche.[53]

In order to immerse himself fully in this other world, Cobb believed in walking: absorbing the history of a place through the archive of the feet. Cobb's method of city walking was completely different from Trevelyan's unplanned wandering through the English and Italian countryside. Being shy and insecure, Cobb enjoyed a "rigid adherence to a daily itinerary."[54] Walking the same city routes at the same times each day, eating at the same restaurants, and taking the same trains had several advantages. They gave him a sense of purpose, a feeling of security, and above all the feeling that he was part of the heartbeat of the city, part of the natural ebb and flow of city life.[55]

These scheduled walks gave Cobb a feeling of belonging to the city, a feeling of community, and a sense of involvement. But beyond this, the walks heightened his historical imagination. They allowed him to sense the past, to catch glimpses of the 18th century in the 20th, to experience the rhythms of the seasons in a city, and to develop "a sympathetic susceptibility to the innumerable nuances of local ambience."[56] In other words, they allowed him to see and hear beyond the limitations of the official documentary records from the period and to make up for the historian's disadvantage "of not being able to hear his subjects."[57]

Cobb's historical borderlands were the places that allowed him this privileged glimpse into the past. In French cities, he deliberately sought out the abandoned, run-down, semi-derelict areas away from the official show places "of frozen orthodoxy" and "official unanimity."[58] He searched on foot, walking along abandoned railway lines or little-used canal paths, in the cemeteries, behind breakers yards, and in abandoned cottages. These semi-abandoned places of the city's underside helped him to imagine the town two centuries back in time. Like a detective searching for clues, Cobb believed the historian must always be alert for tiny pieces of material evidence: "the texture of the stone, the coldness of metal, the rough feeling of fustian, the cadence of a local accent behind reported speech."[59]

Cobb exhibits his interest in the lower classes and the hidden subterranean world of French history in his remarkable book *Death in Paris, 1795-1801.*[60] The subject of this book are 404 dead, who committed suicide or died suddenly either in the River Seine or on its banks between 1795 and 1801. Cobb's remarkable reconstruction of the lives and last hours of these unfortunates reveals his powers of imaginative reconstruction at their height. He works like a dream analyst, following the tiniest clues, which at first sight may seem trivial, in order to unravel the last days of the poor and downtrodden. Just as a tiny detail in a dream, like a mole on a nose or a dirty fingernail can provide an important key to understanding the dreamer, so the laundry marks on the clothing of the Parisian suicides provided Cobb with the key to understanding their lifestyles.

From the detailed records of the clothing and personal effects of the suicides, Cobb was able to reconstruct the "close and uncomfortable proximity" of the Parisian poor.[61] The laundry marks are perhaps the most striking visual clue. They show that those who died often wore other people's clothes, either passed down or stolen. For example, "Anne Marmet, 19, is drowned wearing a red-striped headscarf marked, in red letters, L. D.; Marguerite Merle, 21, is clothed in a man's shirt marked P. H. in blue,"[62] and the list goes on. Cobb tells us we should be careful about reading the story of the shared clothing with rose-tinted spectacles. The fact that a trio of building workers at Limousin took it in turns to wear a shared suit on Sundays could be seen as a sign of fraternity and shared hardship, but such conditions also produced "wary watchfulness even at the expense of much needed sleep,"[63] as the occupants of common lodging houses tried to hold onto their best clothes and possessions.

Cobb's Parisian walks and his eye for unusual clues helped him to reconstruct this remarkable tale of the Parisian underworld, sweating together in August, shivering together in January. It was the "language of clothing"[64] which provided him with the best clues, but the whole work is clearly inspired by his years of walking around the poorer areas of Paris, listening to the language of the laundrymen, observing the workers eating their lunch together, and feeling the fustian, silk, and corduroy on sale in Parisian tailor shops and haberdasheries. The archive of the feet laid the groundwork for this vivid historical account.

SIMON SCHAMA'S JOURNEYS THROUGH LANDSCAPE AND MEMORY

Richard Cobb's legacy lives on today through the work of his famous student, Simon Schama, professor of the humanities at Columbia University and celebrity TV historian. Out of our quartet of historians, Simon Schama is undoubtedly the best known today. His most famous works include *Dead Certainties*,[65] which plays with the boundaries between history, literature, and imagination, and *Landscape and Memory*,[66] which examines the relationship between creativity and nature. At the beginning of his labyrinthine epic *Landscape and Memory*, Schama pays tribute to Cobb: "one of my best-loved teachers," who "always insisted on directly experiencing 'a sense of place,' of using 'the archive of the feet.'"[67]

The central thesis of Schama's book is that landscape inspires the Western imagination. To support his thesis, Schama cites numerous examples: the German artist Anselm Kiefer and the American walker/writers, John Muir and Henry David Thoreau, as well as Jung and Trevelyan—are just a few. But what chiefly interests me are the personal anecdotes, which illustrate the intersection between nature and the historical imagination at play in Schama's own life.

Landscape and Memory begins with Schama as a child walking "for what seemed miles" along the banks of the Thames in Essex, England, paddling his bare feet in the mud and ooze and staring out to the great river's mouth: towards the place where the river met the sea.[68] Here, in this maritime place of inspiration and ancient memory, the fledgling historian imagined the long boats of England's Viking invaders with their dragon heads at the prow, sliding menacingly upstream in search of wealth to plunder.

Later, when Schama has his own young children to entertain and educate, he takes them to the redwoods in Mendocino County in Northern California. Here, once more, as his children walk on the forest floor under a thick canopy of leaves, Schama feels himself fall back through time. He describes this strange experience as "the sensation of time warp in the vegetable kingdom."[69] As the family walks deeper into the woods looking for the cathedral grove, the children become frightened. Schama struggles to understand their fears. He sees that the trunks of the giant sequoias must appear to the little ones like "the torsos of dinosaurs, and possibly of the devouring rather than the grazing variety."[70] What Schama had expected might evoke wonder and excitement in his children instead evokes primal fear. The children want to escape from the darkness and ghostly trees in the "reptilian tomb of prehistory" and enjoy sandwiches in the sunlight and open air.[71]

It is also possible that Schama's children were experiencing some of their father's fears about the sinister landscape of forests. Earlier in *Landscape and Memory,* we learn that Schama's ancestors were Hasidic Jews who made a living by logging in the wild woodland which borders Lithuania and Poland. Schama's maternal grandfather was driven out of the area by "the horseback terror of the Cossack pogroms."[72] When Schama walks in these ancient Eastern European forests, he remembers the more recent terrors, which have left their mark on the landscape. He visits Giby in Lithuania, where a raised mound memorializes the death of five hundred Poles who were killed in 1945 by Stalin's secret police: the NKVD. Then he takes a detour to a cemetery in Punsk (now in Poland), where he digs for traces of his Jewish ancestors who were murdered in the Holocaust. Finally, he sleeps in a hotel built on the site of an old royal palace deep inside the haunted woodland. Here the harsh history intrudes on his sleep, which is interrupted by "nightmares of deportation."[73] No wonder a trip to the California redwoods turns into an awakening of primal fears for the Schama family!

Many passages in *Landscape and Memory* have a haunted, dream-like quality about them. It is as if Schama's own troubled memories and vivid historical imagination guide the reader around a meandering tour through menacing forest groves, up rivers which carry invaders hungry for pillage and plunder, and down into the "rich loam of memory."[74] Many reviewers commented on the dream-like quality of *Landscape and Memory*. Writing in the *National Review*, Eric Gibson compared reading the book to "peeling away the layers of an onion" or "counting the rings inside a tree."[75] The whole work is like a giant excavation, working down "beyond history and into the most inchoate zones of our collective psyche."[76]

When we walk in nature the boundaries between past and present become permeable. When we walk we might carry a backpack, containing items for our journey. We might pack water, trail mix, maps, and a camera, but Schama believes we also carry an invisible psychic backpack bulging with myth and recollection.[77] As we walk, the "rich loam of memory"[78] enters our body, history both personal and collective begins to unravel, and the psychic baggage we are carrying starts to peel away. It is as if the earth itself is a type of psychic compost, fertilizing the frozen and barren parts of the psyche and restoring ancestral memories.

The image of the historian walking in a foreign landscape and carrying a backpack of myth and recollection, which can be activated at any point by the atmosphere of a shady forest grove or a river's flow, is highly evocative. It adds to the experiences of Wordsworth, Trevelyan, Rowse, and Cobb by creating an image for the repressed personal memories and the cultural and ancestral myths, which we carry with us as we walk into the landscape of history. If we allow ourselves to slow down and saunter through the landscapes of memory which call us, we may find a wood, a clearing, or a quiet stream where the boundaries between past and present collapse and our historical imagination has space to saunter with us.

Schama is fascinated by those boundary places where the past collides with the present. Just below his house there are dry stonewalls, standing testimony to the vanished world of sheep rearing a century ago.[79] When he was just 10 years old, the young historian discovered a strange-looking mound in his local London park. Eventually he discovered an abandoned air-raid shelter containing empty cigarette packs with exotic brand names, now extinct, a dirty bottle that once contained the British soda pop named Tizer, a dirty sock, and a half-buried nine of diamonds, perhaps left behind from an air raid game of gin rummy.[80] I remember a sunny picnic on Blackheath in South East London, lying down on the manicured grass, and then suddenly sitting bolt upright when my friend told me that this area was used as a plague pit at the time of the Black Death. The past is closer than we think.

The final words of *Landscape and Memory* are a quotation from the nature writer and walker extraordinaire, Henry David Thoreau. Thoreau did not feel healthy unless he spent at least four hours a day sauntering through woods, hills, and fields. He reminds us that the boundaries we draw between the inner and outer worlds are false lines of demarcation. We may think that the landscape of history is something abstract "out there" in a history book or in a quaint photograph, but the landscape we see mirrors the landscape inside our bodies.

> It is in vain to dream of a wilderness distant from ourselves. There is none such. It is the bog in our brain and bowels, the primitive vigor of Nature in us, that inspires the dream.[81]

SUSAN GRIFFIN: PLACING THE BODY IN HISTORY

Henry David Thoreau's words remind me of the work of the American feminist writer, Susan Griffin. Her work bears testimony to the idea that nature is at work inside of us and that boundaries between inner and outer, personal and political, personal history and collective history, are not only false, but harmful, as they distance us from the pain and suffering of our human family and the natural world,

In a strange way, Griffin's work carries threads of continuity reaching back to the work of Richard Cobb and Simon Schama and, even further, to A. L. Rowse, G. M. Trevelyan, and William Wordsworth. She believes, "We forget that we are history."[82] The lives of our ancestors live on inside us. Our bodies carry the memories of past suffering and joy. Griffin will take a bodily symptom and trace it back in time in order to see it in a broader context. When she was struck by a mysterious illness which left her unable to work and reliant on the care of others, she began a quest to understand the roots of her disease.[83]

When Griffin was diagnosed with Chronic Fatigue Immune Deficiency Syndrome (CIFIDS), Paris began to exert a magnetic pull on her psyche. In a quest for understanding, she found herself looking for mirrors into her own illness through the eyes of Camille, a fictional 19th century French courtesan who died from tuberculosis after a meteoric rise to fame and fortune as the lover of a wealthy man.[84] Although Griffin's wanderings around the streets of Paris in search of Camille are more haphazard and far less organized than the rigid itineraries of Richard Cobb, discussed earlier, they nevertheless share the same overall purpose, namely to absorb more fully the atmosphere of the city and thereby to receive a clearer understanding of their research subjects.

Griffin discovered that the fictional story of Camille was based on a real courtesan named Marie Duplessis. Although Griffin's heroine did not commit suicide in either of her incarnations, she shared her existence in her early years in Paris with the same downtrodden group of suicides whom Cobb investigated in his book *Death in Paris, 1795-1801*.[85] Although Griffin was still weak, she felt compelled "to wander through the grimier parts of the ninth arrondissement, home to street walkers."[86] Like Cobb, she wanted to reach out and touch history, to feel it at work in her own body, and eventually from this strange chemistry she birthed two books.[87]

Like Cobb, Griffin is fascinated by the language of clothing, the feel of different fabrics against the skin, the clues that a pair of antique gloves or the touch of silk lingerie might offer as a pathway to the past. The inspiration that she gained from her Parisian wanderings can be seen in her latest work, *The Book of Courtesans*.[88] Here the walks through the Parisian streets and the imaginary reconstruction of the life of Marie Duplessis comes to fruition in a sensual romp through the boudoirs of some of the most famous courtesans in history. The bodies of the courtesans are glowing with an eroticism which reaches the reader through rich descriptions of the feel and textures of their clothing: breasts pouring out from glistening satin, a glimpse of thigh surrounded by a bejeweled garter belt, or the contours of a small waist under a riding jacket. These walks through the streets of Paris clearly helped to inspire Griffin's vivid and imaginative descriptions of the lives of the courtesans.

Thus Griffin's work carries the ideas of these earlier male poet/ historians into a more modern feminine context. Griffin gives her body permission to enter imaginatively into history and to speak, telling us what it feels and thinks. She is aware of the physical need to reach out and touch history, to allow her feet to absorb the history from the stones of the Parisian streets, to feel the touch of an antique pair of gloves against her skin.

Artist Maya Lin instinctively understood this need when she designed memorials to the Vietnam War and the Civil Rights Movement which can be touched. By placing our fingers on the cool black reflective marble of the Vietnam War Memorial or by dipping our fingers in the film of water flowing over the round table of the Civil Rights Memorial, we are reaching out to touch history. We can find great comfort through walking in the footsteps of our ancestors through the landscape of memory, and many of us have a physical need to touch with our feet or our hands the places where they walked, the earth where they died, or the clothes that they wore.

Although the archive of a library is the more traditional place of historical inspiration, my reading of the lives of many historians suggests that walking into the soulscape of history is an equally powerful source of creativity. Entering into the imaginal world of history is a challenge for any historian. Walking is perhaps one of the more enjoyable ways of entering Clio's realm.

NOTES

1. Alfred Leslie Rowse, *A Cornish Childhood: Autobiography of a Cornishman* (New York: Clarkson N. Potter, 1979), 17.

2. William Wordsworth, "The Prelude," in *William Wordsworth: A Critical Edition of the Major Works*, The Oxford Authors Series, ed. Stephen Gill (Oxford, England: Oxford University Press, 1984), 375-590.

3. *Ibid.*, 577.

4. *Ibid.*

5. *Ibid.*

6. C. G. Jung, *Memories, Dreams, Reflections*, ed. Aniela Jaffé, trans. Richard and Clara Winston (London: Fontana Press, 1995), 315-319.

7. *Ibid.*, 274.

8. Sigmund Freud, *A Disturbance of Memory on the Acropolis*, ed. and trans. James Strachey (London: Hogarth, 1960).

9. Sigmund Freud, *Delusions and Dreams in Jensen's Gradiva*, ed. and trans. James Strachey (London: Hogarth, 1959).

10. George Macaulay Trevelyan, *Clio, A Muse and Other Essays* (London: Longmans, Green, 1949).

11. David Cannadine, *G. M. Trevelyan: A Life in History* (New York: W. W. Norton & Company, 1992), 147.

12. Trevelyan, *Clio*, 12.

13. Hesiod, *Theogeny & Works and Days*, trans. M. L. West (Oxford, England: Oxford University Press, 1988), 3-6.

14. Dianne Skafte, "Creativity as an Archetypal Calling," in *Depth Psychology: Meditations in the Field*, ed. Dennis Patrick Slattery and Lionel Corbett (Einsiedeln, Switzerland: Daimon Verlag, 2000), 36.

15. Trevelyan, *Clio*.

16. James Hillman, *Anima: An Anatomy of a Personified Notion* (Dallas, TX: Spring Publications, 1985), 65.

17. *Ibid.*, 19.

18. Trevelyan, *Clio*.

19. *Ibid.*, 149-150.

20. *Ibid.,* 150.

21. Nor Hall, "Channel a Muse," *Spring 70* (2004):105-115.

22. Hesiod, 3.

23. George Macaulay Trevelyan, *An Autobiography & Other Essays* (London: Longmans, Green, 1949).

24. *Ibid.,* 28.

25. *Ibid.*, 31.

26. Cannadine, 191.

27. James Hillman, *Re-Visioning Psychology* (New York: Harper & Row, 1975).

28. *Ibid.*, 233.

29. Alfred Leslie Rowse, *The Diaries of A. L. Rowse*, ed. Richard Ollard (Penguin, London, 2004), ix.

30. Rowse, *Cornish Childhood.*

31. *Ibid.,* 17.

32. *Ibid.,* 18.

33. *Ibid.*, 17.

34. Alfred Leslie Rowse, *The Use of History*, rev. ed. (New York: Collier, 1963), 46.

35. *Ibid.,* 45.

36. Alfred Leslie Rowse, qtd. in Sydney Cauveren, *A. L. Rowse: A Bibliophile's Extensive Bibliography* (Lanham, MD: Scarecrow, 2000), xxvi-xxvii.

37. Rowse, *Use of History.*

38. *Ibid.,* 34.

39. Alfred Leslie Rowse, qtd. in Cauveren, xxvii.

40. Rowse, *Cornish Childhood,* 220-223.

41. *Ibid.,* 221.

42. Richard C. Cobb, *Still Life: Sketches from a Tunbridge Wells Childhood* (London: Hogarth Press, 1984), 27.

43. Richard C. Cobb, *People and Places* (Oxford, England: Oxford University Press, 1985).

44. Richard C. Cobb, *Death in Paris, 1795-1801: The Records of the Basse-Geôle de la Seine, October 1795-September 1801, Vendémaire Year IV – Fructidor Year IX* (Oxford, England: Oxford University Press, 1978).

45. Cobb, *Still Life.*

46. Richard C. Cobb, *A Second Identity: Essays on France and French History* (London: Oxford University Press, 1969).

47. Cobb, *Still Life.*

48. *Ibid.,* 63.

49. *Ibid.,* 130.

50. *Ibid.,* 131.

51. *Ibid.*

52. *Ibid.,* 27.

53. Cobb, *Second Identity,* 50.

54. *Ibid.,* 8.

55. *Ibid.*

56. Richard C. Cobb, *Promenades: A Historian's Appreciation of Modern Literature* (Oxford, England: Oxford University Press, 1980), 3.

57. *Ibid.*

58. *Ibid.*

59. *Ibid.,* 2.

60. Cobb, *Death in Paris.*

61. *Ibid.,* 86.

62. *Ibid.,* 83.

63. *Ibid.,* 84.

64. *Ibid.,* 86.

65. Simon Schama, *Dead Certainties: Unwarranted Speculations* (New York: Vintage, 1991).

66. Simon Schama, *Landscape and Memory* (London: HarperCollins, 1995).

67. *Ibid.*, 24.

68. *Ibid.*, 4.

69. *Ibid.,* 241.

70. *Ibid.,* 242.

71. *Ibid.*

72. *Ibid.*, 27.

73. *Ibid.*, 74.

74. *Ibid.*, 574.

75. Eric Gibson, "Landscape and Memory," *National Review*, 47, no. 14 (1995):59-61, <http://galenetgroup.com/servlet/BioRC> (accessed July 17, 2004).

76. *Ibid.*

77. Schama, *Landscape and Memory*, 574.

78. *Ibid.*

79. *Ibid.,* 577.

80. *Ibid.,* 518.

81. Thoreau, qtd. in Schama, *Landscape and Memory,* 578.

82. Susan Griffin, *A Chorus of Stones: The Private Life of War* (New York: Doubleday, 1992), 11.

83. Susan Griffin, *What Her Body Thought* (San Francisco: HarperSanFrancisco, 1999).

84. *Ibid.*

85. Cobb, *Death in Paris, 1795-1801.*

86. *Ibid.,* 123.

87. Griffin, *What Her Body Thought* and *The Book of Courtesans: A Catalogue of Their Virtues* (New York: Broadway, 2001).

88. Griffin, *Courtesans.*

JUNGIANA

ZÜRICH . . . REVISITED:
AN INTERVIEW WITH MURRAY STEIN

ROBERT HENDERSON

MURRAY STEIN is a former President of the International Association for Analytical Psychology (2001-2004), the author of *The Principle of Individuation, In MidLife, Transformation, Jung's Map of the Soul,* and *Jung's Treatment of Christianity* as well as the editor of *Jungian Analysis.*

A graduate of Yale University (1965) and Yale Divinity School (1969), he received his Diploma from the C. G. Jung Institute in Zürich in 1973 and his Ph.D. from the University of Chicago in 1985. He is a founding member of the Inter-Regional Society of Jungian Analysts and was the first President of the Chicago Society of Jungian Analysts (1980-85). From 1980 to 2003 he maintained a private practice in Wilmette, Illinois and was a training analyst with the C. G. Institute of Chicago. Since 2003, he has lived in Switzerland and is a training analyst with the International School of Analytical Psychology in Zürich.

Robert Henderson: You have made a big career change by moving from the United States to Switzerland. Why did you move and what has it been like for you so far?

Rev. Dr. Robert Henderson is a pastoral psychotherapist in Glastonbury, Connecticut. He and his wife, Janis, a psychotherapist, are the authors of *Living with Jung: "Enterviews" with Jungian Analysts* (New Orleans: Spring Journal Book, 2006). This interview took place in the spring of 2006.

MURRAY STEIN: The move to Switzerland was for me, and to some extent for my wife too, a natural and logical progression. It was also because of a love affair with this place, which began at first sight when I passed through Zürich as a college student and was smitten. My wife and I had rented an apartment in Zürich in the mid-90's and spent most of our vacations here. Gradually our time in Switzerland lengthened until it seemed just another step to take the leap and move over entirely. I felt the move marked the end of a period in exile. Exactly 30 years, nearly to the day, after leaving Zürich as a student at the Jung Institute and moving to the States, I was able to return "home." It was the fulfillment of a dream. The move back to Switzerland was, and continues to be, the source of immense pleasure and meaning. I am grateful for every day here. Zürich is, for me, the most wonderful city in the world, and Switzerland is an idyll, though certainly not without its problems and faults, i.e., its shadow. As far as my career is concerned, nothing essential has changed. I continue to function as a Jungian analyst, though with a much reduced practice. I have more time now to read, to do research, and to write. I am just finishing a book called *The Principle of Individuation* and am beginning to put together another on Jungian psychology and modern spirituality. I also continue to be very active in the programs of the International Association of Analytical Psychology (IAAP) and from here am able to travel quite easily and conveniently to IAAP groups throughout Europe and to developing IAAP groups in Eastern Europe and elsewhere. Within the past couple of months, I have been in Hong Kong, Belgrade, London, Amsterdam, and St. Petersburg.

Henderson: There are many notable places for Jungian psychology and training around the world. Given your new home, how do you see some of the uniqueness of the Jungian community in Zürich?

Stein: One has to speak of Jungian communities (plural) in Zürich at this point in history. The "Jungian community" that you refer to is in fact quite fragmented, with several centers of interest and activity. One thing I have been trying to do since arriving is to work toward forming an open and cooperative attitude among them. To this end, several of us created what is called the "Zürich Think Tank." About 20 analysts, coming from the five major Jungian centers in Zürich, gather every other month for an evening of sharing and discussion. This has been going on for a year now and is showing good results. The spirit is lively and friendly and not without sharp edges and disagreements. What continues to hold, in my view, as a symbolic center is Zürich itself. The name continues to connote a "home" for Jungians. The specialness of Zürich, the city, lies in the atmosphere, the culture, the streets, and buildings. This continues to occupy the center of the Jungian world's consciousness as a sort of *axis mundi*. One should add that it is a great place to dream and to introvert. For some people this is restful and centering, for others it stimulates creativity. Many people find it healing and enriching to spend a few weeks or months (if possible) here in analysis from time to time. This is part of the old tradition, when people would come from the earth's far corners to be in analysis with Jung or one of his students for a couple of weeks each year or so.

As far as training opportunities today are concerned, Zürich now has several options, including the possibility to train in psychodrama, mythodrama, sandplay, and other modalities. The Psychological Club, too, is active and offers regular lectures that are open to the public. For Jungian work in general, Zürich is a very active and dynamic place to be. What is needed is an information center to direct people according to their interests and proclivities. This does not exist at present.

Henderson: If Zürich stands as a sort of *axis mundi* in the Jungian world, how is that impacted now by the presence of two training centers, the C. G. Jung Institut, Kusnacht and the International School of Analytical Psychology, Zürich?

Stein: In Zürich there are a number of Jungian groups active in various things, as I said above. Some of these groups speak to others and carry on in a collegial way, while others are more isolated and keep to themselves. I would not say that the *axis mundi* is splintered, but the Jungian community here is certainly quite fragmented. Over the years and decades, there has been a continuous process of creativity in Zürich, with new groups emerging (such as the sandplay group, the psychodrama institute, the von Franz Stiftung [von Franz Foundation], and others) and old groups dividing. In the 1990's the von Franz Zentrum [von Franz Training Institute] formed in reaction to changes that had been instituted in the training program of the Jung Institut. In response, a new training program was set up based on the original

Jung Institut model and with the support of Dr. von Franz. Today this organization continues its activities and appears to be doing quite well. In more recent times, a large number of Swiss analysts left the Jung Institut, nowadays located in Kusnacht, and formed the International School of Analytical Psychology, which is located in Zürich. This was the result of a change in the leadership of the Jung Institut, that is, in the Curatorium, around 1998 and of new directions taken by the members of the Curatorium in the years following. Along with these analysts, quite a large number of students left the Jung Institut and transferred to the new International School of Analytical Psychology. So there are in fact now three training programs functioning in Zürich, each with a different set of instructors and its own program.

Each of these splits has created emotional trauma in the local Jungian community. On the other hand, they have also produced new bursts of creativity and energy. The von Franz Zentrum has, for instance, been very productive not only in teaching and training but also in publishing. The new International School of Analytical Psychology now has 70 students enrolled and is planning new programs to attract international candidates for Jungian training. The Jung Institut is active in the local community with courses offered to interested professionals from medicine, theology, social work, etc. With the creation of the new Think Tank in 2005, we hope that some of the steam will go out of the old conflicts and be channeled into more creative activities.

Henderson: What impact do you feel in the environment around Zürich given the fact that Dr. Jung lived and died there?

Stein: The life and work of Jung remain the touchstone of the analytic community in Zürich, as they do for the International Association for Analytical Psychology worldwide, though perhaps to a lesser extent in most places because of the fact that Jung lived here and not there. There has been much discussion in recent years among Jungian analysts about mourning Jung, about going beyond his views and works and becoming "post-Jungian" with more critical distance from the founder, and in some quarters and for some individuals this has been the program. There are institutes where Jung is hardly read, unfortunately, in my opinion. In others, however, where the drift away from the Jungian canon has been strong and even strongest, there is now a return afoot.

In Zürich, some of the groups remain very close to core Jung, while some go in other directions to a degree, though less so than in most other Jungian centers. And it is of course precisely because of Jung's presence here that Zürich is "Zürich" in the Jungian world, that is, the Mecca, the Jerusalem. Students are still thrilled to visit the tower in Bollingen with a Jung grandson. Sometimes it is possible to have a tour of the house on Seestrasse in Kusnacht, which includes Jung's library and consulting rooms and will eventually be turned into a Jung museum of sorts. This can be a numinous experience. The rooms of the Psychological Club on Gemeindestrasse, where Jung introduced so many of his seminal ideas and where he gave his famous seminars in the 1930's, remain as they were since the Club's inception and, as an institution, the Club continues to act as a sort of lighthouse in dark and troubled times in the local Jungian community. So, yes, I would say the spirit of Jung (the Great Father) continues to hover over "Zürich" and invest the Jungian programs and institutions here with an archetypal aura.

Henderson: I am sure you have had some personal experiences in Zürich that have touched your heart.

Stein: There are many such experiences, Rob. I wouldn't know where to begin. Most have little or nothing to do with Jung, though, at least not directly. They are synchronicities around Zürich itself. For me, Zürich is bigger than Jung. Jung was contained in Zürich. Of course in other respects he is bigger than Zürich, too, for those of us who train and practice analysis.

My wife, daughter, and I visited Franz Jung [C. G. Jung's son] in the Jung house on Seestrasse two days before he died so unexpectedly. He was not terribly ill, only suffering from a slight cold, as he told us. We chatted in the library for a couple of hours, the window to the lake open, and a early July breeze billowing the curtain into the room. He showed us Jung's working spaces and the shroud of Turin across from his writing desk. At the end he invited us back for another visit when he was feeling better, to have a homemade fruit tart for which he was quite famous locally. We wished him well and went on our way out the front door with the famous inscription above and up the alley of blossoming cherry trees to the Seestrasse. That was a Friday afternoon. On Monday I learned that he had died on Sunday, in his sleep. I think we were the last people to see him, other than his daughter-in-law who was caring for him in the home at the time. He looked strong and well, with a good sense of humor and great warmth. I have been back to the house since then and felt his presence there still.

Henderson: As you stated, there have new bursts of creativity and energy from the various splits in the Zürich Jungian community. In your opinion, what have been some of the vital issues involved in the splits?

Stein: In the first split, the main issue was clearly theoretical and ideological. Some of the Zürich analysts felt that the Institut was losing touch with the basic principles of Jungian psychology and analysis. They saw a drift toward accommodation with the psychological mainstream, with governmental and social controls taking over the field of psychotherapy, with the post-Freudians, the developmental schools, etc., and away from the symbolic, archetypal, and classical perspectives in which they were steeped. These analysts simply left the Swiss analytical society and the Institut and started their own program, under the guidance of Marie-Louise von Franz. To date they maintain an active training program based on the Zürich Institut model of the 1950's and 60's.

The second split seemed to have some ideological components as well, with a large group of analysts feeling that the new Curatorium (beginning in 1998 and continuing to date) was making too many accommodations to changes in the legal standing of psychotherapy in Switzerland, which now requires a university degree in a clinical field, among other things. They felt the Institut was in danger of losing its soul and had many meetings to discuss this problem. This was somewhat reminiscent of the first split some ten years earlier. But the real fire behind the movement toward creating an alternative international training center in Zürich was generated by a perceived attitude of gross insensitivity on the part of the new Curatorium to the preferences and desires of a majority of the members of the Swiss analytic community. The abrasive style of the Curatoruim leadership hurt peoples' feelings and set many analysts' teeth on edge. An intense conflict developed over several years between the Curatorium and what finally amounted to a large majority of the analytic community in Switzerland. This came to a head in early 2003 when the Curatorium announced that it had incurred huge financial deficits in recent years and was now in danger of going bankrupt. The Curatorium requested financial help from the analysts, at first voluntary and then on a mandatory basis. At issue was control of the Institut and its programs as well as the pursestrings. A kind of "no taxation without representation" feeling took hold among many analysts as the Curatorium sought to require training analysts to pay an annual fee in order to retain their faculty status and to sign a pledge of allegiance to the present and future decisions of the autocratic Curatorium. This created a firestorm of protest. As President of the International Association of Analytical Psychology at the time, I offered to form a "round table" that could perhaps have provided a forum for discussion and possible mediation. This offer was rejected by the Curatorium. Then a significant attempt at mediation between the Curatorium and the Swiss Society for Analytical Psychology took place in 2003-4 under the leadership of Prof. Osterwalder of the Swiss Federal Institute of Technology in Zürich (ETH), a member of the Board of Patrons of the Jung Institut, but this broke down after a few months in mutual accusation and recrimination. A number of Swiss analysts have chosen to stay apart from both sides ("a pox on both your houses") and to participate quietly from time to time in teaching and training activities on all sides, but it has been nearly impossible to maintain the preferred Swiss attitude of neutrality in the midst of this burning conflict.

In 2004, the leaders of the Association of Graduate Analytical Psychologists (the IAAP member group made up of graduates of the Zürich Institut) took action and instigated a revamping of their Constitution. At the same time, they sought and received overwhelming approval from their membership to begin a new training program in Zürich, the International School of Analytical Psychology, under their auspices and control. Many students of the Institut had become unhappy with the tensions and conflicts swirling around them. Some of them chose to transfer to the International School of Analytical Psychology when it opened its doors, while others chose to stay and finish training where they had begun. New students now seem to be showing up in both places these days, but I am not sure of the numbers. By all reports I hear, the inflow has slowed to a trickle at the Jung Institut, while at the International School of Analytical Psychology it is still too early to tell how attractive this program will be to international students. At this time, there are about 70 students enrolled at International School of Analytical Psychology. I do not know the number at the Jung Institut. It is certainly way down from its high point of 350, reached in the early 90's.

At the moment, things seem to be settling into a new form in Zürich. There are now three training programs coexisting side by side. One hopes the feelings will turn more positive in the future and some level of cooperation can develop.

Henderson: Given the issues that have arisen in Zürich and the splits with the training programs as well as the new work on the unpublished materials of Dr. Jung with the Philemon Foundation, what are some of the things you see for the future of analytical psychology?

Stein: Analytical psychology must do two things at the same time— develop and deepen itself internally and meet the challenges of social and cultural changes externally.

On the internal front, the mission of the Philemon Foundation is vitally important. It is critical that Jung's unpublished writings be catalogued for scholarly work and as far as possible published. More historical studies of the highest quality need to be encouraged. Secondly, Jungian theory needs to continue to be restated in contemporary idioms. This means that connections need to be made with what is going on in various branches of scientific research (importantly, in neurological research concerning the brain, in artificial intelligence modeling, in infant research, in geriatrics) and with philosophy, anthropology, culture, and religious studies. These need to be brought into critical relation with established Jungian themes so that new or renewed versions of analytical psychology can find a voice. In other words, the field needs to continually deepen, revise, and renew itself through dialogue. This is the model we inherited from Jung. I think the Jungian journals bear witness that all of this is taking place actively and vigorously at this time in our history. Where Zürich fits into this project is to hold firm as the *axis mundi* of all this ferment and transformation. I am hoping that energy spent locally on splitting and creating new institutions will become channeled into projects like forming a history seminar, a cross-cultural forum, and some new directions in training. On the other front, i.e., dealing with the challenges being forced on analytical psychology by changes in social policy, licensure laws, and other treatment modalities that claim higher efficiency and greater effectiveness, it is incumbent on the institutes and societies to design new and better models of training, to carry out research that either confirms our present methods or shows us some ways to improve them, and to support movements in fields like organizational management, academic studies of all sorts (literary, art, and film studies; cultural and religious studies; law, anthropology, etc.) and other fields, like trauma studies, victim and abuse assistance, etc., that are finding ways to use analytical psychology's insights and methods in their own endeavors. Here Zürich could be a key player, especially with regard to reinventing analyst training for the twenty-first century. The present training programs are designed along old and outmoded models inherited from psychoanalysis, by and large. These are cumbersome and no longer adjusted to the needs and possibilities of potential students. I also think we need to reconceive the idea of "Jungian analyst" to be more flexible and adaptive in the present world. Perhaps the conflicts in Zürich will yield some new ideas along these lines. I hope so.

Henderson: It is apparent to me from all your wonderful writings that Carl Jung has meant a great deal to you, and perhaps that is another reason in this time in your life it is a privilege for you to live in Zürich. What has Jung meant to you?

Stein: As it happens, I am responding to this question on Thanksgiving Day (2005), so it seems most appropriate to say that I am very thankful for Jung's life and works. I have never tired to reading Jung's writings since I first opened *Memories, Dreams, Reflections* in the spring of 1968. I find his mind endlessly fascinating and stimulating. Living in Zürich, I now read him in German, which is for me a whole new Jung, earthier and more immediately present than comes across in Hull's English rendition. For me, Jung provided a way to live meaningfully (though certainly not painlessly!) in the modern and now postmodern world.

FILM REVIEWS

Tsotsi. Presley Chweneyagae, Mothusi Magano, Terry Pheto, Ian Roberts. Written and directed by Gavin Hood, based on the novel, *Tsotsi*, by Athol Fugard.

REVIEWED BY JOANNA DOVALIS AND JOHN IZOD

T sotsi, slang for "thug," tells the story of six days in the life of a motherless nineteen-year-old boy. The film is set in Johannesburg's labor sink, Soweto, a township which mainly consists of miles of shacks. Seeking to answer the question what, in the face of terrible poverty, decency can be, it shows how a collective experience of mother loss can distort a culture. Focusing on the great divide

Joanna Dovalis, a practicing psychotherapist, is co-author of "*Million Dollar Baby*: Boxing Grief," *Kinema* 24 (Fall 2005) and "Grieving, Therapy, Cinema and Kieslowski's *Trois Couleurs: Bleu,*" *San Francisco Jung Institute Library Journal* 25, 3 (2006). Her Ph.D. thesis *Cinema and Psyche: Individuation and the Postmodern Hero's Journey* was accepted by Pacifica Graduate Institute in 2003.

John Izod is Professor of Screen Analysis and Head of the Department of Film & Media Studies, University of Stirling. He is the author of numerous articles and the following books: *Reading the Screen* (Longman, 1984); *Hollywood and the Box Office*, 1895-1986 (Macmillan, 1988); *The Films of Nicolas Roeg* (Macmillan, 1992); with Richard Kilborn, *An Introduction to Television Documentary* (Manchester University Press, 1997); *Myth, Mind and the Screen: Understanding the Heroes of our Time* (Cambridge University Press, 2001); and *Screen, Culture, Psyche: A Post-Jungian Approach to Working with the Audience* (Routledge, July 2006).

between rich and poor in post-apartheid South Africa, it engages the audience in the characters' hope and despair.

This, then, sketches the social backdrop to Gavin Hood's screenplay. As the only semi-educated member of the gang tells his leader, "Tsotsi" (Presley Chweneyagae) is not a real name (but our anti-hero refuses to admit to any other). It makes him as much a social type as an individual. His story focuses on both societal and cultural inequity; but as Tsotsi feels stirrings in his soul, it also follows his journey out of self-blindness to the point of recognizing that becoming a human being with moral dignity is a feasible and worthy goal.

The story begins with the shaking of dice. Tsotsi's gang relax in a shebeen, biding time before their next raid. The music track "Mdlwembe" that accompanies the gaming captures a triumphant African paradox—the vigor and passion of its people in the face of their lives' dire circumstances. The ivories fall on four and five. "Eleven!" someone shouts. Right from the start, the rolling of dice displays the game of fate.

The gang take a train to central Jo'burg and meet the evening rush of Sowetans commuting home. In the terminal concourse Tsotsi scopes the crowds and spots a complacent businessman purchasing a colorful scarf to take home to his woman. The contrast between the exuberantly colored fabrics (not to mention the intimate affection) that the well-to-do can afford and the dull russets and browns of the township catches the spectator's eye. Meanwhile the gang, ignoring fripperies they cannot afford, focus on their intended prey, follow him onto a crowded train, and surrounding him with silent skill, lift his wallet. Warning the target not to protest the theft, one of the gang pokes a sharpened steel instrument against his chest. But when the victim strains to contain his outrage, Butcher (Zenzo Ngqobe), needlessly true to his name, slips the rod between his ribs, killing him instantly. It makes a harsh snapshot of the young men's world.

In the aftermath of the murder, Tsotsi singles out Boston in a brutal fight, the gang ruptures, and Tsotsi is isolated, losing all sense of time and place in the pouring rain. Shaking with cold or fear, he picks his way under a hectic sky that mirrors his bursting emotions. As he walks through a suburb of immense prosperity, a flashback hits him: rows of children living in a stack of cement pipes, with his childhood self dwelling among them. While in memory he stares at his former survival shelter, in raw contrast the present finds him gazing at the costly and pleasant home of well-paid professional people. As he muses, a car drives up to the gate. The woman driver (Nambitha Mpumlwana) gets out and calls for someone within to open the security gate. Tsotsi seizes the moment, holds her off at gunpoint, and jumps into the driver's seat. In panic, the woman opens the passenger door. Tsotsi reacts, shoots her, and speeds away, his habitual pattern of fleeing from crisis now becoming apparent.

He has not gone far before a baby starts to cry from the back seat. Lacking driving skills, he lets the car go off the road and crash. Although he gets out unhurt and starts to walk away, this time it does not prove so easy to escape. The baby's cries escalate and something about the intensity of the noise calls him back. He finds a grocery bag and places the baby inside. The African rain clouds have disappeared as fast as they came, leaving a full moon lighting the wasteland that divides the rich folks' mansions from the poor hovels way below. Tsotsi, shopping bag in hand, makes his uneven way across this empty no man's land. He seems, like some underworld pilgrim compelled to hellish business, to know it well. Yet the moon is a powerful presence, invoking the lunar archetype at what seems a most unlikely moment, when the infant has been snatched from its mother. Richard Tarnas remarks that the feminine dimension comes to light whenever a re-birth is about to occur. And the significance of the birth to come is in direct relationship to the degree of suffering that precedes it.[1] Tsotsi's relationship with this motherless child will lead us into the themes this film sets out to explore.

The next morning, a bewildered Tsotsi awakes to the sound of the screaming infant which is in urgent need of care. Yet a sweetness surfaces in his nature when he dances to soothe the baby. To substitute for a diaper he uses the only material he can lay hands on, a newspaper. With its fragment of headline saying "MOTHER," it makes a bizarre swaddling. The equally bizarre new "mother" finds a can of condensed milk and does his best to pour it into the child's mouth. It makes a fine sticky mess, but Tsotsi's eyes turn soft while feeding him. The baby's powerless neediness has indeed ignited his own maternal instincts. It is the first hint that empathy with the baby's demands may have brought him into contact with the hidden baby part of himself.

Borders, divisions, and liminal spaces crisscross the film. In one scene, Tsotsi is leaving Jo'burg on foot, walking under a smoky brown sky along the railroad track. It is as though he has entered a borderline area on the threshold of his unconscious. Wrye remarks that a psychological threshold

> may be understood as a particular kind of narrative space, which requires [of the individual entering it] a new logic and perspective beyond conventional orders of causality, sequence and selection. A threshold is a particular, often ephemeral, set of consciousness, in which the limits of familiar sameness and reputed difference are extended and enriched by holding simultaneously in mind a glimpse of other and self... The new way is... transitional in the sense of promoting change.[2]

Murray Stein augments this in describing such liminal space as a cultural-psychological interstitial field in the imagination that predominates during periods of change in an individual's life cycle. It links the old and new fixed identities between which the person is in transit.[3] Such a liminal state holds the potential to nurture an imaginal environment in which redemption from grief may be found.

Tsotsi's floundering attempts at baby care reveal to him that he needs a mother for the infant, just as, since early childhood he has lacked his own. This child's present and his own past run in significant parallel—never more so than when the next morning he goes to seek a substitute mother and soon notices a young mother dressed in golden fabric with her baby wrapped to her back in the traditional manner. She is waiting in line to get water. This is Miriam (Terry Pheto). With his baby concealed in its bag Tsotsi follows the young woman to her door where he pulls his gun, making Miriam drop her full pail. The image of the spilled water makes an eloquent emblem how the life-giving feminine may be overturned by an overly aggressive masculine presence. Tsotsi pushes Miriam indoors and, confident of the pistol's authority, instructs her to feed his baby. But then, when he sits and watches her breastfeed, hearing the baby's satisfied gulps, his eyes soften.

In Miriam's room, Tsotsi swings between different states of mind. Mobiles hanging from the ceiling arouse his curiosity; but when she speaks of the emotions they evoke, he looks at her like a curious child who doesn't understand. Her artistry stretches his comprehension of people's spiritual potential. Amazed that she can sell for good money the mobiles that to him are nothing but pieces of junk and broken glass, he has to learn that there are experiences to which he is blind in enjoying color and light. Later, when Miriam speaks of her mobiles, a prism of light glows like hope on Tsotsi's face. It is a pigment in the broader emotional spectrum that she knows well but he has never felt. He has learned to evade emotional experiences. In his life survival has been paramount, the dread of vulnerability must be avoided at all costs—yet for a moment he falls asleep, seduced by the security that the young mother radiates. Then he jerks awake again in order to maintain the vigilance of his ego: it is psychologically too dangerous for him to regress. But when Miriam washes the baby, talking to it melodiously, the comfort in watching her actions hypnotizes him into another reverie. This time he remembers his own mother turning her sick face toward him. Once again he switches back into brutal survival mode and leaves with the baby in the bag warning Miriam that if she tells anyone he will kill her.

Tsotsi's encounters with the baby, a crippled man he runs into at the station, and Miriam the "healthy mother" occur synchronously. Synchronicities may appear at times of crisis, births, and deaths. Here these synchronistic events call Tsotsi to engage with the full mother/child archetype and provide an opportunity for him to correct his one-sided attitude. Through the inexpressible, magical quality that these interventions have in breaking the deeply inscribed routine patterns of his social and psychological life, they furnish him with space to dissolve the intense suffering he holds.

In both Tsotsi's encounter with Miriam and the alternating moods of the landscape, solar and lunar energy (masculine and feminine) move back into balance. It is worth recalling that the baby brings to mind the numinous offspring of such a union, the Divine Child. The latter can be interpreted as "a symbol of future hopes, the seedling, the potentiality of life, newness. . . .[4] Tsotsi's baby signals that potential in him, even though he has not realized it consciously. Appositely, according to Jung, the Divine Child as an archetypal image brings light and points to the conquest of the dark, yet its birth is troubled: "Abandonment, exposure, danger, etc. are all elaborations of the 'child's' insignificant beginnings and of its mysterious and miraculous birth."[5]

It is easy to perceive that, psychologically speaking, there are two babies on Tsotsi's bed.

Tsotsi remembers his sick mother calling him to her bedside to hold her hand. His mind releases the core, repressed trauma of his young life. His drunken father enters the hut, yelling at him to keep away from his mother lest he catch her sickness. For the first time we hear the boy's name, David. He runs away into the wasteland and finds refuge from his father's endless shouting and drunken violence in the pipe stack alongside other homeless children. We can now read Tsotsi's as a story about a child whom AIDS has made motherless. By extending our gaze beyond his own life, we see too that the collective experience of mother loss has significantly shaped the national culture and the morality by which great numbers of its people live.

Tsotsi has begun to grieve his loss. Mourning, as Greg Mogenson suggests, is an intensely creative process: "Much of what we mistake for psychopathology is unconscious mourning."[66] Tsotsi now has an opportunity to create a healing emotional environment in the liminal space occupied by the interplay of reveries. Here he may begin to shift his suffering from the painfully concrete repetition within which he has been locked. The grieving over his past advances when Tsotsi takes the baby across the wasteland to see the abandoned children who live in the cement pipes. He has returned to his original place of mourning to touch not only his personal loss but also his cultural history. The image of rows of cement pipes, cold wombs containing hungry, motherless children, captures a collective pain.

Miriam stimulates the young man's capability for active interior existence and gently guides him toward accepting that he must return "David." She even offers to take the great risk of delivering him to his parents on Tsotsi's behalf. Finally, when Tsotsi gathers the baby to leave (accepting moral responsibility for his own actions), she gives him hope. With traditionally demure demeanor she allows him to see that he may visit her again after the child has been restored to its parents.

Tsotsi has had a first glimpse of the latent potential for his psychological growth in Miriam's entering his life. She is the anima who encourages him to move forward. At the last moment of their time together his relationship with her has shifted from a fixation on the anima as mother to the beginnings of perceiving her in another guise of the anima—as a possible lover.

That opening throw of the dice gave the game away: through it, the players could have addressed either the known or the unknown world. Since shamanic spiritual healing practices remain common to this day among African peoples, the false addition of four and five as eleven might have been read by the players as having mystical significance—but no such interpretation of these "bones" occurs to them. It is a symptom that, although the men in *Tsotsi* are largely governed by the unconscious, they have lost through desuetude the means of gaining access to the images, ideas, and other emanations that surface from it. Where shamanic practices would have guided their grandparents, these young, savagely impoverished urban dwellers have lost that advantage. The only character with confident and controlled access to unconscious impulses that feed her emotions (and thence her conduct) is Miriam. In her life the arts have substituted divination. Her civility, her moral dignity, and her stature as the giver of life remind us that only when we become aware that emanations from the unconscious counterbalance what the conscious mind seizes on can we be reasonably sure of being able to find an understanding and deal with those intrusions. Just as making her mobiles has helped Miriam gain a deeper knowledge of self, so the moving sounds and images that make up *Tsotsi* have comparable power to help its Southern African audiences.

NOTES

1. Richard Tarnas, "Jung, Cosmology, and the Transformation of the Self." Paper delivered at Pacifica Graduate Institute, 2006.

2. H. K. Wrye, "Borders, Boundaries and Thresholds: Establishing the Frame and Setting Fees." Unpublished lecture, (2002).

3. Murray Stein, "Liminality," *San Francisco Jung Institute Library Journal*, 1980 (Autumn), 21. Cited in Joanna Dovalis, "Cinema and Psyche: Individuation and the Postmodern Hero's Journey," unpublished doctoral dissertation, Pacifica Graduate Institute, (2003), 99.

4. Robert H. Hopcke, *A Guided Tour of the Collected Works of C. G. Jung* (London: Shambala, 1992), 107.

5. C. G. Jung, *The Collected Works of C. G. Jung*, trans. R. F. C. Hull (London: Routledge, 1968), vol. 9i § 167.

ADDITIONAL REFERENCES

"City of Johannesburg, official website," http://www.joburg.org.za/soweto/overview.stm, accessed 28 April 2006.

Lebo Mogotsi (2005), "Challenges Facing the South African Gold Mining Industry," *The Alchemist* (38) 15-17, http://www.lbma.org.uk/publications/alchemist/alch38_safrica.pdf, accessed 30 April 2006.

"Sophiatown" entry in Wikipedia http://en.wikipedia.org/wiki/Sophiatown2C_Gauteng, accessed 29 April 2006.

BOOK REVIEWS

BLAKE W. BURLESON. *Jung in Africa.* Continuum, 2005.

REVIEWED BY ROBERT A. SEGAL

In the 1920's Jung travelled—to Africa, to the American Southwest, and to India. He travelled twice to Africa—in 1920 to North Africa and then in 1925-26 to East Africa. It is this second, far longer (five-month) journey, taken when Jung was fifty, that Blake Burleson retraces. Burleson, who teaches religion at Baylor University, knows Africa firsthand and describes Jung's journey in detail. He identifies every place, person, and people Jung encountered. His glossary and his chronology are especially useful. And the dozen photos bring the story alive.

At the same time Burleson psychologizes Jung's journey—in Jungian terms. The outward journey becomes an inward one, and Jung, through his experiences with native Africans, encounters his own blackness, which stands in opposition to his "civilized," European consciousness. Like everyone else, the master needs to experience blackness out there in the world in order to encounter it within himself.

Robert A. Segal is Professor of Religious Studies, University of Aberdeen. He is the author or editor of *Myth: A Very Short Introduction* (2004), *Theorizing about Myth* (1999), *The Gnostic Jung* (1992), *Jung on Mythology* (1998), *The Myth and Ritual Theory* (1998), *Hero Myths* (2000), and the *Blackwell Companion to the Study of Religion* (2006).

The detail aside, what does Burleson's book add to those of others who have written about Jung's travels—notably, his various biographers? While most of the standard biographers, including Gerhard Wehr, Barbara Hannah, Frank McGlynn, Vincent Brome, Deidre Bair, and Sonu Shamdasani, had or have presumably never been to Africa, Laurens van der Post was a native South African who devoted his life to promoting Africa to the modern West. Furthermore, van der Post was a Jungian devotee and eagerly interpreted everything in Jungian terms. But his hagiographical biography of Jung, *Jung and the Story of Our Time* (New York: Vintage Books, 1977 [1975]), discusses Jung's time in Africa in only a few pages (46-53), and no one till Burleson has written an entire book on the subject.

Still, Jung himself devotes some pages to his trip to Africa in *Memories, Dreams, Reflections* (New York: Vintage Books, 1963), and his own psychologizing of his adventure leaves scant room for anything to be added to it by the Jungian Burleson. To quote Jung:

> In traveling to Africa to find a psychic observation post outside the sphere of the European, I unconsciously wanted to find that part of my personality which had become invisible under the influence and the pressure of being European. This part stands in unconscious opposition to myself, and indeed I attempt to suppress it. (*MDR*, 244)

To quote Burleson:

> For Jung, "primitive" referred to an undifferentiated layer of the human (and animal) psyche which had evolved out of the ubiquitous unconscious. As "civilized" man left the collective consciousness of the "tribe," he developed a differentiated ego and, thereby, became more fully conscious as an individual. Yet Jung believed that this stage had come at a price—in this evolutionary process "civilized" man had lost his soul as he abandoned this "primitive" layer.... Jung's journey to [East] Africa, the longest of his life, was an intensely personal quest to recover his own "primitiveness." (*Jung in Africa*, 16)

Burleson is at his best when he challenges Jung's own interpretation, even if he never dares entertain an interpretation other than a Jungian one. Of Jung's sole dream of a "Negro" during the whole trip, Jung writes:

> Finally it came to me: he had been my barber in Chattanooga,
> Tennessee! An American Negro. In the dream he was holding a
> tremendous, red-hot curling iron to my head, intending to make
> my hair kinky—that is, to give me Negro hair.... I took this
> dream as a warning from the unconscious; it was saying that the
> primitive was a danger to me. At that time I was obviously all too
> close to 'going black.' (272)

Burleson dutifully quotes Jung but then, citing Michael Adams,
suggests that the dream could have been intended to "tempt" Jung *to*
"go black" rather than to warn him *against* going black (see 201-202).
Immediately thereafter, however, Burleson observes that in Jung's day
"the phenomenon of 'going black' was more than an adjustment—it
was a full-scale abandonment of one's culture." (202) It was an attempt
to escape from the everyday world altogether. In Jungian terms, it was
inflationary. Burleson thus finally accepts Jung's own interpretation of
the dream—and of Jung's whole mission to Africa.

Burleson documents Jung's reliance on the French armchair
anthropologist Lucien Lévy-Bruhl for his, Jung's, characterization of
"primitives" (see 121, 133-136). Beginning in 1910, Lévy-Bruhl wrote
six books on primitive thinking, which he argued is unlike modern
thinking. Primitives have a mentality all their own. They harbor
conceptions of all things as at once identical and distinct. Their
conceptions shape their perceptions, so that they actually experience
themselves as at once identical with the world yet distinct from it.
They simultaneously "participate mystically" in the world yet
differentiate themselves from the world. Insofar as primitives identify
themselves with the world, they are like mystics the world over—
specifically, mystics of a world-affirming, extrovertive kind. Insofar as
primitives simultaneously distinguish themselves from the world, they
are "prelogical," for they fail to see the contradiction between their
oneness and their separateness.

Lévy-Bruhl was struck more by the prelogical mentality of
primitives than by their *participation mystique*, on which, to be sure,
prelogical thinking builds: one must deem all things identical in order
to contradict oneself by simultaneously deeming them distinct. Yet
Jung, who continually cites Lévy-Bruhl, was struck far more by their
mysticism, which indeed he conflates with their prelogical thinking.

Following Jung in all things, Burleson blithely makes the same conflation. He takes Lévy-Bruhl's, and so in turn Jung's, chief claim to be that primitives identify themselves with one another and so are incapable of distinguishing themselves as individuals:

> Based on Lévy-Bruhl's conclusions, … Jung understood that what set the 'primitive' apart was his inability to differentiate himself from others.… Just as the 'primitive' felt that he was no different from his neighbor, so he felt that his people were no different from any other people. (134)

Burleson is doubly wrong: Lévy-Bruhl stressed the identification of primitives with animals and plants more than with fellow human beings, and he then stressed the simultaneous differentiation from those same identifications. The belief in the identity of all things is hardly unique to primitives.

In Africa, Jung found confirmation of his assumption, which he had firmly held prior to his trip, that Africans embody exactly what Lévy-Bruhl had claimed they do. Nowhere did Jung chance upon anyone who veered from the depiction he brought with him to the field. Far from questioning Jung's managing to find only confirmation of his views, Burleson simply recounts it. While Burleson properly notes the "near universal rejection" of Lévy-Bruhl's ideas about primitives (134) and thereby implicitly criticizes Jung for never challenging those ideas, he is never perturbed by the irony that Jung's long, arduous, dangerous trip to the world of primitives merely bolstered the views that he had had before ever embarking on it. Those who disputed Lévy-Bruhl's contention that primitives harbor a distinctive mentality were professional fieldworkers, who spent years living among the peoples they wrote about. Jung went to the field to see firsthand what primitives are really like and learned nothing. He projected onto primitives exactly what he already believed. Burleson, who touts his own familiarity with Africa, never even blushes. Jung's delight in always finding confirmation of his views provides an embarrassingly stark example of the limits of verification vis-à-vis falsification as the best means of proving a theory.

As earnest as this book is, it is undone by its insularity. Jungian psychology is enlisted to analyze Jung, and Jung's own application of his psychology, while questioned, is finally accepted. The anthropology that Jung enlists is likewise questioned but finally accepted. Like so much else written by Jungians about Jung, this book presupposes the near-omniscience of its subject.

BOOK REVIEWS

TOM CHEETHAM. *Green Man, Earth Angel: The Prophetic Tradition and the Battle for the Soul of the World.* Foreword by Robert Sardello. Albany: State University of New York Press, 2005.

REVIEWED BY DENNIS PATRICK SLATTERY

Tom Cheetham's book could just as easily be titled: *A Brief but Involved History of the Writings of Henry Corbin.* Corbin (1903-1978) was director of Studies in Islam and the Religions of Arabia in Paris and held other teaching posts at the University of Teheran, lecturer at Eranos, and others.

Robert Sardello's Foreword to Cheetham's research and insights is on point in revealing the imaginal link between the thought of C. G. Jung and Corbin's insights on Islamic mysticism. Where the two thinkers converge is in their respective explorations of the imaginal quality of psyche. Yet, as Sardello makes clear, in part through his own teaching and writing on the soul of the world, the realm of spirit is that which separates Jung from Corbin's interests: "the *Mundus Imaginalis* is the imaginal world of the spirit" (xiii).

Dennis Patrick Slattery, Ph.D., is Core Faculty, Mythological Studies at Pacifica Graduate Institute. He has authored or co-edited 9 books, including his latest publication: *Harvesting Darkness: Essays on Literature, Film, Myth and Culture* (2006). He is completing a second collection of essays: *A Limbo of Shards: Essays on Memory, Myth and Metaphor* for publication in 2007.

The five chapter titles, carrying initially their own cryptic weight, delineate the themes of this challenging text: 1. "We Are Now in Heaven:" The *Mundus Imaginalis* and the Catastrophe of Materialism; 2. Consuming Passions: The Poet, the Feast, and the Science of Balance; 3. Black Light: Hades, Lucifer and the Secret of the Secret; 4. Within This Darkness: Incarnation, Theophany, and the Primordial Revelation; 5. Harmonia Abrahamica: The Lost Speech and The Battle for the Soul of the World. This last carries the apocalyptic urgency of the subtitle, excavated from Corbin's own world view. Nowhere does this far ranging and sophisticated survey of the loss of the world soul allow for easy summary; it is far too baroque in architecture and in thematic interests: history, religion, imagination, abstraction, language, culture, myth, poetry, alchemy, mysticism, depth psychology, philosophy, human embodiment—enough to rattle anyone's caged thoughts into new territory. A glance at the extensive bibliography confirms such.

I take as my platinum bar when I read a book the following: what does this work allow, coax, persuade, and provoke me to think about? What individual or sets of analogies begin to emerge and coalesce through the alchemy of this text? Cheetham's excursus forced dozens of associations to the fore, most especially the poetic imagination's workings. I say this because of Cheetham's deft treatment of that space between psyche and myth:

> we uncover here in mythic space, in psyche, the primal conjunction of the concrete and the uncertain; the fecundity of the void. It is just here, at this origin, where mystery and certainty coincide…it is here, in the realm of the inhuman, both divine and demonic, where meaning is born. This is the *mundus imaginalis*. (7)

Influenced deeply, Cheetham admits, by the work of David Abram's *The Spell of the Sensuous,* he is attracted to this more-than-human realm where the imaginal pulses, however weakly, in these pedestrian times.

At times too preachy for my tastes, and often with a predilection to use the pronoun "We" with strident abandon—and makes me wonder who this "we" refers to—nonetheless, as the subtitle of the book expresses without apology, the battle today is for the *anima mundi* as it is continually trodden by a world descending into further abstractions and its source, rationality, which Cheetham believes, ignores most of life's weighty experiences. One of his clarion calls is to return to thinking as an imaginal act, and to ideas as

> openings onto other worlds, tangential to ours. They demand
> the attention of the whole person; they demand attention to
> subtleties we have almost wholly forgotten. (11)

This idea too I like: "Myths, or mythic moves, open spaces. Rational accounts limit them...Both are necessary." (9). His call is not rabid; it is balanced but frequently hyperbolic in the way poetry is hyperbolic, full of exaggerations, even distortions, in order to bring attention to the insight. Cheetham's approach, style, and manner is scholarly-poetic for he calls on the reader to imagine his work with him, to be a traveler in tandem to his developing thesis, and to imagine it for oneself. I enjoyed this participatory rhetorical angle he so cogently creates. He wishes us to become fellow hermeneuts of the Word, as he calls such a partnership in reading and thinking.

A section of the book I found particularly provocative is his discussion of the Christian dogma of Incarnation, which he reimagines through Corbin's thought: It is this fall of the divine into the historical, material world which provides the necessary condition for the projection of God into matter in which Jung found the seeds of modern science. It is the dogma of the Incarnation that underlies the alchemist's inabilities to distinguish spiritual birth and material transformation" (59). The limitation of such an act of divinity into the historical world, Cheetham asserts, is that it deified the human and demythologized the divine, eliminating effectively the intermediate realm "of the *anima*, of the elusive, symbolic soul" (59). The author agrees with Corbin that "idolatry" sprung from such a confusion of the two realms which has led the modern world into a split between two conditions: the person has "nearly disappeared in favor of biological and historical descriptions" at the same time "we fancy ourselves as Masters of the Earth in a final, fatal narcissistic frenzy of attempted control" (60).

One way out of such a narrow porthole for Corbin and Cheetham is through a theophanic imagination originating in the "Abrahamic tradition" (77), so different in intention from "a dogmatic, literal consciousness" (83) which freezes thought and disallows insight. By contrast, and this is the heart beat of the book's many themes, is that "the imaginal world is the realm of the symbolic, the alchemical, the visionary, the wonder-ful. The imagination is a mediating function, an organ of the subtle body" (83) that puts us in more, not less, intimate contact with the world of things.

Cheetham's development from here through most of the remainder of the text of epistemology and theoria is crucial to grasp for anyone interested in the most fundamental question: What does one know and how does one know it? For Corbin, as Cheetham adumbrates it, is through developing a "sacramental sensibility" or a "Catholic sacramental attitude toward the beauty of the earth"...that perceives the world as "'haunted by a sense that the objects, events and persons of daily life are revelations of grace'" (92).

It is important for Cheetham to reveal the thought of Wolfgang Giegerich's interpretation of the Christian myth as ending logically not only in the creation of modern technology but more devastatingly in the creation of the nuclear bomb (100). Corbin, Cheetham is convinced, would be horrified at Giegerich's conclusions because it italicizes Giegerich's failed initiation" (105); Giegerich, Corbin would assert, fails to understand the "imaginal" for such a disposition in "Corbin's theophanic cosmology, 'image' always implies an interplay between immanence and transcendence [which] guarantees the angelic function of beings and prevents idolatry" (105). To his credit, Cheetham names the enemy with civility; he then exposes, through Corbin's mythos, what is lacking in the other's point of view.

As one who pays close attention to the magical, alchemical qualities of words, I enjoyed and learned from Cheetham's riffs on language towards the end of his study. With the intention to words continually dissolving in a culture-wide pandemic, Cheetham takes up the cudgel of language's "ontological force, its ability to transform the soul and the world" (112). Language offers, he reveals, a disposition towards things of the world that is nothing short of mythical. But language's importance and its abilities will be retrieved, he believes, only if it is once again linked to "cognitive sympathy that lies at the root of religion" (112). He calls such an attitude "a poetics [that] could help us to live in the mythological present, in what Corbin called a realized eschatology: that is, one that occurs *right now*" (112). Further on he insists that "the language of poetry is as close as we can get to the language of the angels. It is a language of images, of imagination" (121) that is central to Corbin's sense of a psyche-cosmology.

The Western imagination has been the theatre, believes Corbin, "for the battle for the soul of the world" (121). The world, as he envisions it, will be redeemed only by the forceful mythic and imaginal presence of mind and its articulation in language that respects the innate now-ness of the world's matter. Without this stance, as Cheetham argues, the world will continue to lose its place as something that matters to all of us. The world's languages need to be heard once more by ears grown deaf by dogma, closed by arthritic credos and waxed over by wandering abstractions that bypass the world soul's desire to be recognized on its own terms.

BOOK REVIEWS

ROBERT SEGAL. *Myth: A Very Short Introduction.* Oxford University Press, 2004.

REVIEWED BY VICTOR FAESSEL

Who can be surprised that Robert Segal was called upon to prepare a "very short" introduction to the subject of myth? His scholarly output on the subject has been wide-ranging and prolific. His work demonstrates what one is tempted to call a taxonomist's penchant for logically surveying the "data" before him. In this instance, the data is not a body of myths, not a cross-cultural sampling of a type of myth or a figure from myth. Instead, what Segal undertakes here is to organize roughly a century and a half of theories about myth. A staunch comparative religionist known for the tough-minded logic he brings to the debates on method in religious studies, in this small book Segal displays his formidable chops as a comparativist of modern myth theory itself.

Each of the book's main chapters presents a general theoretical optic on myth and a few of that approach's representative theorists,

Victor A. Faessel, Ph.D., has studied at Pacifica Graduate Institute and at the University of Vienna, Austria. He is English-language publications editor for CISMOR, the Center for Interdisciplinary Study of Monotheistic Religions at Doshisha University in Kyoto, Japan, and coordinator of programming for the Orfalea Center for Global & International Studies at the University of California, Santa Barbara.

delivered in clear, compressed prose. Segal adopts the heuristic of testing
every theory on a single myth—the myth of Adonis, in the versions of
Apollodorus and Ovid (other myths do receive mention). Already tried
in part in his earlier and in many ways similar *Theorizing About Myth*
(1999), this useful innovation helps Segal to demonstrate how each of
the theories might illuminate a particular myth. Quotations and
bibliography provide the book's general interest audience tantalizing
entrée into the major works of the theorists, while, to a reader better
versed in modern mythography, the survey will be most interesting—
or frustrating, as is probably inevitable—for how its author tackles the
challenge of taking in so much theory through his selection,
organization, and "set toward" the material.

   As befits the taxonomist, there is something grid-like about the
way Segal lays out and compares his theorists. The primary criteria for
distinctions are their answers to the questions of myth's origin,
function, and subject matter (or "referent"). Another level down, he
scrutinizes how theorists situate myth's function in relation to etiology
and science: myth will be either a primitive antecedent or proto-form
of science, or else it serves no explanatory or etiological purpose at all.
Emerging with this taxonomic animus is thus a tendency to binary
kinds of dichotomies. It is relevant to note here that Segal calls his
approach in *Theorizing* "argumentative,"[1] for in this book, too, theorists
are aggressively and iteratively compared, maximizing contrasts.

   One is astonished by how much of nineteenth- and twentieth-
century theory Segal is able to fit into the space of this compact book,
and how well his system works to present it. At times the compression
necessitated by the format does frustrate, though. For one thing, it
squeezes out a lot of historical context; for another, it means providing
just a gloss of many figures. Clearly, the art of generalization is
demanded of anyone who undertakes this kind of survey, and Segal is
a most deft practitioner. Still, at times he tends to handle such glosses
in a way that may cause readers familiar with the material to cry foul.
That is, the book's main weakness has to do with how the virtue of
concise contrasts breaks down when theorists' ideas resist a too-narrow
classificatory scheme.

   This difficulty can be seen in Segal's treatment of the German
philosopher Hans Blumenberg's *Work on Myth*. Somewhat like Vico,
Blumenberg postulates an originary context for myth in the origins of

language, under the adaptive pressure of a lifeworld to which humans are poorly adapted biologically. For Blumenberg a principal function of myth has been, before all else, reducing *anxiety* (about things unknown) to tameable *fear* (of known factors) by imposing meaning on a random flux of events.

Myth, for Blumenberg, is thus bound up with an existential constant of human experience: "doubt" about the degree to which we enjoy mastery over external factors impinging on our affairs. Such doubt lingers because of what he calls "the absolutism of reality," how the experiential world's vastness, complexity, and unpredictability never cease to render problematic just this issue of control. So myth, not unlike ritual as a form of propitiatory magic, has long been about "control." But it is so in a basic sense that is not first about explaining (controlling) known factors, but rather, about managing indeterminacy. What accomplishes it is metaphor—the substitution of names, stories, meanings.[2]

For Blumenberg, then, myth "explains" the exterior physical world, but not as etiologies that tend toward science, as schematized by Segal. Myth's referent is not the known world whose quotidian details are explained in etiologies that do succumb to science. Rather, myth refers first to the *unknown*: that part of experience which vexes because of its incomprehensibility, its unpredictability. A chaotic, exigent world provokes explanations in the first place, and of first things like "cosmos" or "nature," while calling forth heroes to hold back the monsters (or even unreliable gods, as in Prometheus' case) at work behind its opaque visage.[3] Myth gets taken up anew, and so perdures, because this basic situation scarcely changes—even in the age of science.

Segal gives Blumenberg all of a few sentences in the present work. Yet even in his extensive treatment of him in *Theorizing*, just as here, he insists that Blumenberg offers no adequate answers regarding the referent of myth or the reason for myth's ongoing life parallel to science—when *Work on Myth*, if indeed digressive, is all about this referent and this reason. It is a philosophical anthropology that thinks in part through an existentialistic psychology. Might the disconnect stem from Segal's premises about myth vis-à-vis explanation, so that this theory eludes his taxonomy's either/or binarism?

Segal has cited Jung espousing a similar-sounding "existential" role for myth, and rightly presents it as Jung's perspective on myth's pre-modern function. The passage is not quoted in the work under review, but appears in both *Theorizing* and his *Jung on Mythology*.[4] In a context dealing with the effectiveness of religious myth in ages marked by "brutality," Jung says that it gives us "the security and inner strength not to be crushed by the monstrousness of the universe." (*Collected Works of C. G. Jung* [hereinafter "*CW*"] 5 § 343) It is worth remembering that Jung once proposed, and allowed to stand, an at least partial "origin" of the archetype in lived human experience: it is a "precipitate...of certain ever-recurring psychic experiences," a "condensation of the living process," the "expression of the physiological and anatomical disposition;" it is a "deposit" of repetitive human responses to life situations, sedimented across vast expanses of time. (*CW* 8 § 748) But Jung also says here: "As a mythological motif, it is a continually effective and recurrent expression that reawakens certain psychic experiences, or else formulates them in an appropriate way."

When Segal arrives at Jung in the chapter "Myth and Psychology," it follows a discussion of the post-Freudian Rank on myths of the hero. He opens by noting that for the two Viennese psychoanalysts, "heroism involves relations with parents and instincts," while for Jung it has to do with these in addition to relations with the unconscious. (The unconscious, Segal reminds us, is the referent of both myth and dream for Freudians and Jungians alike.) The reader's first exposure to Jung on myth has its context in depth psychology's interpretation of hero mythology—the hero as analogue (Jung would insist, "symbol") of the ego's relationship with components of the unconscious. While this presentation does parallel the emergence, in *Wandlungen und Symbole der Libido* (1912), of Jung's distinctive psychology, in Segal's book heroism looks like the touchstone of the Jungian approach to myth generally: "Like Freudians, Jungians at once analyze all kinds of myths, not just hero myths, and interpret other kinds heroically. Creation myths, for example, symbolize the creation of consciousness out of the unconscious." (p. 102)

Little more is said in these first pages about Jung's ideas on myth. After some paragraphs contrasting Jung/Jungians and Freud/Freudians on the unconscious and stages of life, the discussion turns to Joseph Campbell. He, so we learn, provides the "classically Jungian counterpart" to Otto Rank's *The Myth of the Birth of the Hero*. In contradistinction to Rank's study, which situates the heroic work in the first half of life, Campbell's *The Hero with a Thousand Faces* places it entirely in the second. This is a bit confusing, inasmuch as Segal just a few lines earlier had stated that Jung allowed for heroism in both halves of life.

The emphasis on heroism in the presentation of Jung continues in the section testing Jungian theory against the myth of Adonis, who, framed here as an archetypal *puer*, becomes the "opposite" of the hero, even a "failed" hero. (p. 111-12) This might have been an occasion to introduce the most influential of "post-Jungian" theorists, James Hillman. In numerous papers Hillman has pushed the discussion of the *puer* far beyond Marie-Louise von Franz, who gets credit for developing Jung's few comments on this figure; alas, Hillman is never mentioned. But then again, Hillman is wary of "heroism" in psychology. His *The Dream and the Underworld* criticizes Freudian and Jungian approaches to the dream precisely for their insistence on translating its signs into the ego's naturalistic "day world" perspective. That perspective is "heroic," at war with a Hadean "underworld" vision that sees past any firm literalism to its flittering shadow or shade, Hillman's metaphors for the images through which a less than determinate psychic nature expresses itself. The Hillman book is exemplary of post-Jungian approaches, and this part of Segal's discussion seems the right place to have mentioned them.

When Hillman, and David Miller, do appear, it is not in the section on Jung at all but in that part of the chapter "Myth and Literature" devoted to Northrop Frye, whose theory has also been called "archetypal." The placement has its logic, given the common moniker (Frye adapted the Jungian term) and the status of poetics for both Hillman and Miller as they pursue the archetypal beyond the sources and reflexes of "traditional" Jungian theory. But still, Jung has always been a key point of departure for these two theorists, so some discussion of them in the section on Jung would have been expected.

Segal ends this book with a stimulating discussion on the future of the study of myth. A central question, he says, is "whether myth can be brought back to the external world" while avoiding postmodernism's dismissal of the "authority of science." His answer leans on D. W. Winnicott's theory of transitional objects and phenomena. Like the child at play, the adult too may "cling to an internalized object" such as a hobby, interest, value—or, Segal suggests, a myth. The adult recognizes that it is not reality, but it helps him or her to "deal with a much wider world" since, as Winnicott is quoted as saying, "no human being is free from the strain of relating inner and outer reality."

At the risk of misrepresenting him, I am inclined to read Segal's treatment of this imaginal space or world of play as it relates to myth as a tacit nod in the direction of the post-Jungians, even though it builds on Winnicott's ideas. The idea is certainly consonant with the best of post-Jungian theory (one thinks especially of Miller) which agrees that myth, like play, provides a "transition"— it might prefer to say, a metaphorical *carrying over*—from what Segal calls the "known outer world to the unknown one." (p. 139)

The human reflex that fills intermediate spaces or objects with things imaginal has an obvious parallel in Blumenberg's argument about myth. If play facilitates this under conditions seemingly less dire than the absolutism of reality, some pressure or "strain" (even if an unconscious mandate or urge) of creating significance is arguably still at work. This suggests a vibrant nexus involving play, terror, and poesis, a zone where myth is indigene, habitué. It is a region, always mediated by psyche, that—together with theories of myth rooted in problems of power, ideology, and what anthropologist Michael Taussig has called the "space of death"[5]— remains crucial to explaining the ongoing life and future prospects of myth.

Fittingly, and importantly, Segal near the end insists that not all contemporary myths are treated in the manner of play or make-believe. He names as among the most enduring and salient of these myths those of eschatology ("myths of the end of the world") and a few others usually taken for *real*: "progress" and "ideologies." Here Segal points to some unsavory ways in which myth shapes current historical experience. Concluding on a lighter note, observations on how adult make-believe makes film actors into "stars" and modern-day heroes close the book.

With *Myth: A Very Short Introduction*, Robert Segal more than fulfills the stated aim of the Oxford series to which it contributes: "a stimulating and accessible way in" to a new subject. What he achieves is part handy field guide, part playbook of holds for wrestling with this protean phenomenon, surprising for its exhaustiveness in impossibly tight quarters. Hemming in myth theories to facilitate comparison of convergent and divergent traits, the book invites readers to the expansive exploration of their subtler nuances and ambiguities—where the real fun lies.

NOTES

1. *Theorizing About Myth* (Amherst: U of Massachusetts, 1999), 3.

2. *Work on Myth*, trans. Robert M. Wallace (Cambridge: MIT, 1985), 3-7, 34-43.

3. *Ibid.*, 59-67, 307-311.

4. *Jung on Mythology*, *Encountering Jung* (Princeton: Princeton UP, 1998), 19; *Theorizing*, 78.

5. *Shamanism, Colonialism, and the Wild Man: A Study in Terror and Healing* (Chicago: U of Chicago, 1987), 3-11, 127-135.

PHILEMON
FOUNDATION

P HILEMON FOUNDATION is preparing for publication the *Complete Works of C.G. Jung* in English and German. In distinction to the widely known *Collected Works*, it is intended that the *Complete Works* will comprise manuscripts, seminars, and correspondence hitherto unpublished or formerly believed "lost" that number in tens of thousands of pages. ✳ Among our funded projects are Jung's legendary *Red Book*, the Children's Dreams Seminar, the ETH Lectures from 1933 to 1941, and Jung's remarkable correspondence with Father Victor White. ✳ Given the magnitude of our task, the Philemon Foundation invites all those who value the work of C.G. Jung and appreciate its importance to our personal and collective journeys to join us by making a donation. For further information, please contact Dr. Stephen Martin. ✳

PHILEMON FOUNDATION
119 COULTER AVENUE, ARDMORE, PENNSYLVANIA 19003 USA
FAX 610-660-9219 TELEPHONE 610-896-0344
SMARTIN@PHILEMONFOUNDATION.ORG
WWW.PHILEMONFOUNDATION.ORG

Harvesting Darkness
Essays on Literature, Myth, Film and Culture

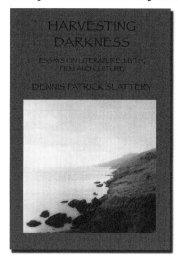

**ISBN 0-595-38452-8 • Price: $24.95 (USD) • Paper
Publishers: iUniverse, 2006**

Harvesting Darkness gathers essays, both scholarly and cultural, written during the past 25 years, all of which have been published previously in books, journals, and other periodicals. They span a wide arc, exploring subjects as diverse as writing, the imagination, grief, poetry, prayer, loss, and silence, as well as address specific literary works and films, such as Sophocles' *Antigone*, Dante's *Commedia*, Mark Twain's *Huckleberry Finn*, Dostoevsky's *The Idiot*, Melville's *Moby Dick*, Joseph Campbell's mythology, Wim Wenders' *Wings of Desire* and Philip Leacock's *Three Sovereigns for Sarah*. Drawing upon the theories of phenomenology, depth and archetypal psychology, and mythology, these essays develop a theory of mythopoiesis.

A Limbo of Shards
Essays on Memory, Myth and Metaphor

**ISBN 0-595-41925-9 • Price: $24.95 (USD) • Paper
Publisher: iUniverse, 2007**

Both literature and culture coalesce in the three main arenas of this volume: memory, myth, and metaphor. As Peter C. Phan, Chair of Catholic Social Thought at Georgetown University, writes in the Foreword to this volume, the fields of literature and depth psychology "function for Dennis *as modes of knowing*, or more precisely, *modes of imagining*, and hence *modes of being and acting* in the world." *A Limbo of Shards* is a study of literature, psychology, mythology, culture, and nature in its various shears that, taken together, fashion a single image of the imagination's diverse expressions.

ABOUT THE AUTHOR:
Dennis Patrick Slattery, Ph.D., is Core Faculty, Mythological Studies at Pacifica Graduate Institute in Carpinteria, California. A teacher for 39 years, he is author/co-editor of 9 books, including two volumes of poetry and accompanying CDs. His work witnesses intimate and sustained marriages between poetry, literature, spirituality, phenomenology, and depth psychology.

Order online at: www.amazon.com
or contact Pacifica Graduate Institute Bookstore, (805) 969-3626, ext. 141

New Publications
from Spring Journal Books

Psyche and the Sacred
Spirituality Beyond Religion
Lionel Corbett
Foreword by Murray Stein

ISBN 1-882670-34-5 • Price: $23.95

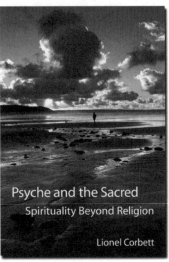

Psyche and the Sacred
Spirituality Beyond Religion
Lionel Corbett

Corbett describes an approach to spirituality based on personal experience of the sacred rather than on pre-existing religious dogmas. Using the language and insights of depth psychology, he describes the intimate relationship between spiritual experience and the psychology of the individual, revealing the seamless continuity of the personal and transpersonal dimensions of the psyche. For those seeking alternative forms of spirituality beyond the Judaeo-Christian tradition, this volume will be a useful guide on the journey.

About the Author:
Dr. Lionel Corbett teaches depth psychology at Pacifica Graduate Institute, Santa Barbara, CA, and is the author of *The Religious Function of the Psyche*.

Living with Jung
"Entirviews" with Jungian Analysts, Vol. 1
Robert & Janis Henderson

ISBN 1-882670-35-3 • Price: $21.95 (USD)

The first in a 2-volume set, this collection of interviews with leading Jungian analysts—past and present—draws upon a wealth of memories and experiences, many of which go directly back to first-hand encounters with Jung. Through their eyes, we catch a rare glimpse of Jung not found in his writings. Featured in this volume are: Adolf Guggenbühl-Craig, Murray Stein, Jane and Jo Wheelwright, John Beebe, Joseph Henderson, Patricia Berry, Thomas Kirsch, C. Toni Frey-Wehrlin, James Hall, Russell Lockhart, Fred Gustafson, and Gilda Franz.

About the Authors:
Rev. Dr. Robert S. Henderson is a pastoral psychotherapist and Janis W. Henderson, M.A. is a psychotherapist. They live in Glastonbury, Connecticut, and have studied Jungian psychology together since their marriage in 1969.

To order, please visit our online store at
www.springjournalandbooks.com or call *504.524.5117*

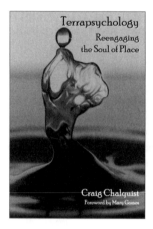

**Foundation for
Mythological Studies (FMS)
&
Spring Journal**

present

*Nature and Human Nature
Changing Perspective*

March 16-18, 2007, Santa Barbara, CA.
www.mythology.org

The Nature and Human Nature Conference will explore how the sciences and the humanities can work in tandem to achieve a shift in consciousness with respect to our current environmental ethos.

Scientists, psychologists, and cultural mythologists are increasingly addressing the toughest and most perplexing global issues, yet critical dialogue is required so that we no longer ignore the human factors or the ecological facts.

Experience extraordinary presentations and conversation led by experts in various fields that will increase your knowledge of environmental and human issues seen from a long-term perspective.

The aim of this Conference is to contribute to constructing new worldviews about the interactions between humans and nature. In this way, we hope to motivate educators, policy makers, and entrepreneurs to devise attitudes, policies, and corporate responsibility for the future of our planet and humankind.

Co-Sponsors: Pacifica Graduate Institute, Santa Barbara City College, Joseph Campbell Foundation, International Association of Jungian Studies (IAJS), Sustainable Santa Barbara.

For more information: www.mythology.org